Following Franco

MANCHESTER
1824

Manchester University Press

Following Franco

Spanish culture and politics in transition,
1962–92

Duncan Wheeler

Manchester University Press

Published by Manchester University Press
Altrincham Street, Manchester M1 7JA
www.manchesteruniversitypress.co.uk

British Library Cataloguing-in-Publication Data
A catalogue record for this book is available from the British Library

ISBN 978 1 5261 0518 9 hardback

First published 2020

The publisher has no responsibility for the persistence or accuracy of URLs for any external or third-party internet websites referred to in this book, and does not guarantee that any content on such websites is, or will remain, accurate or appropriate.

Typeset by Newgen Publishing UK
Printed in Great Britain
by TJ Books Ltd, Padstow

Contents

Contents

Acknowledgements

In the nearly ten years it has taken me to complete this book, I have accrued countless debts of gratitude. The School of Languages, Cultures and Societies at the University of Leeds has provided a convivial and supportive academic home, whilst I am indebted to the Department of Media and Audiovisual Communication at the University Carlos III – Concepción Cascajosa Virino, Carmen Ciller, Ana Mejón, Alejandro Melero, Tamara Moya Jorge, Manuel Palacio, Xosé Prieto Souto, Rubén Romero Santos *et al.* – for providing me with an academic home-from-home in Madrid. In my travels, the following have kindly opened their doors to provide more hospitable billeting than any hotel could provide: Betlem Soler Pardo in Valencia, Noelia Iglesias Iglesias in Santiago de Compostela, Mila López Casellas in Granada, José Luis Alonso de Santos and Marga Piñero in El Puerto de Santa María, and Fiona Melville in Sotogrande. María Bastianes, Ben Bollig, Maria Delgado, Stuart Green, Helena Miguélez-Carbeilla, Rebecca Jarman and Vicente Rodríguez Ortega all generously gave of their time to read draft sections of the book. The critiques of the anonymous reader from Manchester University Press were similarly constructive and smart. Caroline Wintersgill, Jonathan de Peyer and Alun Richards have been first-rate and patient editors.

I carried out over 300 interviews, and am very grateful to all of those who gave of their time freely to talk with me. I have rehearsed various sections at talks delivered at the following institutions: the Universities of Cambridge, Malaga and Oslo; Trinity College Dublin; King's College

Acknowledgements

London; Universitat Pompeu Fabra; and UCL. The comments and feed-back I received have fed into this book in myriad ways, as have the responses of my students on my final-year undergraduate module at Leeds on the Transition. Invitations to provide commentary on the inde-pendence debate in Catalonia by BBC Scotland and the *London Review of Books* helped sharpen my thinking on Spain's autonomous communities. I am similarly grateful to my editors at *Political Quarterly* and *Jacobin* for commissioning publications based on my interviews with Alfonso Guerra and Felipe González. I would like to record my debt to the librarians and archivists at the following institutions: the British Library; the Brotherton Library, Leeds; the Biblioteca Nacional (Madrid); the Archivo General de la Administración; the Fundación Juan March; the Archivo Partido Comunista (Madrid); the Arxiu Nacional de Catalunya; Tate; the Fundación Pablo Iglesias; the Fundación de la Transicion; the University of Navarra; the Centro de Investigaciones Sociológicas; the Fundación Francisco Franco; the Institut del Teatre; the Museo Picasso; the Fundación Joan Miró; the Fundació Gala-Salvador Dalí; the Archivo General de la Comunidad de Madrid; the Biblioteca de la Plaza de Toros de Valencia; el Museo Reina Sofía; the Fundación César Manrique; the Casa del Carnaval, Santa Cruz; the Biblioteca militar, Toledo; the Ministerio de Cultura; the Municipal Archives of Almería, Baix Llobregat, Barcelona, Bilbao, Burgos, Castellón, Córdoba, Fuengirola, Granada, Gerona, Ibiza Town, Oviedo, Pontevedra, San Sebastián, Teguise, Valencia, Valladolid and Vigo; and the Provincial Archive of Zaragoza.

Wilma Wheeler kindly acted as an ad hoc and unremunerated research assistant on various occasions. Conversations with the following individuals have, with or without their knowledge, provided ideas that go uncredited in the book: Gregorio Alonso, Andrés Amorós, Peter Anderson, Xosé Manuel Blanco, Paul Castro, José Luis Castro de Paz, Mercedes Cebrián, Javier Cercas, Richard Cleminson, Guillem Collom-Montero, Álvaro Delgado-Gal, Steph Dennison, Sarah Ferguson, Soledad Fox Maura, David Frier, Asier Gil, Ángeles González-Sinde, Belén Gopegui, Jim House, Germán Labrador, Javier López Alós, Federico López Terra, Isabelle Marc Martínez, Karl McLaughlin, Rosa Navarro

Acknowledgements

Durán, Ruth Patiño, David Penton, Marina Pérez de Arcos, David Platten, Gonzalo Pontón, Alma Prelec, Carles Puigdemont, Hayley Rabanal, Paula Rebuelta García, Elena Rueda Ruiz de Austri, Vicente Ruiz 'El Soro', David Sánchez, Marta Sanz, Max Silverman, Angel Smith, Mike Thompson, Gisela Tomé Lourido, Miguel Torres, Maite Usoz de la Fuente, Mario Vargas Llosa, Steve Wheeler, Tom Whittaker, Andrew Windsor, Sarah Wright and Pablo Zavala.

Note on translations

All translations are my own unless otherwise noted. For quotations from unpublished archival sources, the original text is also included.

Political parties and formations

Agrupaciones de Independientes de Canarias	Independent Coalition of the Canary Islands
Alianza Apostólica Anticomunista	Anti-Communist Apostolic Alliance
AP	Alianza Popular (People's Alliance)
Centro Democrático Social	The Democratic and Social Centre
CiU	Convèrgencia i Unió (Convergence and Union)
Ciudadanos	Citizens
Coalición Galega	Galician Coalition
Comisiones Obreras	Workers' Commission
Fuerza Nueva	New Force
Grupo Independiente Liberal	Independent Liberal Group
Guerrilleros de Cristo Rey	The Warriors of Christ, the King
Izquierda Unida	United Left
Junta Democrática	Democratic Junta
Más Madrid	More Madrid
Más País	More Country
Partido Socialista Popular	Popular Socialist Party

List of political parties and formations

Plataforma de Convergencia Democrática	Platform for Democratic Convergence
PNV	Partido Nacionalista Vasco (Basque Nationalist Party)
Podemos	We Can
PP	Partido Popular (People's Party)
PSOE	Partido Socialista Obrero Español (Spanish Socialist and Workers' Party)
Soria ¡Ya!	Soria Now!
Terra Libre	Free Land
Teruel Existe	Teruel Exists
UCD	Unión de Centro Democrático (Union of the Democratic Centre)
Unidos Podemos	United We Can
Unión del Pueblo Canario	Union of the People of the Canaries

Introduction

In May 2007, riots took place in and around Madrid's Second of May Square when the police attempted to end unregulated parties consisting of teenagers drinking in the open air ('botellón'). Leaving aside the extent to which the police's response was (dis)proportionate, this was seemingly the manifestation of a depoliticised society in which commitment to democracy co-existed with a general disillusionment with mainstream politics. Since Felipe González's landslide Socialist victory in 1982, the Partido Socialista Obrero Español (Spanish Socialist and Workers' Party; PSOE) and the Partido Popular (People's Party; PP) had alternated in government. Unaccustomed to serious competition, the major parties had become complacent. If young people had once run from the police to oppose the regime of General Francisco Franco (1939–75) and to fight for democratic rights, their sole objective in the twenty-first century appeared to be the right to party. Protests, in other words, were no longer what they used to be.

This would all change with the financial crisis, which exposed the political elites as being singularly unimpressive at providing moral or economic leadership. Unemployment rates rocketed from 1.8 to 6 million, peaking at 27 per cent of the workforce.[1] Cuts to social spending alongside rising joblessness have been held accountable for increased suicide rates, especially amongst young men.[2] In a highly regulated two-tier labour market, the young were disproportionately affected by the financial crash: the share of under-30s living with their parents would reach 80 per cent, with 1 in

1

4 Spaniards aged between 18 and 29 being in neither education, training nor employment, one of the highest rates in the developed world.[3] Anger against the culprits and consequences of a global recession, whose effects have been particularly devastating in an economy overly dependent on the construction boom, crystallised in the 15-M movement, an attempt to hold a largely discredited establishment to account. As Kostis Kornetis notes: 'In the summer of 2011, the trend of evoking Francoism as a direct precedent of repression and accusing the transition of creating weak democratic foundations and a feeble political system was consolidated as a protest frame with the appearance of the *indignados*.'[4] Pablo Iglesias – Secretary General of the political start-up able to translate the energy and ideals of the 15-M into electoral currency – has stated that 'The Transition is probably the most important subject of Spanish-based reflection in Podemos. Our political point of departure is, in reality, a critical analysis of the Transition.'[5] Rapidly evolving political and socio-cultural realities ensure that this book intervenes by default and design in ongoing debates on whether the so-called 'culture of the Transition', alongside an associated nomenclature, the 'regime of '78' – the year in which the new democratic Spanish Constitution was signed – remain, if indeed they ever were, fit for purpose.

Francoism's aftermath was, in many respects, a different world from that of twenty-first-century post-recession Spain. There are, however, structural parallels that can shed light on our understanding of the past and present. Principal amongst these is the need to pay greater attention to broader ideological fissures that have been reflected and refracted through generational conflict. Foreigners frequently observe with envy the ostensibly harmonious nature of Spanish family relations, and yet Oedipal dramas were ubiquitous in the cultural production of the Transition. Representations of children were privileged and nuanced to a greater extent than ever before or after in the national cinema.[6] As Marvin D'Lugo notes of Carlos Saura's films: 'he dramatized individual characters in the throes of their submission to the social apparatus of the family and other social institutions that reproduce the ideology of the state.'[7] *El desencanto* (*The Disenchantment*) (Jaime Chávarri, 1976) profiles the Paneros, whose paterfamilias, Francoism's poet laureate, died in 1962.

The documentary exposes the façade of the ideal family, its members depicted as dysfunctional, albeit photogenic, misfits. *La guerra de Papá* (*Daddy's War*) (Antonio Mecero, 1977), a cinematic adaptation of a Miguel Delibes novel that did not immediately lend itself to a politicised allegorical reading, was largely ignored by critics but was the period's biggest box-office hit, more than 3.5 million Spaniards paying to see a cinematic depiction of mutual miscomprehension between parents and children. There is a widespread tendency to relegate family dysfunctions to allegory, politics gliding over the very real generational conflicts that Parts I and III of my book suggest were instrumental to a Transition in which young people were alternatively vilified for apathy and subversion.

In the present day, the most qualified ever generation of Spaniards are increasingly forced into economic exile, often taking on the low-paid, non-professional jobs in Northern and Western Europe that their grandparents' generation held during the 1960s when Spain's economic miracle relied on emigrants sending foreign currencies back home. In a letter dated 18 November 1965 from Belgium, where he was studying on a university exchange programme, future President Felipe González (1982–96) wrote to his then girlfriend:

> Honey, how disappointing Europe is, the immense solitude of the emigrants. Nobody looks out for them, they are repressed, oppressed and, to top it all, hated as inferior beings, as a cursed race … Thousands of bars in Brussels have a sign saying entrance prohibited to Spaniards, Africans and Latin Americans.[8]

Shedding the ghosts of the Civil War (1936–39) and boosting national self-esteem so as no longer to feel second-class citizens of Europe were interwoven aspects of democratisation.

Evolving narratives of the Spanish Transition

The Transition, both at home and abroad, has traditionally been construed as Spain's success story, the suture of the wounds of a bitterly cruel fratricidal conflict, which cleared the way for the country's belated modernisation and European integration. Locked into a co-dependent relationship with the Civil War, the Transition was a success because of the previous bloody failure. Spain provided a 'new template for survival' for reformists in Eastern Europe as the Berlin Wall fell.[9]

Against the backdrop of 'the cosmopolitan liberal Europe that 1989 had served to mythologise'[10] and the tragic events unfurling in the Balkans, historians in the 1990s quite understandably celebrated the exemplarity of the relatively peaceful Spanish antecedent. If, however, as Pamela Beth Radcliff notes, 'the "Spanish model" has been a ubiquitous positive presence in comparative democratization studies', this is clearly a double-edged sword in terms of Spain's place in the global pecking order:

> The reason there is a 'Spanish model', as opposed to an Austrian, German or Italian model, is that the Spanish version was assumed to be more accessible to developing nations. If Spain could transition successfully from a (backward) authoritarian regime to a modern democracy, then so could any number of similar countries.[11]

A recognition of the limits of the Spanish model does not, however, imply that it no longer has lessons to impart. Quite the contrary; as Clive Barnett notes: 'The meanings, values and risks of democracy are most clearly exposed and problematized when applied to new contexts.'[12] Podemos's leader has taken the more recent crisis in Spanish society and disillusionment with politics as an invitation to debunk the mythical origins of the current status quo and translate the energy of popular protests into electoral currency:

> The 15-M symbolised the existence of an organic crisis in Spain, questioning the official political narratives and representing the clearest political expression of that crisis, managing to impose new interpretations of the situation and new possibilities for transformation via the actions of subaltern sectors of society ('the masses'). The implementation in Spanish political languages of the term 'casta' to indicate political and economic elites is a good example of the hegemonic politics of Podemos.[13]

It is not necessary to subscribe to such an ideological agenda to recognise that Podemos, at least at first, instilled a new-found optimism into segments of a disillusioned electorate – one campaign slogan read

'¿Cuándo fue la última vez que votaste con ilusión?' (When was the last time you were excited to vote?) – by challenging the hegemony of the PP and the PSOE.

In a book aptly titled *La Transición contada a nuestros padres* (*The Transition Told to Our Parents*), academic and founding member of Podemos Juan Carlos Monedero refers to 'a pious tall story, a family lie that concealed a far-from heroic past and helped the country to feel better than it was'.[14] In *El futuro* (*The Future*) (Luis López Carrasco, 2013), the filmmaker looks back at the euphoria and optimism of his parents' generation, a mock-documentary style recreating a party in Madrid just after the Socialists' first general election victory, the first time the left had controlled the Spanish Government since before the Civil War. This was seemingly not just a victory over the forces of political conservatism, but also of the young over the old. As a result of the demographic boom of the 1960s, more Spaniards celebrated their eighteenth birthday in 1982 than at any time before or since. Armed with the campaign slogan 'Por el cambio' (For change), González's Government was the youngest in Europe, the first time the generation of 1968 had gained power. The Movida, the drug-fuelled youth movement that put Pedro Almodóvar and his adopted city of Madrid on the (inter)national cultural map, provided an ideal showcase for rapid change, a desire to leave the past behind and career optimistically into the future.

Culture and education were understood to be key to this brave new world, the PSOE investing heavily in the arts, and the creation of new universities resulting in an explosion of jobs for young academics. According to a national survey conducted in 1994, three-quarters of Spaniards were satisfied or extremely satisfied with the Transition and the socioeconomic changes of the past two decades;[15] approval rates were highest amongst university-educated urban dwellers.[16] This is the same profile as the demographic for Podemos, a party that emerged from the political sciences faculty of Madrid's Complutense University. As Concepción Cascajosa Virino and Vicente Rodríguez Ortega note: 'Although it bound together a variety of social groups and activists coming from diverse backgrounds, a majority of its supporters were urbanite, middle-class, cultivated, Internet-savvy, young individuals.'[17] Many of Podemos's leading lights, Iglesias included, had cultivated the CVs and personal connections that normally allow access into the highly paternalistic Spanish university system, only for the financial crash to debar them from gaining tenure. Rising youth unemployment and precarious job opportunities for the professional as well as manual workers have made graduates less predisposed to endorse the logic of late capitalism.

When the major parties agreed with uncharacteristic speed and efficiency to amend Article 135 of the Constitution in 2011, thereby introducing a cap on the structural deficit of the State, the betrayal felt was as much psychological as political: successive generations had been raised to believe the text to be sacred and untouchable. An attempted coup that took place on 23 February 1981 was a potentially lethal threat to Europeanisation, averted through the fortitude and quick thinking of King Juan Carlos, who steered the country towards a stable monarchical democracy, built on the bedrock of the free market and barring memories of the past from dictating the future. At least that is what young Spaniards were brought up to believe: from 1981 to 2008, the Transition and the King were sanctified as guarantors of democracy and modernisation, terms that became conflated and confused.

In the 1990s, Spanish coverage of Prince Charles and Princess Diana's separation had depicted the British royal family as 'backward, anachronistic, repressive and out of touch' in comparison with the Bourbon dynasty, 'dynamic, democratic and European'.[18] Since being photographed on a hunting exhibition in Botswana in 2012 at the height of the financial crisis, Juan Carlos has gone from being mollycoddled as the guarantor of a democracy to being seen as a liability for the royal family and Spain alike. Engulfed in corruption scandals and speculation surrounding adulterous affairs, the King abdicated in favour of his son, Felipe VI, in 2014. In a salacious tract, Amadeo Martínez Inglés calculates the Emeritus King had 4,786 lovers, peaking with 2,154 between the years of 1976 and 1994.[19] It is remarkable that he found the time to amass his unexplained fortunes,[20] Juan Carlos embodying for an increasingly broad section of the Spanish population what Joan Ramón Resina characterises as 'the impregnation of society with Francoist values through the capillary dispersion of corruption'.[21]

In May 2018, Prime Minister Mariano Rajoy (2011–18) became the first leader of Spanish democracy to be ousted by a vote of no confidence supported by the PSOE, regional nationalist parties and Unidos Podemos – a new formation between Podemos and more long-standing left-wing parties, principally Izquierda Unida – after many of the PP's senior officials were dragged through the courts, a number being found guilty of fraudulent practices. Pedro Sánchez, leader of the PSOE, was sworn in as a caretaker President on 1 June 2018, with promises of reform. It took two further general elections for a government to be formed, Sánchez eventually retaining his position by entering into a coalition, the first of the post-Franco period, with Iglesias. It remains to be seen if Parliament will uphold the retired King's legal immunity, but Juan Carlos has already lost the affection of his former subjects, and the privileged positon by which, for example, the then President of the regional Government, Jordi Pujol, apologised after writer Quim Monzó parodied royalty on Catalan television.[22]

Cultural production has performed a key role in articulating a new discourse around disquieting aspects of Spain's recent political past. *El rey* (*The King*), a production by Teatro de barrio – a cooperative theatre company based in Lavapiés, a multicultural district of Madrid, at whose base Podemos was officially launched as a political project in 2014 – offers a revisionist take on the Transition, in which the masses were hoodwinked by a monarch who privileged personal interests over political statesmanship. A trilogy – *Grupo 7* (*Unit 7*) (2012), *La isla mínima* (*Marshland*) (2014) and *El hombre de las mil caras* (*The Man with a Thousand Faces*) (2016) – by filmmaker Alberto Rodríguez examines the human and ethical costs of Spain's transformation into an ostensibly modern democratic state. In the post-15-M context, it should come as no surprise that Podemos and *El País* – alongside a generation of established writers and intellectuals who both bestowed and received prestige from inclusion within its pages[23] – have behaved in mutually hostile fashion. Simultaneously a chronicler and beneficiary of the 'regime of '78', the latter, in Laura Desfor's words, 'self-consciously set out to be the newspaper of the democratic transition ... Modelled after *Le Monde*, *El País* "revolutionized" the Spanish media with its modern layout and print technology.'[24] Over the course of 2013, Spain's major newspapers were taken over by major corporations, and long-standing editors dismissed. Amidst fears the country was heading the same way as Greece, steering from above was called on once again.

Spain is undoubtedly a more plural, modern, democratic and prosperous nation in 2018 than it was in 1978. The same claim was made in 1975 in relation to 1939. Symbolic and financial investment by the Franco regime in commemorating the '25 años de paz' (twenty-five years of peace) in 1964 provides a textbook example of a broader phenomenon, articulated as follows by Michel-Rolph Trouillot:[25] 'Celebrations straddle the two sides of historicity. They impose a silence upon the events that they ignore and they fill that silence with narratives of power about the event they celebrate.'[26] Historians have long queried the extent to which the dictatorship could claim credit for Spain's growing prosperity, 'as if somehow Franco had engineered the European/Western economic boom of the 1960s, or indeed the sunny weather which together underpinned the country's success in the new era of mass tourism'.[27] There are unfortunate echoes of the dictatorship's glib triumphalism in titling a municipally funded exhibition that opened in the provincial town of Albacete in 2018 as '40 años de progreso' (forty years of progress), paying tribute to the chief architects of the Constitution at the national and local level. In rural Aragon and Castile, platforms Teruel Existe and Soria ¡Ya! claim that lack of investment in some of the most depopulated areas of Europe is evidence of the authorities reneging on their responsibilities and progress not being equal for all. A few short years before Spain's first high-speed train, of dubious economic sustainability, to connect Madrid and Seville was inaugurated in 1992, a series of unprofitable train-lines were suspended, the closure of the near-centenary Valladolid to Ariza line leaving towns such as Soria and Aranda de Duero cut off from major transport links.[28] In the words of the Soria ¡Ya! newsletter published in advance of the 2016 national elections: 'It beggars belief how little we matter to any of the parties and how little they try and hide the fact.'[29] Charges of centralism are no longer reserved for Madrid, with Soria ¡Ya! generally reserving their harshest critiques for the seat of regional government in Valladolid.

During the Second Republic, federal statutes were introduced for Catalonia and the Basque Country with another in Galicia in the process of being approved. The equation of dual identities with the purported disintegration of Spain constituted one, if not the, chief justification for the military coup of July 1936. The self-proclaimed 'nacionales' (nationals) and 'nacionalistas' (nationalists) – the two terms were interchangeable in Francoist rhetoric – fought in the name of a Spain that was 'una, grande y libre' (unified, great and free). Even on his deathbed, the Caudillo remained obsessed with the separatist threat. Read on television by tearful Prime Minister Carlos Arias Navarro, Franco's final address to the nation commanded: 'Maintain the unity of Spanish lands, exalting the rich variety of its regions as a fortress for the unity of the Patria.' The democratic Constitution of 1978 faced the near impossible challenge of keeping Spanish nationalists on side whilst at least playing lip-service to those championing the interests of the recently christened autonomous communities. Adopting far more caution than had been exercised during the Second Republic, a concession to this democratic precedent and the interests of some of the most potentially conflictual regions of Spain was made in acknowledging Catalonia, the Basque Country and Galicia as historical nationalities whose passage from regions to autonomous communities would be fast-tracked. A referendum was offered in Andalusia to allow its citizens to decide if they wanted to be afforded similar privileges.

The creation of seventeen autonomous regions has devolved some political power, also laying the foundations for a 'quasi-nationalism of comparative grievances',[30] and one-upmanship. The promise of prestige and employment opportunities led, for example, Catalonia, Madrid and Barcelona to compete with each other for the opportunity to provide a home for Euro-Disney, a themed resort that ended up in Paris. As Jesús López-Peláez Casellas notes, 'Francoist ideologues consistently tried, between the 1940s and 1970s, to empty flamenco music and dance of their specifically Andalusian (political and cultural) content,[31] offering a folkloric display of Gypsy culture for internal and external consumption. In the early twentieth century, Blas Infante's German-inspired Andalusian nationalism had, by contrast, posited flamenco 'as the expression of regional sentiment rather than the art form of an ethnic minority.'[32] Following the creation of the Andalusian regional Government in 1980, attempts were made to patent this artistic patrimony. Such exclusionist tactics were understandable but often counter-productive: UNESCO acknowledged flamenco as an example of Intangible Cultural Heritage in 2010 following an initiative that, unlike previous bids, had not sought to exclude Extremadura and Murcia,[33] the two other autonomous communities to have a long tradition in this music and dance.

In the words of Omar G. Encarnación, the devolution of powers to regions was 'the most politically sensitive and organizationally complex outcome of the politics of compromise that accompanied the transition.'[34] As President of the Catalan Generalitat from 1980 to 2003, Jordi Pujol pursued an accommodationist approach to central government in Madrid, seeking to negotiate further concessions and to consolidate Catalonia as a cultural, as opposed to a sovereign, entity. Although not free of tension, this was a more peaceful form of nationalism than that manifest in the Basque Country by Euskadi Ta Askatasuna (ETA) prior to their announcing the end of their armed struggle in 2011. The financial crisis gave central government the excuse it had arguably been looking for to bring an increasing quantity of the expenditure of local and regional administrations under its purview.[35] Whilst many in Catalonia believed that they were subsidising the rest of Spain, greater fiscal autonomy in the Basque Country helped make it the autonomous community with the lowest debt-per-capita rate.[36] This has been instrumental in a reduction of hostilities.

The most culturally significant manifestation of what Helena Miguélez-Carballeira has termed 'post-ETA poetics'[37] is the film *Ocho apellidos vascos* (*Spanish Affair*) (Emilio Martínez Lázaro, 2014), which broke all records at the domestic box office. Amaia, a young Basque woman, visits Seville for the first time. Rafa, a local Don Juan, who has never left Andalusia, follows her back home, unaccustomed to a woman resisting his advances. A sequel, *Ocho apellidos catalanes*, appeared the next year, and is set in a small town outside Gerona (Amaia is now going out with a Catalan) whose inhabitants pretend Catalonia had gained independence from the Spanish State in order to please an ageing matriarch. The follow-up was less popular and not so funny, but it shows how quickly the Catalan situation escalated: the gag in which an aghast Spaniard calls the police because he thinks the town has illegally declared independence soon lost all comic appeal. On 1 October 2017, the police and civil guard followed central government orders to disrupt voting in the referendum on independence that the Catalan Parliament had approved but that Spain's courts and national Parliament had declared illegal. This resulted in Spain's most serious crisis of state since the Transition, triggering Article 155 of the Constitution, which reverted rule of Catalonia from the Generalitat to the Spanish Parliament in Madrid. Rajoy's strategy for dealing with Podemos and Catalan separatists alike has been to dismiss them as unruly kids.

The European Union treated the reaction to the Catalan referendum as an internal affair, but images of violent police action were negative publicity for the Spanish State in the international arena. Elected political representatives who had organised the illegal referendum were arrested for sedition; the President of the Generalitat, Carles Puigdemont – a former journalist and Mayor of Gerona who had been unusual amongst the political and intellectual classes in having advocated Catalan independence since the 1980s – escaped prison by going into exile in Brussels. Rajoy was rightly chastised for his intransigence, which did much to prompt the constitutional crisis, but it has never been part of his game-plan to ingratiate himself with voters he knows will never support him. The PP was more troubled by the rise of Ciudadanos as a party with national prospects, from its grass roots in Catalonia where it represented the interests of anti-independence citizens. When Puigdemont addressed the Oxford Union in May 2019, he received a warm welcome, and presented himself as a bulwark against extremism, claiming that Basque and Catalan nationalists were responsible for keeping the rise of the far-right Vox Party in check. Formed in 2013 by PP members disillusioned with Rajoy's regime and what they perceived to be the ills of twenty-first-century Spain – immigration, feminism, regional nationalism, animal rights – Vox secured the largest number of votes of any political group in the 2018 Andalusian regional elections. In the November 2019 general elections, their position consolidated: the most successful post-Franco far-right party overtook Unidas Podemos and Ciudadanos, coming third behind the PP and PSOE. Contrary to Puigdemont's claim, the independence movement has been instrumental in the rising acceptance of Vox's conservative and nostalgic appeal to centralist nationalism.

The end of Spain's long-standing bipartidism has led to Spaniards going to the polls a record four times between 2015 and 2019. The voting in April 2019 revealed the extent to which Spain was split between left- (Unidas Podemos, PSOE) and right-wing (Ciudadanos, Vox, PP) parties, the former block securing a marginally greater number of votes. Pablo Iglesias and Sánchez were unable to negotiate a deal, and a largely disillusioned electorate were forced back to the polls in November. Unidas Podemos won far fewer seats, and the PSOE lost a few. Pragmatism forced their respective leaders to negotiate, Sánchez granting Iglesias the vice-presidency in exchange for a more moderate line, including negotiations with Catalan factions being underpinned by the framework of the Constitution. The narrow victory of the left required the support, or at least abstention, of smaller nationalist forces in the Basque Country and Catalonia. Ongoing support will require that the PSOE make concessions that will result in a backlash not only from political opponents but also voters and the media. The tightness of the situation was such that Sánchez's successful investiture was dependent on the support of Teruel Existe's sole MP, Tomás Guitarte. A newcomer to parliamentary politics, he endured a baptism of fire when police protection was required following threats of violence from anti-PSOE militants in the build-up to the divisive vote.

A rare point of consensus in an increasingly divided socio-political landscape is that, for better or worse, the institutions and individuals that contemporary Spain comprises are the products of the Transition. Traditional political parties and commentators speak of the longest period of stability, development and democracy in the country's tumultuous and frequently tragic history; by contrast, detractors question to what extent the 'regime of '78' prevented Spain from realising its democratic potential, with much of the infrastructure and institutions of sociological Francoism left in tact. Frequently lost in debates surround the merits (or lack thereof) of the Transition is the need to distinguish between critiques of how it was handled at the time as opposed to what Carlos Closa and Paul M. Heywood presciently characterised as 'the almost fetishistic character of the 1978 Constitution'.[38] A central premise of this book is that it is possible to be critical of the latter whilst offering an ambivalent or even positive assessment of the former. In disentangling the two claims, I trace a genealogy of how and why they became confused and conflated under González's fourteen-year presidency.

Reform, not rupture: consensus and the pact of silence

David Rieff's provocatively titled book *In Praise of Forgetting* problematises the 'present golden age of collective memory' to critique 'the moral free pass that remembrance is usually afforded today'.[39] He concludes that the 'takeover of history by memory is also the takeover of history by politics'.[40] As Ignacio Fernández de Mata remarks: 'It is no exaggeration to say that Spanish twentieth-century politics have been completely shaped by memory'.[41] After Franco's death, Henry Kissinger was optimistic about democratic possibilities under King Juan Carlos but noted that the USA's 'principal concern was whether a society still riven by the memory of the civil war could transcend its rancorous past and learn to co-exist with political opponents in a pluralistic system. There was no precedent in recent Spanish history for such self-restraint'.[42]

The prototype of two Spains – one traditionalist, conservative and inward-looking; the other progressive and modern, its eyes firmly set on Europe – was firmly entrenched by the nineteenth century. Intellectuals and politicians were fixated on the national problem, the question of how and why the former imperial powerhouse had been relegated to the status of a European backwater, losing its last vestiges of empire in 1898 following defeat in the Spanish-American War. According to Santos Juliá: 'in the same way that the Civil War inevitably split Spain into two, the division of Spain into two was the inevitable cause of the Civil War'.[43] Viewed as the antechamber to an international showdown between democracy and fascism – 'one of the last theatres of political romanticism', to borrow a phrase from Laurie Lee[44] – the Civil War often played out as the dress rehearsal for the battle between Allies and the Axis powers.

It is not necessary to subscribe to the 'collective madness' theory, propounded by some apologists for Francoism, which bypasses the fact that the Civil War has a very specific origin – an illegal uprising against a democratically elected Government – to recognise, as so many foreign volunteers discovered too late or not at all, that the two sides were far from homogeneous, nor was everyone fighting for the same objective. Franco was a ruthless and canny operator, able to convince a diverse array of monarchists, social conservatives, religious groups and the Falange – the fascist movement that combined a cult of violence and intimidation with a genuine desire for aesthetic experimentation and rejection of what it construed to be the undemocratic and unjust practices of capitalism – that, even if they did not necessarily trust or respect him, he was the safest bet in terms of protecting personal and national interests. Beyond the immediate demands of the battlefield, a pedagogy of violence during and after the Civil War was indicative of the regime's commitment to ex(or)cising 'anti-Spain' so as to forge a nation state declared as 'una, grande y libre'. Acknowledging this cultural and political genocide ought not to blind us to the fact that the discourse of two Spains is an umbrella term that diverts attention away from an array of hybrid identities.

If there is any truth to poet Jaime Gil de Biedma's claim (later put to music by Paco Ibáñez) in *Triste historia* (*Sad History*) that 'Of all the histories that make up History / the saddest of all is that of Spain / because it ends badly', then the Transition's reputed success is inextricably linked with its ability to reverse this millennial curse. The first inklings of a breakdown of consensus over the consensus paradigm emerged at the beginning of the twenty-first century, when debates surrounding historical memory in civil society gained momentum and began to interrogate critically how and why the victims of the Civil War were remembered in the present day. Amnesty (some would say amnesia) constituting the sine qua non of the Transition cannot be understood without reference to what had gone so wrong in the past and the potential for archaic differences to jeopardise the relative peace and prosperity of the present. Accepting that this may have been the case in the 1970s does not automatically commit us to subscribing to the same ethos in the twenty-first century: 'how we weigh up the human need for remembrance against remembrance's dangers must take place in the context of how we live now and who we are as human beings'.[45] Supporting the decision by Pedro Sánchez's Government to remove Franco's body from the Valle de los Caídos (Valley of the Fallen) does not necessitate discrediting the Transition, although the two often go hand in hand in an increasingly polarised and polarising public sphere.

In the late 1950s, the last-minute decision to allow some, although by no means all, victims of the Civil War who had fought for the Republic to be transported and laid to rest in the recently inaugurated Valle was indicative of how and why it provided psychic and physical artillery for the regime's revisionist doctrine of peace and reconciliation.[46] A tourist brochure, whose sentiments continue to be echoed in the twenty-first century in official publications and sermons by the abbot,[47] opens as follows:

> The Monument to all who fell in the Spanish Civil War, the erection of which was considered while the war was still in progress and decided upon when it was ended, should be regarded by all Spaniards as a just tribute to the meaning of all those who gave their life for their ideals. No man can give more.[48]

This anodyne account underplays the fact that this pharaonic mausoleum, built by forced labour,[49] was for Franco yet 'another monument devoted to perpetuating his victory'.[50] The decision to make it both the burial ground for the martyred Falangist leader José Antonio Primo de Rivera – who was removed from his previous grave in nearby El

Escorial – and the future resting place for Franco, thirty-six years after the end of the Civil War, bears testament to Slavoj Žižek's observations on how and why the 'materialization of ideology in external materiality reveals inherent antagonisms which the explicit formulation of ideology cannot afford to acknowledge';[51] 'the political, religious and funerary profile of the Valley … is definitely codified as a monument to Francoism in which both its tensions and vision of the world are inscribed'.[52]

This may have been a call for peace but it was not a call for peace at any cost: it was a carefully guarded peace in which the Caudillo's (re)telling of history retained a posthumous elocutionary force. Schoolchildren, alongside some official state visitors, continued to be taken to the Valle well into the 1980s,[53] whilst the prodigious architectural feat predated the Transition's so-called 'pacto de olvido' (pact of forgetting) in embodying a trade-off whereby the right did not obstruct Spain becoming more politically moderate in exchange for the bodies of the vanquished and the biographies of the victorious remaining disinterred. What always draws my attention on visiting the Valle are the fresh flowers that appear perpetually to adorn the tombstones of both Franco and Primo de Rivera; such tributes are off-limits to the thousands of casualties of the Civil War whose whereabouts remain unknown. Axiomatic to the eradication of anti-Spain in symbolic as well as real terms was denying Republic victims of the War and the subsequent dictatorship the chance to mourn what Judith Butler has critiqued in a different but often analogous context as 'ungrievable lives':

> What is the relation between the violence by which these ungrievable lives were lost and the prohibition of their public grievability? Is the prohibition on grieving the continuation of the violence itself? And does the prohibition on grieving demand a tight control on the reproduction of images and words?[54]

Strategic post-grief amnesia is not the same as never having the opportunity to grieve at all.

The Transition demanded that all sides of the political divide make an effort not to instrumentalise the past in the present, but that does not imply that the weight of sacrifice was evenly distributed. In Part IV, I am particularly interested in critically analysing this dynamic in relation to the cultural and political separatist demands made throughout a pluralist nation state, most prominently in the Basque Country and Catalonia. Franco's last wishes stressed the need to preserve the unity of Spain, and the aggressive centralism of the dictatorship ensured that many progressive members of Spanish society sympathised with the nationalist demands of ETA, who struck a vital blow against the regime with the meticulously planned assassination of the General's right-hand man, Admiral Carrero Blanco, in 1973.

The equation of ETA with democratisation, coupled with the repressive kneejerk reactions of the State, imbued the terrorist organisation with a legitimacy it would not otherwise have accrued. As can be seen in the documentary film *El proceso de Burgos* (*The Burgos Trial*) (Imanol Uribe, 1979), the detention of ETA's leadership in 1970 by the Francoist State exposed the corrupt and corrupting practices of the latter at least as much as of the former. Divisions nevertheless arose after the bombing of the Rolando Café in Madrid in September 1974, which, unlike previous attacks, targeted innocent bystanders as opposed to those explicitly aligned with the regime. This led the majority of ETA members 'to form ETA Político-Militar (or ETA-PM), which, though not rejecting the use of force, laid more emphasis on mass action and the political arena. The military front, on the other hand, became known as ETA-Militar (or ETA-M) and centred its activities on the "armed struggle".[55] Set against a pan-European context in which terrorism was on the rise, the actions of ETA-M was used by the Spanish armed forces to argue that democracy was, at best, not working and, at worst, inherently flawed; events in the Basque Country constantly threatened to derail the Transition. The paradoxical role of ETA in the democratisation process can be gauged from the Spanish–Italian co-production, *Ogro* (*Ogre*) (Gillo Pontecorvo, 1979), about the assassination of Carrero Blanco. As Alan O'Leary and Neelam Srivastava note: 'this act of terrorism under Franco had to be carefully distinguished from the actions of ETA under the nascent Spanish democracy, and by analogy from the actions of the Brigate Rosse under Italian post-war democracy, however imperfect'.[56]

17

Following the first democratic elections of 1977, the discourse of reform, not rupture, became firmly entrenched across the spectrum of mainstream political parties with the consequence that those not willing to moderate their positions found themselves increasingly ostracised. The vast majority of laws passed between 1977 and 1982 were approved with substantial inter-party collaboration,[57] whilst Party members were exceptionally disciplined when it came to voting on such matters as the draft Constitution of 1978.[58] In relation to this specific legislative matter, the recently legalised Spanish Communist Party proved to be the most disciplined of all. Under the leadership of Santiago Carrillo, there was a marked move to the centre in an attempt for the political formation that had formed the most consistent opposition to Francoism to gain democratic and electoral legitimacy in a new age. In an article for *El País* titled '¿Dónde estoy?' (Where am I?), dissident playwright Alfonso Sastre – a former Party member and ETA sympathiser whose partner, Eva Forest, was involved in the Rolando Café attack – accused the current crop of democratic politicians of opportunistically embellishing their anti-Francoist biographies, and questioned to what extent being to the left of Carrillo was the equivalent of being exiled to an ideological Siberia, bereft of comrades in arms.[59]

In an interview with the leader of the Spanish Communist Party originally published in *El País*, Rosa Montero noted how 'he lets slips phrases like "one of the most beautiful things in the world is a woman" or subtle jokes about homosexuality that evoke old conventional echoes'.[60] In her debut novel, *Crónica del desamor* (*Absent Love: A Chronicle*), first published in 1979, Montero mapped the personal onto the political and vice versa: 'Elena lived through the falling out of love in melancholy fashion, without tears, only with that nauseating tiredness, that conviction of the irreversible, of the definitive loss: the same exhaustion as when she abandoned the Spanish Communist Party.'[61]

If *La caza* (*The Hunt*) (Carlos Saura, 1965) constitutes a satire on the discourse of '25 años de paz' by reuniting a series of Civil War veterans to suggest that the foundational violence of the Francoist State is detrimental not just to the vanquished but also to the ostensible victors,[62] Montero carries out a similar re-evaluation of gender roles. The novel suggests that men and women alike have been stunted by ingrained gender hierarchies and the inability to forge relationships on an equal footing. As late as 1973, women were legally required to leave paid employment on marrying and to seek their husband's approval before accepting payment for non-domestic labour.[63] Francoism encouraged the reproduction of the State's paternalism in the home, but ingrained hierarchies did not die alongside the dictator. Casting an outsider's eye on the Transition, the narrator of *Madrid Underground* by David Serafin – a pseudonym for Oxford don Ian Michael – observes of María Rosa Pérez: '[s]he had enjoyed seeing Buñuel's *Viridiana*, so long banned in Spain, but she was feeling guilty at getting home late to cook her husband's supper'.[64] Since its creation in 1977, the Ministry of Culture has supported Gibraltar's efforts to enter the 'Miss World' competition, construed as an important symbol of self-determination.[65] Various female MPs elected in the 1977 elections resigned because of the prevailing machismo in their parties whilst, in 1979, the number of women candidates presented by each of the parties appeared to be inversely proportionate to their chances of winning.[66]

Patronage, permissiveness and prohibition neither began nor ended with the dictatorship. In his study of translations into Catalan of literary texts published from 1962 onwards, Jordi Cornellá-Detrell notes how the circulation of censored texts in the present day has largely gone unnoticed as a result of the firm line drawn 'between censorship and non-censorship, equating Franco's regime with the purging of books and democracy with freedom of expression'.[67] Part II here is concerned with expanding the remit of this premise to trace how and why democracy and freedom of expression have come to be viewed as synonymous, resulting in misguided historiography and, I will contend, the surreptitious continuation of censorial practices. A book such as Shirly Mangini's *Rojos y rebeldes: la cultura de la disidencia durante el franquismo* (*Reds and Rebels: The Culture of Dissidence during Francoism*) narrates a series of heroic actors and acts – 'a dramatic testament to try and survive within a cultural vacuum'[68] – distorts the historical record and, in the process, offers easily dismountable myths for revisionist historians who downplay the repression of the Francoist regime to argue that the coercive use of subsidies by democratic governments is as bad if not worse.[69] We require a more sophisticated heuristic model than prohibition for dictatorship, permissiveness for democracy.

It has become a commonplace to speak of Spaniards travelling to Perpignan to watch *Last Tango in Paris* (Bernardo Bertolucci, 1972) or soft-porn films, but much less frequently referred to is the fact that the musical *Jesus Christ Superstar* and its cinematic adaptation (Norman Jewison, 1973) were authorised in Spain, unlike in a number of neighbouring states, as was the ultra-violent *A Clockwork Orange* (Stanley Kubrick, 1971), albeit belatedly with advertisements appearing in many of the major newspapers the week the Caudillo died. Amidst the correspondence held in the Francisco Franco Foundation – a publicly funded archive located close to the Real Madrid Stadium frequented by few researchers and generally only cited in reactionary publications – is a series of letters to the Caudillo from various Catholic organisations that adopt an almost accusatory tone in their observation of the decline of moral values and licentiousness pervading society, culminating in the cinematic release of *Jesus Christ Superstar*. In a missive dated 20 June 1974, Luis María Chico de Guzmán writes: 'Una vez más pedimos que no se autorice la proyección de esa película ni de otras igualmente hirientes para el pueblo que si V.E. tuviera ocasión de ver, también se sentiría herido como español y como católico' (We ask once again that neither this film nor others equally harmful for the people be authorised. If Your Excellency had the chance to see them, he would also feel wounded as a Spaniard and a Catholic).[70]

Art, power and governance: cultural and political agency

Democratisation in the 1970s and 1980s was, if not predetermined, at least preconditioned, by the cultural politics of the previous decade. Manuel Fraga's appointment as Minister of Information and Tourism in 1962 was both the symptom and cause of a liberalisation of the regime, whilst the so-called 'contubernio de Munich' (Munich conspiracy) constituted the most professional and comprehensive meeting of the various wings of the

Francoist opposition united in an attempt to undermine the dictatorship's attempts to gain respectability through European integration.[71] Loose alliances of this kind provided the basis for the Junta Democrática and subsequently the Plataforma de Convergencia Democrática which, in a period with countless political parties, provided a collective voice for the mainstream opposition during the transfer of powers from Franco to Juan Carlos. The complex and contradictory demands of compromise and opportunism, friendship and skulduggery, statesmanship and self-interest, which acquired epic proportions in the mid-to-late 1970s, were in rehearsal the previous decade as factions jockeyed for power via strategic and often unexpected alliances. Fraga promoted himself as the spokesman for the reformist centre, bringing other like-minded spirits into his orbit through various means, including dinner parties with carefully curated guests.[72] In a card dated June 1966, Marxist academic and future Mayor of Madrid, Enrique Tierno Galván, presented himself as the 'pensador no 1 del Socialismo' (foremost thinker of Socialism) before issuing an invite to a 'cena de confraternidad tierno-falangista' (dinner of co-fraternity between Tierno and the Falangists); prominent disciples of Primo de Rivera were said to be coming, with the regulatory blue shirt declared optional.[73]

A recurring theme in democratisation studies is the extent to which success can and should be attributed to elites. Torcuato Fernández-Miranda, the young King's mentor, once said that the Transition had an impresario, Juan Carlos; a scriptwriter, himself; and an actor, Adolfo Suárez, President of Spain from 1976 to 1981. Hagiographic narratives that emerged in the mid-1990s, when the Transition's stock was riding high, foreground individual and collective agency to an extent that belies the fact that Franco died in his bed. Titles such as *Cuando la Transición se hizo posible: el contubernio de Munich* (*When the Transition was Made Possible: The Munich Conspiracy*)[74] and *Nosotros, la Transición* (*Us, the Transition*)[75] – alongside Victoria Prego's lavish television series and accompanying book *Así se hizo la Transición* (*This Is How the Transition Was Done*)[76] – foreground narratives of 'great men' who navigated Spain into safe waters. This model of agency has since been repurposed for cultural figures; hence, for example, Esther Pérez Villalba refers to 'singer-songwriting and political singers as cultural pro-democracy agents'.[77] The increased caution surrounding the Transition's success has done little to halt the ever-expanding cast of candidates staking their claim as protagonists, or to develop a theory of agency through which we can critically assess the role of individuals or collectives.

In the words of Ben Highmore, studies of the everyday demand an 'ability not to let the extraordinary overcome the world of the ordinary'.[78] Entertaining the possibility that culture can be understood to encompass not just spiritually nourishing high art but also, in Raymond Williams's terms, 'a whole way of life' offers the possibility of revisiting the relationship between elites, the masses and agency throughout the Transition. 'Theoretically, a period is recorded; in practice, this record is absorbed into a selective tradition; and both are different from the culture as lived'.[79] As the title suggests, John Hooper's *The Spaniards* (1986), later revised and updated as *The New Spaniards*,[80] was written as an account of how citizens lived in a newly formed democratic state and was assembled from material the correspondent had prepared that could not find a home in the *Guardian*, largely because it transcended what former editor-in-chief Alan Rusbridger (1995–2014) characterises as 'the worthy, very masculine core of what a broadsheet newspaper had been for most of the nineteenth and twentieth centuries'.[81] Taking celebrities as its focus, Part I of the current volume charts how and why the exclusion and feminisation of mass culture are inextricably linked to its absence from canonical accounts of the Transition, as well as making the case that successful political figures have been more alive to the possibilities of the popular than most intellectuals.

In the 1960s, the lives of everyday people changed beyond recognition through the influx of tourists from abroad, a rural exodus to the urban metropolises and economic emigration. Europe in general enjoyed an economic boom and rising living standards, but this process was exaggerated in Spain where, following decades of economic stagnation, the 'country's GDP, at constant prices, grew by 7.2 per cent per annum between 1960 and 1973, compared with the OECD average of 5 per cent'.[82] It cannot be taken for granted that the general population was invariably more progressive than the regime. Sasha D. Pack has, for example, documented evidence that 'authorities in coastal locations were often so fearful of foreign tabloid accusations of Spain's inquisitorial customs that affronted locals frequently denounced their failure to enforce the laws.'[83] Geoffrey Huard has shown that, much to the consternation of a zealous Barcelona-based magistrate, officialdom turning a blind eye ensured levels of homosexual activity in the Raval neighbourhood during the 1960s and 1970s were not dissimilar to those during the Second Republic or, for that matter, in the Paris of 1968;[84] sex tourism in hotspots such as Lloret de Mar during the late Francoist period resulted in arrests but not criminal charges.[85] There are two dangers in discussions of 1960s Spain: under- or overstating the effects of repression at a time when democracy was not a high priority for the general public.

As the dictatorship neared its end, those opposing the regime and auditioning for leading roles in a hypothetical Transition thought of little else other than politics. Conversely, however, the carefully orchestrated depoliticisation of a society in which aspiration had replaced self-abnegation as the national ideal constituted one of Francoism's major coups. In the words of José M. Magone: 'The opening up of the media market was paralleled by major reforms of the authoritarian regime in the economic sector. The new middle classes that emerged in the 1960s clearly represented new markets for the expanding media landscape.'[86] An increasingly urban consumer-based society ensured there was more work for women in the burgeoning service industries, and female demographics were prime targets for the expanding advertising industry. The first consumer rights society was established in 1963, but had less to say about contractual obligations than providing a forum to assist couples and working mums prevented from having a social life because they had nobody to leave their children with.[87] As was reflected in the in-house bulletin for employees of the Galerías Preciados department store,[88] the material and the moral were often presented as an indissoluble package.

With the exception of Part I, which simultaneously charts the role of celebrity in the Transition and historicises a critical habitus that favours the dismissal, as opposed to the critical exegesis, of popular culture, the remainder of the book combines analysis of 'high' and 'low' art to offer a more holistic overview of Spanish cultural production over a thirty-year period than has hitherto been available. Twentieth-century icons such as bullfighter Manuel Benítez ('El Cordobés') and crooner Julio Iglesias are, for example, critically examined in relation to a broader cultural and political sphere for the first time. The fact that *¡Hola!*, Spain's one major contribution to international journalism, has received no serious academic interest when its future currently seems far more secure than that of *El País* requires explanation. Franco was not only a fan of popular culture himself – he had a private cinema in his primary residence, the Pardo Palace, and he later became addicted to watching television in his bedroom – but also controlled his public image in the manner of a media-savvy celebrity. In 31.9 per cent of episodes of the NO-DO – the official newsreel service shown before all cinema performances – he makes an appearance;[89] 'Franco became the leading man of the NO-DO, its greatest actor.'[90] From 1962 onwards, the Caudillo began addressing his subjects in their homes via television. In the so-called information age, Fraga increasingly eclipsed the ageing Caudillo's star billing, becoming a perennial feature on television, greeting dignitaries and inaugurating tourist sites. Suárez, who beat many ostensibly better qualified candidates to become Spain's first democratically elected President since the Second Republic, quickly became wise to the power of popular culture in his role as Director-General of the State broadcaster (1969–73); a characteristically shrewd and self-interested early move was persuading the scriptwriters of *La casa de los Martinez* (1966–70), the most popular prime-time television series of the time, to make the eponymous protagonists – ostensibly an everyday family who welcomed a celebrity into their home every week – spend their holidays in his home province, Avila.[91]

As Part I documents, a doctrinaire, Marxist-inflected opposition was predisposed to dismiss mass culture as the opium of the people, a modern-day 'bread and circus'. There was some empirical justification for this position, but it often reinforced, as opposed to counteracting, dictatorial policy. In the words of Helen Graham and Jo Labanyi: 'What Francoism discouraged was not popular and mass culture, but the exercise of independent thought necessary to the development of any form of cultural analysis.'[92] Applying a psychoanalytic approach to Walter

Benjamin's notion of the dustbin of history as a privileged site for locating the detritus from which the past can be recomposed, Labanyi has later drawn on Jacques Derrida's notion of the spectral – 'often a matter of pretending to certify death there where the death certificate is still the performative of an act of war or the impotent gesticulation, the restless dream, of an execution'[93] – to argue that:

> critical writing on modern Spanish culture, by largely limiting itself to the study of 'high culture' (even when the texts studied are non-canonical), has systematically made invisible – ghostly – whole areas of culture which are seen as non-legitimate objects of study because they are consumed by subaltern groups.[94]

Advances have been made in Spanish cultural studies over recent years, but rich pickings are still to be found amongst the spectres at the feast, 'the traces of those who were not allowed to leave a trace; that is, the victims of history and in particular subaltern groups, whose stories – those of the losers – are excluded from the dominant narratives of the victors'.[95] The cultural concerns of working-class women will, for example, come to the fore in the discussion of the production and reception of the little-studied romantic novels of Corín Tellado, who, like Britain's Barbara Cartland or France's Delly before her, wrote for and enjoyed massive sales in a society tensed between, on the one hand, the inexorable development of modernity and, on the other, a deep-rooted social conservatism.

One of the pitfalls of the discourse surrounding the two Spains is that it b(l)inds disparate vectors of oppression. To what extent, for example, can the Catalan bourgeoisie lay claim to (post)colonial status when their riches have depended in no small measure on the labours of Castilian-speaking migrants? Following the 2017 independence referendum, I asked Ventura Pons for his thoughts. Barcelona's cinematic laureate, born into a bourgeois family made wealthy by the textile industry, responded with a quasi-evangelical redemptive narrative: 'I voted "Yes" and I'm extremely pleased and happy. I've waited 72 years (I was born in '45) to see my nation free. The oldest parliament in Europe, six years before Westminster.'[96] This depiction of a small nation wrestling the shackles of an incompetent centralist state is not necessarily representative, but neither is it entirely atypical. As addressed in Part IV, Catalonia is more than Barcelona, and Spain cannot be reduced to Madrid, but the global fascination with the rivalry between the Real Madrid and Barça football teams is symptomatic of the antagonism between complex and frequently contradictory notions of Spain and Catalonia often being channelled through their two major urban centres. In the words of Richard Lehan: 'Textualizing the city creates its own reality, becomes a way of seeing the city – but such textuality cannot substitute for the pavement and buildings, for the physical city.'[97] Part III relates textual affects back to the asphalt of Barcelona and Madrid to offer a class- and gender-inflected spatial analysis of two capitals that, in spite of their frequent animosity, have faced many of the same challenges, from rural migration in the 1960s to rising levels of crime, unemployment and drug consumption in the post-Franco period. Extending the parameters of the period referred to as the Transition until 1992, the year Spain celebrated its democratic consolidation for domestic and international consumption – Barcelona hosted the Olympic Games and Seville the Universal Exhibition, and Madrid was European City of Culture – facilitates a broader purview for engaging with the ethics and aesthetics woven into the fabric of Spain's two major cities.

Culture has constituted a privileged medium for both competition and (re)conciliation. On the one hand, it provided a vehicle for Catalan nationalist expression that helped to ensure that the increasingly unjustifiable actions of ETA – a particular nadir being the 1987 bombing of the Hipercor shopping centre in Barcelona – were not replicated. Conversely, however, this was always a delicate equilibrium, and a more steadfast maintenance of a non-folkloric national(ist) culture than in any of Spain's other autonomous regions constituted both the means and ends for pro-independent demands that gained momentum following the ousting of the right-of-centre pragmatist Jordi Pujol from the presidency of the Generalitat in 2003 – after twenty-three years in power, yet another of the 'great men' of the Transition was hoist with his own corrupt petard. As David Chaney notes: 'Culture is not a neutral or self-evident term but one that has been developed through an enormous overlapping literature of theoretical reflection, descriptive survey and ethnographic report.[98] Part IV explores what is at stake in different notions of culture in a context where the Ministry of Information and Tourism being rebranded as the Ministry of Culture was construed as a key stepping stone towards democratisation. The return of Pablo Picasso's *Guernica* to Spain is employed as an emblematic case-study to explore the means by which culture was a means of suturing the wounds of the Civil War.

The execution of Federico García Lorca constituted Francoism's original sin, the precursor to the aerial bombing of innocent civilians depicted in Picasso's most famous painting. If the dictatorship was uncivilised and uncultured, post-Franco Spain has fetishised culture as an absolute good and hallmark of the modern pluralistic, democratic state. What this utopian vision disregards is the potential that culture holds to exclude as well as to include. The Transition was undoubtedly accompanied by an explosion of creativity in the arts ranging from the resurrection of local festivities across the Peninsula to the arrival of rave culture in Valencia but, I will suggest, unequal power relations were upheld rather than dispelled by expanding the remit of culture to encompass activities as diverse as torturing animals and injecting heroin.

The ostensible democratisation of popular culture served to reiterate a hierarchical division of an excessively earnest state (read universal) high culture with the carnivalesque of the local. On this model, it was entirely logical that *Guernica* was not returned to the Basque Country but formed the cornerstone of the Reina Sofia Art Museum, officially inaugurated in 1992. Culture was employed both to conceal and to compensate for the human costs of Spain's leap into (post)modernity: with the gulf between rich and poor increasing, crime rates were high whilst rates of HIV infection and heroin consumption topped European rankings. The recent investigative turn in cultural production has begun to grapple with the ghostly underbelly of 1992. As recalled in *Urtain*, a play premiered at the Centro Dramático Nacional (National Drama Centre) in Madrid in 2008, the eponymous protagonist, a former European featherweight boxing champion and popular celebrity from the Basque Country, committed suicide just four days before the commencement of the Olympic Games in Barcelona. At the time of writing, Luis López Carrasco is in the process of completing the follow-up to *El futuro*, a documentary about the frequently violent strikes against industrial reconversion that took place in 1992 in Cartagena (Murcia). A quarter of a century on from Spain's *annus mirabilis*, the democratic structures of the State appear to be simultaneously underdeveloped and outdated. Spain finds itself at a crossroads, torn between nostalgia for a time when anything and everything seemed possible, and genuine anger against the unrealised potential of a calcified Transition. One advantage of Spain no longer seeing itself as a country in perpetually forward motion is the unrealised potential for a collective and individual reflection on the country's recent history, an overdue recognition of the need to move beyond the Manicheanism detrimental to scholarship and culture alike.

The alternate beatification and condemnation of the 'regime of '78' is both paradoxical, given the ostensible consensus that grounds its mythical origins, and wholly consistent with broader historical patterns. Both individually and collectively, the sections that follow reveal how and why an awareness of the cultural politics of the thirty-year period between 1962 and 1992 is as vital for understanding contemporary Spain as the three years of the Civil War were for the passage from dictatorship to democracy. The Transition was no fairytale, but neither was it the nightmare it could have been: critically engaging with the revenant of culture in its myriad guises is a necessary prerequisite if Spanish society is ever to aspire to a genuine, as opposed to pharaonic, self-confidence in its past, present and future.

Part I

Celebrity

Introduction

On returning to the United Kingdom in 1962 to complete an under-graduate degree in Spanish following her year abroad, Lucia Graves – the daughter of the poet Robert, raised in Mallorca – recalls Conchita, a woman running a dressmaking school, who was obsessed with listening to radio agony-aunt Elena Francis, and wonders: 'Could all this world of Madrid be encompassed in an Oxford translation class?'[1] The answer was clearly no. If, as Joke Hermes contends, '[p]opular cultural texts and practices are important because they provide much of the wool from which the social tapestry is knit',[2] then the principal aim of this part is to show the importance of celebrity to the cultural politics of a period when the 'distinction between an ascetic Spain and an indulgent West rested on a distinction of consumer values that, if they [had] once existed, no longer did'.[3]

Over the course of the 1960s, the combined sales of women's magazines *Lecturas, Semana, ¡Hola!* and *Diez minutos* eclipsed the rest of the market combined.[4] Spaniards were not avid newspaper readers: the first serious market research suggested the country had 107 newspapers, but that only 5 per cent had a circulation of over 100,000.[5] The pro-monarchist *ABC* sold best (192,000 copies), a far cry from the 5 million copies of the *Daily Mirror* sold in the UK;[6] the combined sales of newspapers in Spain in 1967 were around 2.5 million.[7] The interpellation of (un)willing subjects in a culture of non-inquisitiveness was evidently one of Francoism's chief political triumphs, but work remains to be done on critically interro-gating the information available to everyday Spaniards alongside a more nuanced understanding of how this both shaped and reflected their interests. During the nascent democratic period, a number of canonical cultural texts – most eminently the documentary film *Canciones para después de una guerra* (*Songs for after a War*) (Basilio Martín Patino, 1976) and Carmen Martín Gaite's 1978 novel *El cuarto de atrás* (*The Back Room*) – resurrected the popular culture ostensibly patented by the Franco regime in the 1940s and 1950s. As Stephanie Sieburth notes, '*El cuarto de atrás* teaches us that the effects of role-play through mass-culture can be positive, negative, or both at once.'[8]

This part has been designed as an academic counterpart to such creative enterprises. In the first chapter, I employ two case-studies – the bullfighter 'El Cordobés' and pop singer Raphael – to explore the gender- and class-infected discourses that emerged around celebrity culture in a period described by Nigel Townson as the 'transition to the Transition'.[9] I will analyse how and why these figures provided evidence for the oppositional left to understand mass culture as the opium of the masses, a surreptitious form of depoliticisation. A dogmatic desire to denigrate rather than engage with celebrity culture nevertheless proved counter-productive for their progressive ideological agenda. Politics and celebrity culture are frequently construed as antithetical, but they share the common trait of being ubiquitous and invisible in late-twentieth-century Spain, everywhere and nowhere at the same time. Chapter 2 critically interrogates the extent to which remodelled formations of power and influence were forged and contested though a generational shift as embodied by a series of aristocratic figures from the royal and Franco families. The third and final chapter hones in on the leading lights of the 1980s Spanish media-scape – Isabel Preysler, Isabel Pantoja and Julio Iglesias – to suggest that Spain's reputed jump from pre- to postmodernity was not as clear-cut and absolute as it often assumed to be, and that this is inextricably linked with the political and diplomatic power celebrities continued to wield at home and abroad.

Chapter 1

Fandom and mass-culture in late-Francoist Spain

Manuel Benítez 'El Cordobés' and Raphael

Modern celebrity culture predates Hollywood and the Internet. The public began taking a strong interest in a large number of living authors, artists, performers, scientists and politicians in the eighteenth century.[1] In Spain, celebrities first arose when bullfighting ceased being an exclusively aristocratic practice to become a form of mass popular entertainment. As Tara Zanardi remarks, '[l]ike the actors of the British stage, bullfighters in part acquired their new stature from their performance of aristocracy'.[2] Celebrities simultaneously reflect and transform the societies from which they emerge.

In what follows, I chart how and why the two most important male celebrities of 1960s Spain bear testament to Justin Crumbaugh's claim that Manuel Fraga, the incoming Minister of Tourism and Information (1962–9), advocated 'a conscious re-politicization of society through the symbolic channels made available by Spain's emergent information age'.[3] Combining tradition and modernity in terms of biography, public persona and performance styles, Manuel Benítez 'El Cordobés' and Raphael were simultaneously exploited and exploitative in their attempts to present a benign image of a dictatorial regime for domestic and international consumption. The humble origin of many Andalusian stars was a long-standing celebrity trope, but a saccharine 'rags to riches' narrative became ubiquitous at a time when, with the exception of Japan, Spain had the fastest growing economy in the world.[4] The bullfighter and the melodic pop singer constituted ego-ideals for millions of Spaniards moving from the country to the city, as aspiration replaced austerity as the national ideal. In an increasingly urban consumer-based society, celebrity media-reports were fixated by jet-set lifestyles: frequent plane trips, stays in Hilton hotels, rides around different cities in convertible sports cars, etc.

As Larry Collins and Dominique Lapierre wrote in their international best-seller, a 'factional' novel titled *Or I'll Dress You in Mourning: The Story of El Cordobés and the New Spain He Stands For,* 'love of art may drive a man to a bullring's ticket window, but it is hunger that drives him onto its sands'.[5] Born in 1936, Benítez suffered the after-effects of the Civil War first-hand: his father died in the prison into which he had been thrown for his Republican sympathies. Raised in social care, the orphaned child did whatever was necessary to improve his fortunes: teetering on the edge of starvation and criminality, he made a name for himself in small towns and villages by taking on bulls in ramshackle and frequently lethal festivities from a young age. On 21 February 1961, Pipo – El Cordobés's ruthless and ambitious manager – organised the first bullfight to be held in Franco's principal residence, the Pardo, as part of a charity event organised by the Caudillo's wife, Carmen Polo, to raise funds to build housing for the poor.[6] El Cordobés would never have succeeded – or, at least not to such a great extent – in an age prior to the arrival of mass media and the package holiday. To the consternation of purists, he was more a consummate celebrity entertainer than an orthodox matador. His crowd-pleasing antics included a series of well-rehearsed tricks: chief in his arsenal was a gymnastic display of bravery in which he ostensibly allowed himself to be dominated by bulls that frequently tossed him high in the air. Performances outside the ring were similarly stage-managed. On 4 May 1965 he was flown on his private light aircraft to Tenerife;[7] greeted at the airport by fans and reporters, he then opened a renovated cigarette factory, whose owners sponsored the bullfight that brought him to the Canary Islands. Curro Romero, a classical bullfighter, has complained of sensationalism, 'when many of us came from the same place, but didn't have that kind of marketing'.[8] Benítez's appeal was boosted by fabled tales of generosity; having once been denied medical treatment after a serious goring for not being a union member, he was reputed to have used his position as the world's foremost matador to insist that all injuries be treated.[9] The legend was amplified in hagiographic biographies[10] and *Aprendiendo a morir* (*Learning to Die*) (Pedro Lazaga, 1962), a saccharine cinematic star vehicle in which Benítez played himself;[11] the star reputedly did not read the script as he had yet to learn to read.[12]

Television enabled more Spaniards to witness the national *fiesta* than ever before, whilst mass tourism transformed it into an increasingly lucrative industry. In 1962, the then Director-General of Tourism, Don Manuel de Urzáiz, claimed that 70 per cent of requests for information received by his office from abroad related to bullfighting.[13] The Mayor of Fuengirola justified using public funds to subsidise the construction of a bullring that same year by a private concern with recourse to the argument that it would attract tourists to the municipality on the Costa del Sol.[14] In 1963, there were 360,000 television sets in Spain; this figure had risen to 1,250,000 in 1965 and to over 3 million in 1968.[15] Whenever a televised bullfight was announced in advance, factory workers requested (and usually received) permission to start work two hours earlier to be able to finish in time to watch the event.[16] Pepín Toboso, owner of the Galerías Preciados chain, complained that revenue plummeted, and unsuccessfully petitioned the State to delay the transmission of Benítez's bullfights until after his department stores had closed.[17]

According to Kenneth Tynan, El Cordobés was 'arguably the highest-paid individual performer in European history':

> This cool uncaring boy, with his disdain for tradition and dignity and balletic 'line', was a Spanish embodiment of something I had already met under several other names. In France, the *blouson noir*; in Britain, the Mod; and in America, the hipster. Nonchalance, love of danger for kicks, casual contempt for conformity: these were the attributes that made *El Cordobés* the first hip bullfighter.[18]

Following the breakthrough success of the Beatles, the first holiday manager Brian Epstein took was to Spain in 1964 to meet with Benítez. Epstein's travelling companion, Peter Brown, recalls:

He was this handsome kid who wore his hair long and he became the Beatle bullfighter that everyone knew and there was talk about him being part of the next Beatle movie. Brian and I went to visit him at his farm in Cordoba where we were treated like very important people. They were all very courteous. But Pipo was a monster and Cordobes was very tied up with him. We did examine the whole business about whether it was possible to do the movie. It just didn't work out, but it was wonderful to go to his farm.[19]

The project may not have materialised, but Epstein's fascination with the taurine world did not end there. According to Nat Weiss, his American business partner: 'Bullfighters were to Brian what the Beatles were to music fans. They were his idols.'[20] Epstein indulged his fantasies by managing British bullfighter Henry Higgins and hanging a photo of El Cordobés in his London bathroom.[21] The Beatles performed to a half-empty Las Ventas bullring in 1965 shortly after receiving their MBEs from Queen Elizabeth II. The connection between British pop aristocracy and El Cordobés would be revitalised in the 1980s when Tom Jones recorded 'A boy from nowhere', based on Benítez's life, from the otherwise unsuccessful musical *Matador*, subsequently staged in London in the early 1990s.

Benítez was an idol not because he wanted to change society, but rather because he suggested it was possible for one to change position within the social hierarchy. Frank Evans, the son of a Conservative councillor, who would go on to become footballer George Best's informal manager in Manchester and a matador in Spain, recalls tales told to him as a teenager in northern England by family friend Paco Montes: '*El Cordobés* lived the life. I wanted to be part of it but had absolutely no idea how to get there or what to do.'[22] In *El espontáneo* (*The Rash One*) (Jorge Grau, 1964), for the film's eponymous protagonist (a hotel bell-boy unfairly dismissed after being sexually molested by drunk foreign female guests) flicking through a magazine with glamorous images of Benítez is instrumental in his deciding to try his own luck in the ring. Harassment was treated here in a comic vein but it frequently had tragic real-life consequences when the 'widespread practice of sexual objectification of female domestic servants ... was a typical habit of middle-class men across Western Europe'.[23] Spanish employment law offered young women little protection in the workplace at a time when they were increasingly in demand in the service industries whilst still being subject(ed) to antiquated hierarchies of gendered social roles. As depicted in *Chica para todo* (*A Girl for Anything*), Alfonso Paso's popular theatrical play – rapidly adapted for the cinema (Mariano Ozores, 1963) – a culture shift ensured that female servants went from living with families for their whole working lives, often a cloistered form of self-abnegation, to a situation of short-term contracts being given to rural migrants.[24] The correlative to a greater freedom of movement for employees was that their situations were more precarious and open to exploitation. In 1963, a nineteen-year-old young woman from the small Catalan municipality of Granollers wrote to popular radio agony-aunt, Elena Francis, to say she had a fraught relationship with her mother, and wanted to move to Barcelona to work as a maid; she received a reply to say that it was a shame that she could not make an effort to improve family relations, but that a contact for a training centre for domestic labour was enclosed.[25] Many of the roughly 500 letters sent daily to the radio station referred to the sexual harassment of young women in their new homes.[26] In an act of transventriloquism, Juan Soto Viñuelo replied in the name of Elena Francis between 1961 and 1984, also scripting the radio-shows. He claims to have sometimes invented letters to raise awareness around the subject: in his opinion, 'the only way not to be bothered by the man of the house was to be ugly'.[27] El Cordobés's proletarian roots were central to his sexual allure, but he exploited the opportunity to exercise his *droit de seigneur* in the houses of friends and, in 1968, a young maid working in Madrid gave birth to Manuel Díaz,[28] an illegitimate child raised in poverty before going on to be a successful bullfighter in his own right. Benítez always denied kinship, even taking Díaz to court for using his artistic name, until DNA tests offered near-definitive proof of paternity in 2016. The paternalism of Francoist press laws prevented Benítez's private misdemeanours from becoming public knowledge.

In the same year Díaz was born, his father's professionalism was put into question when fellow matador Miguel Mateo 'Miguelín' illegally jumped into the ring at Las Ventas on 18 May when El Cordobés was performing. Embittered by what he believed to be Benítez's unwarranted popularity, the less successful matador from Algeciras grabbed and caressed the horns of a young bull that had been fed up to give it the veneer of an older, more aggressive beast. This was an effective piece of theatre in itself, an easier manoeuvre for a professional bullfighter to carry out than lay spectators might suspect. After being arrested and spending a night in jail, Miguelín immediately paid the requisite fine and apologised in public, expressing gratitude to the police for the good treatment he had received. The ruse seemingly worked in his favour. Miguelín was contracted to take on six bulls in one afternoon at Las Ventas (the standard although by no means unique format of a *corrida* is for three matadors to take on six bulls), receiving multiple trophies, thanks in part to the good will of the audience.

The authorities, worried that Miguelín might establish a precedent, replaced the traditional fine with a prolonged prohibition from working as a professional bullfighter.[29] According to a report in bullfighting magazine *Fiesta nacional*:

> The French are worried about strikes, the English think of nothing other than maintaining the strength of the pound, the Italians about elections and the North Americans peace negotiations. Meanwhile, we Spaniards invest all of our media and even political energies into two figures who ostensibly have nothing to do with public life: Raimón, the Valencian singer, and Miguel Mateo 'Miguelín', a bullfighter from Algeciras.[30]

The veracity of this statement hinges largely on what is understood by 'public life'. Against the backdrop of an increasingly politicised Europe, the case for bullfighting as modern-day 'bread and circuses' is easy to make. Chronicles from 1898 indicate that, on the same day the Spanish navy lost the final vestiges of empire, Madrid was filled with well-heeled men and women excited to attend a *corrida*.[31] In the so-called information age, bullfights and football matches were televised on 1 May, Labour Day, to reduce the chances of workers demonstrating.[32] Conversely, however, the media dedicating more attention to Miguelín's imprisonment than to student uprisings in Paris was not solely the consequence of press censorship. What went on in Las Ventas was more familiar to most Spaniards than the Sorbonne or even Madrid's Central (now Complutense) University, the product and cause of bullfighting providing a recognisable terrain on which injustices could be more clearly perceived. After a televised *corrida* in 1968, matador Jaime Ostos openly accused commentator Lozano Sevilla of extorting money from bullfighters for positive commentary,[33] which led to the latter's dismissal. These were battles very different from but not necessarily less parochial than the ones increasingly being fought on university campuses. After the dismantling of the Francoist students' union in 1965, the principal source of student unrest over coming years concerned what was to be put in its place.[34] From 1967 onwards there was an almost constant police presence on the campuses of Madrid and Barcelona,[35] with Blas Piñar's Fuerza Nueva Party flexing its muscles by bussing in vigilantes from Valladolid, a fascist stronghold. Raimón's concert in aid of workers' rights at the Economics Faculty of the Complutense, which ended with police intervention, has been described as 'the most symbolic anti-Franco public event that Spain had yet to see', and crystallised a rising tide of protest.[36]

The march for democratisation in the university and Spain more broadly were presented as inextricably linked missions. Militants expressed sympathy for the proletariat but, in a situation that was hardly unique to Spain (see, for example, Pier Paolo Pasolini's 1968 poem, 'Vi odio, cari student (Il PCI ai giovani!!)'), the most optimistic estimates suggest that a maximum of 6 per cent of the undergraduate population came from working-class families;[37] it was also largely impossible to mobilise campus protests unless the issue being contested related specifically to the university.[38]

Spanish student leaders travelled to Paris regularly,[39] and the events of May had a clear effect on ongoing struggles in Madrid.[40] Álvaro Fleites Marcos's study of press coverage in Spain reveals that French student uprisings were reported, but that journalists adopted an almost universally condemnatory attitude,[41] fearful their actions might be replicated in Spain. Outlets diverged in their attribution of blame to the French authorities. The liberal *Madrid* newspaper received a 250,000 peseta fine and two-month publication ban, not for its calls for General de Gaulle to resign, but for the parallels it suggested between the French premier and General Franco.[42]

Over the course of the decade, the Spanish Communist Party increasingly courted students, whilst repeated attempts to call a national strike failed. Paul Preston attributes this failure to their leader Santiago Carrillo misinterpreting the workers' struggles in Asturias during 1963 and 1964 as being about ideology and class struggle as opposed to wages.[43] The efforts of the Francoist opposition were frequently scuppered by the inability to engage with the masses in concrete, as opposed to abstract, terms. Looking back on his time in the student theatre group of the Faculty of Medicine at Seville University, Joaquín Arbide recalls that the politically committed actor Francisco Rabal – whose father and uncle had been forced to work in the construction of El Valle de los Caídos – horrified the assembled audiences by suggesting that, if they wanted to make a genuinely popular theatre, then they ought to hire performers such as Lola Flores,[44] 'a component of singular importance in that *back room*, as Carmen Martín Gaite would put it, that makes up the history of popular culture in contemporary Spain'.[45] A regular at the Pardo, Flores was the leading proponent of the *copla* (traditional Spanish popular song).[46] As she noted in an interview with film and music magazine *Fotogramas*, she, unlike the Fab Four, had managed to fill Las Ventas bullring: 'In Spain, I'm bigger than all those international long-haired types who come from abroad.'[47] That the Beatles graced the front cover of the 20 November 1964 issue of the same film and music magazine that included a glowing report on the premiere of biopic *Franco, ese hombre* (*Franco, That Man*) (José Luis Sáenz de Heredia, 1964) – 'a kitsch fiction masquerading as a document of truth'[48] made to coincide with the celebration of twenty-five years of peace – is a striking manifestation of Spain's 'entanglement of temporalities'.[49]

In both musical and iconographical terms, Raphael, the poster-boy of late Francoism and bête noir of much of the oppositional intelligentsia, operated somewhere between the folkloric superstar and the long-haired hit-makers from Liverpool. Inspired by the international company Philips, the 'niño de Linares' (lad from Linares) replaced the 'f' of his first name with 'ph' to sound more modern at home and familiar abroad. He was quickly promoted to a headliner at the televised Christmas fundraising concerts organised by Carmen Polo.[50] The singer had been born into a working-class Andalusian family, but had moved to the capital as a child when his father came looking for work in construction. Raphael frequently recounts the tale of their being evicted from their flat in Cuatro Caminos (one of the capital's principal immigrant districts), and the callousness with which neighbours reacted when his family were left humiliated alongside their mattresses in the stairwell.[51] Much was made of the house the young star bought for his parents, alongside his frustration with his father for refusing to accept money from him and continuing to work in a dangerous industry. In his film appearances, Raphael repeatedly played an aspiring singer or a celebrity struggling with the pressures of fame. In the former category, there is invariably a scene in which the character transcends his social origins through a combination of hard work and raw talent in the live environment.[52]

Raphael's performance style is sufficiently idiosyncratic to render comparisons difficult, but mannerisms of walking onto the stage almost as if he were a bullfighter, holding his arms out to emphasise particular phrases, and demonstrative facial gestures owe more to the tradition of male flamenco song than to Anglo-American pop. Radiating youth, with an impeccably conserved fringe and invariably dressed in dapper, generally black, clothes, he nevertheless embodied a new male archetype for Spanish popular music. In 1966, 'Yo soy aquél' (I am he) – his signature tune to this day – represented Spain in the Eurovision Song Contest. Raphael was doing military service at the time but, as the singer recalls in his memoirs, his management convinced Fraga to grant him leave with the following rationale: 'that I did more service for my country singing than being locked up in barracks.'[53]

As Ivan Raykoff and Robert Deam Tobin note, '[m]odernity characterizes the ideal of post-war Europe to which the Eurovision Song

Contest provides literal and figurative access: a society that is democratic, capitalist, peace-loving, multi-cultural, sexually liberated and technologically advanced'.[54] Spain's participation since 1961 was construed as partial compensation for the regime's failed bid for associate status to the EEC, providing entry into what was then considered an exclusive club, whilst an internal document from 1966 for Spanish State television on techniques for optimising 'eficacia política' (political efficiency) suggested that, from 19 May onwards, news programmes used reports on the song contest as a pretext for reporting on news from around Europe, investing in purchasing footage from foreign broadcasters in the hope they would reciprocate.[55]

'Yo soy aquél' was the best-selling single at home in 1966, and expectations for victory in Luxembourg reached fever pitch.[56] The song came seventh but, in some respects, this benefited Raphael, who was treated as a national hero sabotaged by nefarious foreign conspirators; he was greeted by cavalcades of fans at Barajas airport, let off military service and automatically entered as the (unsuccessful) Spanish entry in 1967. Massiel, a former 'Miss Madrid with Glasses' champion,[57] won the coveted trophy in 1968, albeit amidst rumours persisting to this day that the Francoist television authorities used bribes authorised from above to secure a Spanish victory.[58]

Irrespective of the veracity of this claim, the regime's interest in the contest is intimated by Massiel's being ordained into the Order of Queen Isabel the Catholic Queen (although she never picked the award up), and investment into Madrid's hosting the competition the following year with a high-profile gala at the Teatro Real for which Salvador Dalí provided the publicity materials. Only black-and-white television was available in Spain until the mid-1970s, but the German television broadcaster lent TVE a mobile production unit to broadcast the colour signal to the rest of Europe.[59] Austria was the sole country to withdraw as a result of the competition's being held in a country that remained a dictatorship. A state of emergency, declared in January 1969 following student revolts, which led to the closure of universities and the death of Enrique Ruano in police custody, was suspended shortly before over fifty international journalists arrived at the Costa del Sol as guests of Fraga's ministry prior to an international event designed to showcase a different side of Spain to the European community. Work remains to be done on the special treatment given to celebrities by the regime, but it is clear they were often afforded freedom of movement as a tacit reward for their role as international ambassadors used to whitewash the continued violence of the Francoist State and develop international links in Europe and beyond.

The legitimacy of the Caudillo's victory in the Civil War alongside the limited international respectability subsequently accrued by Spain were predicated on anti-Communism and yet, even here, cultural ties never disappeared. By 1964, important sections of the Spanish media advocated the normalisation of relations between Spain and the Soviet Union.[60] Luis Miguel Dominguín, the matador who had no compunction about hunting with his friend Franco and dining with dissidents such as novelist Juan Goytisolo and exile Jorge Semprún – the Buchenwald concentration camp survivor who had carried out undercover work for the Spanish Communists prior to being expelled from the Party by Carrillo in 1964 – in Moscow,[61] organised bullfights behind the Iron Curtain in Tito's Yugoslavia. On becoming Minister of Foreign Affairs in 1969, Gregorio López Bravo de Castro has stated that a major priority was establishing trade links with the Eastern Bloc.[62] Following the condemnation of the Soviet invasion of Czechoslovakia by the Spanish Communist Party, the Kremlin sold Franco's Government much-needed coal during the 1969 miners' strike in Asturias.[63] The location of the Oscar-winning film *Z* (Costa-Gavras, 1969) is never explicitly stated, but the script co-authored by Semprún implicitly references the Spanish context with a brutal anti-Communist police and vigilante violence juxtaposed against bigwigs courting the Soviets with a performance by the Bolshoi ballet. A decade after expelling Semprún for questioning the Soviet party line, Carrillo's subsequent turn towards Eurocommunism was the logical consequence of political opportunism combined with a sense of personal betrayal. When López Bravo travelled to the Philippines in 1970, he stopped off in Moscow allowing for the first official meeting between a Francoist politician and senior members of the Soviet administration.[64]

That same year, the Communist State appreciated the same qualities in Raphael that they saw in Early Modern playwright Lope de Vega – who from the 1930s to the 1960s was amongst the most staged dramatists of any nationality on the Soviet stage, audiences and critics alike being seduced by the passion of Spain and its national playwright[65] – catapulting star-vehicle *Digan lo que digan* (*Let Them Talk*) (Mario Camus, 1968) into a box-office sensation.[66] At a time when there were still no official diplomatic links, Raphael performed his first concerts in Leningrad and Moscow in 1971. Fans queued overnight to secure tickets and, according to the recollections of one, police on horseback were deployed to retain order.[67] The growth of Spanish in Soviet universities has been attributed to the entry of women coinciding with Raphael's success, with the publication of pedagogical guides to learning the language of Cervantes using the lyrics to songs performed by the lad from Linares.[68] Claims of this kind lend themselves to exaggeration, but publications and websites bear testament to the professional and personal gateways Raphael's largely female fan-base believe their idol has opened for them.[69]

As Lawrence Grossberg notes, the 'fan can only be understood historically, as located in a set of different possible relations to culture.'[70] As recent research into China and Taiwan has brought to the fore, fandom is particularly ripe amongst adolescents undergoing the transition away from childhood into adulthood in societies that combine tradition with an accelerated rate of change.[71] The first fan phenomenon in Spain was pop group Dúo Dinámico in the early 1960s,[72] celebrities receiving an increasing volume of correspondence.[73] *Raphaelitis* (Raphael Fever), the moniker given to the Spanish equivalent of Beatlemania, took hold when he entered Eurovision.

In the first issue of a new fan bulletin, *Club Raphael*, the editor, Maribel Andujar, highlights her desire to form a global community.[74] The announcement of an official fan uniform – a red short-sleeved top with a black skirt and belt – based on Raphael's personal colour preferences was announced in issue 4; in issue 6 a hymn that was to be sung at all meetings of members was published. It contained the following lines:

Raphael, you are the best
your song is our hope
and, in this moment,
we swear an oath.

In line with the star's liminal identity, Raphael's fan club was a manifestation of what Rosario Coca Hernando refers to as 'a new ambivalent femininity which combined both the traditional and the modern'.[75]
It perpetuated traditional female gender roles, as was demonstrated by
Andujar's piece addressed to Raphael's mother, 'A Doña Raphaelita', which
compares the singer's progenitrix to the Virgin Mary before proceeding
to say how all of his fans consider themselves to be his mother (Club
Raphael, issue 10);[76] it is, in fact, striking how many fan accounts from
across the globe, now readily accessible online,[77] refer to him not only
as 'el niño' (the lad) but also as 'mi niño' (my lad). The club organised
events such as *Operación abuelo* (Operation Grandparent) that, in line
with the kind of initiatives promoted by the regime's Women's Section
(the Sección Femenina), encouraged female teenagers to carry out good
works in the community, and also echoed the development of a new
kind of paternalistic civic society as evidenced though the exponential
growth of pedagogical and community projects that emerged around
television clubs, subsidised by the Ministry of Information and Tourism,
that sprung up around the Peninsula.[78] For the oppositional left, Raphael
constituted a surreptitious form of depoliticisation, a textbook example
of the totalitarian impulse Theodor Adorno diagnosed at the heart of
mass-produced popular music, organised 'into a system of response
mechanisms wholly antagonistic to the ideal of individuality in a free,
liberal society'.[79]

As Tania Modleski remarks: 'It is one of the greatest ironies in the
development of mass-culture theory that the people who were first
responsible for pointing out the political importance of mass art simultaneously provided the justification for slighting it.'[80] Dissidents under
Franco believed cultural theory to be a corrective force, but a puritan-
ical intelligentsia simultaneously under- and overestimated the effects of
popular culture, remaining oblivious to the fact that 'there are in fact no

masses, but only ways of seeing people as masses'.[81] Fans were thereby construed as what William W. Kelly terms 'the most duped and ignorant of the already co-opted audiences of Culture Industry spectacles'.[82] In a journalistic report, Francisco Umbral noted how:

> Something's going to happen, they are waiting for something, expecting to receive something at Raphael's house, when these young women who look like employees or workers, almost never university students, put up with being stood up by their hypothetical and collective boyfriend. They arrive punctually for their date with nothing, a meeting with the doorman … He is the anti-ideological singer, the romanticism of the record company, and diluted eroticism.[83]

Umbral proceeds to posit Raphael and Madrid, the psychic and physical capital of the Francoist State (see Part III), to be in cahoots and similarly inauthentic: the singer exploits his fans in a manner akin to the way that the regime deceives its subjects. A similar vision is on display in the documentary film *Rafael en Raphael* (*Rafael in Raphael*) (Antonio Isasi-Isasmendi, 1975) which juxtaposes queues of hysterical fans for sold-out concerts in the centre of Madrid and interviews with law students. As the director recalls: 'The most charitable thing to be heard there was him being dismissed as an unbearable and anachronistic kitsch phenomenon.'[84] What this class- and gender-inflected reductive vision fails to acknowledge is the very human needs to which both the star and his fans responded. In a letter to Elena Francis dated 27 April 1968, eighteen-year-old Maite complained she had worked in Madrid for three months but had yet to make any friends, and that on Sundays she entertained herself by going to the cinema or watching television, whilst her hobby was collecting celebrity photos.[85] The entry of women into higher education is depicted as a positive manifestation of female emancipation but there is no sense that friendship between fans provided a new generation of less-educated women, with a hitherto unknown level of economic independence in the expanding service industries, with group outings, social networks and reconfigured identities.[86]

By the time of *Rafael en Raphael*'s release, the star had married the journalist Natalia Figueroa,[87] daughter of the Marquis of Santo Floro, effectively marking the union of a traditional and new form of aristocracy. In the film, both the singer and his friend El Cordobés are shown to have framed pictures of Franco in their respective condominiums. Raphael combined a common-sense belief in Francoism with the purported absence of an ideological agenda when asked about his political views:

> If I think there are political problems here? There, you've got me: I don't understand any of that stuff! And it's not a pose: I am absolutely apolitical, absolutely. I don't know what socialism is, I don't know what is – what other things are there? – well, communism – what other things? There are other things – democracy and the reign of rhinos, he, he, he! I swear to you that I don't know anything. Not even what they want to say with these words … I admire and adore Generalísimo Franco madly, I love him very much and with a very profound kind of love. He inspires in me a great respect … Now, if suddenly, King Juan Carlos or … and if he comes and behaves like Franco, then he would also warrant my respect in the same way John Kennedy deserves my respect for the way in which he treated the American people. Do you understand what I'm saying?[88]

That this view is so unintelligible is not solely the result of Raphael's self-serving logic, as confused as it is confusing. It is also the symptom of a society divided between the majority who ostensibly saw politics nowhere and a minority who reduced everything to politics.

In a book comprising a conversation between Carmen Sevilla – the Spanish face of Philips electrical appliances and perennial fixture in Francoist charity events – and Francisco Rabal titled *Aquella España dulce y amarga: la historia de un país contada a dos voces* (*That Bitter and Sweet Spain: The History of the Country Told by Two Voices*), the two actors reminisce about the 1960s. After discussing Sevilla's performing at the Pardo Palace in front of Franco and television cameras, Rabal notes: 'But what seems strange to me is that it doesn't bite away at your conscience now. Because it's as if you didn't realise what was going on this country at that time.' She responds as follows: 'Conscience? About what? If I was happy with life and everything around me. If I took a salary home and started to earn and have a much more comfortable position in life … Conscience about what, Paco? I was very young.'[89] An ethical appraisal of celebrities' complicity with the Francoist regime requires a more serious critical engagement with popular culture than has traditionally taken place within the public sphere in Spain or the academic discipline of Hispanic studies. The celebratory nature of much scholarship carried out under the rubric of cultural studies aside, taking popular culture seriously does not exonerate it of political responsibilities. Not only is there labour to be done in (de)politicising celebrities but, as the next chapter will explore, the celebritisation of the major political players underpinned a regime change predicated on evolution, not revolution.

Chapter 2

Aristocracy and generational change

The houses of Alba, Franco and Bourbon

Beginning life in 1940s Barcelona, *¡Hola!* became a social phenomenon when the magazine moved its centre of operations to Madrid, began publishing in colour and expanded national distribution: weekly sales rose from 250,000 in 1962 to 470,000 in 1974.[1] The fixation on royalty by 'the most conspicuous commercial success of Franco's Spain'[2] was symptomatic of a contradiction at the heart of the regime: the trappings of aristocracy, without noble lineage. Cayetana Fitz-James Stuart, the Duchess of Alba, always retained an aristocratic disdain for what she considered to be gauche imposters. The roll-call of European nobility who attended her 1947 marriage to the Duke of Sotomayor's son was absent from the 1950 wedding of Franco's daughter, Carmen, to playboy doctor, Cristóbal Martínez Bordiú – awarded the title of Marquis of Villaverde – even if the 'wedding itself was on a level of extravagance that would have taxed any European royal family'.[3] Readers developed a taste for such displays; the 1959 marriage of the Shah of Iran to third wife Farah Diba – wearing a Yves Sant Laurent dress and a tiara by jeweller Harry Winston – was one of *¡Hola!*'s best-selling issues at the time.[4] The Shah's *demi-monde* similarly constituted a parvenu royal family, albeit with more genuinely aristocratic credentials than the Franco clan, whose ostensibly shocking lifestyles were reported on more candidly in Spain.[5]

Iran was similarly transforming from a rural to an urban society, becoming 'one of the fastest industrializing authoritarian countries in the world'.[6] Under the dictatorship, Spain maintained close socio-political ties with Arab countries (never recognising the Israeli State), which could be relied upon to endorse membership bids to the United Nations.[7] In 1965, episode 1175B of the State newsreel, NO-DO, featured Fraga going to Iraq and Turkey to make tourism deals; the following year, in episode 1204A, viewers witnessed Carmen Polo, Franco's wife, greeting the Shah at Barajas airport.

Carmen's attempts to replicate the fashion Cayetana established for gala events for those in need (parodied in the 'Sienta un pobre a su mesa' (Sit a poor person at your table) campaign in Luis García Berlanga's 1961 film *Plácido*) were pale imitations. In diplomatic terms, the Duchess was a far less contentious figure for western figures to be photographed alongside. In 1966, she hosted Princess Grace of Monaco and Jackie Kennedy in Seville during the April Fair, the latter donning a traditional mantilla to accompany her to watch El Cordobés,[8] bullfighting and mon-archy being two subjects Cayetana refused to enter into discussion on, believing them to be absolute goods. If the trajectory of upwardly mobile matadors and singers often took them from Andalusia to the capital, the Duchess's trajectory had taken place in reverse: born in Madrid, she reputedly felt most at home in Seville, which allowed her to maintain a diplomatic distance from the epicentre of Francoism.

In 1972, Tico Medina – an ¡Hola! reporter who scripted *Aprendiendo a morir*, the cinematic star-vehicle for El Cordobés (see Chapter 1) – published a book on the Duchess, noting how this media-friendly figure was renowned for having both the common touch[9] and refined cul-tural tastes: 'she once said that in the case of a global catastrophe she would save the Parthenon and the complete works of Federico García Lorca'.[10] The outbreak of the Civil War that led to the assassination of Andalusia's greatest poet (see Chapter 10) resulted in Cayetana's moving to London, her father appointed as Franco's ambassador to the UK. More broadly, the Spanish royal family clearly saw their interests to have better prospects with the rebels than under the Second Republic. Franco had been Alfonso XIII's gentleman-in-waiting, and the King honoured the young General by agreeing to be best man at his wedding.[11] After a plebiscite opted for a republican as opposed to monarchical form of government in 1931, Alfonso voluntarily went into exile; his son, and heir to the throne, Don Juan, was quick to return to Spain following the coup. He crossed the French border in a chauffeur-driven Bentley determined to join the rebels in Burgos. In transit, however, he met General Mola, an anti-monarchist who, without consultation, ordered him to leave the country. This rash move led many monarchist officers to switch their allegiances from Mola to Franco.[12] Presciently aware of the threat Don Juan posed to his unifying position within the broad church of anti-Republicanism, Franco accepted donations to the war effort from Alfonso XIII but made sure to keep members of the royal family out of the fratricidal conflict.

Frequently giving the impression he would relinquish his role as Head of State following victory, Franco never delivered upon this promise. Against this backdrop, the Bourbon family's vocal commitment to dem-ocracy is better understood in pragmatic, as opposed to ethical, terms. In a possibly apocryphal story, Juan Carlos is reported to have asked as a child: 'And why does Franco, who was so good during the war, treat us so badly now?'[13] Exiled from the dictatorial regime, Don Juan found democracy an expedient tool, his best chance of returning to the throne being to present himself as a force for stability, normalising the socio-political fabric of what, especially in the wake of the Axis defeat, was an anachronistic, totalitarian state. This was anathema to Franco, who had no intentions of relinquishing his pseudo-monarchical position, but knew not to repeat Mola's mistake of rejecting the royal family out right. The resulting compromise was for the young prince to be brought to Spain, and educated away from his family and under the tutelage of the regime. In the words of Paul Preston, Juan Carlos was 'little more than a shuttlecock in a game being played by Don Juan and Franco':[14] 'Franco was viewing the Prince as a direct heir while his father saw him as a pawn in his own strategy to reach the throne.'[15] In the meantime, Juan Carlos learnt some valuable lessons. Attending the military academy in Zaragoza, he realised that most officers would never forgive his father for having spoken out against the regime.[16]

If Franco had exercised what arch-monarchist José María Pemán referred to as 'cautious passivity'[17] in relation to the royal family since the end of the Civil War, a new phase commenced with the marriage of Juan Carlos and Sofia, the future Queen of Spain. Luca de Tena, chief editor of *ABC*, successfully petitioned to become Spanish ambassador to Greece in advance of the wedding in an attempt to smooth relations and ensure positive coverage.[18] This public-relations exercise faced challenges from the outset. The Falange press was critical of what it perceived to be her opportunistic decision to convert to Catholicism.[19] According to Jaime Peñafiel, the Spanish media received a missive from the Ministry of Information and Tourism ordering them not to pay unwarranted attention to the wedding or to focus on the fact that it would be a meld of a Catholic and a Greek orthodox ceremony.[20] As a result, the State broadcaster, TVE, underplayed what Andrew Morton suspects was the biggest congregation of European royalty since Elizabeth II's coronation in 1953.[21] Don Juan's role was sidelined; he would probably have been excised entirely if the Spanish broadcaster had not been reliant on footage from Greek public broadcast television.[22] *¡Hola!* nevertheless ignored Ministry recommendations, and provided extensive coverage,[23] whilst the wedding struck a sufficient chord with everyday Spaniards that a young girl aspires to have a dress like Sofia's for her first communion in *La gran familia* (*The Big Family*) (Fernando Palacios, 1962), the year's feel-good cinematic Christmas hit. The Princess's ability to charm both Franco and the Spanish public was instrumental in Juan Carlos becoming an increasingly tenable future Head of State, as were contacts made whilst abroad.

Antonio Garrigues y Díaz Cañabete, the Spanish ambassador to the USA, was perplexed on receiving no instructions from Madrid. Aware of their potential to bolster the image he wanted to present of Spain as an atypical but nevertheless liberal nation state (see Part II), he ensured they were granted an audience with John F. Kennedy and treated as visiting heads of State.[24] Recalling her honeymoon, Sofia noted how:

We were greeted very positively by the authorities in all of the countries we visited. Maybe because we were who we were, but we weren't going as Franco's representatives. People saw us as the future. We could already see what they were thinking: 'This is something new. Something's beginning to change in Spain.'[25]

This generated ambivalent feelings at home: Juan Carlos was variously seen as posing competition to Franco's popularity, or as the best chance of Francoism outliving its chief architect. Sofía and Juan Carlos's inter-national stature was rendered in the celebrity press more in personal than political terms, a special feature from *Garbo* following the birth of their first child, Elena, reporting on her being surrounded by a multitude of languages: her mother speaking Greek, her father Spanish and her nanny being English.[26]

In 1968, Juan Carlos was appointed President of the Spanish World Wildlife Fund, but he had no major official roles beyond being Franco's potential future heir. Following the birth of Prince Felipe that same year, Alfonso's widow, Queen Victoria Eugenia, visited Spain for the first time since going into exile in 1931. The road from Barajas airport to the Liria Palace, the Duchess of Alba's central Madrid property, was lined with cars and cheering crowds. The monarchist press dwelt on the effusive response, but State television dedicated just seventeen seconds to the visit.[27] In 1969, Franco named Juan Carlos his successor. The Prince's first official visit was in October, to Iran, to which he would return in 1971 and 1975. Oil-rich Arab states whose position on the world stage was limited by socio-economic development not being aligned with rights for its citizens made logical trade and political interlocutors in the twilight years of the dictatorship and beyond.

Although few perceived it at the time, the upcoming Transition was set on a new course when Adolfo Suárez's appointment as Director-General of TVE in 1969 coincided with Fraga's removal from the Ministry of Information and Tourism. The latter's control of the media was such that his star rivalled that of the increasingly infirm Franco; in 1966, for example, a carefully orchestrated campaign to reassure the nation that radioactive contamination resulting from the crash of an American B52 in the fishing village of Palomares was nothing to worry about showed Fraga wading into the sea alongside the US ambassador.[28] Suárez, by contrast, pulled strings behind the scenes and always sought to privilege the personal over the political in his public profile.[29] From humble beginnings in the Castilian backwater of Cebreros, the future President ingratiated himself with the various Francoist families, but endeavoured not to allow his ambition to be perceived as a threat. After presiding over the youth section of the national Catholic Action group, Suárez's stock rose in June 1969 when, in his capacity as Civil Governor of Segovia, he joined and apparently led a rescue mission following the collapse of an illegally constructed banqueting suite that resulted in 58 deaths and 147 injuries.[30]

As Juan Francisco Fuentes notes of the friendship that quickly developed between Suárez and Juan Carlos: 'They were similar in many ways, starting with age, which functioned as a kind of vital ideology, capable of making up for the none-too-subtle gaps in their respective educations.'[31] In the prologue to a 1972 publication titled *La generación del príncipe* (*The Prince's Generation*), comprising interviews with political stakeholders too young to remember the Civil War, Juan Carlos wrote: 'The important thing for a generation is for it to have clear ideas about the future of the country and for it to have a fervent desire to serve the national community.'[32] Youth compounded by calculated quietude ensured Suárez and Juan Carlos were repeatedly underestimated. A coalition of the major opposition parties, the Junta Democrática, took Don Juan's post-Franco accession to the throne as almost inevitable. At the opposite end of the political spectrum, hardline Francoists did not trust Juan Carlos, tainted by his father's liberal credentials.

Javier Memba is right that the 'frequently bloody debate between the bunker and the reformists had no impact whatsoever on the happiness reported in women's magazines'.[33] Conversely, however, the fact that reportage was far from politically neutral came into focus when the 35-year-old Alfonso de Bourbon, Alfonso XIII's grandson and Spanish ambassador to Sweden, became an alternative pretender through his courtship of the 19-year-old Carmen Martínez Bordiú, Franco's grand-daughter and a pseudo-royal since birth: there was a photo-shoot of her first birthday,[34] and she had been a staple of NO-DO ever since.

The nascent romance was aggressively marketed as the stuff of fairytale. In a book produced in 1971, José María Bayona noted how, like 'any young girl, she was awaiting her Prince Charming'.[35] Although he had previously had some inconsequential flings – 'But what young man doesn't' – Alfonso reportedly knew immediately that Franco's grand-daughter was different: she displayed 'responsibility and culture, unusual for a girl of her young age, especially in an era in which frivolity has taken hold of so many a young girl's heart'.[36] According to the cover story from *¡Hola!*, published on 25 December 1971:

> *¡Hola!*'s millions of readers were overjoyed by the exclusive we gave last year surrounding the announcement of the engagement of Carmen Martínez-Bordiú Franco to Alfonso de Bourbon after he asked for her hand. All of Spain welcomed this happy occasion with a remarkable warmth, leading our switchboard to receive hundreds of telephone enquiries about the date of the wedding, the presents, the wedding dress and other details about which we will fulfil our obligations by informing our readers.[37]

In a feature for *Teresa*, the bride was asked if the media frenzy and public interest were more down to her or the groom. Martínez Bordiú replied: 'I don't know, it has all come about by chance, coincidences that happen in life. It just turns out that Alfonso is Alfonso XIII's grandson and I'm my grandfather's granddaughter. I think we've both contributed to our wedding being newsworthy'.[38] Carmen Polo was reportedly over-joyed: 'To perpetuate Francoism with Bourbon pedigree. What more could one ask for?'[39]

Invitations to the wedding of Franco's granddaughter and His Royal Highness, Prince Alfonso (a title to which he had no right) were sent to all European heads of state and royal households, but most were politely declined.[40] Alfredo Sánchez Bella, the then Minister of Information and Tourism, commissioned a poll to gauge public opinion on the match: 89 per cent of those surveyed knew about the marriage, with 76 per cent aware that Alfonso was the Spanish Ambassador in Sweden. Asked if the groom had a claim to the throne, 47 per cent responded affirmatively, with 69 per cent believing he satisfied the formal conditions to succeed Franco. Nevertheless, Juan Carlos was reported to have greater support from State institutions, most noticeably the army and the financial sector.[41] A new publication, *Gentleman* – designed to be a Spanish hybrid of *Playboy* and *Esquire* – published an interview with Alfonso's father and Don Juan's brother, Don Jaime de Bourbon, in which he said he was unwilling to renounce his dynastic rights in favour of his son; the already-printed issue was taken off sale and banned by the authorities.[42] Suárez refused to televise the wedding on TVE,[43] but an officially sanctioned version can be seen in episode 1524B of the NO-DO, dedicated to the marriage and, unusually for the time, broadcast in colour. A visibly blushing, retiring bride is given away by her grandfather. At Juan Carlos and Sofia's wedding, the biggest ovation from the public outside was given to Grace Kelly, the film-star turned aristocrat.[44] Here, the NO-DO voiceover emphasised the presence of her husband, the Prince of Monaco.

Although Juan Carlos remained the international community's favoured choice to succeed Franco, his mandate to rule came not from them but from the Caudillo's final written testament, in which he defied the wishes of his wife and revealed greater level-headedness and political maturity than might have been expected. According to Queen Sofia:

> In that situation, that document was key, because in one of its paragraphs the Caudillo said that Spaniards should align themselves 'alongside the new King'. Franco has dictated it to his daughter, we don't know when. She typed it up and guarded the document on her father's instruction. She could have chosen not to hand it over, but Carmencita, an intelligent and noble woman, didn't just not stand in the way, but facilitated things. Soon afterwards, the King granted her the title of Duchess of Franco and, to be honest, she's more than earned it.[45]

This would be the document the tearful President, Carlos Arias Navarro, read out on TVE.

The only prominent members of the international community to attend Franco's funeral were Vice-President Nelson Rockefeller, Imelda Marcos and General Augusto Pinochet.[46] The Spanish Caudillo was a role-model for the Chilean dictator even after the Francoist regime had actively resisted 'American pressure to isolate Dr Allende's government, or to influence it'[47] – Francoist policy was to prioritise links with former colonies irrespective of ideological persuasion. It was made clear to Pinochet that he was unwelcome at Juan Carlos's coronation,[48] where representatives of the major democracies, amongst them President Giscard d'Estaing, President Scheel and the Duke of Edinburgh, were present.[49] The incoming King secured international support by constituting the best chance for democratisation and stability. Domestically, the latter was the priority. If democracy was to establish itself as a political system in a country lacking in a strong tradition in this form of governance, it was paramount that it not be seen to place in jeopardy the peace and prosperity the Francoist regime purported to have secured for Spanish citizens. Juan Carlos's mantra that he wanted to be King of all Spaniards was simultaneously an attempt to leave behind the wounds of the Civil War and to transform his royal figure into the embodiment and guarantor of democracy.

As Charles Powell notes, the Spanish monarch faced 'the daunting challenge of winning over the hearts and minds of the left whilst retaining the support of the right'.[50] This was impossible to achieve with Arias Navarro as President, and the King's championing of Suárez is symptomatic of how and why political sympathies had long been reflected and refracted along generational divides in various ambits of public life. Hence, for example, by the time of the Second Vatican Council in 1962, a recruitment hiatus in the 1930s had ensured that the Spanish priesthood was largely split into those over 60 and those under 40, and '[m]any – though by no means all – of the older generation retreated to an ideological bunker defined by the certainties of the Caudillo's confessional state'.[51] In conversations with Carrillo, Suárez claimed that both he and the King were keen to legalise the Communist Party but that the army was an obstacle:

> In Spain, the army is not a pyramid in structure. there are more chiefs that Indians, lots of 60-plus generals about the place. From Lieutenant Coronel and above, the mentality of men who fought an extremely cruel war, and

defeated Communism. That was the crowning event of their youth, what they've lived off and what continues to keep them going. They believe that legalising the Spanish Communist Party and handing over to them the right to live with full civil and political rights an affront, a revenge on the part of history they refuse to accept. Young officers don't think in this way, but they're not the ones to have control of the arms.[52]

If visceral responses were at least as important as rational thought throughout the Transition, then any attempt to understand both the cultural production and the politics of the time demands the tracing of a genealogy of affect that goes beyond cataloguing dates and laws.

A brief survey of mass-produced print culture serves to illustrate the benefits of such an approach. Fernando Vizcaíno Casas, described by Manuel Fraga in his diaries, after introducing him at a book launch in 1980, as 'the most popular of our writers',[53] was the publishing sensation of the Transition, dominating best-seller lists throughout 1978, and also finding a receptive audience in translation in Portugal. The revisionist nostalgia of Vizcaíno Casas's texts was often adapted for the silver screen by Rafael Gil, the dictatorship's cinema laureate. Following Franco's death, Arias Navarro reputedly spent time at his place of burial, seeking counsel from the recently deceased Caudillo and praying he would return to rescue Spain from the abyss.[54] In the farcical *Y al tercer año, resucitó* (*And The Third Year, He Rose Again*) (Rafael Gil, 1980), Franco is resurrected, and aghast to see the chaos into which his beloved *patria* has been plunged: young people take drugs; participate in pointless demonstrations; and engage in perverse sexual practices, including bearded men kissing or the making of pornographic films in which actresses seduce dogs. On news spreading of the Caudillo's return, young and old congregate to welcome their saviour, although the newspapers report that only a few nostalgic oddballs turned up. In real life, an audience in Valladolid implored the cinema's projectionist to rerun the scene in which Franco returns.

Propaganda camouflaged as popular entertainment this may be, but Vizcaíno Casas's broad appeal cannot be denied and warrants explanation. As Sara Ahmed notes: '[a]ttention to emotions allows us to address the question of how subjects become invested in particular structures such that their demise is felt as a kind of living death'.[55] Vizcaíno Casas's preferred mode of address is melodrama, a genre that, in the words of Peter Brook, 'starts from and expresses the anxiety brought by a frightening new world in which the traditional patterns of moral order no longer provide the necessary social glue'.[56] The front cover of *Hijos de papá* (*Spoilt Kids*) consists of a photo of visibly intoxicated young people on a dance-floor; the prologue laments the plight of parents in their fifties:

> Those who, as youngsters, wanted to sign up for public duties were rejected for being immature, for lack of expertise. Years later, they thought, quite logically, that their political moment had arrived; but then they were told that they belonged to a bygone or, sorry, as they like to say nowadays, obsolete age. In other words, they are past it for those tasks that are the exclusive preserve of the so-called 'Prince's generation'.[57]

The book is structured in two halves, the first describing the courtship and actions of adolescents in 1946 and the second showing those same characters struggling to understand their own increasingly wayward adolescent children in 1978. This clearly struck a chord when so many Spaniards were concerned about the generational gap: according to a Government sociological study, arguments about how to bring up and educate children constituted the chief source of conflict between part-ners,[58] whilst agony-aunt Elena Francis frequently mediated between parents and their offspring.[59] Drawing on Ahmed's notion of 'affective economies where feelings do not reside in subjects or objects, but are produced by effects of circulation',[60] I would like to suggest that litera-ture produced for the mass market was not always as unreconstructed as Vizcaíno Casas's texts might suggest, and that its role in negotiating the psychological, as opposed to legal and constitutional, break from Francoism, a prerequisite for a successful Transition, has been insuffi-ciently acknowledged.

In a discussion of Carmen Martín Gaite, Kathleen Doyle remarks on how '[p]opular literature through its methods of remembering and reconstructing the past, nurtures the dialogue between personal history and official historiography, giving prestige to the former and debunking the latter.'[61] *El cuarto de atrás* constituted 'a self-conscious attempt to rescue the disappearing world of the narrator's childhood from the risk of oblivion during a time of social and political upheaval',[62] 'which merges the narrator's personal history with the social and cultural history of the period, becoming a type of collective memoir for the women of Martín Gaite's generation'.[63] The at-least-semi-autobiographical protagonist recalls seeing Carmen Franco and, 'influenced by the reading of romance novels, which used to put a tearful emphasis on the dissatisfaction of rich heiresses, I thought of Franco's daughter as a prisoner who had been put under a spell'.[64] The prize-winning novel has rightly accrued canonical status as a defining text of the Transition for its mediation of the past and the present and engagement with popular culture; this has not, however, prompted interest in how and why romance literature was both constituted by and constitutive of changing mores.

Corín Tellado's writing may not be realistic, but she created fictional worlds with which her readership identified. Poverty and sexual harassment are, for example, recurrent themes in her novellas from the 1960s.[65] Tellado's epigraphs derive from a broad range of sources ranging from the Bible to Flaubert, but most of her reading consisted of newspapers and women's magazines, from which she seemingly gleaned inspiration. In 1968, Andrés Amorós noted that her books were unique in regularly selling over 100,000 copies a week. After criticising colleagues for not engaging with her literary output, this academic based at the Complutense notes: 'These novels reflect, perhaps, modes of thinking and acting typical of those sections of Spanish society that are "stuck in the past", and don't show any signs of leaving it in the immediate future. Our criticisms are directed more at them than the novels themselves.'[66] By contrast, if we entertain seriously Diana Holmes's claim that romance 'provides a narrative form in which to address the difficult reconciliation of personal desire with social imperatives, and the particular form that this takes for women',[67] Tellado's vast literary output is ripe for non-condescending critical reappraisal.

One of Amorós's most pointed criticisms was that: 'There are naturally none of the tensions between parents and children, nor are there those strange stories of the breakdown between generations. Everyone forms parts of the same social group and is happy in the role to which they have been assigned.'[68] This was not, however, the case in much of her production from the 1970s and 1980s, when the best-selling Spanish-language author of all time performed an important pedagogical labour, introducing her readership to new mores within a familiar idiom that struck a balance between being non-threatening and suggesting that new times require different models of conduct from those with which her generation was inculcated. In *Déjanos vivir* (*Let Us Live*), for example, a nominal setting in New York is a clear surrogate for Spain. Two students, Urfe and Katia, scandalise their respective parents by living together without being married. The son recriminates his adulterous father Peter for his life and relationship being founded on deceit:

> How many times have the two of you thought about divorce? I haven't … I'm not going to think about divorce. I don't want to live with that weight, that absurd tying down. I don't live for society. I live for the woman I love and for me, and I form part of that society in the hope that it understands me; if not, I forgot about it.[69]

Pursuing a similar theme from a different angle, *Hay algo que se muere* (*Something Has Died*) features Marcela, a motherless child in her early twenties who lives with her aunt and works in a bank. César, a good-natured young man, asks for her hand in marriage, but she distances herself, scared to admit she is not a virgin. As a teenager, ex-boyfriend Martín had fooled her with promises of becoming her husband, before running off to England where, it is implied, he was further corrupted by notions of moral relativism. Martín reappears and blackmails Marcela but, encouraged by a friendly priest to be honest, she tells César her secret. He is accepting, stating that what interests him is not her past but their future.

The ambivalent narrative retains traditional gender norms but nevertheless implies that sex outside marriage does not have to be punished or equate to social death. This is typical of Tellado's tendency salaciously to depict new customs without renouncing the moral certainties of yesteryear. In her own life, the queen of Spanish romance challenged convention, separating from her husband in the late 1950s, shortly after their two children were born. In her later novels, politics were often played out on a generational battlefield that threatened the reconciliation and stability so vital for democratic consolidation. In *El pasota* (*The Dropout*), a young bourgeois couple, Bea and Tomás, live together with his parents in Marbella. After travelling to Ibiza to work as a teacher, he grows a beard, begins smoking pot and becomes inculcated with Marxist ideologies, returning home to accuse his father of amassing money and describing his parents' domestic servant as a slave. Claiming marriage is a bourgeois convention, he talks of how he practised free love when abroad and acted as a 'gigolo for a rich lady'.[70] He heads back to the hippy enclave, where 'many of his friends in the commune had been born in orphanages, some were the children of divorcees and others had been raised in the gutter amongst drunks and reprobates'.[71] Befitting the romance tradition, love, for Tellado, often performs the role of reintegrating individuals into society, functioning as the best antidote to inter-generational conflict. The prodigal son returns home and, without explicitly renouncing the Ibiza lifestyle, on discovering that Bea has another suitor, says that if the choice is between being a free spirit and losing her, he would rather relinquish the former. Tellado's novellas preached tolerance within circumscribed limits, reassuring her readership that changing mores were not as apocalyptic as they might appear at a time when, as Pablo Sánchez León remarks, the media broadcast images of the young as simultaneously disorderly and apathetic.[72]

Her principal contribution to the politics of consensus, the leitmotif of a Transition predicated (in theory if not always in practice) on dialogue and mutual respect, is manifest through an incessant return to the clash between parents and children in an attempt to forge a common language. Novellas that admittedly failed to satisfy most basic requirements for canonical inclusion nonetheless participate in what Terence Cave characterises as literature's role in the 'human conversation', forming part of 'a cognitive ecology'.[73] Tellado's prose bears empathetic testament to Ahmed's claim that '[e]motions may be crucial to showing us why transformations are so difficult (we remain invested in what we critique), but also how they are possible (our investments move as we move)'.[74]

This dichotomy was also on display in the popular press. On the one hand, ¡Hola!, in the words of Jaime Peñafiel, 'knew how to change without changing. Because if, during the regime years, it focused on Franco and his family, now it would do so on the King and his'.[75] Conversely, however, for the first time, a mass audience was found for overt discussion of politics, albeit sold as a sugar-coated pill: Interviú, which combined salacious celebrity interviews and erotic photo-shoots with current affairs, quickly became the most popular cultural magazine, read by a fifth of all Spaniards.[76] The roles allocated to women were limited and sexist (see Chapter 5) but it provided a lexicon for icons of Francoism to reinvent themselves. Lola Flores, for example, appeared on one front cover claiming she enjoyed taking cocaine and made love on a daily basis. Carmen Martínez Bordiú effectively remodelled herself for a new age, retaining her celebrity status more effectively than any other member of her family. If the widowed Carmen Polo became something of a recluse, only occasionally going out to visit her friend Raphael, her granddaughter actively sought out the company of visiting rock-stars such as Supertramp.[77]

In 1979, Martínez Bordiú left Alfonso, now the Duke of Cadiz, and their two young children to move to Paris with Jean-Marie Rossi, a millionaire antique dealer. She subsequently received custody of the children when Alfonso, who would himself later be killed in a skiing accident, fell into a coma after a car accident in which their eldest son died;[78] a sensational press frenzy ensued over speculation that the Duke of Cadiz would face criminal charges for dangerous driving. This is not the biography viewers of NO-DO would probably have predicted on first seeing episode 1147B, in which a nervous and awkward adolescent girl sits on the stage in her role as 'reina de la fiesta' (queen of the party) for the poetic jousts organised as part of the twenty-five years-of-peace celebrations.

According to a hagiographic biography by Paloma Barrientos:

> At the time, Carmen epitomised the kind of woman raised to get married, to have children, to put up with her husband's infidelities out of love for a false family unity. She didn't do it. In spite of what people might say,

the criticisms, charged with being frivolous – who isn't? – lacking self-reflection, immature, it has been her against the world. Some will never forgive her for the fact.[79]

Before divorce laws were passed, her first marriage was, on Alfonso's insistence, annulled on the grounds of her psychological immaturity when she took her vows.[80] Her by-then ex-husband claimed she was superficial for renouncing family life once the novelty wore off,[81] whilst her father, who had told her it was her duty to endure an unhappy marriage in silence, did not speak to her again until his grandson's tragic death.[82] Sex and scandal imbued her celebrity status with a malleability that allowed it to outlive the socio-political conventions underpinning her grandfather's regime.

Ostentatious rebellion allowed her to foreground generational affiliations over biological origins. In a book first published in 2001, Carmen mixes generic traits from self-help manuals and popular sociology to make claims such as the following:

> Our generation has been – and let's not forget it – the one that has piloted one of the most important changes in mentalities of all time. From the 1960s onwards we have ensured that society was gradually less inhibited, freer, less corseted. The facts are there: May '68, 'make love, not war', the fashion revolution with the mini-skirt, new musical rhythms, with the Beatles heading the bill, the beginning of television, the explosion of Pop Art.[83]

Tendentious and misleading as such claims are, her evocation of the generation divide is a useful reminder that the discourse of the two Spains (the victorious and the vanquished) can blind us to other divisions operative within the framework of the Transition, something that a sustained engagement with primary texts from the period reveals in an unequivocal manner.

Regally indifferent to changes in political mood, the Duchess of Alba, embodying the bohemian and the patrician, had little problem adapting. Cayetana's first husband died in 1972, the couple's last public appearance together being the wedding of Carmen and Alfonso.

Husband number two was Jesús Aguirre, the son of a single mother, who later trained as a Jesuit priest. In the 1960s, he became 'a cultural reference point for religious progressiveness amongst Madrid society',[84] reputedly holding a clandestine mass in the chapel of the Complutense for Julián Grimau, the undercover member of the Spanish Communist Party executed by the regime in 1963,[85] whilst his publications included a reconciliatory tract from 1969 titled *Cristianos y Marxistas* (*Christians and Marxists*).[86]

A confidential report sent to Fraga on a lecture given to students in Lisbon offers an inkling of *¡Hola!* potential: after saying Aguirre's ideas might have been subversive if the audience had been larger and with more cohesive political objectives, the informant referred to him as 'un sacerdote o fraile, muy elegante, por cierto, con un traje bien cortado y una corbata a rayas de gran calidad' (a priest or friar who was, incidentally, extremely elegant, wearing a high-quality fitted suit and striped tie).[87] In one of her most iconic statements, Cayetana boasted that 'Jesús was a real man and I still maintain that we made love every day'.[88] In the words of Juan Luis Cebrián, a friend and former colleague of Aguirre on *Cuadernos para el diálogo* (*Notebooks towards Dialogue*), who, as founding editor-in-chief of *El País*, was given exclusive access to the 1978 union of the dandy and the Duchess:

> Jesús and Cayetana's wedding seemed in many ways to be a metaphor for the Transition. That Adorno's translator, a priest who had renounced the cloth, an illegitimate child whose father was in the armed forces, a homosexual incapable of coming out of the closet, married the Duchess of Alba, the foremost representative of the Spanish aristocracy, renowned for her amorous versatility and unpredictable character, constituted a veritable symbol of the many Spains that emerged following the dictator's death.[89]

The couple first met in Marbella in 1975, a place the Duchess usually snubbed in favour of Ibiza. Neither made a good impression on the other. Romance later developed when Aguirre was invited in his capacity as the recently appointed Director-General of Music and Dance to a dinner Cayetana hosted at the Liria Palace for his former neighbour and friend Francisco Fernández Ordóñez,[90] the then Minister of Tax.[91]

This might not have been the most glamorous of cabinet positions, but multi-millionaires were well advised to keep this crusading Harvard graduate on side. In spite of the economic miracle of the 1960s, an efficient welfare state was never introduced in Spain.[92] Fernández Ordóñez had become aware of the unequal spread of wealth in Spain when he was posted to Huesca in Aragon in his first job as a young tax inspector;[93] in the epilogue to the Spanish translation of a Flemish ecclesiastical publication, he complained that 'the average Spanish tax evader is not an anarchist or a Communist, and neither is he a rabble-rousing student. He is a right-wing man, a defender of established law and order.'[94] Even for those paying their taxes, Spain was a relative fiscal paradise, actor Sean Connery, for example, buying property in Marbella in order no longer to be a UK tax-payer.[95] Fiscal revenue in 1975, including contributions to the social security system, represented 18 per cent of national GDP, a smaller proportion than in any other OECD country.[96] Employees had tax deducted from their wages, but this was not the case for businessmen and investors – failure to declare assets was not even classified as a crime under the dictatorship; 'there are no equal opportunities for evasion.'[97] Charitable events such as those hosted by Franco's wife or the Duchess of Alba were necessary because of underlying structural inequalities, the creation of a more equitable (or at least less inequitable) tax system being one of the most understudied aspects of the democratisation project: 'Fiscal reform was already the great myth, the great test, the maximum indicator that something was going to change in the solid structures of the Spanish economy. It was the promise never forgotten but never completed.'[98] To encourage civic behaviour, a publicity campaign was launched with the slogan 'Ahora Hacienda somos todos. No nos engañemos' (We are all part of the tax system. Let's not kid ourselves).

The House of Alba Foundation was created in 1976. Aguirre was a great asset, ideally placed both personally and politically to safeguard this patrimony by effectively placing a private collection in the public domain. On the one hand, this can be seen as a democratisation of one of Spain's great art collections (with works by Goya, Velázquez and Rubens); conversely, it proved financially advantageous, removing tax burdens, and with the State taking on many of the maintenance costs. Until the end of the Duchess's life, the Liria Palace was only open to the public on Fridays, and featured in few listings or tourist publications, relatively few Spaniards or foreigners knowing they had the right to visit the city-centre locale in which some of the finest examples of Mengs are on display, alongside gauche trinkets in the Goya room. Shortly before her death, Cayetana attended a pop-art exhibition dedicated to her own iconic figure. Across the street from the Dueñas Palace in Seville a posthumous tribute has been painted onto a garage door: the front cover of British punk band the Sex Pistols' 1977 single 'God Save the Queen' superimposed with her image and the message 'God Save the Duchess'. A less affectionate picture was painted in the autobiography of her son, Cayetano Martínez de Irujo,[99] a publishing sensation in 2019, who claimed that she and Aguirre combined the coldness associated with aristocrats and the irresponsibility of bohemians; left socially isolated and psychologically vulnerable, he sought out love and company with his pet lion and on cocaine-fuelled nights out with Pocholo Martínez-Bordiú, Carmen's cousin, who would later marry one of Adolfo Suárez's daughters.

Cayetana never became embroiled in the kind of scandals that beset the Duchess of Franco when she was caught smuggling State jewels out of the country, or Lola Flores who failed to submit tax declarations between 1982 and 1985. When the latter stood trial in a high-profile test case in 1989, she prefigured crowd-funding by asking on television that every Spaniard donate a peseta to enable her to settle her debt, whilst publicly asking President Felipe González to intervene. The petition went unanswered. In contrast, the Spanish aristocracy maintained excellent relations with the Socialist administration, both a cause and a consequence of the fact that, as Brad Epps notes,[100] attention to the return of democracy to Spain has taken as given another seismic change, the restoration of the monarchy. As Juan Francisco Fuentes observes, the relationship between González and Juan Carlos 'went beyond that of a mere marriage of convenience'.[101] Juan Carlos's warmth and lack of formality in comparison with other European monarchs are frequently remarked upon. Less commented upon is the relative absence of royal discretion when it comes to political commentary: Sofia has, for example, spoken of how she considers González's Vice-President, Alfonso Guerra, one of the great statesmen of Spanish politics and to have been unfairly maligned.[102] The Duchess of Alba never made any secret about voting for González, and a personally signed photo of the former President remains on display in the Liria Palace.

The PSOE achieved a landslide victory in 1982. Like the King, González and Guerra had a popular touch, expressing themselves in ways that could be understood across social and generational divides. It is no coincidence that Guerra, who masterminded the electoral campaign, had carried out surveys amongst housewives and female factory workers about their cultural habits in the 1960s.[103] Long before Tony Blair and Bill Clinton got wise to the trick, the PSOE were expert at exploiting popular culture as a means of ex(or)cising residual fears of radicalism. Guerra proudly employed the popular idiom that Spain's own mother would not recognise the country after their term in office, but González's appearances in ¡Hola! alongside his family told a different story. That he targeted the magazine as the media outlet for one of his first interviews as President is as counter-intuitive and revealing as El País having the exclusive to the marriage of Cayetana and Aguirre.

In an issue with the Pope's visit to Spain on the front cover, readers are reassured that González, 'apart from [being] an experienced politician with a proven track record, is a married family man who spends all of his free time with them, even if this is less than he doubtless wishes'.[104] His wife, Carmen Romero, is also interviewed, depicted as a modern but non-threatening working woman.[105] She champions women's rights, but does not consider herself a feminist and thinks it unnecessary for her to resign from her job as a school-teacher: 'The only First Lady in this country is the Queen; the rest of us are women, nothing less, nothing more.'[106] A few weeks later, González is interviewed again, celebrating his first Christmas in the Moncloa Palace, the presidential residence, claiming theirs is a Christmas typical of the middle class, the social group to which he believes the vast majority of Spaniards belong. He makes sure to note that his first official act was to attend an infantry parade, and that dialogue with and respect for the armed forces are a priority.[107] When asked for his festive wishes, his first is that 'citizens from all over Spain live in peace, that they live without the heartache of violence';[108] his second that the social classes he grew up with, the dispossessed and poor, know that his thoughts are with them and that there is shelter from the storm, relief from the recession. Leading the first Government to be formed primarily of politicians who belonged to the generation of 1968, Spain's first progressive President for nearly half a century was taking the country into uncharted waters, but did so by appealing to the same core values most highly prized since Franco's death: peace, prosperity and fair play. What remained to be seen was how he would deliver on such promises and the faith invested in him not only by the Party faithful but also by a broad cross-section of the electorate who, a decade earlier, had probably never heard of a 30-year-old activist going by the clandestine name of Isidoro, or contemplated voting for a party with a Marxist tradition (see Chapter 6).

Chapter 3

¡Hola! in the age of champagne socialism

Isabel Preysler, Miguel Boyer, Julio Iglesias, Francisco Rivera 'Paquirri' and Isabel Pantoja

In some but not all respects, Spain skipped modernity and went from being a premodern to a postmodern society. That said, a tendency to overstress the traditionalism of late Francoism is replicated in a blindness to the continuities still in place in the 1980s, the decade in which Spanish democracy was consolidated. This can clearly be evidenced in the production and reception of popular culture. Raphael and Corín Tellado saw their popularity wane at home, even as their stock rose in Latin America. Conversely, however, the dominant assumption amongst the intelligentsia that icons of popular culture from the dictatorship period owed their success to the regime's patronage and the infantilisation of its subjects is undermined by their frequent resilience in democratic Spain alongside international success. A homage to Lola Flores organised by Julio Iglesias in Miami and broadcast by TVE in 1990, at a time when the creation of private television channels meant the State broadcaster no longer had a monopoly, enjoyed an audience share of 39.2 per cent.[1]

According to a poll conducted by the National Centre for Sociological Research in 1992, Isabel Preysler was the most famous woman in Spain, followed in descending order by Isabel Pantoja, Carmen Romero and Lola Flores, with Queen Sofía lagging some distance behind.[2] The continued success of the (inter)national celebrity press was inextricably linked to the amorous adventures of Preysler and Pantoja, whose emotional peaks and troughs provided as fantastical reading as any romance novel. The former arrived in Madrid from her native Philippines to study, and, in 1970, aged 18, met the man who would become her first husband: Julio Iglesias, the future multi-millionaire 'Latin lover', who rose through the ranks in privileged Francoist fashion, subsequently becoming an ambassador for Spain throughout the democratic period. Having trained in the Real Madrid youth team until a traffic accident rendered a professional sports career untenable, he wrote 'La vida sigue igual' (Life goes on) whilst in recovery. It was the Spanish entry for the 1968 International Song Contest in Benidorm. The recording did not initially find favour with the organisers, but his well-connected gynaecologist father (responsible, amongst other things, for introducing the epidural to Spain) intervened with the Secretary-General of the National movement, José Solís Ruíz, to secure his son's inclusion. In his autobiography, Dr Iglesias justifies nepotism on the basis that Julio Jr was at an unfair disadvantage because Adolfo Suárez and his team held a personal grudge against his father.[3] 'La vida sigue igual' won in Benidorm, and was employed as the basis for a semi-autobiographical cinematic star-vehicle with the same title (Eugenio Martín, 1969). The young star's manager, Alfredo Fraile, contracted adolescents to provide choreographed enthusiasm, and to shatter the glass of the windows of the cinema where the premiere took place.[4] Iglesias was adept at transforming himself into a prototypical celebrity, participating in a benefit football game on 25 December 1968 between pop-stars and bullfighters to raise funds for a housing charity presided over by Carmen Polo.[5]

Fraile's next goal was for his client to represent Spain in Eurovision. Behind-the-scenes negotiations were once again required that cast doubt on the future President's reputed animosity towards the Iglesias clan. If Fraile's memoirs are to be believed:

> As a result of their summer holidays in Peñiscola (Castellón), Dr Iglesias Puga had become a personal friend of Fernando Herrero Tejedor, one of the Regime's fat cats, with very good contacts in government. These included a great influence on Adolfo Suárez, whom he had taken by the

hand right to the higher reaches of the Falange.[6] Through his negotiations, we were able to negotiate a meeting with Suárez.[7]

Following a successful meeting, Julio represented Spain in Eurovision. 'Gwendolyn' beat Raphael's record, coming fourth in the same year that Iglesias met his future wife. Their wedding further boosted the singer's profile in Spain as the young couple and their new family – Chábeli (b. 1971), Julio (b. 1973) and Enrique (b. 1975) – becoming staples of ¡Hola!.

Although they initially set up house near Malaga, Dr Iglesias soon found them a Madrid flat in a block purpose-built for the regime's elite. The singer was rarely home as he pursued the dream of becoming a transatlantic superstar. According to Fraile's memoirs, Nicaragua's military dictator, President Samoza, treated Iglesias and Fraile as visiting dignitaries, inviting them to his home where he proclaimed himself a fan of Spain and of Iglesias's music before leading them to his bedroom where there were framed pictures of Franco and Spanish balladeer Rocío Jurado on the bedside table. Elsewhere, Iglesias has claimed that Fidel Castro kept a cassette recording of his song 'Un canto a Galicia' (A song for Galicia) in his car.[8] His music was elsewhere used to torture prisoners in Pinochet's Chile, where the singer played a free concert in a prison before breaking records by playing to over 100,000 people in the National Stadium.[9] In an autobiography, Iglesias claimed Chile had a special place in his heart, making reference to a benefit concert he did with Priscilla Presley.[10] Asked two years later if he had any reservations about playing at the site of the massacre of civilians, including singer-songwriter Víctor Jara, he replied: 'I'm not involved in politics. I just sing to allow people to switch off and relax. My conscience is so clear that I sleep eight hours a night. I've got nothing to hide.'[11] In a sensationalist exposé, his ex-butler Antonio del Valle claimed politics and song could not be so easily divorced: 'he felt a terrible aversion towards the new politicial situation in Spain. The Iglesias clan were visceral Francoists, and maintained close friendships with numerous South American dictators.'[12] The continually unfaithful Iglesias attempted unsuccessfully to convince Preysler to move the family to the USA. During his long absences, she became a high-profile celebrity in her own right, photographed on nights out with Carmen Martínez Bordiú, her neighbour and new best friend. At an invitation-only screening of *Saturday Night Fever* (John Badham, 1977), she met Carlos Falcó, the Marquis of Griñón,[13] a divorced aristocrat related to the Duchess of Alba. The title track of Iglesias's first album to receive a Grammy nomination, *Hey*, seemingly lamented mistreatment at the hands of his ex-wife. Throughout the 1980s, Iglesias and Preysler competed over which of them could accrue the best contacts and grace the most covers of *¡Hola!*.

The down side of fame came to the fore in December of that same year when Basque separatist organisation ETA kidnapped Dr Iglesias, who was held hostage for over two weeks before being rescued by the police. The Spanish President, Leopoldo Calvo Sotelo, phoned Julio in Miami to say how pleased he was that the mission had been successful;[14] the global press were invited to witness father and son reuniting at the singer's US residence. A picture of the pair with their arms around one another graced the front page of *¡Hola!*, the recently released prisoner talking of his ordeal in an exclusive interview. Dr Iglesias claimed he could cope with the cold and solitary conditions, but that he was tortured by 'an obsessive and terrible idea: I knew that if anything happened to me, my son wouldn't sing again'.[15] He need not have worried. Julio's next album, *Momentos*, catapulted him to global superstardom, lead single 'De niña a mujer' (From a girl to a woman) (featuring Chábeli on the front cover) shifting 1.2 million units in six months in China and two million in Brazil within a year.[16] Iglesias was the only domestic star with sufficient cachet to be booked alongside the Rolling Stones for stadium concerts to coincide with Spain's hosting of the World Cup in 1982. In Barcelona, he was greeted by Jordi Pujol, and the singer brought both tenor Plácido Domingo and football superstar Diego Maradona out on stage with him. Shortly after being elected to government, Felipe González invited Iglesias to Moncloa, where the singer reputedly complained of the lack of attention paid by the State broadcaster to ambassadors for Spain such as himself, Montserrat Caballé, Domingo or golfer Severiano Ballesteros, as well as lobbying for the introduction of private television channels.[17]

If political connections facilitated his rise, Iglesias's international success allowed him to become one of Spain's most important unofficial diplomats and a major broker of electoral currency back home. In 1983, Fraga travelled to the USA to ingratiate himself with the Reagan administration. On 14 December, a memo was sent from the National Security Council's Europe advisor, Peter Sommer, to colleague Robert McFarlane. Cautioning against the political advisability of a photo call, an exasperated Sommer notes that the leader of the Spanish opposition had missed an appointment with the US Vice-President and that:

> What I call the 'Fraga saga' continues … Despite our strong recommendations that Fraga pursue his Washington meeting through official channels (i.e. via the US Embassy in Madrid or the Spanish Embassy in Washington), Fraga relied on world renowned singer Julio Iglesias to set up the appointments. In a nutshell, Fraga's requests were not well handled.[18]

Mishandled they may have been, but Fraga's Galician compatriot was well placed to hustle on his behalf: the singer had been contracted for ten concerts at Los Angeles's Universal Amphitheatre to coincide with the 1984 Olympic Games and to perform at the White House for the state visit of French President, François Mitterrand. By the time Reagan visited Spain in 1985, only Juan Carlos could rival Iglesias's international political connections.

Fraga's autobiography features a photo with the US President taken in the Pardo (where, like many visiting dignitaries, Reagan was billeted) under a boastful sub-heading 'Larga entrevista' (Long interview), in which section he highlights that his interlocutor refused to meet with Enrique Tierno Galván,[19] as a result of the Mayor of Madrid's Marxist credentials.[20] The uproar surrounding the US President's visit, a year before a divisive referendum on Spain's NATO membership was held (see Chapter 6), nevertheless undermined Fraga's attempt to present himself as a global player in modern-day democratic conservatism. Before touching down in Madrid, Reagan courted controversy by criticising Spain's unwillingness to follow US policy on Nicaragua, and the claim that most of his countrymen would agree with him that Americans who

74

came to Spain to fight Franco were on the wrong side.[21] Political considerations were ignored by the celebrity press, which was more interested
in Nancy, the First Lady, dancing to flamenco alongside the Spanish
Queen. Sofia has claimed that Reagan was the best President the USA
has ever had,[22] but a rise in anti-American sentiment facilitated the re-
emergence of Adolfo Suárez – who had always opposed the King's nurturing of US–Spanish relations – as a major political player ahead of the
1986 general elections. To optimise the chances of his new party, the
Centro Democrático Social – who had won just two seats in 1982 – he
contracted Iglesias's manager to run his campaign.

Fraile faced an uphill battle with party barons, who still referred to
Suárez as President and, in his view, were preventing him from converting
personal charisma into political currency: 'It wasn't easy, but we ended up
convincing him, and managed to turn his rallies into a spectacle, which
was our aim. He ended up taking off his jacket and projecting himself
to the audience as if he were Julio Iglesias.'[23] Even the campaign slogan,
'Contigo, yo puedo' (With you, I can), sounded like the title of a romantic
ballad. Suárez's party came third in the 1986 elections, gaining seventeen
new seats, a success neither the former President nor his new political
formation would ever subsequently come close to replicating.

If Iglesias flirted with politics, Preysler went one step further: 'The
woman in the Spanish public sphere with the greatest erotic charm'[24]
left the aristocratic Falcó for the child of an eminent Republican family,
Miguel Boyer, whose imprisonment for political dissidence under Franco
did not debar him from holding top positions in academia and industry.
Appointed director of the National Institute for Industry in 1974, Boyer
went on to combine working for the National Bank of Spain with mili-
tancy in the PSOE. Drawing on R. I. M. Dunbar's claim that '[w]ithout
gossip, there would be no society',[25] I would like to suggest that what
Francisco Umbral has characterised as the 'great love story of our democracy'[26] constitutes an ideal case-study to interrogate the claim that '[g]
ossip greatly expands the opportunities for cultural learning, because one
can benefit from the experiences of others outside of one's field of vision
and sometimes even outside one's circle of friends'.[27] It simultaneously

provides a privileged peephole into understanding how and why democracy, a 'promiscuous and often purely rhetorical word',[28] became embedded in 1980s Spain. Embroiled in a romance with Preysler prior to the 1982 general elections, González ordered his incoming Minister of Economy, Business and Tax to keep the matter secret, concerned as he was by the reputational damage already caused by Alfonso Guerra's extra-marital affair.[29] Boyer and Preysler's infidelity to their respective spouses was common knowledge amongst Spain's political and media elites but the press, cautious of potential reprisals, kept quiet, and it only became public knowledge in 1985 after Boyer resigned from government to take on more lucrative roles in the Spanish banking sector.

Having seen the dismal results of Mitterrand's nationalisation of the French banking system in 1981, the Socialist administration did not attempt the policy in Spain,[30] but they regulated it more firmly than Suárez's Unión de Centro Democrático (Union of the Democratic Centre; UCD). Following the collapse of the bank that was run by Jordi Pujol, who has always attributed the Bank of Spain's intervention to anti-Catalan sentiment, as opposed to financial irregularities,[31] the expropriation of holding company RUMASA, owned by business magnate and Opus Dei member José María Ruiz Mateos – 'a right-wing *enfant terrible*'[32] – in 1983 was, in Ernesto Ekaizer's words, the Government's 'baptism of fire'.[33] In the twenty-first-century Spanish public sphere, populism is primarily associated with the emergence of the anti-austerity Podemos as a major political force. The pioneer populists of post-Franco Spanish democracy such as Ruiz Mateos came, however, from the right of the political spectrum. As Cass Mudde and Cristóbal Rovira Kaltwasser note: 'almost all successful populists are insider-outsiders: men and women who have never been members of the political elite, i.e. the inner circle of the political regime, but have (strong) connections to them'.[34] In line with this conception, what could be seen as the Socialists' attempt to bring the financial elites who owed much of their fortunes to the laissez-faire approach of Francoism in line with the Constitutional order also lent itself to being interpreted as an unconstitutional attempt to retain exclusive licence over the banks and business.[35] Boyer regularly escaped from this maelstrom to Paris for rendezvous with Preysler. She had become a fixture in the French capital ever since her best friend Carmen Martínez Bordiú had set up home there with her second husband (see Chapter 2). Franco's granddaughter had also recently been appointed correspondent on French fashion for *¡Hola!*.

In her first column, Martínez Bordiú claimed she had to be persuaded to take on the role, only accepting when she realised that her privileged view of fashion, so important to the modern world, might be of interest to the magazine's readers: 'I hope to achieve this through the eyes of a daughter, of a modern woman and wife, of our time. A woman who, as well, lives fashion directly in Paris, where I am regularly invited to fashion shows and launches'.[36] Preysler retained the habit of selling exclusives to her separations as well as marriages. She and Falcó appeared together to discuss their divorce in *¡Hola!*, with whom she secured a lucrative deal as a celebrity interviewer. Her first subject was Julio Iglesias. Subsequent interviewees included Clint Eastwood; Gregory Peck; and Mario Vargas Llosa, the Peruvian writer often photographed alongside his wife socialising with Boyer and Preysler. The latter couple's marriage lasted until Boyer's death in 2014. Shortly afterwards, Vargas Llosa left Patricia, his wife of five decades, for Preysler, and many *¡Hola!* readers came into contact with the Nobel laureate for the first time. In the late 1980s, features on Preysler's marital home in the Puerta de Hierro (when Adolfo Suárez was first passed over for a ministerial role under Franco, he laconically claimed he did not satisfy the two vital prerequisites of having studied in the independent school El Pilar or having property in the exclusive Madrid neighbourhood), and the couple's holidays with the jet-set in Marbella, converted her into a metonym for the chic and glamorous fortunes that surrounded a government whose policies and style were increasingly the very embodiment of champagne socialism.

Predating British New Labour's Peter Mandelson by over a decade, Boyer's successor in government, Carlos Solchaga, boasted that Spain was one of the countries where one could get rich quickest,[37] but did not include the British politician's caveat that this was fine as long as millionaires paid their taxes. The Madrid Stock Exchange saw increases of 200 per cent between 1986 and 1989, and went in parallel with 'the first attempt in continental Europe at growth by means of a financial and property-asset-price bubble that would have a positive knock-on-effect on domestic consumption and demand without any significant support from industrial expansion'.[38] Between 1982 and 1996, investment in the public sector rose from 38 per cent to 46 per cent of GDP,[39] but what Richard Maxwell terms the 'inconsistent geography of Spanish capitalism' was both the product and cause of unemployment rising from 16 per cent to 22 per cent over the course of the decade.[40] In real terms, wages decreased on average between 1979 and 1986.[41] The spread of salaries was significantly higher in 1988 than a decade previously, the numbers of those on the minimum wage having reduced purchasing power.[42]

Ruiz-Mateos thereby presented himself as a modern-day Robin Hood, waging a public-relations war against Boyer and the glamorous Preysler. He dressed up as Superman to attend court hearings, and his stunts included visiting their condominium with an entourage dressed as Preysler's three husbands, and defacing the famous Osborne bulls that adorn the Spanish highways to indicate that Boyer was a cuckold. Physically assaulting his nemesis outside court, footage of which received heavy rotation on the State television channel, aided the fortunes of his anti-González, anti-European party – both he and his son-in-law became MEPs in 1989[43] – establishing a new brand of populism in Spanish politics whereby martyred businessmen claimed to be representing the real interests of the people. Mario Conde, a self-made millionaire with political aspirations (and, at one time, possibilities) rose through the traditionally endogamous Spanish banking system, entering Juan Carlos's inner circle to become an icon and threat to González's Government by dint of a counter-intuitive but nonetheless effective anti-establishment public persona. In his memoirs – written when serving a prison sentence for fraud – Conde maintains his innocence and claims his downfall was orchestrated because 'Felipe didn't want to share with anyone, at least not with anyone important, the glory of "modernizing" Spain.'[44] In his first set of memoirs, future President of the PP José María Aznar speaks repeatedly of the PSOE's hegemony – in terms that anticipate to a greater extent the rhetoric of Podemos and Pablo Iglesias than either man would admit – paying particular attention to their control of the media (see also Chapter 6).[45] The subsequent deregulation of Spanish television constituted a new chapter in the reporting of politics and celebrity, providing a breeding ground for a new brand of populism.

Jesús Gil y Gil, the builder responsible for the collapse of a banqueting suite instrumental to Suárez's initial rise (see Chapter 2), spent two years in prison before receiving a pardon from Franco. He was never made to relinquish the leisure complex where the tragedy occurred. Los Ángeles de San Rafael currently doubles up as a resort for predominantly lower-middle-class patrons and a training ground for the players of Madrid's Atlético football team (of which Gil y Gil was President from 1987 to 2002). In spite, or perhaps because, of his vocal racism – he referred to his team as FC Congo following the signing of foreign players, and once threatened to call on the Ku Klux Klan after an under-par performance – his funeral in 2004 was attended by over 20,000 mourners. *El pionero* (*The Pioneer*), a sympathetic biographical documentary, premiered in 2019 as the first in-house production by HBO Spain. Gil y Gil's political career took flight when his party, the Grupo Independiente Liberal, took control of Marbella town council in 1991, the same year his chat programme *Las noches de tal y tal* debuted on Telecinco. The commercial television channel was launched by media tycoon Silvio Berlusconi, whose interests in Spain were represented by Alfredo Fraile.

Spaniards had traditionally rejected tabloid publications, the sensationalist *Claro* launched in 1991 folding soon afterwards,[16] but televisual content of this kind found an audience. This had repercussions for previously sacrosanct notions of decorum in public broadcasting. Canal Nou, the Valencian Autonomous Community's bilingual channel, broke the tradition of journalists treating celebrities with kid gloves in its flagship programme, *Tómbola*. In the first episode, broadcast in 1997, Martínez Bordiú looked on in shock as Chábeli Iglesias walked off set disgusted at being questioned over the ethics of exploiting her private life for profit. If *Tómbola* marks a new chapter in Spain's television that falls beyond the time-frame of this book, TVE's *Juncal* (Jaime de Arminán,

1989) can retrospectively be viewed as the end of an era. Francisco Rabal appeared as the eponymous ex-matador in the last series to exert such a tight hold on the national consciousness prior to the diversification of viewing options and the concomitant segmentation of audiences. Filmed in Seville just prior to the gentrification that hosting Expo '92 entailed (see Chapter 12), the popularity of a series featuring Lola Flores in a secondary role was indicative of European integration not precluding bullfighting from retaining a privileged place in the (inter)national psyche.

In the late 1970s, *La clave* (*The Key*) – a televised discussion show[47] – questioned whether folkloric stars such as Lola Flores still had a place in contemporary Spain, but no such equivalent debate was framed in relation to taurine activities. More generally, bullfighting was criticised less for animal cruelty than for the people and business practices involved. Various press articles rallied against bullfighting as the natural habitat of the relics of the corrupt Francoist establishment.[48] In Fuengirola, the local town council recognised they had been swindled by a local former matador who had run the bullring since its construction as a limited company, but had wheedled his way out of paying municipal taxes. An expert's report concluded the local authority had the right to expropriate the bullring, but no action was taken.[49] A drawing of a bull was an official mascot for Spain's hosting of the World Cup and the World Swimming Championships in 1982 and 1986 respectively.[50] González and Guerra, being natives of Seville, favoured a quintessentially taurine Madrid–Andalusia axis, whilst Tierno Galván had published celebratory tracts on the bulls.[51] The Mayor of the Spanish capital believed traditional festivities such as San Isidro to be crucial to reviving civic pride (see Chapter 8), and he invested tax-payers' money in subsidising both *corridas* and concerts by local and major international acts such as Tina Turner. Aficionado Juan Carlos said the day that the EU required Spain to give up the bullfight would be the day Spain left the EU;[52] Julian Pitt-Rivers concluded in a report originally commissioned by the European Parliament that the 'cult of the bull is not disappearing today, either in popular Spanish culture nor in the bull-fight of the national culture – despite the enormous cost of seats, comparable to that of the opera in other countries ... For it is inherent in the Spanish mentality.[53] The notion of boxing as more barbaric was prevalent in the nineteenth century,[54] and was upheld by *El País*. Spanish democracy's flagship newspaper gave extensive coverage to *corridas* in its culture sections, but advised contributors not to write about boxing, that cruel and indefensible sport.[55]

An increasingly drink-dependent Manuel Benítez was coaxed out of retirement in the late 1970s.[56] In a letter dated 18 April 1980, the company running the bullring in Cordoba wrote to the town council seeking support, on the grounds of their social and community initiatives (e.g. reduced-price season tickets for pensioners) and the claim that tourism would benefit from the presence of El Cordobés and Francisco Rivera.[57] The latter, popularly known as Paquirrí, had a classic biography: from humble beginnings, he entered taurine aristocracy – as well as the front cover of *¡Hola!* – through his first marriage to Carmen Ordóñez, the daughter of matador Antonio Ordóñez, whose professional rivalry with brother-in-law Luis Miguel Dominguín had been immortalised in Ernest Hemingway's *That Dangerous Summer*. Paquirri was a different character and *torero* from El Cordobés; more interested in technique and discipline than showmanship, he allegedly considered changing profession when an audience accustomed to more polished pyrotechnics responded coolly to his debut performance in Madrid's major bullring.[58] Though he was fond of money and attractive women, there were none of the sordid tales of drunken binges and sexual misdemeanours that were increasingly common in relation to Benítez.

The end of Rivera's first marriage was attributed to his not sharing his wife's penchant for the jet-set lifestyle, preferring to remain at his rural retreat, honing his art. He nevertheless begun an affair with Lola Flores's daughter, Lolita, and went on to marry Isabel Pantoja, a folkloric singer from humble beginnings in Triana, a traditional working-class neighbourhood of Seville. Performing a genre associated with an older generation, Pantoja was in many respects an anachronistic figure.[59] The early years of their romance coincided with his worst performances in the ring,[60] but their celebrity cachet rose after she nursed him back to health following a serious goring in April 1981.

The engagement was prolonged so that he could have his previous marriage annulled and be wed again in and by the Church. When this eventually took place in spring 1983, the event was televised and, in the words of Ana Baeza, 'all of the most folkloric clichés were dressed in white to turn into reality the dreams of that Princess from Triana'.[61] What transformed Paquirri and Pantoja into legends was his fatal goring in Pozoblanco where, like Manolete before him, a great bullfighter met his death in an ill-equipped lower-tier bull-ring; Rivera would probably have survived if more adequate medical facilities had been on hand.[62] The funeral was another national (and televised) event attended by politicians, dignitaries, celebrities and everyday people alike:

> The coffin with the mortal remains of the bullfighter Francisco Rivera *Paquirri* journeyed through the streets of Seville, in a remarkable fare-well ceremony … Hundreds of people broke through the police barrier that closed off access to the ring to shout, with tears in their eyes, 'torero, torero'. The coffin was removed from the funeral car and carried on the pallbearers' shoulders to the sand, where the master from Barbate gave his final victory lap, while numerous individuals struggled to touch the wood coffin draped by a *capote* adorned with a giant crucifix.[63]

Within this carefully choreographed national melodrama, Pantoja – who always claimed to have been a virgin on her wedding day[64] – took on the role of a tragic heroine straight out of Lorca's rural tragedies. After becoming the world's most interviewed and photographed recluse, she was rebaptised as 'la viuda de España' (Spain's national widow), raising a seventh-month-old son alone. According to a description by Francisco Correal:

> The widow entered via Saint Geronimo's gate – 'the false gate', in local slang – at quarter past eight in the morning. Her wails were recorded for the radio-waves. Within a few hours, the tomb was inundated with a varied and epitaphic array of flowers. There was ever a chorus of cardboard cut-out mourners improvised in order to move the readers of that press to whom one could apply the nomenclature employed by Karl Marx in relation to religion: the heart of a heartless world.[65]

Paquirri's death transported traditional paradigms into a changing media-scape, over which the protagonists often exerted very little control.

Footage of Rivera in a makeshift infirmary shot by TVE was broadcast widely and, despite his widow's objections and a landmark court
case, commercialised through the new medium of VHS.[66] As Francisco
Umbral noted: 'There wasn't the medical science to help him (that's why
he left us), but there was the technology to film his death.'[67] Central to the
torero's legend was the stoical attitude with which he faced severe pain
and human mortality.

Pantoja returned to the stage in November 1985 at a televised gala performance in Seville organised by Queen Sofia, in which her and Rivera's
son, Kiko, presented his mother with a rose on stage. She then released
a multi-platinum comeback album, which dealt almost exclusively
with her late husband. Spain was split between those who empathised
with the young widow's grief, and those for whom she was shamelessly
capitalising on her husband's premature death. This national soap-opera
was exacerbated by ongoing legal battles with Carmen Ordóñez, who
made claims on Paquirri's estate for herself and on behalf of her two sons,
Cayetano and Francisco. Encarna Sánchez delighted in contrasting the
natural talent and professionalism of Rocío Jurado (also married to a
bullfighter, Ortega Cano) with Pantoja's (over)reliance on personal tragedy. The most popular voice of the Spanish airways subsequently did an
about-turn and became one of the widow's closest friends and strongest
advocates, a move widely construed as confirmation that the broadcaster was a closet lesbian. If Pantoja's music conflated what Simon Frith
characterises as 'the double enactment' by which pop-stars 'enact both a
star personality (their image) and a song personality, the role that each
lyric requires',[68] the fact that 'her film approximated a script from a film
from the post-war period'[69] was capitalised upon in a shameless elong-
ation of her star persona with the release of cinematic vehicle *Yo soy esa*
(*I'm the One*) (Luis Sanz, 1990).

This 1940s period piece cast Pantoja as a folkloric star. Taking its name
from the title of 'Yo soy esa', a much-loved *copla*, it constituted a return to
the kind of cinema that the heavily subsidised heritage films of the 1980s
(see Chapter 6) were intended to make obsolete, and coincided with the
death of Concha Piquer, 'unforgettable because of her incomparable

ability to act in song; because of her compelling, astringent voice; and because of the tragic stories she told with such emotion'.[70] Rumours of a real-life romance between Pantoja and co-star José Coronado, 'the epitome of the old-style leading man',[71] built expectation for what Terenci Moix refers to as 'the most anticipated kiss since Deanna Durbin was inducted into adolescence through her little kiss with Robert Stack'.[72] The more than 1.3 million spectators to buy tickets for the film included many who had not been to the cinema in years. Keen to capitalise on the phenomenon, a more political follow-up, *El día que nací yo* (*The Day I was Born*) (Pedro Olea, 1991) was rushed into production, but was markedly less successful.

Pantoja can be seen as the last in a long line of traditional celebrities, or the pioneer of a new breed where celebrity became an end in and of itself – and for whom performance on the stage and in the ring became of only secondary importance. Besieged and sustained by an increasingly intrusive celebrity culture, Carmen Ordóñez died, like her ex-husband, in the public eye, alcohol a more drawn-out and less dignified killer than a bull's horns. Her two sons had, by this time, followed in their father's professional footsteps. Aficionados in Las Ventas never rated Francisco Rivera Ordóñez, but his celebrity – enhanced by marrying and then divorcing the Duchess of Alba's daughter, Eugenia Martínez de Irujo – ensured he was able to pack out rings throughout Spain until his retirement in 2017. To boost ticket sales, towards the end of his career he began to advertise himself as Paquirri. Half-brother Kiko Rivera (popularly known as Paquirrín) is a DJ and reality-TV star. Pantoja was imprisoned for money-laundering in 2014, following a disastrous romance with Julián Muñóz, Gil y Gil's successor in the GIL Party as Mayor of Marbella. Spain was once again divided on the national widow: was she an innocent victim who had been duped, or was she guilty of avarice, an unforgivable sin at a time of national recession in which fellow citizens were enduring job-losses and cuts to basic public services. At the time of writing, she is marooned in Honduras as part of the 2019 edition of the *Supervivientes* (*Survivors*) reality show, a financial necessity to pay off her debts, according to the disgraced 63-year-old.

Other survivors of Francoist celebrity culture have fared better. The premature obituary of mass culture from the dictatorship carried out by the oppositional left has proved to be both glib and counter-productive. It has impeded the development of a heuristic artillery capable of understanding, let alone combating, a twenty-first-century media-sphere in which Carmen Martínez Bordiú competes on the Spanish version of *Strictly Come Dancing* and is interviewed on the State television channel at home in front of an original photograph of model Naomi Campbell's naked buttocks and a portrait of her grandfather in military attire who, she claims, like all human beings, was bisexual.[73] Franco's granddaughter became a duchess after her mother died in 2017 by virtue of a legislative change championed by Natalia Figueroa to make male and female aristocrats equal before the law,[74] thereby ensuring that her son with popstar Raphael will one day be a marquis. The performer Rodrigo Fresán, described as 'the orgasm that never stops',[75] continues to thrill his original fan-base whilst courting lucrative gay and youth markets. In a relatively young parliamentary democracy, the television specials of the lad from Linares are at least as much part of Christmas as speeches by Franco; Juan Carlos; and, now, Felipe VI. Over the last decade, his 1968 hit 'Mi gran noche' (My big night) has become a classic last song in nightclubs, and is popular amongst the brass bands that help fill the 20,000 seats of Pamplona's bullring during the nine days of the San Fermín festivities. Headlining the Sonorama Music Festival in 2014, the septuagenarian singer performed for over two hours in front of indie music fans with banners that proclaimed 'Raphael es el puto amo' (Raphael is the fucking boss) and 'Vota a Raphael' (Vote for Raphael). It is highly improbable that inebriated revellers articulated such slogans with this in mind, but they unwittingly provide an illustrative coda to the principal thesis of this section: it is as quixotic to take celebrity out of political discussion as it is to take the politics out of celebrity culture.

Part II

Censorship

Introduction

In the ambitiously titled *Franco's Crypt: Spanish Culture and Memory since 1936*, Jeremy Treglown makes a spirited case against 'what's supposed to have been a uniformly traditionalist and repressive official culture'.[1] Helen Graham's review for the *Guardian* spoke of an 'elegant but deeply flawed book', an 'antiquarian rerefurbishment of Francoism, done in patrician British style'.[2] The author, former editor of *The Times Literary Supplement* and a recent convert to Hispanism, identifies a disciplinary misconception, put to work to advance a conclusion by means of a non-sequitur: the Franco regime did not police cultural production as harshly as common wisdom dictates, and it was not therefore as bad as we have often been led to believe. Treglown inherits from those he critiques a blindness to the ramifications of the fact that, as Steven Lukes notes, '[p]ower is a capacity, not the exercise of that capacity (it may never be, and never need to be, exercised); and you can be powerful by satisfying and advancing others' interests'.[3]

Filtering this insight through Foucault's notion of the archive as 'the general system of the formation and transformation of statements',[4] this Part traces the history of censorial practices in relation to cultural production over three decades. As Paul Allain notes: 'Good or bad, archives are always partial but even that partiality needs careful editing and curating. We should approach them with caution and always be prepared, for an archive is to some extent only as good as what it is used for, ultimately reflecting the abilities of its explorer'.[5] Timothy Garton Ash's research into the Stasi records (including his own) leads him to contemplate 'how a file opens the door to a vast sunken labyrinth of the forgotten past, but how, too, the very act of opening the door itself changes the buried artefacts, like an archaeologist letting in fresh air to a sealed Egyptian tomb'.[6] In comparison with the former East Germany, Spain invested fairly limited human and financial resources into the surveillance of its subjects, or into the subsequent exegesis of said surveillance. There is nevertheless an expanding body of scholarship that alternates between two dominant visions of the Francoist censor: the ubiquitous and draconian fascist oppressor, and the easily hoodwinked bureaucratic buffoon. If, as I will suggest, repression often resides more in the constant possibility of recrimination than in specific examples of prohibition, then there is a pressing need to go beyond the routine practice of cataloguing case-studies to become more self-reflective about what is at stake in the relationship between narrating censorial practices and the development of canonical accounts of the Transition.

Chapter 4 charts evolving systems of control during the final thirteen years of Francoism, whilst seeking both to situate and to deconstruct the academic field of censorship studies in the Spanish context. The tense years between 1975 and 1982 – when cultural production and press freedoms were seen as a litmus test for democracy – are documented in Chapter 5. I make a case for 1981 being more significant in many respects than 1978 on the grounds that it marked the end of a period in which the consolidation of this particularly political system was far from a foregone conclusion. Chapter 6 covers the ten years of Socialist rule from 1982 onwards.

In a decade when it was sometimes difficult to know if Franco was more discredited at home for being old-fashioned or for being a dictator, I suggest that an unreflective and self-satisfied celebration of freedom of expression camouflaged the prolongation – and, in some cases, intensification – of non-democratic practices, an almost carnivalesque idolatry providing fast-track access to (post)modernity alongside a first-class platform on the international stage.

Chapter 4

The regulation of cultural production during and after Manuel Fraga (1962–75)

Irrespective of whether Fraga's prime contribution be understood as the liberalisation or the legitimisation and prolongation of Francoism, his appointment as Minister of Information and Tourism in 1962 was indicative of the regime increasingly seeking international respectability, and he was responsible for a radical overhaul of how journalism and cultural production were regulated in both ideological and bureaucratic terms. Hardline Francoist Gabriel Arias-Salgado had previously held the position since the Ministry was created in 1951. Shortly after his appointment, José María García Escudero was dismissed as Director-General of Theatre and Cinema in 1952 for awarding *Surcos* (*Furrows*) (1951), made by Falangist director José Antonio Nieves Conde, a National Interest Prize when the film was overtly critical of poverty and exploitation in Madrid. Fraga's reinstating of García Escudero was symptomatic of the fact that, to borrow a phrase from Pamela Beth Radcliff, the country was no longer 'held together by the blood pact of the Civil War and the implacable marginalization of anti-Spain'.[1] If, in the 1940s, a staple of children's comics was 'rojos' [reds] being beaten up, the censor became increasingly concerned by the 1960s with the psychological effects such content might have on young impressionable minds.[2] My hypothesis is that we need to become more methodologically self-reflective and consult a wider range of archival resources than has traditionally been the case if we are to make serious headway into developing an understanding of the mechanisms by which culture and control fed into the forging of a new social contract. In what follows, I will make a first attempt at carrying out this endeavour and, in the process, hope to convince the reader that such an approach has the potential to enhance understanding not only of censorship but also of the culture and politics of the Transition.

A BBC radio broadcast from 16 January 1962 on contemporary Spanish painting, timed to coincide with three exhibitions in London (Tooth's, Marlborough and the Tate),[3] claimed 'we have the almost unheard-of spectacle of a thoroughly rebellious and non-conformist artistic movement being smiled upon by a thoroughly reactionary and autocratic regime'.[4] Antoni Tàpies was, against his express wishes, included in a group show at the Tate organised by the Spanish Embassy. The Catalan artist believed the regime to be deliberately tarnishing his reputation by including under-par paintings, and refused to lend anything in his possession. In a letter dated 21 November 1961, Sir John Rothenstein, the museum director, wrote to him: 'I am particularly disappointed, not only as an admirer of yours, but because of the hope the exhibition held out of enabling the Tate Gallery to consider the purchase of one of the works included.'[5] An exasperated Tàpies later threatened legal action. On 5 January 1962 Rothenstein replied:

> You will appreciate that it is very difficult for us to intervene in a diffe-rence of opinion regarding an official exhibition coming from a foreign country, especially as it is being presented here under the auspices of the Arts Council and not of the Tate itself. However, I have asked the Arts Council to convey to the organisers that we have never before had a case of an artist being included at the Tate Gallery contrary to his express wishes and that this places us in an extremely embarrassing position.[6]

Tàpies's stance was an unusually blatant manifestation of a broader phe-nomenon. Similarly fearful of becoming pawns in the regime's attempts to export a liberal veneer, some artists refused to be included in the Spanish entry to the Venice Biennale from 1962 onwards.[7] They wanted nothing to do with the Francoist State's growing sophistication in appropriating culture as a form of reputation-enhancing soft power.

In a letter dated 16 July 1962, Antonio Garrigues wrote to congratulate Fraga on his new position. After cattily remarking that 'no tendrás que esforzarte mucho para mejorar a tu predecesor' (you won't have to make much of an effort to do better than your predecessor), the Spanish ambassador to the United States specifies that, alongside the Foreign Office, Fraga's ministry represents the outward image of Spain, and 'si queremos embellecer esa cara habrá que poner manos a la obra' (if we want to improve that face, we have to get to work).[8]

The profile of censors became more enlightened and professionalised as García Escudero made a deliberate effort to recruit writers, critics and intellectuals alongside younger clerical advisors: members more aligned with the spirit of the Second Vatican Council than the Civil War crusade.[9] Under his watch and, to some extent, patronage, the Nuevo Cine Español (New Spanish Cinema) emerged. Madrid-based filmmakers collaborated with Basque producer Elías Querejeta who, in Virginia Higginbotham's words, 'was able to package the violence and distortions of the Spanish experience in a style both visually interesting to a foreign audience and, more importantly, permissible by the Franco regime'.[10] In a letter dated 10 September 1963, Foreign Minister Fernando Castiella forwarded to Garrigues correspondence received from the Spanish ambassador in Italy about a screening of the film *El verdugo* (*The Executioner*) (Luis García Berlanga, 1963) with the following cover note:

> He mandado hacer reproducciones, en una tirada reducidísima, de una carta del Embajador Sánchez Bella [Alfredo]. Creo que es interesante que la conozcan algunos de nuestros Jefes de Misión. Por razones obvias, te agradeceré que la consideres como secreta y, a poder ser, la destruyes en cuanto la hayas leído. Si te remito este documento es porque creo que puede ser de utilidad para nuestro mejor Servicio.[11]

> I have ordered some reproductions, in a very limited run, of a letter from Ambassador Sánchez Bella [Alfredo]. I think it would be interesting for some of our Heads of Mission to be aware of it. For obvious reasons,

> I would be very grateful if you considered it confidential and, if possible, if you could destroy once read. If I am sending you this document, it is because I think it could be of use for our greater Service.

Garrigues and Castiella were orchestrating a campaign of soft power, actively petitioning Franco on the benefits of freedom of expression as a privileged form of cultural diplomacy.[12]

Unaware of the Foreign Minister's involvement, Sánchez Bella's letter, dated 30 August 1963, complains of one of the most incredible libels ever committed against Spain. The ambassador claims that, on arriving in Italy, García Escudero realised he had been hoodwinked but felt it better to go ahead with the screening of the tragicomic film about a reluctant executioner to avoid negative publicity. Sánchez Bella is unconvinced because of the tremendous inopportunity of the subject matter; an international outcry had not saved under-cover Communist agent Julián Grimau from execution by firing squad a few months previously. The pathos of Berlanga's film is in the contrast of happy-go-lucky tourists in Palma de Mallorca and the regime's unreconstructed brutality. Both characterised 1960s Spain, liberal credentials in a perpetual state of flux.

The creation of cultural magazine *Cuadernos para el diálogo* (*Notebooks towards Dialogue*) in 1963 by Christian Democrat Joaquín Ruiz-Giménez Cortes – a former Minister of Education (1951–5) who, increasingly disillusioned with the regime, became Franco's only minister ever to resign – was both cause and consequence of an increasingly pluralistic public sphere. That it was aimed at an elite educated audience ensured that greater leniency was shown: various authors published materials banned when presented elsewhere.[13] New press legislation implemented in 1966 (replacing emergency legislation from 1938, when the country remained at war) was couched in the discourse of individual rights and the free market: 'the principal inspiration for this law comes from the idea of optimum development and the greatest possible outlay of a person's freedom'.[14] Prior censorship was excised, but Fraga's office retained the right to seize offending publications and impose heavy fines, effectively sub-contracting censorship out to a range of gatekeepers.

Newspaper editors were made responsible for content but were guaranteed a salary for a year if dismissed by the owners.[15] Most cases were brought against weeklies/monthlies with limited runs, which were more willing to risk being taken out of circulation.[16] The major privately owned newspapers (*ABC, Ya, La Vanguardia*) were the biggest benefactors, as the close relationship between the owners and key figures within the regime generally, although by no means inevitably, allowed them to avoid reprisals for the publication of potentially contentious material.[17] Writers and editors were in theory encouraged to contact the Ministry informally if they had questions or concerns, but this did not always work out in practice. In the words of Miguel Delibes, the novelist who edited regional newspaper *El norte de Castilla* from 1958 to 1963: 'Before they didn't allow you to ask anything. Now they do but they don't answer.'[18] Patricia O'Connor, a North American scholar, did receive a response after contacting Fraga in 1965 in advance of a trip to Spain to ask for permission to write on theatre censorship; he responded affirmatively, enclosing a leaflet containing details of new censorship norms.[19] She was initially granted permission to consult any files she wanted in the Ministry's basement, but this decision was subsequently revoked. O'Connor was then informed that she could only request information on specific plays; this was a slow process, and she had no idea if she was being granted access to all the documentation or if a prior screening process had taken place.[20]

As I will later discuss, Fraga was replaced by the intransigent Sánchez Bella in 1969. O'Connor returned to Madrid in 1972 to find a note at her hotel ordering her to report to a police station, where she was intimidated by officers who claimed to know she was the daughter of Spanish Communists in exile, and that the Party was funding her research. O'Connor was not, however, tortured, as was suspected by playwright Antonio Buero Vallejo, actress Nuria Espert and critic Francisco García Pavón when she missed appointments. This was not a far-fetched supposition. In 1968, a well-documented dossier of police repression with multiple testimonies documented torture in prisons and police stations across the country.[21] A covering letter, signed by 1,200 individuals – including cultural dissidents Carlos Barral, Joan Miró and Enrique Tierno Galván, as well as Ana Fraga Iribarne (the Communist-sympathising sister of the Minister of Information and Tourism) and Alfredo Mayo (the leading man of early Francoist cinema) – demanded action in respectful but unequivocal terms:

> los funcionarios tanto de la Brigada de Investigación Social como de la Guardia Civil o de la Policía Armada que no practiquen tales reprobables métodos y Vd. mismo que con seguridad los ignora (pues no es pensable que, conociéndolos, los apruebe) son, sin duda, los primeros más interesados en que la investigación que aquí solicitamos se realice.

> civil servants from the Social Investigation Brigade as well as the Civil and Armed Guards who do not carry out such reprehensible methods, and you yourself, who are surely unaware of them (it being unthinkable that, if aware of such practices, you would give the go-ahead) are undoubtedly the first to have a vested interest in the carrying out of the investigation for which we call.

As with a letter sent to Fraga by a group of Spain's leading artists and intellectuals in September 1963, protesting about the violent repression of strikers in Asturias, the petition seemingly went unanswered. Torturous practices outlived Franco. Traumatising as the ordeal must have been for O'Connor, it benefited her research: 'several theatre figures I had never met contacted me with invaluable information about their censorship experiences.'[22]

O'Connor's correspondence, now held at the Juan March Foundation in Madrid, bears testament to her admirable tenacity. It also offers a snapshot into how and why practitioners sought to present themselves as representing both Spanish theatre and the opposition. Writing from exile in Paris, Francisco Arrabal claimed the censor, and its allies in theatre magazine *Primer Acto*, were in cahoots, attempting to veto his presence on the Spanish stage: 'El único teatro escrito por españoles que tiene un eco en el mundo entero (Picasso, Alberti, Max Aub y más modestamente el mío) está rigurosamente amordazado en la España de hoy' (The only theatre written by Spaniards to be globally renowned (Picasso, Alberti,

Max Aub and, on a more modest scale, my own) is rigorously gagged in present-day Spain).[23] The extent to which playwrights whose works have not been tested in the theatre are worthy of canonisation remains a moot point. This is why, for example, Diego Santos Sánchez's quasi-evangelical defence of Arrabal's 'panic theatre' is careful to complement an explanation of the dramatist's expulsion from the Spanish stage with a case for the plays' formal unities.[24]

As reflected in the pages of *Primer Acto*, the major division in theatrical circles was between the strategies of *posibilismo* and *imposibilismo*, as championed by Antonio Buero Vallejo and Alfonso Sastre respectively.[25] The former advocated pragmatism, writing works that were critical but not to an extent that militated against their being staged: 'Sometimes, self-censorship is not a deformation, but a means of seeking communication.'[26] Sastre, by contrast, construed any compromise as betrayal, placing his faith in the possibility of retrospective vindication.[27] In a letter to O'Connor dated 5 July 1969, Buero Vallejo cautioned against taking Sastre seriously, noting that close attention would reveal that he did in fact seek recourse to camouflage tactics (e.g. setting the action abroad or the use of philosophical abstraction), and that censorship alone did not keep his plays off the stage.[28]

In relation to censorship in fascist Italy, Guido Bonsaver has argued that 'insistence on episodes of open opposition have tended to produce a rather dualistic vision of the historical picture and to discourage the exploration of the so-called grey zone occupying the vast space between vocal opposition and full collaboration.'[29] The principal bone of contention between *posibilismo* and *imposibilismo* was as to whether said 'grey zones' existed, but such liminal spaces remain uncharted terrain in Hispanic studies, critics disproportionately focusing on dissident playwrights at the expense of figures such as the prolific and much-lampooned Alfonso Paso. The holdings of the Arxiu Nacional de Catalunya in San Cugat contain reports on plays that had almost always been reviewed previously in Madrid, but now required permission to be performed in and around Barcelona. Counter-intuitively, dissident playwrights such as John Osborne and Bertolt Brecht were seemingly censored less than Paso, whose plays rarely escaped cuts of one kind of another and were, even then, generally only approved for those aged 18 and over. Most of the objections relate to sexual content, such as the use of contraception,[30] prostitution[31] and Spanish taboos,[32] but others provide insights into particularly sensitive subject-matter. Paso is repeatedly chastised for making references to political corruption[33] and, remarkably, given information coming to light about State kidnapping of children under the dictatorship, the following lines from a comedy titled *Como está al servicio* (*The State of the Servants*), staged in 1968 but set at the end of the Civil War: 'Intervino una cosa que se llama Tribunal de Menores que es un organismo que les quita los hijos a las que los han parido y se los pasa a las que tienen buena conducta' (Something called the Court for Minors got involved. It's an organism that passes children from their birth mothers to women of good character).[34] The lack of uniformity in the Francoist censorship apparatus clearly cautions against subscribing to general principles.

On the one hand, a number of landmark publications ensure we have a much clearer idea of the relevant censorship legislation and its victims than when O'Connor first embarked on her research.[35] As Raquel Merino notes, improved access to archives has constituted a 'privileged "balcony"'[36] from which to view the terrain. Elsewhere this critic speaks of archival 'traces' employed as building blocks for 'potentially accurate' accounts of censorial practices.[37] Conversely, however, the limitation of a positivistic approach resides in the reluctance 'to reflect on the archive as an epistemological structure that produces the very history it is archiving'.[38] The deification of dissidents in post-Francoist Spain has been the product and cause of what Derrida terms 'archive fever'.[39]

Located in Alcalá de Henares, a commuter town outside Madrid, the Archivo General de la Administración (AGA) is the first, and frequently only, archival port of call for the growing number of scholars working on censorship in Francoist Spain. Bearing testament to Derrida's precept that 'archivisation produces as much as it records the event',[40] the cataloguing process is complicit in a system of canonisation and hierarchy. Files relating to iconic victims of repression (e.g. *Viridiana* (Luis Buñuel, 1961)) have been digitised, whilst books, plays and films – unlike, say, television programmes or popular-music recordings – have been indexed. Limited opening hours (8.30 a.m.–2.30 p.m.) compounded by the slow delivery of materials have encouraged researchers to concentrate on more readily accessible files. The unearthing of silenced voices has become a quasi-spiritual star, couched in the rubric of a naïve positivism that bypasses the extent to which a 'spectral messianicity is at work in the concept of the archive and ties it, like religion, like history, like science itself, to a very singular experience of the promise'.[41] To cite just one example, Luis Vaquerizo García's book on the Nuevo Cine Español[42] reproduces plot summaries and much of the correspondence housed in the AGA, but makes little attempt to articulate the complex and frequently contradictory dynamics at play. In comparison with the vast bibliographies on literature, press, theatre and cinema, relatively little attention has been paid to the censorship of popular music. The first comprehensive study, Xavier Valiño's *Veneno en dosis camufladas* (*Poison in Camouflaged Doses*), is authoritative on bureaucratic process:

> In principle, all of the submission of texts in English, French and Italian – the latter two occupied a tiny proportion in comparison to English – were revised by one of them [the four censors]. All of the texts in Castilian, Catalan, and possibly also in Basque, were then supervised by a second reader, aided in the other languages by the other two. Their superiors also contributed to the revision of submissions when their participation was needed.[43]

Valiño also unearths a series of anecdotal gems: 'She makes me warm', by teenyboppers the Osmonds, was banned for its pronounced eroticism,[44] presumably a result of linguistic conflation – 'caliente' means both 'warm' in temperature and 'hot' in sexual parlance. The Velvet Underground's debut album was released minus 'Venus in furs' – banned for references to masochism[45] – but included 'Waiting for the man', a song about the procurement of class-A drugs, which the censor nevertheless believed to narrate the story of a young woman left waiting by an unpunctual boyfriend; she has other suitors, but he is special to her, and she just incidentally happens to be carrying $26 in her hand.[46]

Veneno en dosis camufladas provided the basis for a touring exhibition titled *Vibraciones prohibidas* (*Prohibited Vibrations*), a visual and sonic mnemonic feast that received heavy media coverage.[47] Valiño's methodology is, however, beset with a series of familiar pitfalls. First, he simultaneously assumes the censors to be omniscient and ignorant. Second, there is no recognition that censorship was hardly the unique preserve of Spain;[48] nor any sense that there might be grounds for, say, censoring the image of a naked adolescent girl on the front cover of the Scorpions' *Virgin Killer* album from 1976[49] or, more pressingly, that censorship is frequently a process of (pacted) negotiation. Censors retained the right, for example, to approve songs for inclusion on LPs alone,[50] thereby precluding the possibility of release as a single or playing on the radio. Valiño would have been well advised to examine the lengthy documentation contained in the AGA on the Beatles star-vehicle *A Hard Day's Night* (Richard Lester, 1964).[51] In February 1969, concerned internal memos were exchanged amongst high-ranking officials about stories being run by both the *Sun* and the *Daily Sketch* claiming the Spanish censor would only allow the release of a Beatles film if a striptease scene was cut. The ministerial bureaucrats had no memory of this, but decided to investigate their own records; on locating the file relating to the film, they discovered *A Hard Day's Night* was initially awarded the rating of 'for patrons of 14 years and over', but also noted the inclusion of a letter dated 25 August 1964 from the distribution and exhibition company, Filmayer, offering to make any cuts that were required to ensure the Fab Four's cinematic outing could be seen by viewers of all ages. They concluded a deal must have been reached, as had been standard practice for the star-vehicles of Raphael and Julio Iglesias.

Under Fraga's watch, explicit and detailed documents with the criteria for assessing films and plays were made available to practitioners for the first time. This move towards transparency in principle militated against the sympathies and whims of individual censors. In relation to the stage, however, as O'Connor noted at the time: 'the official committee following specific norms has been more difficult to predict than the action of the readers. A reason for this apparent inconsistency is the importance of the political atmosphere as a major factor in determining the fate of prospective theatrical offerings.'[52] In 1968, Adolfo Marsillach staged a version of Peter Weiss's *Marat-Sade* at the Teatro Español. Then, when the state of emergency was declared at the beginning of 1969 (see Chapter 1), Weiss prohibited the continued performance of his work because of 'the persecution and imprisonment of students and intellectuals that was taking place in Spain.'[53] The Spanish practitioner was in the process of contacting Weiss when he received a call from Fraga's brother-in-law and right-hand man, Carlos Robles Piquer, who ordered him to continue performing the play to provide a semblance of normality.[54] Weiss refused to yield, and the run was curtailed. Marsillach claims the next time the Minister summoned him to his office, Fraga pointed to the Spanish flag and said 'Whilst I represent this flag, Mr Weiss will not be staged again in this country.'[55]

As artistic director of the National Theatre, Marsillach then discussed with Fraga the possibility of an updated version of *Tartuffe*, in which Molière's sycophantic flatterers would be members of Opus Dei. The Catholic organisation, founded by José María Escrivá in 1928, was on the ascent, championing, in the words of Joan Estruch, 'the rationalization of the state apparatus, with the goal of placing it at the service of the economy (contrary to the strategy of the Falangists who throughout the history of the Franco regime tried to subordinate the economy to policy).'[56] Fraga shared their discourse of rationalisation and modernisation yet, both personally and politically, was more closely allied with the Falangists. Animosity towards the Opus Dei technocrats predisposed him to greenlight Marsillach's latest venture, reputedly telling him: 'Get on with it, lest there be some kind of ministerial change.'[57] *Tartuffe* opened in Madrid on 3 October 1969. Before the month was out, Fraga had been replaced by Sánchez Bella in a cabinet shake-up favouring sectors aligned with Opus Dei, despite, or perhaps because of, their laundering of State funds through the MATESA holding company.[58] That Fraga afforded the press free rein to cover the scandal was thought a greater betrayal of trust than the fraud itself. *Tartuffe*, a success amongst critics and audiences in the capital, had a national tour booked. According to Marsillach, theatre owners around the country pulled out after receiving threats from a high-ranking civil servant who claimed there would be consequences if they hosted the Molière production.[59]

The compelling but simplistic equation between prohibition and opposition often places an overemphasis on the written record, both in terms of an underrepresentation of non-textual cultural production and an (over)reliance on textual traces of said repression. *Castañuela 70*, a dissident collaboration between independent theatre group Tábano and musical troupe La madre del cordero, was, for example, initially approved despite its parodies of charity events and popular culture alongside a concentrated attack on the exploitation of folk-lore by the regime to camouflage the survival of feudal relations in Andalusia.[60] Armed with generally positive reviews,[61] the production was a sell-out success in Madrid during August and September (chal-lenging months for theatre), much to the consternation of the more reactionary sections of society. The most convincing account of what then happened is that the Guerrilleros de Cristo Rey – an ultra-right terrorist organisation that had bombed cinemas showing films such as *Ana y los lobos* (*Ana and the Wolves*) (Carlos Saura, 1973) – vio-lently interrupted a performance, thereby providing the grounds for the production to be banned in the name of public order.[62] In 1972, Miguel Narros, a former artistic director of the National Theatre, travelled with Víctor Manuel and Ana Belén to Mexico to stage the musical production *Ravos*, after applications for it to be staged in Spain had been repeatedly declined. A media witch-hunt began back home when a rumour originating from an anonymous source claimed the production featured a Spanish flag being trodden on and thrown into a garbage can. On 22 December, a telegram was sent to all local radio stations from the directorial offices of Spanish radio and televi-sion saying it was now prohibited to play any songs by Víctor Manuel because of his 'actitud anti-patriótica' (anti-patriotic attitude).[63] He and Belén were concerned about returning to Spain, but Julio Iglesias, a personal friend who had seen the production in Mexico, assured the authorities that the accusations were false.[64]

The nebulous zone of personal sympathies and connections often counted as much if not more than politics per se. Catalan publisher Carlos Barral had a man in Madrid on the payroll to bribe and negotiate with censors.[65] Spain's first major professional musical promoter, Gay Mercader, recalls that the challenges he faced were more logistical than ideological, and that a small bribe was sufficient to receive a licence for international rock bands to play in Spain.[66] As Antonio Cazorla Sánchez notes, in a regime that had initially shown no compunction about shooting hundreds on a daily basis, only one official was ever executed for corruption.[67] Paternalism fomented a patronage system with endogamy and corruption at its very core. Juan Cobos Arévalo, an altar-boy at the Pardo Palace, claims in his memoirs that Admiral Carrero Blanco – a champion of the Opus Dei technocrats, and Franco's Vice-President from 1967 onwards – was the staff's favourite minister for being the most amenable to advancing the interests of their friends and relatives.[68] As head of the Generalissimo's Military House, Juan Castañón de Mena received frequent requests from figures such as an architect who complained that, in spite of being persecuted and imprisoned by the reds, he was now being taken to court for a building constructed in Lerida some seventeen years previously that had recently collapsed, causing five mortal casualties.[69] Castañón de Mena was promoted in the October 1969 reshuffle to become Minister of the Armed Forces. In a letter dated 14 May 1973, he sent a list of recommendations to the director of the Zaragoza military academy (where Juan Carlos had trained), including a recruit for whom Don Luis expressed a special interest in his passing his exams.[70]

A fluctuating combination of patronage, permissiveness and prohibition characterised the regime until its very end, different aspects coming in and out of focus. Due to Franco's ailing health, his number two took over presidential duties on 9 June 1973, and addressed a cabinet meeting as follows:

> It is incumbent upon us to bring morality back to streets, to discos and to performances, and we must prevent drug trafficking; and with the same care the sale and distribution of books and magazines with opposing or immoral ideologies … We need to raise men, not poofs, and those intrepid long-hairs that are sometimes to be seen hardly serve to this end – quite the contrary.[71]

On 20 December, Carrero Blanco was assassinated, his rigid routine making him an easy target. ETA left a bomb under the car that picked him up at the same time every day from mass. As Catherine O'Leary notes, turmoil 'during the period from 1973 to 1977 was reflected in the many changes in personnel at the MIT [Ministry of Information and Tourism], and none of the ministers who succeeded Sánchez Bella lasted long'.[72]

The regime was in accelerated free-fall, ETA having struck a potentially lethal blow against the long-term possibilities for post-Franco Francoism. According to an internal Government report: 'Los demás hombres políticos del régimen estaban – y siguen estando – varios escalones por debajo de Carrero' (No other politician from the regime was, nor indeed is, in anywhere near the same league as Carrero).[73] Eva Forest, the wife of Alfonso Sastre, was arrested, accused of carrying out the lethal attack. The dramatist, although not implicated, was detained, as Spanish law dictated that a husband was responsible for crimes committed by his wife.[74] When Alfonso Paso subsequently died in 1978, an obituary in the magazine of the Spanish Legion lamented that some wanted to dismiss him in a manner akin to the period he represented.[75] From the pages of *ABC*, Natalia Figueroa was similarly aghast:

> The other evening I was left speechless in front of the television. Two people – a critic and a playwright – had been chosen to speak on television about Paso on the occasion of his death. Both ended up saying more of less the same: 'Paso was a product of the Francoist regime … He lived through the age of repression. His superficial theatre is an indictment of Francoism's subculture.' The playwright ended with these words: 'May both the period as well as Alfonso Paso rest in peace.'[76]

In his twilight years, he had combined writing for the stage with a column in *El Alcázar*, a newspaper closely affiliated with the most reactionary sectors of the regime, the bunker. This earned him appreciative letters from Carlos Arias and Saddam Hussein, who expressed gratitude 'por sus nobles sentimientos hacia Irak y la nación árabe' (for your noble sentiments towards Iraq and the Arab nation),[77] but relations with theatrical colleagues were less warm.

Unlike, say, Raphael, there has been no revival in Paso's fortunes. He is rarely staged on the contemporary Spanish stage, much to the consternation of his youngest daughter, Almudena, who – married to a Clark Gable lookalike she met at Universal Studios in Los Angeles – combines running a celebrity-impersonator's business with attempts to vindicate her father's reputation, petitioning mayors, without much success, to name streets in his honour.

Almudena's rationale for not including the letter from Saddam Hussein (a scanned copy of which she emailed me) amongst her father's papers, donated to the Juan March Foundation, was that it would provide additional artillery for his enemies. When I met with her, she referred to the major injustice of the dismissal of her father – a friend and collaborator with Sastre in their younger days – as a puppet of the regime when, she claimed, he suffered repression. She recalled being in Franco's company as a child: her father would ask him to intervene on his behalf, but the Caudillo would divert the conversation, claiming it was Fraga's department and not his concern. Almudena's logic stands or falls on the equation of direct censorship with opposition. There may be more cuts to his plays than to those of other playwrights, but the files housed in the Catalan archive suggest greater leniency in policing the productions, the censor rarely indicating the need to be vigilant at the dress rehearsal or to ensure that instructions have been followed in subsequent performances.[78] A counter-argument is that it was proximity to the regime (how many other writers were granted personal audiences with Franco?) that allowed Paso to test limits without fears of reprisal.

As Michael Thompson argues, '[t]he act of resorting to explicit censorship confirms that the control mechanisms are not working automatically, making the suppressed work of art all the more effective in highlighting fault lines in the discursive order'.[79] One of the relatively few documents to relate directly to censorship in the papers of the Francisco Franco Foundation is a letter to Fraga from Robles Piquer dated 21 December 1965, concerning the potential publication of Manuel Hedilla's memoirs alongside reports by the censor, and containing the following request: 'Por tratarse de un libro que afecta directamente a la historia del

Movimiento Nacional juzgo conveniente, si lo tienes bien, que entregues a S[u] E[xcelencia] Jefe del Estado, fotocopia de las páginas que contienen párrafos especialmente delicados' (Because it is a book that directly affects the National Movement, I deem it appropriate, if it meets your approval, to deliver a copy of the pages containing especially delicate paragraphs to H[is] E[xcellency], the Head of State).[80] Hedilla, the provisional leader of the Falange following the execution of José Antonio Primo de Rivera by Republican forces in 1936, was charismatic competition for Franco, rousing troops with speeches on the need to limit the excesses of capitalism and their destiny to do so once the crusade against anti-Spain had been won. Franco had him jailed on 25 April 1937. After the war, Hedilla's mother pleaded with the Caudillo, who had earlier commuted an initial death sentence, to release him; Franco reportedly claimed Hedilla was an innocent bystander but did not issue a pardon until May 1947.[81]

By the 1960s, Hedilla was keeping a low profile, staking out a modest living working for the State airline, Iberia,[82] but his biography – eventually published in Paris as opposed to Spain – remained incendiary. He was both an insider and an outsider, capable of besmirching the regime's mythical origins and auditing its failure to deliver. Economic progress and rising living standards for an aspirational middle class had not necessarily translated into improvements in social equality or the eradication of poverty, a blight clearly visible in the shanty towns that emerged on the peripheries of the major industrial cities to which frequently starving rural émigrés flocked (see Chapter 7).

The one major exception to the general relaxation of censorship under Fraga was references to social exclusion and poverty. Drawing upon his experiences of making *Cuadrilátero* (*Boxing Ring*) (1970), filmmaker Eloy de la Iglesia recalls that 'certain things were approved without question if the actors were well and correctly dressed, but not if they appeared like people in the street': 'we had much greater knowledge of a street in Manhattan than of one in Madrid'.[83] Featuring a botched illegal abortion and set in alcohol-strewn taverns on the capital's streets akin to 'a cyst within the great city',[84] Luis Martín-Santos's novel *Tiempo de silencio* (*Time of Silence*) was initially submitted to the censor's office in 1961.

Prior to its first edition in 1962, numerous cuts were made in relation to questions of morality (especially prostitution) and the use of taboo language, but criticisms of the regime and harsh living conditions went relatively unscathed. Andrea Bresadola attributes this comparative tolerance to the experimental prose style and elite readership.[85] This is plausible but it is not self-evident that *Tiempo de silencio* would have been approved under Fraga's ostensibly more liberal watch. The decade's closest equivalent to *Surcos* was *Los golfos* (*The Hoodlums*) (Carlos Saura, 1961), about a group of young lads who are led into crime to fund one of its members in testing his luck as a bullfighter; again, it was released just prior to Fraga's appointment. Based on a social-realist novel published in 1960 by Juan Antonio de Zunzunegui about family tensions and moral and financial impoverishment, Fernando Fernán-Gómez's *El mundo sigue* (*Life Goes On*) (1965) was only awarded a classification after numerous cuts were made and, even then, the film had limited distribution.[86] In relation to Buero Vallejo's *El tragaluz* (*The Skylight*), the censor requested that references to the hardships of the post-Civil War period be softened, but sceptical comments about Spain's reputed modernisation and development had to be excised completely.[87]

Neo-realist film director Francesco Rosi publicly asked for his name to be removed from the credits of Spanish–Italian co-production *Il momento della verità* (*The Moment of Truth*) (1965) following numerous cuts, prompted by what was shown outside rather than inside the bullring.[88] The offending scenes were arguably less damning than those on show a decade earlier in *Mi tío Jacinto* (*Uncle Hyacinth*) (Ladislao Vajda, 1956), a film about an impoverished, retired bullfighter that shows decrepit shanty towns not far from Las Ventas bullring. In his memoirs, García Escudero cites *Juguetes rotos* (*Broken Toys*) (Manuel Summers, 1966) – a documentary about various former celebrities (music-hall stars, boxers, footballers, bullfighters) now living on the fringes of society – as one of the few films to have been heavily censored under his watch.[89] A report for *Cuadernos para el diálogo* praising Summers's honesty was, unusually for this publication's articles on culture, censored.[90] *Juguetes rotos* was only approved for over-18s following the excision of references to bull's testicles, sequences mocking priests and what were considered tendentious scenes of children begging.[91] Cut dialogue included 'Opportunity has come to be nothing more than a taurine term in Spain.' *La oportunidad* was a popular television talent show established by matador Luis Miguel Dominguín's brother, Domingo, in Madrid's second largest bullring, and sponsored by *Pueblo*, the regime's flagship newspaper. Contestants from all over Spain came in the hope of being discovered. As is on display in star-vehicle and biopic *Nuevo en esta plaza* (*New in This Ring*) (Pedro Lazaga, 1965) – seen by 3 million viewers on its initial release in Spain, and a blockbuster hit across Latin America – the programme was a launch pad for Sebastián Palomo 'Linares' to escape a life of poverty in rural Andalusia.[92] His fellow contestants included future flamenco star Camarón de la Isla, and ballet dancer Antonio Gades, but the matador nevertheless claims to have been the only one amongst the approximately 1,200 contestants to have genuinely triumphed in front of a bull. Dominguín had strong Communist affiliations, had acted as a producer on *Viridiana* and unsuccessfully attempted to negotiate Picasso's return to Spain (see Chapter 10). According to his son, Domingo's intention was to spotlight not only potential matadors, but also the conditions that brought them forth:

> More or less once a year, Spanish Television would pull the festivities and *Pueblo* its support. The matter had turned into a social scandal, because newspapers and magazines started to carry reports on lads who told all sorts of stories: that his mother was a prostitute, his father in prison … The matter entered public opinion and Franco's long arm pulled the plug.[93]

If becoming a matador was the Spanish equivalent to the American Dream, control of the myth and the reality was of particular concern to the establishment because it reached the masses, tourists and dignitaries. New legislation replacing earlier laws dating from 1930 (which had not been updated since) were brought into force on 15 March 1962 in an attempt to curb corruption[94] and to prevent comic bullfights being used as a pretext to caricature individuals and institutions or to make an apology for any vice or crime 'that promotes hate or animosity between social classes'.[95] The rhetoric of peace and progress had become official orthodoxy as the State grounded its legitimacy through recourse to a technocratic criterion of delivery as opposed to what William Viestenz has characterised as Franco's 'political theology'.[96] Ricardo de la Cierva, a former Director-General of Popular Culture, responded to a question about the dictator's legacy as follows: 'the secular blight that has always weighed down on us, even during the Golden Age, has disappeared: the hunger of the Spanish population'.[97] This tendentious political narrative had been safeguarded at any cost to prolong Francoism well past its sell-by date, yet the transfer from the metaphysical to the material preconditioned the Transition: disrobing the sacred origins of the 'regime of '36' meant that competing models of governance could and would be laid out to tender.

Chapter 5

Key performance indicators

Democratisation and freedom of speech
(1975–81)

In the words of Paul Rae, 'many (mainly Western) governments and human rights NGOs use freedom of expression as a standardized metric for assessing the political status and global rights rankings of states world-wide. It is an important principle, but a blunt instrument.'[1] Blunt as it may be, a critical analysis of censorial apparatus between 1975 and 1981 can help articulate the means by which democracy was conceptualised and exercised alongside a greater appreciation of what were formulated as key performance indicators for the Transition and new forms of government. As British Prime Minister Harold Wilson communicated to US President Gerald Ford: 'I recognise, even if it cannot be put bluntly in public that King Juan Carlos has a very hard row to hoe. So we shall encourage him privately to move as fast as possible, but try to avoid public condemnation when we can, if the pace is slower than public expectation here may demand.'[2]

Prior to the Caudillo's death, the future King endeavoured to establish contacts with all the major political players. After having met the Romanian President Ceauşescu at an event organised by the Shah in Iran, he employed Luis Miguel Dominguín as an intermediary to facilitate his envoy, Manuel Prado y Cordón de Carvajal, to meet with Santiago Carrillo, leader of the outlawed Spanish Communist Party, in Bucharest.[3] Juan Carlos talked – and, perhaps more importantly, listened – to as many people as he could, but he also clearly had his favourites. Towards the end of the dictatorship, Suárez held no significant role but Juan Carlos asked

Luis María Ansón to promote the future President's public image through his publication *Blanco y negro*.[4] In the words of Walther L. Bernecker, 'Juan Carlos did not assume all the powers enjoyed by Franco; but he was far more powerful than any other monarch in Europe.'[5] The Spanish King was also the royal Head of State least likely to retain his position at that time. He had inherited a disciplined army brought under governmental control by the dictatorship but, as Bonnie N. Field notes, the 'intact military and security apparatus represented a potential veto player should the transition go too far or too quickly'.[6]

A document on public order, dated 21 October 1976 and marked confidential, from Home Secretary Rodolfo Martín Villa to civil governors instructed zero tolerance of events organised by the Spanish Communist Party and adopted the following rule of thumb: 'Se actuará con prudencia en cuanto se refiere a las ideas, pero se reprimirá, en todo caso y con la máxima energía y despliegue de medios, cuanto atente contra la unidad de España, la forma monárquica del Estado y las Fuerzas Armadas y de Orden Público' (Prudence can be applied in relation to ideas but, by all means possible, assaults on the unity of Spain, the monarchical basis of the State, the armed forces and public order should always be stamped out as firmly as possible).[7] By 1977, it was common knowledge that Communist leader Santiago Carrillo was regularly to be found in Spain, not too subtly disguised in a wig. There were strategic advantages to Juan Carlos legalising a party predisposed to accept the monarchy in exchange for the opportunity to participate in elections. Their participation would take votes from the PSOE and exert pressure on Felipe González not to be the one major player unwilling to endorse the King's role in the new political landscape. Conversely, however, generations of Spaniards had been indoctrinated with the belief that the Civil War had saved them from Communism, and the security forces were likely to construe electoral recognition as proof that democratisation could not to be trusted. Alongside Carrillo's followers, ETA had provided the most sustained opposition to Francoism in its twilight years, and the nascent democracy was characterised by an escalation of violence between the security forces and the Basque separatist movement.

In a report for *Index on Censorship*, James Burns marshalled evidence to suggest that 'a year after Franco, coverage of the Basque country by the Spanish press is more extensive than that of Northern Ireland by the British mass media'.[8] He also noted how right-wing groups called for the prohibition of a cartoon from *Cambio 16* – a publication financed by figures close to the PSOE leadership such as Enrique Sarasola (a Basque businessman who had made his fortunes in Colombia) – of Juan Carlos on a trip to New York 'looking like a cross between a fairy godmother and Fred Astaire, waving a magic wand and dancing over the Statue of Liberty against a star-studded Manhattan skyline',[9] but that the King laughed it off and ensured no action was taken. In the issue of the Spanish Legion magazine dated October 1977, José A. Mondría Beltrán confirms their unconditional allegiance to Juan Carlos as Franco's successor alongside 'the total dedication of thousands of men' who have 'as the means and ends to their lives a love for SPAIN, that blessed Spain that now finds itself so mistreated by those who not long ago boasted of being the faithful depositories of historical traditions'.[10]

The aftermath of Franco's death could have been more violent than it was, but the notion of a peaceful Transition is pure revisionism: according to Ignacio Sánchez Cuenca's calculations, including victims of State violence (e.g. five strikers killed by police in Vitoria in 1976, or the death of an innocent bystander following violence in the Pamplona bullring in 1978),[11] there were 718 mortal casualties of political violence between 1975 and 1982.[12] Of these, 54 per cent belonged to the military or the police, the preferred targets of left-wing terrorist groups, whilst victims of right-wing terrorist groups were predominantly civilians.[13] Recalcitrant fascists were accused of both infiltrating and usurping the identity of radical left-wing group GRAPO, which adopted the slogan 'Despues de la Constitución, La Guerra' (After the Constitution, War). On 5 March 1976 the police deactivated a bomb at the editorial offices of *Cambio 16* but, on 26 June 1977, GRAPO blew them up – amazingly, there were no injuries.[14] The security forces provided protection against vigilante groups but it was not always clear if they saw their duty as safeguarding human rights or preserving their own jurisdiction. On 20 September 1977, a bomb was left by a group calling itself the Alianza Apostólica Anticomunista at the offices of satirical comic *El Papus*; it exploded prior to being taken to its intended recipient, resulting in the doorman's death and twenty injuries. The Barcelona press went on strike in solidarity, Madrid (with the exception of *El Alcázar*) quickly following suit.[15] Disciplined and readily mobilised militants were Carrillo's principal bargaining chip. The restraint demonstrated after five Communist lawyers were killed in the Atocha massacre of 24 January 1977 was a turning point in public perception and instrumental in the legalisation of the Communist Party, Carrillo overnight becoming a leading player in the democratic game.[16] Suárez's centrist programme had forced Fraga to the right, his traditional role as the mouthpiece for moderate reform usurped by the King's favourite. Carrillo adopted the opposite policy, distancing himself from the iron grip of Soviet control. Attempts to occupy less radical electoral space were scuppered by the German Labour Movement's investing in the PSOE so as to raise their electoral profile, whilst simultaneously lobbying for them to become international auditors of the Transition.[17]

El País, established in 1976, provided relatively balanced reporting on the first post-Franco democratic Spanish elections, thereby establishing its reputation and unique selling point within a heavily politicised media landscape. As intimated by a mock-Francoist poster that proclaimed Suárez's victory year of 1977 in satirical magazine *Por favor*,[18] the incumbent Prime Minister had an unfair advantage: the director of the State television channel was a personal friend, Rafael Ansón,[19] and he was the King's favourite. The pragmatics of democratisation could be seen to justify Juan Carlos's championing of Suárez to oust Arias Navarro – a man who had earned the nickname 'the butcher of Malaga' for his actions in the Civil War – in July 1976,[20] or his appointment of his former tutor, Torcuato Fernández-Miranda, as head of Parliament and the Council of the Realm.[21] Harder to defend is the complete lack of impartiality he demonstrated when, leaving nothing to chance, he wrote personally to the Shah of Iran and the Prince of Saudi Arabia to request funds to support the UCD's election campaign, playing up the then-antimonarchist PSOE's Marxist credentials.[22] The King's political survival being tied to non-radical democratisation ensures his role is better assessed in tactical, not ethical, terms. A tightrope was required to mediate between Francoists with scant democratic or international credibility, who nevertheless held power, and an opposition whose principal negotiating card was the ability to imbue the Transition with legitimacy.

The all-too-real cartoon villainy of the unreconstructed right legitimised a Manichean narrative hardly conducive to more progressive sections of society being self-reflective about their own undemocratic practices. In May 1976, *Interviú* magazine, 'an intriguing mix of unenlightened pornographic titillation and a forum for serious anti-establishment commentary',[23] appeared in kiosks for the first time. Issue 6 featured a fully clothed trade unionist, Marcelino Camacho, on the cover, but this was the exception rather than the rule; the magazine's chief selling point was female flesh. Editorials spoke of vendors threatened by the far right; editor-in-chief, Antonio Álvarez Solís, boasted of publishing photos of a topless Brigitte Bardot in the following terms:

> It gives us great pleasure to have been able to publish them. And not just for commercial reasons, something that is dealt with by another department. It satisfies us at least as much as the hundreds of thousands of readers who have been able to contemplate them. And that, even taking into account that the most common comment – amongst men and women – might have been: 'how saggy they've become!'. Yes, Sir, saggy but important. And the only shame – both for us as for Spanish readers – is not to have been able to publish them ten or fifteen years ago, when they were in their full splendour.[24]

Issue number 16 provided the magazine with its most iconic cover: a naked grown-up image of Marisol, Francoism's Shirley Temple,[25] appeared under the headline 'El bello camino hacia la democracia' (The sweet path to democracy). The issue tripled average sales within three days and, in a week, *Interviú* became the first Spanish magazine to sell a million copies; the photos had been taken and published without the consent of the former child-star, who received no payment in exchange.[26] The rules of sexual and political engagement were clearly changing.

Irrespective of what reactionary conservatives and the ostensibly progressive left might have contended, albeit from radically different positions, female exploitation did not begin or end with Franco's death. Paloma San Basilio recalls how, in the 1960s, a publicist rang her asking to do a photo-shoot for an international drinks company. A Mercedes was sent to pick the singer up, taking her to a remote location before demands were made for pornographic images: 'I had two options: shout and run away (there were five of them, and I was alone) or try and get past the obstacles and escape from there as soon as possible. It was torture, they looked at me lasciviously and I tried to cover myself up as much as possible.'[27] The photos first appeared in *Interviú* years later; San Basilio received no payment and was unable to veto their publication.[28] Less than a decade earlier, actress Carmen Sevilla had gone directly to Fraga when a journalist implied she was sleeping with her future husband; the then Minster confiscated the offending reporter's press card.[29] On 28 October 1970, *Garbo* magazine published an exposé of Luis Miguel Domínguín's affair with his teenage cousin; Maruja Torres was fined 3,000 pesetas for the 'dissemination of the love-life of a married man, with a woman who was not his wife'.[30] In a country where anyone over 30 could remember a time when the bikini was outlawed, *Interviú* fast-tracked the normalisation of explicit material.

The publication of erotic novels took off in 1977 and peaked in 1978.[31] As Santiago Fouz-Hernández notes, a new 'S' classification for cinema releases 'served the double purpose of promising some sexually explicit content while preventing the alienation of audiences who may not yet be ready to watch porn, at least not in a public space'.[32] Rape was often trivialised. In *Gusanos de seda* (*Silkworms*) (Francisco Rodríguez Fernández, 1977), an over-domineering mother marries her emasculated son off to a rich industrialist's daughter, who has learning difficulties. The protagonist will only receive his father-in-law's fortune on producing an heir and, coerced by his mother, rapes his wife, causing her visible pain before prostituting her out to local figures of authority. Publicity material for *Los violadores del amanecer* (*Dawn Rapists*) (Ignacio F. Iquino, 1978) encouraged rapists to attend the premiere, promising the presence of the actresses;[33] the plot for the film, seen by over a million viewers in its initial theatrical run (and still available on DVD), is bereft of plot or character development, merely recounting pruriently the rapes of teenage girls in and around Barcelona. Feminist publications complained of the nascent democracy's objectification of women,[34] but it was a challenge for isolated voices to counteract an ingrained culture of gender-bias amongst the anti-Francoist opposition. As Ursula Tidd, for example, notes in her study of Jorge Semprún, '[t]here is an assumption on his part that if democratic values triumph then gender equality will somehow naturally follow without any dedicated steps needing to be taken to achieve it'.[35]

The continued universalisation of the heterosexual male perspective was a symptom and cause of the fact that discrimination faced by gays in 1978 was not all that different from that of 1975.[36] TVE refused to broadcast an episode of the debate show *La clave* on homosexuality, a more taboo subject than previously aired topics, such as divorce or abortion.[37] *El diputado* (*The Deputy*) (Eloy de la Iglesia, 1978) details the travails of a married anti-Francoist lawyer turned congressman, blackmailed by an ultra-right group for his sexuality. De la Iglesia, a card-carrying Communist, claims that the rumour he was making a film based on a real-life case in Enrique Tierno Galván's Socialist Party was sufficient for the future Mayor of Madrid – a committed homophobe, for all his liberal credentials[38] – to ask Carrillo to intervene. De la Iglesia reminded the Communist leader of an earlier boast that the Party never censored its membership.[39] Carrillo even attended the film's premiere, and as was the case in 'manifestos of gay associations from the time, *The Deputy* makes it clear that, even if the left isn't as open to collaboration as it ought to be, there is nothing worse than the right'.[40]

The residual intolerance of the Francoist bunker came brutally to the fore in relation to *La torna* (*The Screw*). Els Joglars, whose 'theatrical forms have always transgressed the accommodating shape of traditional performance',[41] had often shared stages with Catalan singer-songwriters in the late 1960s and early 1970s, the frisson of dissent transforming performances into 'happenings'. Two years before the State newsreel NO-DO stopped being produced, episode 1815 from 1977 praised the troupe and features an excerpt from 'their latest hit'; the report neglected to mention that *La torna* was about Heinz Chez, a common criminal executed alongside anarchist Salvador Puig on 2 March 1974. A year before prior censorship ended, *La torna* was approved. As a member of Els Joglars recalls:

> the censorship guy came to speak to us before the performance at the premiere in Barbastro, and then he came in the evening to see the play. But look at what drew his attention; about the scenes with the drunk army guys he didn't say a thing. What he did ask was that the actresses who were playing the waitresses cover up a bit and also that we take out some of the coarse language. The Ministry of Culture's General Direction of Performances approved *The Screw* on 6 September 1977 with the rating 'suitable for all'. And with that official blessing, the tour commenced.[42]

As with the documentary film *Queridísimos verdugos* (*Dearest Executioners*) (Basilio Martín Patino, 1977) – shot clandestinely whilst Franco was still alive – Els Joglars dwelt as much on the farcical and often alcohol-induced incompetence of the executioners of State justice as on the death penalty itself. Deliberately performing in squares and streets in Tarragona named after the Caudillo and Carrero Blanco, scenes mocking the Guardia Civil were greeted with laughter in Catalonia and applauded in the Basque Country.[43]

At a time when the armed forces felt besieged by ETA and betrayed by Suárez, Els Joglars received an anonymous warning not to proceed with a performance in the Catalan town of Reus. Collectively agreeing to go ahead with the show, they were placed under military arrest on 17 December 1977. As their self-appointed leader, Albert Boadella, recalls: 'It soon stopped being an unfinished and chaotic theatre play to become an undisputable symbol of liberty.'[44] Especially in retrospect, Boadella boasts of suffering more at the hands of ostensibly progressive members of the Catalan establishment – he was particularly offended by the director of Barcelona's Theatre Institute suspending his stipend as a visiting lecturer following his arrest[45] – than from the repressive forces of Francoism. Twenty-two theatres in Barcelona did, however, refuse to perform as an act of solidarity,[46] the Liceu Opera House closing its doors for the first time ever. On 10 March 1978, even the establishment *ABC* denounced police charging at a peaceful demonstration in Barcelona, 12,000 people calling for the release of Els Joglars.[47] The report also highlights that the student-let protest insulted the mainstream political parties, singling out Suárez, Martín Villa and Josep Tarradellas, President of the Generalitat, for censure. The front cover of the April 1978 issue of the anarchist magazine *Ajoblanco* was black, with a simple message 'R. I. P. a Joglars'. Editor Pepe Ribas complained: 'Two-and-a-half years and everything remains the same.'[48]

Freedom for cultural practitioners remained contingent on not offending the forces of law and order. Whilst most of the members of Els Joglars sought the services of lawyers affiliated with the Communist Party, Boadella believed they would needlessly prolong proceedings to raise their own profile and instead contracted a specialist in military law. He recalls Tarradellas as the only politician to visit him in prison, where he was confined alongside common, as opposed to political, prisoners, and that the King attempted to intervene on his behalf following pressure from Princess Beatrix of the Netherlands, who had seen Els Joglars when they had performed in Amsterdam.[49] The President of the Catalan Generalitat reported to Boadella that he had heard Juan Carlos enquire about the case to an army general at a dinner, whose response that justice would be served was more chilling than comforting. Boadella and one other Joglar escaped to France from a hospital where they had been receiving treatment whilst their colleagues awaited trial, causing a rift that has never healed.

The Spanish army flexing their muscles was a military operation designed to reinforce their role as privileged auditors of the new regime, ensuring democracy was constantly in the dock between 1975 and 1981. Members of Parliament had little to gain by raising their heads above the parapet: freedom of expression and personal liberties took a back seat to not jeopardising the Moncloa Pacts, a fragile economic and political consensus instrumental in the subsequent drafting of Spain's democratic Constitution. If the pragmatics of democratisation facilitated non-democratic practices, it was reasonable to ask to what extent the ends justified the means.

The Iranian Revolution of 1979 provided an opportunity to explore what Spaniards of the time understood by democracies, alongside their limitations. Juan Carlos offered comforting words to the Shah and the Iranian people: 'Tradition and progress. Combining both is, I think, the key to the affinities and great similarities that exist between our two nations.'[50] *ABC* predictably followed the monarchical line and claimed that Ayatollah Khomeini was a dangerous, repressive and hypocritical demagogue.[51] Conversely, the Marxist-inflected *Tiempo de historia* echoed the stance taken by Michel Foucault, who thought Iran fortunate not to have followed Spain's post-Franco trajectory,[52] by presenting in gendered terms the protagonists of the Iranian Revolution as anti-imperial heroes: 'from being a country "penetrated" by consumerism and television, "Americanised" and alienated, it has managed to transform itself into a country that denounces that penetration.'[53]

Disillusionment with parliamentary democracy existed across the Spanish political spectrum but, for the reactionary right, it was proof of an underlying flaw. As Dick Howard notes: 'Totalitarian ideology, after all, claims that it incarnates the true realization of democracy when in fact it is the attempt to overcome the creative instability characteristic of democratic social relations typical of modernity.'[54] In his diaries, Fernando Vizcaíno Casas raged against 'the gutless resignation with so many murderers let loose and, to make it worse, with a heroic aura'.[55] *Fuerza Nueva*, the in-house magazine of Blas Piñar's fascist party, was temporarily shut down in 1973 for criticising diplomatic links with East Germany and China.[56] When it resurfaced, Pedro Rodrigo evoked what was happening in Iran as a cautionary tale:

[Jimmy] Carter, who wants to export democracy as if it were shipments of peanuts,[57] exerted pressure on the Shah – who had already raised the standard of living of the Persians, and created the most powerful Army of the Near East – to become more 'open', 'a democratisation' with parties and freedom of the press.[58]

As Stanley Payne notes, Fuerza Nueva was 'a noisy feature of Spanish life in the 1970s, even though lacking in popular support'.[59] For more mainstream political parties, stability was priority number one, consensus simultaneously posited as both synonymous with and superior to inalienable democratic human rights. The 1978 Constitution was drafted on this basis: 'Any reference to the democratic legality against which sections of the army rose in 1936 and the repression of the Franco regime exercised for almost forty years was barred from the text as part of the supposed price of democracy.'[60] Despite, or even perhaps because of, the so-called 'pact of silence', best-seller lists were dominated by books about the Second Republic, the Civil War and the Francoist period.[61] Strategic forgetfulness is not the same as amnesia; as Jo Labanyi, drawing on the work of Santos Juliá, notes: 'the consensus politics of the Transition were based, not on a pact of oblivion, but on an agreement not to let the past affect the future.'[62] These politics were, however, predicated on the reasonable but hardly guaranteed assumption that agents of the State would cease to behave as they had in the past.

In 1971, sociologist Amando de Miguel was court-marshalled and imprisoned, ostensibly for an article he had written in *Madrid*, although he believes the real motivation came from a derogatory chapter he had written about the army for the 1970 FOESSA report.[63] Joel Leslie Gandelman, special correspondent for the *Chicago Daily News* and *Newsweek*, was deported in October 1976 for reporting on the torture of Basque separatists by the security forces.[64] The following year, Eva Forest published a clandestine book about the torture of women, including personal experiences of physical and psychological abuse: her interrogator told her that her husband, playwright Alfonso Sastre, had been shot following her arrest for Carrero Blanco's assassination.[65] As Forest wrote, 'We thought that these things no longer happened. We thought they belonged to times gone by but such practices are alive and well, being exercised from the centre of Power.'[66] The producers of *Los violadores del amanecer* – one of the last films to be passed (unanimously) by the censorship board prior to its dissolution – played it safe by stating in the plot summary that 'La policia alarmada por tantas fechorías, actúa incansablemente' (The police, alarmed by such outrages, were tireless in their actions).[67]

In theory, the need for pre-emptive caution was rendered obsolete with the Constitution. Article 20 declared freedom of expression a sacred principle, and prohibited advance censorship. However, as Timothy Garton Ash notes: 'The question "how should free speech be?" is as crucial as the more familiar "how free should speech be?" and, ideally, the pair will be inseparable.'[68] The latter was effectively bypassed because of the legal vacuum in which the deregulation of cultural production took place. In a system predicated on a constitutional penal code, the absence of concrete guidance outsourced responsibility for policing freedom of expression to an often unreconstructed judiciary. The lack of specific provisions is thrown into sharp relief when compared with forms of liberalisation that raised more immediate questions of public order. A radical overhaul of Spaniards' leisure habits and the urban landscape ensued when, in February 1978, bingo was decriminalised by royal decree on moral and pragmatic grounds: 'systems of absolute prohibition have frequently failed in achieving their moralising objectives and have in fact resulted in a widespread toleration of underground gambling ... in settings without judicial protection.'[69] Shortly afterwards, a flurry of practical guides to running gambling joints referencing employment law and contracts appeared.[70] Such guidance may not always have been abided by, but the rules of engagement had at least been articulated in more explicit fashion than in any document available to filmmakers.

After attending a course run by Amnesty International on the after-effects of torture,[71] Lola Salvador began writing about a real-life historical incident from 1910 when, against the backdrop of political unrest, two workers from Oso de la Vega (Cuenca) admit to the murder of a man, who later turns up alive, following beatings and torture by the local Guardia Civil. Producer Alfredo Matas, enthused by the success at the Spanish box office (over 3.5 million admissions) of *Midnight Express* (Alan Parker, 1978) – a Hollywood take on the corruption and brutality of the Turkish prison system – set about making what would eventually become *El crimen de Cuenca* (*The Cuenca Crime*) (Pilar Miró, 1980). The film was more brutal than Salvador's script or subsequent book on the subject intimated. Less Manichean than *Midnight Express*, the torture scenes were nevertheless more explicit: the graphic depiction of teeth and toe-nails being removed and a suspect's penis being stretched would shock in any context. An earlier television adaptation of Galdós's *Tormento* (*Torment*) alluded to the repression of miners in Asturias in the 1960s,[72] but the film, directed by Miró, herself raised in a military family, was perceived as more of an affront for three key reasons: first, the explicit nature of the torture; second, her affiliation with the PSOE (she was González's image consultant for the 1977 and 1979 election campaigns); and third, the planned release date, coinciding with real-life cases of torture in the Basque Country, where the Guardia Civil were increasingly being called upon to leave.

By the time *El crimen de Cuenca* was due to be released, advance censorship had been abolished, but the film was submitted to the Ministry of Culture on 22 November 1979 to receive a certificate to determine potential age restrictions. Matas had sought legal guidance from, amongst others, Joaquín Ruiz-Giménez Aguilar (son of the founder of *Cuadernos para el diálogo*, he formed part of his father's legal firm), whose curriculum included selecting guests to appear on an episode of *La clave* dedicated to judicial errors.[73] A trailer had already been screened, and the film booked into cinemas, but the Ministry of Culture thought it advisable to seek Home Office approval, which was declined. Spectators turning up to see *El crimen de Cuenca* instead had the opportunity to watch *Polvos mágicos* (*Magical Ejaculations*) (José Ramón Larraz, 1979).[74] The security forces had by now been alerted to the film's content and a letter dated 10 December 1979 from the Guardia Civil head office called for prohibition, 'since, as much for its approach, the length of the torture scenes, "the film's central nucleus", as for its crudeness combined with the campaign against torture currently taking place, it constitutes a humiliation of the Corps, intolerable in all respects'.[75] The army was even more intransigent, confiscating the film and placing Miró under house arrest to await a military trial.

Ruiz-Giménez recalls his most personal conversations with Miró taking place when he accompanied her on the obligatory fortnightly visits to report to the military judge. She reportedly confided her fears alongside the shock that, as the daughter of a military man, she was considered the enemy when, in her opinion, the film was simply drawing attention to the kind of isolated incidents that needed to be acknowledged and expunged if the armed forces were to have a viable future in democratic Spain.[76] Miró has always maintained that the torture scenes were not that extreme and that she was shocked by the disproportionate attention they received.[77] *El crimen de Cuenca* was the highest-profile example of dozens of theoretically civil cases to which the military were able to stake a claim because of the tardiness in updating the penal code in line with the democratic Constitution. The resulting controversy helped ensure Salvador's book was a best-seller, selling over a million copies in 1979, the author signing copies – with a dedication and the message 'Libertad de expresión' (Freedom of expression) – on a daily basis at Madrid's book fair, escorted by two municipal police officers for her own protection.[78] The situation became even tenser when ETA kidnapped UCD MP Javier Rupérez and made it a condition of his release that a commission be formed to examine cases of suspected torture in police custody in the Basque Country.[79]

El País published a rigorously researched piece advocating for how and why the filmmaker should have a civil rather than a military trial,[80] although footage from a TVE film programme that referred to a witch hunt was mysteriously excised prior to transmission.[81] A letter dated 4 February 1980 from the incoming Minister of Culture, Ricardo de la Cierva – who had inherited the problem from his predecessor, Manuel Clavero – to Suárez reported on a meeting with Miró and her lawyer:

> Han comprendido la postura de este Ministerio ya que su actual Titular no denunció la película ni ahora la ha secuestrado. Lo único que me piden es que interceda ante la Justicia Militar para que decidido ya el secuestro de la película, no procesen a la directora ni al productor. Creo que debemos interceder, dentro de la Ley con la más exquisita delicadeza ante la Justicia Militar, para que no se decida tal procesamiento, ya que el secuestro de la película es comprensible pero el procesamiento podría dañar gravísimamente nuestra credibilidad democrática.[82]

> They have understood the attitude of this Ministry, since its current head neither denounced the film nor seized it. The only thing they ask of me

is to intervene with the Military Justice so that, now the confiscation has taken place, they prosecute neither the director nor the producer. I think we should intervene, within the law and with the most exquisite delicacy, with the Military Justice, so that they don't take said prosecution forward, given that the seizure of the film is understandable but that the prosecution could do grave damage to our democratic credibility.

Miró received letters of support from internationally renowned filmmakers Rainer Werner Fassbinder, Werner Herzog and Wim Wenders. An invitation came from the Berlin Film Festival to premiere *El crimen de Cuenca* in February 1980. Miró accepted, even though it increased the chances that she and Matas would be charged for libel. Post-Berlin, there were multiple invitations to screen the film internationally, which Miró was more inclined to accept than Matas, who did not want to rock the boat further. The director became disillusioned, however, following a screening in Cannes organised by Amnesty International. She sensed that the moderator of a pre-screening discussion on censorship had not seen the film, whilst chaos ensued when the Spanish critics present vociferously objected to his claim that their country was as repressive as states such as Turkey and the USSR.[83]

One of the largely forgotten facets of life in post-Constitutional Spain was the widespread tendency to judge democracy in terms of results as opposed to its being considered a good in and of itself. A sense of stagnation coupled with record unemployment figures and the violent actions of ETA resulted in disillusionment with a liberal parliamentary system: abstention rates for the first democratic elections in June 1977 were 22 per cent, but rose to 31 per cent by March 1979, a significantly lower turnout than for general elections elsewhere in Europe and, at the time of writing, the lowest in post-Franco Spain.

Amongst non-voters, 36 per cent claimed that abstention was due to a lack of interest in politics, with 20 per cent attributing it to an outright hostility towards democracy.[84] Never forgiven by many in the armed forces for the legalisation of the Communist Party, tantamount to treason in their view, the PSOE similarly developed a grudge against the first democratically elected President since 1936 for shamelessly playing on the electorate's fears, returning incessantly to the Marxist aspects of their Constitution in a televised debate, widely credited with the UCD receiving the mandate to rule for a second term. Willy Brandt advised the PSOE that they needed to destroy Suárez sooner rather than later if they were ever to become viable electoral prospects.[85] Following their loss in the 1979 elections, the PSOE adopted the twin strategy of presenting themselves as less threatening to broad cross-sections of the electorate and actively campaigning to discredit the Government. In May 1980, a group of PSOE MPs interrogated the Minister of Culture over *El crimen de Cuenca*. Alfonso Guerra – one of the chief architects of the Constitution and a personal friend of Miró, who had seen *El crimen de Cuenca* at her flat – claims he was reluctantly persuaded to take on the role of spokesman at the last minute, and that his incendiary speech was largely improvised. De la Cierva found himself against the parliamentary ropes, stating what would be the appropriate course of action were they to abide by the Constitution before Vice-President Fernando Abril intervened to clarify that not offending the armed forces was priority number one.[86] In terms of establishing the PSOE as advocates for culture, and culture as the most effective antidote to repression, Guerra's parliamentary intervention was a theatrical *pièce de resistance* that remains in the popular imagination to the present day. An alternative interpretation would read as follows: Guerra and the PSOE were irresponsibly ridiculing an elected government at a period in which there was an all too real threat of a military coup.

As Javier Cercas notes in the historical novel *Anatomía de un instante* (*Anatomy of a Moment*): 'it is a fact that at least for its principal ringleaders the 23 February coup was not exactly a coup against democracy: it was a coup against Adolfo Suárez; or, to put it another way: it was a coup against a democracy Adolfo Suárez embodied for them'.[87] The author unearths compelling historical evidence that González, having successfully petitioned party members to excise any references to Marxism in their Constitution and electoral manifestos, had conversations with the royal household about heading a provisional government were military means to be used to depose an unpopular President, tainted by links to a former dictatorship.[88] Suárez's subsequent resignation cannot be divorced from a lack of support from his own party and, crucially, the King: the former allies had increasingly clashed over matters of state such as the possibility, and even desirability, of Spain joining NATO, a measure aggressively pursued by Juan Carlos, who believed US support to be instrumental to his own power-base and the country's future.[89] On 23 February 1981, Lieutenant Coronel Tejero entered the Parliament building to hold the elected MPs hostage on the day of the investiture of Leopoldo Calvo Sotelo as Suárez's substitute. The outgoing President, Carrillo and Gutiérrez Mellado – men with very different pasts and political beliefs, who had nevertheless converged on the common goal of legalising the Communist Party – were the only three MPs to defy barked orders to cower on the parliamentary floor.

Fear would have been mitigated for some of the political hostages by the excitement and expectation that they might be asked to form part of some new ruling formation. Cercas distinguishes between a 'soft coup' and a 'hard coup', the difference residing in whether military force was considered a means or an end. A soft coup could potentially offer what the Pacts of Moncloa had four years previously: the best prospect for self-advancement couched within reasons of state. The initial question was not so much whether the coup would be successful as to what kind of coup would unfold, and to what extent the military uprising might be redeemed as a pragmatic concession to democratic consolidation. Tejero's demands and demeanour laid the latter possibility to rest. Unaware that a television camera was still operational, Suárez, the closest Spain ever had to a John F. Kennedy-style President, had a better sense of theatre facing the barrel of a gun than his assailant, exposed as an anachronistic clown. The philosopher Julián Marías, a senator by royal decree, suggested the footage ought to win an award for 'film of the year' and, as Carrillo notes: 'Without that marvellous video I'm not sure that the coup would have inspired the emotion it did in Spain and across the world.'[90]

The King of all Spaniards had an ideal opportunity to exercise his role, condemning the insurrectionists and defending democracy. Conspiracy theories abound surrounding the monarch's possible involvement in the illegal armed uprising. Why did it take him so long to declare himself? Might he have hedged his bets, waiting to see how the day's events unfolded? On Cercas's reading, if Juan Carlos had wanted a coup to succeed, it would have; if the King brought it to a halt, it was simply because he was the only person with the ability to do so.[91] *Anatomía de un instante* has been censured as an 'affectively driven reconstruction of the transition that aims to cultivate a sense of pride and attachment to it as a project', rendered through an 'emotionally persuasive structure of atonement, reconciliation and heroic overcoming of history'.[92] There is, however, an ambivalence in the depiction of a Head of State who is shown to be neither unequivocally anti-coup nor pro-democracy; Cercas's most profound insight lies in his demonstration of how and why these two notions were neither antithetical nor absolute prior to 23 February 1981.

Changes in the military justice code made on 22 December 1980 ensured Miró no longer fell within their jurisdiction.[93] The suspension of *El crimen de Cuenca*'s exhibition licence was lifted on 20 February 1981 but, three days later, this probably seemed a pyrrhic victory: the events of the 23-F, shorthand for the date of the unsuccessful coup, didn't bode well for high-profile dissidents. Furthermore, Miró had given birth to her only child on 13 February – unsubstantiated rumours claimed Felipe González was the father – and she justifiably feared for her life. After the coup was crushed, however, *El crimen de Cuenca*'s being such a high-profile litmus test for Spanish democracy ensured it enjoyed a far greater level of success than it would have done under normal circumstances. Although a licence was granted in March 1981, Matas was keen the film secure an '18' as opposed to an 'S' certificate. He therefore struck a deal with the Ministry of Culture by which the film, cut for international markets,[94] could be released uncensored domestically with a more respectable certificate in exchange for the premiere being held off until August, when the threat of terrorism was perceived to be lower.[95] In spite of being released during a tough month for cinema admissions, purchasing a ticket (over 2.5 million were sold) became a symbolic gesture, and the same ministry that had held back its release awarded the film a monetary prize. A petition signed by 1,740 military wives and widows was presented to Soledad Becerril (the recently appointed Minister of Culture and the first female cabinet member since the Second Republic), expressing puzzlement at why 'we have to pay for the gratuitous offences committed against our husbands',[96] but it had little purchase in the new socio-political landscape. The logical outcome of the upcoming 1982 general elections was the victory of the PSOE: the UCD was in disarray and the televised footage of Tejero and his stooges had done more to discredit the Spanish right at home and abroad than any left-wing party had ever achieved. If a coup could occur under a centrist party's watch, the electorate seemed willing to move to the left, and the PSOE not only won the 1982 elections with an absolute democracy but, armed with the slogan 'Por el cambio' (For change), convinced much of Spain that a vote for them equated to a vote for a democracy now embodied by González.

Chapter 6

The regime of '81

Patronage and permissiveness

In the aftermath of Franco's death, the right allowed the country to move towards the centre in exchange for the bodies of the vanquished and the biographies of the victorious remaining interred. The unsuccessful coup changed the balance of power: new terms of engagement could, and perhaps ought, to have been brought into play. On the one hand, citizens rightly celebrated that they now had more freedoms than ever before. Conversely, however, as Charles Tilly notes, a level of distrust is 'a necessary condition of democracy. Contingent consent entails unwillingness to offer rulers, however well elected, blank checks.'[1] This chapter proposes a cost–benefit analysis of what I have coined the 'regime of '81', a narrative framing through which, I will contend, a suspiciously neat division between freedom and repression was both the product and the symptom of how democracy was celebrated rather than interrogated, paradoxically facilitating the perpetuation of Francoist ills.

If we take Roger Simon's definition of hegemony as 'a relation not of domination by means of force, but of consent by means of political and ideological leadership', then the PSOE under Juan Carlos's patronage were skilled architects of 'the organisation of consent'.[2] Signed in 1978, the Constitution had neither the legal nor the symbolic force it subsequently accrued until it was effectively ratified by the failed coup. In 1981, Valencia City Council commemorated the anniversary of the signing of Spain's democratic Magna Carta by printing posters in both Castilian and Valencian, as well as 30,000 editions of the Constitution and 1,100 adaptations for children.[3] A new Spanish coat of arms was introduced at the end of 1981 to replace the fascistic eagle wings on the post-Constitutional national flag. The unreconstructed right constituted both a cautionary warning against the country's potential involution and a convenient scapegoat, facilitating retrospective redemption by reformed Francoists. In his memoirs, Fraga speaks of an unsuccessful attempt to engage fellow MP Blas Piñar and incorporate him into a national(ist) project. In reference to a last-ditch attempt, he writes: 'I prepared myself with a combination of British-style patience and Galician humour to put up with sarcasm and impertinence. The overriding theme: democracy inevitably ends in chaos.'[4] The memoirs of Carlos Robles Piquer – the former Minister of Information and Tourism's brother-in-law – commenced as follows:

> Why have I begun with the 23-F coup attempt? Because it reflects well, with a concrete example, what these pages wish to demonstrate: that it is possible to have worked – as millions of compatriots also did – with ideas and principles that marked many years of my life during Francoism and then skilfully cooperate in the establishment and consolidation of a very different democratic system.[5]

Robles Piquer was appointed Director-General of RTVE by Calvo Sotelo's short-lived Government, but faced heavy criticism from both the UCD and the PSOE for reactionary political views – his resignation eventually being prompted following the broadcast in June 1982 of a programme seen to justify the coup[6] – and for depicting Fraga as the champion of the modern democratic right.[7] This was a difficult narrative to pitch. Commenting upon Fraga – the ex-Francoist minister who was now leader of Alianza Popular, the main opposition party out of whose ashes the PP would later be formed – Alfonso Guerra wrote: 'the idea of being more or less democratic, I find it very difficult to accept. This is a term, in my view, of the kind they refer to as discrete in linguistics: presence–absence. Either one is democratic or one isn't, but a little bit democratic … That is like being a little bit pregnant.'[8] Irrespective of Fraga's democratic credentials (or lack thereof), the rhetoric of the incoming Vice-President's statement is indicative of the PSOE's intention to patent democracy.

Prior to even forming a government, the PSOE ordered that the anniversary of the signing of the Constitution be commemorated in schools;[9] 6 December was declared a national bank holiday in 1983. Run by Santillana Publishers, the fifth National Competition for School Initiatives, launched in November 1982, departed from the traditional syllabus by calling for projects on such topics as: 'Evaluate the Constitution as a route for resolving long-standing conflicts in our country: the regional problem, the "two Spains" etc'. The winning entry was titled 'Democratic participation by pupils as a didactic exercise in Constitutional values'.[10] Frequently, bilingual school editions (Castilian alongside the local language) of the Constitution were produced,[11] alongside teaching guides with commemorative activities.[12] The Ministry of Education foreclosed debate on the *Ley Orgánica Reguladora del Derecho a la Educación* (LODE), the new school curriculum, by claiming: 'The principles of the LODE do not reflect an ideology specific to the Socialist Party, but rather ideas that can be widely accepted by any citizen with a progressive and democratic outlook'.[13]

Democracies are expected to produce lower levels of corruption because politicians face re-election, which generally results in the separation between political and economic elites.[14] Government control over the financial sector (see Chapter 3) and the lack of a strong opposition party undermined this tendency in 1980s Spain. Given that there had been no purging of the State administration, Francoist relics were deployed in the corridors and offices of the new State – resulting, for example, in museums and libraries often being staffed by veterans of the Women's Section (the Sección Femenina) – there was some justification for keeping allies with clear democratic credentials close at hand. An internal report for the Ministry of Culture was, for example, concerned that most of the security staff had begun their careers in the Guardia Civil. A number had reportedly fly-posted pro-Tejero posters in the build-up to the 1982 general elections and handed out leaflets claiming the PSOE planned to undermine privileges enjoyed by permanent members of staff.[15] Another report claims that, in its short history, the nascent Ministry has served:

> enmascarar algunas vergonzosas administraciones franquistas (Movimiento, Ministerio de Información) y como campo libre para el protagonismo de algunas figuras de UCD. Dicho de otro modo el Ministerio de Cultura no ha empezado a existir como órgano serio para una acción política y seria de Estado.[16]

> to disguise some of the disgraceful Francoist administrative bodies (the Movement, the Ministry of Information) and as a free rein for some leading figures of the UCD to do as they wished. In other words, the Ministry of Culture has yet to begin to function as a serious organ for serious and political State action.

From the materials kept on file, it nevertheless appears that the UCD were either less generous or more ethical than their PSOE counterparts. Requests for favours are usually politely deflected; those that are granted tend to be modest: the Spanish ambassador for Algeria, for example, secures a job in a museum bookshop for a niece who graduated in history and geography before working as a Spanish lector at the University of Leeds.[17]

Following their entry into government, the PSOE's cultural wing quickly adopted the role of enlightened caciques. Those CVs kept on file for candidates belonging to the party faithful were, in general, noticeably shorter. In the case of incoming Director-General of Cinema, Pilar Miró, it states prominently that she had belonged to the PSOE since 1976.[18] Admittedly, the more radical overhaul of the State administration undertaken by the Second Republic (1931–6) had been self-sabotage: disproportionately high numbers of the army officers and middle-class professionals who supported Franco's uprising had previously had their privileges undermined;[19] the dictatorship subsequently used civil servant positions as a means of rewarding the faithful. When the reactionary right had long traded favours with impunity, a case could be made for the retrospective need to level the playing field, modest compensation for the injustices consensus had forcibly put to one side.

Rocío (Fernando Ruiz Vergara, 1980), a documentary denouncing the quasi-feudal relations that continued to exist in rural Andalusia – which implicated the co-founder of the religious Brotherhood of Rocío in atrocities during the Civil War – had briefly been shown prior to being banned.[20] The director subsequently received a two-month prison sentence and a fine for slander. Shortly before the film eventually went on general release – with the two reputedly libellous scenes excised – the producer, Vicente A. Pineda, wrote to Miró in a letter dated 23 March 1985:

> ¿Qué es lo que espero de ti? Tu amistad. Y una posibilidad dentro de la línea más estricta y generosa, a la vez, de que como ha sucedido con otras películas 'mártires' o 'víctimas' se reconsidere en *Rocío* a efectos prácticos su calificación de Especial Calidad y que, naturalmente, no pierda su derecho pleno a la cuota de pantalla por el largo tiempo, más de dos años, que ha estado bloqueada.[21]

> What do I hope from you? Your friendship. And a possibility within the realms on what is both permissible and generous, as has happened with other 'martyred' and 'victim' films, that the candidature of *Rocío* for the Special Quality award be reconsidered and, naturally, that it doesn't lose its right to a screen quota for the long period of time, more than two years, in which the film has been prohibited.

The documentary did not, however, receive preferential treatment, possibly because it did not provide a good fit for the cultural policy of the present.

In her capacity as Director-General, Miró paid symbolic lip-service to freedom of speech, introducing a system still in place whereby certificates are advisory, not compulsory; it is recommended children do not watch violent or sexual explicit material, without its being illegal for them to do so. New funding streams nevertheless favoured less incendiary films than *El crimen de Cuenca* or *Rocío*. Subsidies were concentrated on a small number of producer-led prestige projects. *La colmena* (*The Beehive*) (Mario Camus, 1982) – based on José Camilo Cela's novel set in and around Madrid's famous Café Gijón – was the year's biggest box-office success, and the equivalent of €2.5 million was invested in its promotion at the Berlin Film Festival. *Los santos inocentes* (*The Holy Innocents*) (Mario Camus, 1984) – 'a slow moving but poignant indictment of the misery in which the Spanish aristocracy kept the peasantry',[22] adapted from a novel by Miguel Delibes – was fêted at Cannes. The aesthetic criticism that these heritage films seek to be 'visually pleasing at any cost'[23] is symptomatic of ethical ambivalence: the reluctance to attribute individual blame or to focus on atrocities, co-existing with an evolutionary narrative in which the present is positioned as an improvement on and logical outcome of the past. The execution of the *señorito* and exodus of a young couple from a peasant family in 1960s rural Extremadura to the city at the end of *Los santos inocentes* is cathartic, suggesting a better life lies ahead.

Spanish films enjoying prominence at festivals such as Cannes and Berlin in the late 1970s and early 1980s cannot be divorced from the country's seeking approval and being rewarded for the challenges it had overcome; it is unlikely that the mawkishly sentimental (exaggerated by the use of indirect sound) *Volver a empezar* (*Begin the Beguine*) (José Luis Garci, 1982) – about a Republican Nobel Prize winner, who returns from his privileged exile in the University of Berkeley to his native Asturias where he receives phone calls from Juan Carlos and is reunited with the object of his first love, truncated by the Civil War – would have otherwise won the Oscar for Best Foreign Film. More generally, the recipients of prize-giving during the Transition were at least as indicative of the changing times as of the quality of the figures and works being recognised. As part of Juan Carlos's endeavour to be King of all Spaniards, exiles such as the poets Rafael Alberti and Jorge Guillén were welcomed home to perform 'a totemic and fossilised role in the Transition',[24] their more radical political positions neutralised by the passage of time. In 1975, the jury of the National Francisco Franco Prize for literature sensibly decided not to make an award.[25] The Premio Cervantes was created the following year to recognise the lifetime achievement of a Castilian-language writer. As Sarah Bowskill notes, '[t]here is evidently an unspoken agreement that the prize will be awarded alternately to a Peninsular and a Spanish American author'.[26]

In the words of James F. English, prizes 'serve simultaneously as a means of reorganizing an ostensibly higher, uniquely aesthetic form of value and as an arena in which such value often appears subject to the most business-like system of production and exchange'.[27] Established in 1952, Spain's best remunerated award for an individual novel was and remains the Planeta Prize. In the mid-to-late 1970s, former dissidents were rewarded with disproportionate frequency. Jorge Semprún won in 1977 for *Autobiografía de Federico Sánchez* (*Federico Sanchez's Autobiography*) – an exposé of the Spanish Communist Party based on his experiences as an undercover agent and the most wanted man in Spain. The elderly Falangist protagonist of Juan Marsé's novel *La muchacha de las bragas de oro* (*The Girl with the Gold Panties*), the 1978 winner, sets out to write an autobiography in which he will admit how he falsified his past as an antidote to what he terms the 'opportunistic sprint towards democratic accreditation'.[28] Commenting on the 1979 winner, Manuel Vázquez Montalbán's *Los mares del sur* (*Southern Seas*) (see Chapter 7), Santos Juliá notes the irony of a Communist ex-prisoner lobbying to receive a lucrative commercial reward from a former Captain of the Legion, who had entered Barcelona victoriously in 1939 before transforming himself into a powerful publisher.[29] Prizes, 'a patronage system for the post-patronage age',[30] constituted not only a form of (re) conciliation but also a means by which to whitewash reputations.

In a forensically documented D.Phil. thesis, Enrique Sacau-Ferreira observes how the 'political undertones of Spanish music criticism as well as the promotion of avant-garde music under Franco has been ignored even when they carried out duties that were decidedly at odds with democratic practices'.[31] Jesús Aguirre noted in the diaries of his time as Director-General of Music in the nascent Ministry of Culture that it was a conscious decision to begin awarding lifetime achievement awards in order to bypass what he perceives to be an anachronistic and undignified bartering system previously in place at the Ministry of Information and Tourism whereby composers such as Cristóbal Halffter and Luis de Pablo would petition on behalf of their most recent compositions.[32] Halffter's well-remunerated commissions for the twenty-five-years-of peace celebrations had previously coincided with international promotion for his work.[33] In spite of such trade-offs, 'during democracy, Spanish avant-garde composers have always tried to present themselves as either rebellious or impartial.'[34] One of the composers discussed in Sacau-Ferreira's thesis threatened the University of Oxford with legal action if they did not withdraw details from the institutional web-pages. The chair of examiners looked at the case and concluded the content was fully justified. The complainant was told to pursue legal action if he so wished.

Novelist Javier Marías has repeatedly made the case that Cela – who worked as a censor under Franco long before receiving the Nobel Prize in 1989 – was a collaborator, and that the veneration of his figure is evidence of a lack of rupture in Spain.[35] In *Así empieza lo malo* (*Thus Bad Begins*), Marías's 2014 novel set in 1980 in Madrid, there is a deliberate ambiguity as to whether the original sin refers to what happened under Franco or to how it was dealt with subsequently: 'Nobody is going to be made to sit trial, agreed, and anyway, there would be no way of doing it, and it wouldn't be worth it. Imagine the chaos. But, listen, I'm not keeping quiet about what I know, when things change, so at least they don't give out the medals quite so readily.'[36] Although he believed the equivalent of ethnic cleansing took place in the early post-Civil War years, González claimed he never used his absolute majority to create public debate about the past because, when still leader of the opposition, General Gutiérrez Mellado asked him to wait until the protagonists had all died to avoid unnecessary pain.[37] When, in summer 2018, I asked if he regretted this decision, the ex-President replied negatively, repeating what he claimed was the exact image employed by the 23-F hero: fire still rages under the ashes.

In a closed-doors parliamentary session held on 17 March 1981, both the Government and the opposition agreed that the armed forces ought to be appeased by intensifying the anti-terrorist campaign and the relatively rapid progress towards regional autonomy slowed down.[38] The coup's chief architects received lenient sentences from a military, as opposed to a civil, court, the presiding judges including José María García Escudero amongst their ranks. Juan Carlos delivered a speech in the midst of the trial at his old military academy: he recalled his time in Zaragoza with nostalgia, and made assurances that he would not allow the armed forces to be brought into disrepute by the ill-advised actions of a minority.[39]

Both the incoming President and the King were united in a desire to modernise but not alienate Spain's armed forces. It is not necessary to subscribe to conspiracy theories surrounding Juan Carlos and González's involvement in the coup to acknowledge that it strengthened their respective positions. In the case of the latter, it facilitated an implicit pact whereby he did not shame the right in exchange for the discrediting of any oppositional discourse to the Socialist project. This allowed the President to write himself a blank cheque for the perpetuation of paternalistic practices in democratic clothing. Gutiérrez Mellado was able to live out his post-army career in relative comfort because, in 1986, González made him a member of the Council of the Realm. This decision was taken on the insistence of Enrique Sarasola – the shady personal friend of González who had rushed to take care of the future President's wife and children on the night of the coup – on discovering that the retired General was considering a job in sales because of difficulties paying his mortgage. The Basque entrepreneur reputedly claimed that someone who had served his country as faithfully as Gutiérrez Mellado ought not to be left in a precarious financial position; a more statesmanlike response would have sought structural solutions as opposed to remedies via ad hoc cronyism.

The President's behaviour was replicated throughout society, the cultural industries proving to be no exception. In a letter dated 9 March 1983, the Mayor of Madrid, Enrique Tierno Galván, wrote personally to Javier Solana, the recently appointed Minister of Culture, to request that he take a personal interest in the candidature of Miguel Lezcano as the local delegate for tourism or culture in the municipal town of Guadalajara: 'Me parece justo que este compañero de familia muy perseguida en la ciudad, y ya propuesta en otra ocasión, abrigue esperanzas'[40] (It seems fair to me that this comrade from a family who were heavily persecuted in the city, and who was put forward on another occasion, can harbour some hopes).

This sat uncomfortably with the vision proffered by González in a speech from 1976: 'culture, worthy of that name, is always critical. And that critical freedom should be preserved in relation to all political parties, also in relation to the Socialist Party.'[41] The determining factor as to whether this principle was upheld once in government was the influence of specific media.

An internal report from 1983 on the chain of State-owned newspapers spoke of a financial and political deficit:

> La existencia de una Cadena de periódicos propiedad del Estado es un hecho poco común en los países democráticos del occidente europeo, y sólo se explica entre nosotros por la herencia, aún sin liquidar tras seis años de transición política, de un régimen totalitario.[42]

> The existence of a chain of State-run newspapers is a very uncommon feature in the democratic states of Western Europe, and can only be explained amongst us for the legacy, still not resolved after six years of political transition, of a totalitarian regime.

The Constitution made no explicit reference to television.[43] The PSOE had been unequivocal in opposition: accusations of political manipulation and corruption at RTVE underpinned a vote of no confidence in 1980,[44] Guerra citing a list of cases from the preceding two years, claiming censorship with the UCD to be worse than under Franco.[45] This claim was not without substance. Iñaki Gabilondo had, for example, been suspended from the newsroom after telling journalists: 'The political class is absolutely convinced that television is a twentieth-century invention designed to win elections and they do not understand that it can, on occasions, be used as a mirror to show the reality of the country.'[46] No political party advocated an independent regulatory or advisory board, even once this measure was recommended to member states by the Council of Europe in 1982.[47] The PSOE succeeded in rationalising a State broadcaster, which, in spite of its monopoly, was haemorrhaging money in 1983; from 1984, it ran at a surplus for the remainder of the decade.[48] Nonetheless, in a context where the Director-General of RTVE – alongside many of the country's most influential and well-remunerated positions in the cultural industries – was appointed by the incumbent Government, the charge of a democratic deficit identified in relation to the chain of nationalised newspapers was even more pronounced because of the State monopoly and the greater impact on public opinion.

138

Although most European states have public broadcasting, the Spanish media-scape was unique in that it was funded largely by advertising and there was no competition until the arrival of stations run by the autonomous communities, first in the Basque Country in 1982 and then in Catalonia in 1983. As José Miguel Contreras and Manuel Palacio note, this effectively duplicated the proportion of public television in areas of Spain even once the media-scape eventually allowed for the introduction of private television channels in 1989.[49] Many of the vices of the centralist Government were replicated at the level of autonomous communities, the Catalan TV3 being a platform for President Jordi Pujol, who effectively silenced cultural opposition through a discourse of national martyrdom and generous and frequently untransparent subsidies for the arts.[50] The principal cultural opposition within Catalonia was Els Joglars. A year after Pujol ascended to the presidency of the Generalitat in 1980, they staged *Operación Ubú* (*Ubu Operation*), which, alongside sequels *Ubú President* (*President Ubu*) (1995) and *Ubú President o los últimos días de Pompeya* (*President Ubu; or, The Last Days of Pompei*) (1999), provided acerbic critical commentary on the abuse of power. Boadella claims that, through an intermediary, Pujol asked what he could offer them in exchange for them leaving him alone.[51]

Els Joglars received subsidies from the Ministry of Culture, but their ability to fill theatres alongside a relatively autonomous production model has made them less dependent on patronage or intermediaries than most Spanish or Catalan cultural practitioners. Boadella also highlights that judges in the 1980s almost invariably prioritised freedom of expression over other considerations, thereby providing a creative and legal life-jacket. Barricada, a hard-rock band from the Opus Dei stranglehold of Pamplona, experienced multiple obstacles with a local executive representing multinational label Polygram who vetoed the inclusion of 'En nombre de Dios' (In the name of God) on an album release.[52] Business interests, as opposed to the law, increasingly determined who had the right to say what. Els Joglars and theatre owners were unsuccessfully prosecuted multiple times for blasphemy over *Teledeum* – a satire on the Church in the age of televised mass media – premiered in 1983, but this did not prevent the production from being performed around the country (with the added advantage of free publicity). Given that the number of theatre tickets sold annually in Spain plummeted from 11 to 5 million between 1983 and 1990,[53] few practitioners could afford to bite the hand that fed. Jonathan Mayhew has similarly argued that the vogue for an apolitical 'poetry of experience', with Luis García Montero as its leading exponent, reflected 'a cultural climate favourable to a new model of the writer-intellectual as a servant to the cultural politics of the state',[54] a product and cause of subsidies and prizes: 'poetry can be a quite lucrative career for anyone who is tapped into this pipeline'.[55]

Cinema provides another example of the Socialist predilection not just to counteract but also to control market forces, a tendency prevalent in virtually all media and a fertile breeding group for corrupt practices. In November 1985, Alfredo Matas invited some of the best-known figures in Spanish cinema to lunch to set out plans for the formation of a Spanish Film Academy 'that would act as a mouthpiece for the entire film industry in dealings with the administration and would have prize-awarding rights'.[56] Hence, for example, they preselect the film put forward in the 'Best Foreign Film' category for the American Academy Awards, a gatekeeping function without which Pedro Almodóvar would probably have more than the two Oscar statuettes currently in his possession. José María González-Sinde, the scriptwriter for many of Garci's films, was the Academy's first President, and the first televised Goya Awards – a more conciliatory name than the alternative suggestion of the Buñuel awards – were presided over by the King and Queen in 1987. If the producer and director of *El crimen de Cuenca* now operated a powerful monopoly on the production and reception of Spanish films, this inevitably required exclusions as well as inclusions. Cult horror director Jesús Franco believes the Miró legislation 'sent us all to hell apart from the small body chosen by the new captains of the sea';[57] whilst Mariano Ozores, one of the most commercially successful producers of the 1960s and 1970s, claims she never forgave him for his films opening on city-centre screens when hers did not, and that she blacklisted his films from subsidies on the basis that he made 'cinema for plumbers'.[58] Sally Faulkner has made the counter-argument that Miró's promotion of a middlebrow cinema for the expanding middle-class market needs to be understood in relation to rising social mobility.[59] Without disputing this sociological reality, it was nevertheless unfortunate that the promotion of 'quality' producer-led cinema concentrated vast budgets in a limited number of hands – disproportionately those of friends and veterans of the Nuevo Cine Español (see Chapter 4) – and combined with external factors (diminishing protectionist methods, a rise in home entertainment and inflation) to render a situation in which domestic audiences turned away from their national cinema just as the Goya Awards provided an unprecedented promotional platform for Spanish films. That audiences were more interested in watching stars of Spanish cinema in their most glamorous clothes picking up awards than seeing their films is indicative of the hegemony of television.

There was a furore when, following the broadcast of a documentary critical of Fraga on 19 June 1985, José María Calviño – the Socialist appointed Director-General of RTVE – admitted he would do everything in his power to prevent the leader of the opposition winning an election.[60] A potential conflict of interest is also present in an official letter dated 16 December 1986 and written by Luis Solana, director of the Telefonica communications network, to his brother, Javier, the then Minister of Culture, which stated: 'Te adjunto un documento interno de esta casa sobre las posibilidades de colaboración con RTVE. Creo que te puede ser útil en el proceso de definición de objetivos nacionales y reparto de funciones' (I attach an internal document from here about the possibilities for collaborations with RTVE. I think it might be useful for you as you draft a list of national objectives and division of responsibilities).[61] What stretched the notion of the 'mass communications media' as 'the connective tissues of democracy'[62] to breaking point was the PSOE exercising its control of the media to manipulate public opinion in the referendum on NATO membership in 1986. By this time, Spaniards were spending an average of 207 minutes a day in front of the television, which put them fourth in the world (behind the UK, the USA and Canada).[63]

In opposition, the PSOE had criticised Calvo Sotelo for fast-tracking Spanish entry; the slogan 'OTAN, de entrada no' was central to their election campaign. Most voters understood this to mean 'NATO, no way', but linguistic ambiguity ensured it could also be understood as 'NATO, in principle no'.[64] Ronald Reagan's visit to Madrid in 1985 (see Chapter 3) was greeted by 400,000 protestors; the peace movement – a rallying call for those disillusioned by the PSOE – also recruited well amongst social activists from the 1970s.[65] The professionalisation of the armed forces – sought by González alongside an increasingly pragmatic approach to his and the nation's role in a rapidly changing international landscape, and West German support for Spanish EU membership being contingent upon continued NATO membership[66] – led the Socialist President to join forces with the King and Queen in campaigning for a 'yes' vote.

Javier Krahe's performance of an anti-NATO song, 'Cuervo ingenuo' (Naïve crow), was cut from a live TVE special,[67] the singer-songwriter declining an offer to perform another song in its place. State monopoly of the media was paradoxically enhanced by the presence of deregularisation on the agenda, as the major telecommunications companies courted the Government in the hope of receiving a coveted licence. In the words of Richard Maxwell:

> The quid pro quo for the press was the assurance that the private TV bill would not be rejected because of political caprice. (Remember that the largest dailies, *El País* and *La Vanguardia*, were tightly linked to two major private TV promoters, SOGOTEL and TEVISA.) The press acquiesced … this corporatist collaboration brought together a pro-NATO alliance of both state and private media.[68]

Spaniards were not necessarily fooled, but they were convinced. In the early months of 1986, shortly before the NATO referendum and Spain's becoming a fully-fledged member of the EU, the number of citizens who said that they never believed a word that González said increased, but so too did those who thought he protected the nation's interests.[69]

After the PSOE achieved the referendum result they sought (56.85 per cent voted 'yes'), calls were made for Calviño to be dismissed.

Against the wishes of Guerra, who saw television as central to political strategy, González lobbied for Pilar Miró to be appointed as his
successor.[70] Personal and political allegiances aside, the incoming
Director-General's character was unpredictable as regards the extent
to which she kowtowed to government. An early casualty was *La bola
de cristal* (*The Crystal Ball*), broadcast on Saturday mornings between
1984 and 1988, which 'used contemporary music, sardonic humour
and innovative directing techniques to offer the most original children's
programme in Spain'.[71] According to director Matilde Fernández: 'We
all had great expectations of the Socialist party but then they started
promoting Spain's adherence to NATO, censoring us, which had not
happened before with the UCD government'.[72] After complaints were
made to the Spanish ombudsman – a recently created role in the
Spanish context, occupied by Joaquin Ruiz-Giménez (father), a bulwark of civic society, whose track record involved defending *El crimen
de Cuenca* (see Chapter 5) – by the American Embassy, parents' associations and Islamic groups, Miró insisted on personally approving
content before transmission, and eventually took the programme
off air.[73] On the other hand, under her tutelage, Javier Garruchaga's
Viaje con nosotros (*Travel with Us*) began in 1988, featuring interviews
and performances of guests from the worlds of politics and culture
ranging from Elton John to Fraga, whilst satirical sketches included
puppets of Pujol and González. Miró's most defiant political gesture
occurred on the eve of a national strike against the liberalisation of the
labour market spearheaded by Carlos Solchaga, the PSOE's Finance
Minister: at midnight on 14 December, the late news was interrupted
and a square appeared on a blank screen in millions of Spanish
homes announcing 'It's 00.00 and 14 December is now more than a
success.' As Solchaga noted in his diaries: 'The psychological effect is
tremendous'.[74] The prophetic statement of TVE was instrumental in
the most systematic and successful protest yet mounted against the
Socialist project, the country grinding to a halt.[75] Miró was replaced
by Luis Solana and *Viaje con nosotros* suspended. Shortly afterwards,
concerns auditors raised over expenses were leaked to the press by

factions allied with Guerra. Subsequently acquitted, Miró stood trial for spending public funds on her wardrobe.

In contrast to television, the waning of radio's popularity in the 1960s and 1970s resulted in its being under far less tight Government control.[76] The medium's prestige had been raised by its accurate reporting of the coup,[77] and constituted the mass media's most critical running commentary of the Socialist administration. Encarna Sánchez, 'loved by housewives and feared by politicians',[78] was a former PSOE ally, but she moved far to the right after she joined the religious COPE radio station, her nighttime shows attracting over half-a-million listeners. Through largely successful attempts to co-opt the news Spaniards received, the Socialist administration inadvertently bestowed more legitimacy on populist right-wing media pundits, the effects of which are still to be felt in the twenty-first century through such reactionary outlets as newspaper *La Razón* or multi-media platform *Libertad digital*. It is not necessary to subscribe to the far-fetched belief that right-wing publications in Spain are more democratic than their leftist counterparts to accept the lesser claim that the arrival of a credible right-of-centre alternative to *El País* in 1989 was an important step in the democratisation process. With a less cosy relationship to central government and a commitment to investigative journalism, *El Mundo* revealed the existence of Government-sanctioned hit-squads, the Grupos Antiterroristas de Liberación (GAL), to fight a dirty war against ETA in the Basque Country either side of the French border. This was an important development in a context where it had, for example, traditionally been left to the foreign press to comment upon the hypocrisy of the Spanish State's complaining about a lack of support from Mitterrand's Government in the fight against terror when its special relationship with Arab states and dependency on their oil had stymied actions against ETA's receiving economic support and training from Libya, Palestine and Algeria.[79]

González has argued that 'there is no State without secret areas, susceptible to abuse, but vital for security'.[80] José Barrionuevo, a former Deputy Mayor of Madrid in charge of the municipal police who claims in his autobiography to have never 'participated in the gross anti-military

144

sentiment exhibited by some of our *lefties*,[81] was appointed Home Secretary in González's first Government. Between 1974 and 1982, mercenary death squads had killed more than thirty people.[82] As Fernando Savater and Gonzalo Martínez-Fresneda noted at the time, the Defence of the Constitution Law introduced in the aftermath of the coup was adapted to function as draconian anti-terrorist legislation.[83] Furthermore, in the words of Luis Martín-Estudillo, the '1981 coup attempt brought to a halt the work of the parliamentary investigative commission on torture'.[84] He attributes this and, by implication, 'the disappearance of torture as a topic of political debate within the institutions of democratic Spain in the 1980s'[85] to the fact that 23-F 'reminded those trying to abolish torture that questioning the practices of the armed forces was not without its risks'.[86]

A pedagogy of violent intimidation co-existed with a hegemonic silence that can be framed in relation to a reassuring symbolic discourse by which the unsuccessful coup supposedly heralded both the defeat of the unreconstructed armed forces and the consolidation of democracy. The film *El caso Almería* (*The Almeria Case*) (Pedro Costa, 1984) depicted a real-life incident in which three innocent young men, misidentified as ETA terrorists, were tortured and killed by the Guardia Civil. Torture is described but never explicitly shown. An investigative judge faces opposition and threats for taking on the military but he (and by implication justice) wins the day as the arrogant petulance of the armed forces, deliberately reminiscent of Tejero's behaviour throughout his trial,[87] is slowly chipped away and defeated in the courtroom. In a best-seller about the anti-ETA crusade, Lorenzo Silva, Manuel Sánchez and Gonzalo Araluce make a rare exception to an almost exclusive focus on terrorist atrocities and the heroic actions of the State to reference 'the disastrous and unforgivable actions of the agents' who were convicted of first-degree murder 'by virtue of a sentence as severe as it was warranted'.[88]

No mention is made of two young convicted ETA felons, José Antonio Lasa Aróstegui and José Ignacio Zabala Artana, who, in 1983, were kidnapped by GAL in Bayonne and taken to San Sebastian, where they were tortured and killed. Their remains were found in 1985, but not identified for a decade.[89] Between 1975 and mid-1988 there were between twenty and thirty serious attempts to negotiate between the Spanish State and the Basque terrorist organisation.[90] Nevertheless, ETA's insurgency continued 'because, for nearly everyone involved, the cessation of violence is not the most important thing on their political agenda. Of course, nearly everyone wants an end to the violence; it's just that other objectives are paramount.'[91] Barrionuevo, who holds firm to a belief in the 'generosity of Spanish democracy' alongside the 'enormous danger that the persistent, ferocious and cruel attack by terrorists represents for our living together in peace'[92] was imprisoned in 1998 for misappropriating Government funds to finance the activities of GAL, which resulted in twenty-seven fatally and over thirty badly injured victims, not all of whom were the intended targets. Joaquín Leguina, President of the Regional Council of Madrid from 1983 to 1995, blamed the vanity of investigating judge, Baltasar Garzón, alongside an intrusive media for the conviction when, he claimed, no minister had been incarcerated for equivalent actions in the UK and Germany against the IRA and Baader Meinhof.[93] As Paddy Woodworth notes, however, 'the Spanish courts have stopped short of establishing the full extent of the organizational links between the GAL and the PSOE'.[94] A far-from-transparent non-democratic discourse of 'us and them' is exposed not only by the actions of GAL but also by the Government's communications policy. Jeremy Harris, BBC correspondent to Spain at the time, was informed by the Spanish Home Secretary at an event organised at the presidential office that GAL were working for them and doing a fine job.[95] In contrast, John Hooper learnt of GAL's illegal activities through contacts at *El Mundo*, and went on to speak with Judge Garzón. When González hosted a lunch for eight foreign journalists, the former *Guardian* correspondent claims the President gave specific instructions that he not be invited.[96]

The curtailment of a broader debate on and around torture was symptomatic of a post-coup Socialist culture in which democracy was unencumbered to enact its illocutionary force as a panacea for Spain's ills and a valuable global export. Alongside Portugal, it headed what Samuel Huntington has termed 'democracy's third wave', at least thirty countries undergoing transitions to democracy between 1974 and 1990, sweeping through Latin America before moving to Eastern Europe.[97] Shortly after Franco's death, Spain may have been the first country officially to recognise the new military regime in Argentina,[98] but Juan Carlos made sure to highlight the importance of human rights to General Videla in speeches made during his state visit in November 1978.[99] At a time when CIA intelligence on Iran was outdated and incomplete,[100] Suárez's influence and potential mediating role in the Middle East impressed both Jimmy Carter and Margaret Thatcher.[101] The Spanish President arguably became addicted to being flattered abroad at the expense of running a country back home, a task he increasingly left to Fernando Abril. The closest he came to the controversy unfolding around *El crimen de Cuenca* was in Berlin, when Miró's participation at the Film Festival coincided with his visiting the German capital for a meeting with Helmut Schmidt to discuss dialogue between European and Arab states, alongside the crisis situations in Iran and Afghanistan. Suárez carried out important legwork in raising Spain's international profile, but increasing discord back home and in his own party ensured he was unable to reap the dividends effectively.

González inherited a more stable domestic scenario, and soon put his artillery of personal and political skills to effective use, equating modernity and democratisation in a seductive package that simultaneously enhanced national self-esteem and Spain's global standing. Although he had visited Israel in 1972, the PSOE adopted a pro-Palestine stance that was moderated in the early-to-mid 1980s, Spain officially recognising the Jewish State for the first time in 1986.[102] Juan Carlos, González and incoming Foreign Minister Francisco Fernández Ordóñez, skilfully balancing new diplomatic relations with visits and reassurances to Arab states,[103] helped ensure Madrid was suitably neutral territory to host the 1991 Middle East peace talks. Until 1977, 18 July was the national holiday in commemoration of Franco's illegal uprising. Debates surrounding a suitable replacement date were not settled until 1987. That Columbus's arrival in the New World (12 October) narrowly pipped Constitution Day (6 December) to the post[104] was an ostensibly anachronistic nostalgic glance for a country fixated on the future, but it was symptomatic of a calculated paternalism to position Spain as the missing link between its former colonies and the major western powers (see Chapter 12). With frequent assistance from the impeccably well-connected Sarasola, González had been carefully curating his contacts in Latin America since the dictatorship.

Cuba's declaration of an official period of mourning for the death of Franco,[105] whose regime had survived largely on the basis of its anti-Communism, is a historical irony matched by the fact that the then Vice-President of Iraq, Saddam Hussein, had made sure to receive his induction into the Order of Isabel the Catholic Queen when he travelled to Spain and met with the Caudillo and his chosen heir in 1974. Suárez's attendance at the sixth conference of non-aligned counties in Havana in September 1979 was thought to be a good thing by the USA, which saw him as a potential go-between.[106] In 1990, González claimed to have had 'a good relationship with Fidel coming from a starting point of disagreement since the mid-1970s'.[107] Castro's brief visit to Spain in 1984 had been his first ever to a European capitalist state, but relations were later put to the test when the Spanish Embassy in Havana granted asylum to Cuban nationals seeking to escape the island.[108] When Castro visited Spain for the Barcelona Olympics and quincentenary of Columbus setting sail, the politician he spent most time with was Fraga. The Cuban Commander's Galician heritage aside, ideological differences were ameliorated by a generational affinity between two politicians, who were once the future, now rendered increasingly redundant by the global Zeitgeist. As Apartheid drew to a close, F. W. de Klerk received guidance on negotiations with Nelson Mandela and the African National Congress (ANC) from the Socialist President.[109] In a post-Cold War context, Mikhail Gorbachev cited González as the European leader he felt the closest personal affinity with, and claimed Spain was a model to be emulated.[110] The Spanish premier appeared more comfortable with Fraga-like reformers than, say, incoming Czech President, Václav Havel, whose journey from dissidence to power had exacted a greater personal toll. A notable exception to this general rule was Jorge Semprún: the concentration-camp survivor and excommunicated Communist accepted González's invitation to return to Madrid from Paris to replace Javier Solana – moved in a cabinet reshuffle prior to later being appointed Commander-in-Chief of NATO – as Minister of Culture, despite not belonging to the Spanish Parliament or to the PSOE.

As biographer Soledad Fox Maura notes, 'whenever you hear people who knew Jorge speak about his magnetism, anyone would think they were describing a rock star'.[111] In his autobiographical account of his time in government, Semprún expresses pride in taking the global lead in ensuring Spain boycotted the Tehran Book Fair and published a State-subsidised post-Fatwa translation of Salmon Rushdie's *The Satanic Verses*.[112] The back cover preached of 'our editorial commitment to offering the reader the work of an author of proven literary merit, and the moral duty to defend tolerance as the foundation of our living together in harmony and perhaps the only basis for breaking down antagonisms and controversies'.[113] When the author decided to come out of hiding, Spain was amongst the first countries he visited. Rushdie, often accompanied in public readings by Mario Vargas Llosa, expressed his gratitude for the support and solidarity he had received from the State, and requested that its institutions mediate with the Iranian Government on his behalf.[114] Spain was able to take a lead in 'the most important free speech controversy of modern times'[115] despite, or perhaps because of, the book's content not being an obvious fit with national interests: Beatriz de Moura admits rejecting *The Satanic Verses* for Tusquets publishers because, unable to decipher the Islamic references, she found it boring; accepting that this was a limitation, shared by most Spanish readers, on her part, the Brazilian-born editor nevertheless claimed no post-Fatwa review was offering an honest appraisal.[116] Spain had a relatively small Muslim population but the Shah's celebrity profile ensured the Ayatollah Khomeini was a ubiquitous cartoon-like villain. In 1982, Galician punk-rock band Siniestro Total released a loose reworking of Elvis Presley's 'Blue Suede Shoes' with the refrain, 'Ayatollah, no me toques la pirola' (Ayatollah, hands off my balls).

It is not necessary to claim blasphemy is relative to acknowledge that the UK's significant Muslim population ought to inform debates surrounding the publication of Rushdie's novel;[117] as Simon Lee observed: 'the result of the current woolly argument about free speech has been a general assumption that one either has to be an absolute free speech fanatic or an apathetic free speech cynic'.[118] By 1992, Spain was in thrall to the notion of free speech as a manifestation of democracy, at a time when this political system simultaneously served to modernise society and the lives of individuals but was also evoked, less positively, as an exclusionary mechanism and to revoke criticism.

Part III

Cities

Introduction

A Spanish Government poll from 1982 indicated that 48.2 per cent of retired people were not living where they had been born.[1] Over the course of the dictatorship, people's residences, alongside their everyday practices and sense of identity, were often transformed. The urban population rose from 56 per cent in 1960 to 73 per cent in 1981,[2] Madrid and Barcelona gaining nearly 1.4 million inhabitants apiece during the 1950s and 1960s.[3] 'El clásico' – any clash between Real Madrid and Barcelona Football Club – is a recognisable global brand, 'the motherfucker of them all, a War of the Roses, football against the enemy, the real Glory Game'.[4] If Barça is, as the saying goes, more than a club, Madrid is more than a city – it is a metonym for Spanish national identity. The ferocious talent of the players aside, audiences watching the biggest fixture of international club football respond, with greater or lesser cultural ken, to an epic rivalry that extends beyond the pitch. A year before it joined the European Union, Eugenio Trías claimed Spain has 'to a large degree been an unresolved conflict throughout this century between a civil society without a state – Cataluña – and a state without a civil society – Madrid'.[5]

Spanish nationalists have attributed the outbreak of the Civil War to the separatist demands of the Generalitat under the leadership of Lluís Companys. Following the Francoist victory, the rebel 'region' was put in its place by the dictatorial, centralised State: 25.2 per cent of ministers came from Madrid with only 3.36 per cent being from Barcelona, a lower percentage than those from Ferrol, the small Galician shipbuilding town in which the Caudillo was born.[6] SEAT automobiles, 'an emblematically Spanish business both in terms of nepotism and its organisation,'[7] retained its administrative offices in Madrid despite virtually all production being carried out in factories in and around Barcelona, a situation only rationalised when the by-now flailing company was taken over by Volkswagen in 1987.[8] The two cities have clearly experienced both dictatorship and democracy in distinct, albeit not necessarily antithetical, manners. Reifying specificities runs the risk of lapsing into chauvinism, but almost anyone who has lived in, visited or even read about Barcelona and Madrid tends to concur they are very different cities; disagreements are more likely to follow when it comes to quantifying the reasons for and nature of said particularities.

In his memoirs, Argentine footballer Diego Maradona says his time playing in Barcelona was doomed not just because of illness and injury but 'because of the city as well, because I'm more … more Madrid'.[9] Culture may lack the financial traction of the beautiful game, but it has also chronicled and informed wider debates surrounding Spain's two largest cities, their frequently fraught relationships and (inter)national aspirations. My aim here is to chart a cultural competition in perpetual extra-time, one side grabbing the advantage only for the other to equalise and subsequently take the lead. In Chapter 7, I explore the creative tension between class and national(ist) identity that, I maintain, was instrumental in the consolidation of Barcelona as Spain and Catalonia's cultural capital during the late Franco period. In the following chapter, I turn my attention to how and why Madrid, the dictatorial city par excellence, was able to reinvent itself during the Transition through the drug-fuelled youth movement known as the Movida. The closing chapter compares and contrasts this reinvention with the model of accommodation advanced between Catalonia, Spain and the world through sport and culture in Barcelona's Olympic adventure.

Chapter 7

Urbanisation and development
Class, gender and race

Following the loss of Spanish colonies in 1898, economic prowess and a consolidated bourgeoisie served to convince many Catalans they were being held back by an ineffectual centralist bureaucracy. Barcelona's mercantile trade ensured the city had a class structure and social hierarchies often more legible, although not necessarily familiar, to non-Spaniards than Madrid. As registered in *Homage to Catalonia*, George Orwell was overcome by his initial impressions: it 'was the first time that I had ever been in a town where the working class was in the saddle'.[1] He later wondered if he had been deceived and if the bourgeoisie might have adopted an expedient proletarian disguise, one of the various doubts that began to assail him 'about this war in which, hitherto, the rights and wrongs had seemed so beautifully simple'.[2] Class, as opposed to territorial warfare, ensured the Catalan bourgeoisie had reasons to be both grateful and beholden to the rebels. Josep Maria de Porcioles, Mayor of Barcelona from 1957 to 1973, embodied many of the most exploitative practices of late Francoism and had, in his youth, been a sympathiser with the Catalan Nationalist Party, the Lliga Catalana. I am concerned here with critically interrogating the animosity between Madrid and Barcelona, an animosity that has served to disguise complex and frequently contradictory vectors of oppression. This dialectic has, I will suggest, underplayed the extent to which the two cities faced challenges hardly unique to Spain but exaggerated by the dictatorship's ad hoc modernisation, through which poverty became first mobile and only later mobilised.

In a diary entry dated 12 September 1960, the Catalan poet and industrialist Jaime Gil de Biedma records a road trip through Alicante, Andalusia, Murcia and rural Castile:

> The backwardness, the poverty and the misfortune are even greater than one imagined – our day-to-day life in the city serves to cut us off: here of course there is also poverty *à revendre* but at least we are free of that radical alienation, of that total state of anachronism in which a large part of Spain lives, and which we tend to forget when we think of our country.[3]

Juan Goytisolo, Gil de Biedma's friend and colleague, documented this in social-realist writings of the 1950s and 1960s, homing in on isolated communities around Almeria with premodern forms of sociality. Miguel Delibes depicted rural poverty in his native rural Castile in *Las ratas* (*The Rats*) in 1962, whilst travel photography by Carlos Saura and the North American Bruce Davidson, as well as contributions to *Afal* magazine, bear testament to levels of poverty more habitually associated with Africa than Europe. As Barry Jordan notes, the modernist prose of Luis Martín-Santos's *Tiempo de silencio* was '[s]upposedly the gravedigger of the *novela social*'.[4] The novel's form undoubtedly constitutes a stylistic break, but its subject-matter nevertheless transports anthropological study of abject poverty from the rural to the urban milieu. Set in Madrid, the controversial novel's publication was midwifed by Barcelona publishing house Seix Barral (see Chapter 4).

The squalor that Gil de Biedma glimpsed out of his window remained largely concealed from the urban middle classes in both geographical and symbolic terms. At a time when car ownership was becoming a realistic aspiration for an increasingly broad cross-section of society, a carefully zoned and chronically underfunded public transport system was both the symptom and the cause of the regime's determination psychically and physically to expunge poverty. This carefully concealed underworld is exposed in Alfonso Sastre's play *La taberna fantástica* (*The Fantastic Tavern*) – written in 1966 but not staged until the 1980s – set in a rough and ready tavern near Las Ventas bullring frequented by drunks, criminals, *quinquis* (a derogatory term for impoverished delinquents on the fringes of both society and the law) and the occasional member of the

Guardia Civil, to whom Luis the bar-owner has to give drinks for free. When drunken violence erupts, Luis curses 'Fucking tinkers, you're worse than the Gypsies.'[5] With limited access to sociological context or data, the rare occasions on which more respectable members of society came into contact with marginal(ised) groups were structurally predetermined to reinforce prejudices: in a book credited to Julien Agirre – but, according to Sastre, written by Eva Forest[6] – documenting the assassination of Carrero Blanco (see Chapter 4), the original plan to kidnap as opposed to kill their target was scuppered when *quinquis* robbed their safe house.[7] Poverty and crime were nothing new but urban migration simultaneously reinforced and reinvented existing paradigms.

Spanish Gypsies both replicated and departed from broader patterns. Increasingly concentrated in cities, by the early 1960s most had left their traditionally itinerant lifestyles behind.[8] There were more employment opportunities in Barcelona,[9] with 82.4 per cent of the 12,000 Gypsies estimated to be residing in Madrid in 1971 living in shacks.[10] In 1978, a year after Juan de Dios Ramírez Heredia became the first member of the Romani community to be elected to Spanish Parliament,[11] only 26 per cent of Gypsies formed part of the active population, a statistic inextricably tied to higher birth rates and lower life expectancy than the national averages.[12] In a country lacking a strong tradition in the twentieth century of immigration from abroad, what Lou Charnon-Deutsch refers to as 'the internal colonization of the Spanish Roma'[13] is both symptom and cause of a fluctuation between 'idealized images of "cheerful exoticism" linked to their artistic skills, and the most detrimental stereotypes'.[14] Antonio Sabater, a judge based in Barcelona, wrote the following in his book from 1962, *Gamberros, homosexuales, vagos y maleantes* (*Hooligans, Homosexuals, Vagrants and Lowlives*): 'A group of the population – who constitute a race apart – characterised by their aversion to work, for not bowing to the social order and living principally from theft, con-artistry and other punishable acts, are the Gypsies.'[15] Sabater only retired in 1986.

As David Harvey notes, cities, from their very inception, have 'arisen through the geographical and social concentration of a surplus product' and are, as such, inflected by class, 'since surpluses have been extracted from somewhere and from somebody, while control over the use of the surplus typically lies in the hands of a few'.[16] In 1964, Francesc Candel published a book titled *Els altres Catalans* (*The Other Catalans*), in which he focused on the plight of recent arrivals in the peripheral neighbourhood Can Tunis where he lived, alongside other immigrant areas such as the shanty towns emerging on and around the Montjuic mountain. By 1977, 80 per cent of unskilled manual workers in Catalonia were migrants from elsewhere in Spain.[17] Around 40 per cent of housing units in the Madrid metropolitan area in 1975 had been built after 1960,[18] but this had not served to resolve the capital's housing crisis. When Carrero Blanco's future assassins first moved to the Spanish capital from the Basque Country, they were pleasantly surprised by the lack of security surrounding their target, whose daily routine rarely varied,[19] but an unexpected complication was the near impossibility of finding a place to rent. In 1974, 54 per cent of the 4.3 million people in metropolitan Madrid lived in inadequate housing, whilst 8.1 per cent of housing stock remained empty for reasons to do with speculation.[20]

Barcelona's credentials as Spain's literary centre are attributable in large part to the mapping of an Oedipal drama onto an increasingly sprawling class-obsessed urban metropolis. In a diary entry for 21 October 1962, Gil de Biedma speaks of his father confronting him for having signed a petition against the torture of miners in the Asturian strike: 'The memory of that scene wouldn't be so unpleasant if it wasn't for the clarity with which one discovers the fundamental dishonesty of the class in someone as charming and seemingly humane.'[21] Juan Goytisolo refers in his autobiography to a sentimental attachment to Marxism 'dictated in no small part by the desire to make me forgive the original blight of my class and the infamy of my family's past'.[22] His anti-Francoism, alongside that of his brothers and fellow writers, Luis and José Agustín, cannot be divorced from their father's capitulation to the Franco regime. This extended to falsely attributing their mother's death in a bomb-raid by Mussolini's air force to the Republican enemy. When Luis was imprisoned, his father wrote to Franco begging for clemency in light of their suffering during the war and his track-record as an upstanding right-wing Catholic.[23] The narrator of *Tiempo de cerezas* (*Time of Cherries*), a Bildungsroman by Montserrat Roig first published in 1977, recalls a demonstration against the repression of Asturian strikers: 'Natalia wasn't shouting against that ashen mass of colour that had hit her, nor against the jeeps, nor the water tanks; she didn't shout against the loose dogs who struck out without knowing why; Natalia shouted against her past, against her father's anger, against all that she had been.'[24]

As Catherine Davies notes, Roig's literary project involved writing 'realist narrative fiction, which nevertheless incorporates new techniques to put across in a straightforward language a clear set of ideas and a point of view, and to focus on experienced reality (middle-class family and university life) in Barcelona.'[25] In the words of Doreen Massey: 'spaces and places are not only themselves gendered but, in their being so, they both reflect and affect the ways in which gender is constructed and understood.'[26] Alongside Mercè Rodoreda, 'the undisputed mistress of the narrative of everyday life,'[27] Roig specialised in first-person female narrators, lacking a room of their own, looking back on lives traversing the city (often not by choice) by foot, nuancing the notion of the *flânerie* as 'a metaphor for the gendered scopic hierarchy in observations of urban spaces.'[28] The protagonist of Rodoreda's *La calle de las Camelias* (*The Street of Camellias*), recounted as a stream of consciousness, written in Geneva and originally published in Catalan, recalls her life since she was dumped as a baby just prior to the Civil War. As she drifts in and out of sexual relationships, closer to prostitution than romantic partnerships, her misfortunes are revealed in laconic, non-self-pitying fashion. A married well-to-do father denies responsibility for their unborn child: 'I didn't get annoyed, because it wasn't a reason to become annoyed, but rather to be sad.'[29]

The Liceu Opera House – in the words of novelist Esther Tusquets 'our temple, the temple of a fearful and provincial bourgeoisie'[30] – incongruously located on the Ramblas, Barcelona's proletarian boulevard par excellence, is a running aspirational motif. The protagonist eventually gains access to this bourgeois oasis – a venue at which until well into the 1980s an annual benefit gala concert was held to supplement the meagre wages of the ushers, security and permanent staff[31] – when invited by one of her various sugar-daddies. She soon learns that interior as well as exterior spaces are zoned. Sat alone in the stalls, looked down upon both figuratively and literally from a private box by her bourgeois lover and his family, she leaves almost immediately. Social divisions under-pinned by place of birth were far from gender-neutral. According to a poll conducted in 1969 amongst men in Barcelona between the ages of 14 and 20, 62 per cent had had their first sexual experience with a prosti-tute;[32] a contemporaneous survey of sex-workers indicated that 8 per cent came from Catalonia, 80 per cent from the rest of Spain and that 12 per cent were foreigners.[33]

Catalonia's class system and enforced incorporation into a paternal-istic and dictatorial State ensured the urban culture of Barcelona was unique. A new generation of university-educated middle classes, along-side proximity to France and the sea, meant that, even if the bar was set low, Barcelona was Spain's most cosmopolitan city. Madrid dominated a centralist commercial cinema alongside nascent television and popular-music industries, but the most advanced urban cartographies were clearly of the Catalan capital. Hence, for example, the so-called Barcelona School – 'a heterogeneous group of film-makers and artists who emerged during the 1960s and early 1970s with a characteristically cosmopolitan flair that set them apart from the "official" idiom of the contemporary "New Spanish Cinema" '[34] – was influenced by the cinema of Jean-Luc Godard,[35] and embodied a keen sense of alienation in the modern(ist) world without seeking refuge in some mythical arcadia. In *Brillante porvenir* (*Brilliant Future*) (Vicente Aranda and Román Gubern, 1965), a young man with a boring small-town existence finds employment in a Barcelona construction firm after falsifying credentials as a trained archi-tect; his colleagues repeatedly refer to him as professional and respon-sible – the film's ironic humour derives from the viewer's being made privy to his scams and cluelessness about the job he is meant to be doing. A departure from the proselytising of doctrinaire social realism resulted in the Barcelona School being 'regarded as problematic and politically suspect'.[36] If a film such as *Noche de vino tinto* (*Red Wine Night*) (José

María Nunes, 1966) documents a night of sex, violence and adventure with staged dialogues and minimal narrative beyond the pretext of a small-town girl coming to the city in search of excitement, the School's standing was not abetted by its practitioners belonging to the *Gauche Divine*, 'little more than an endogamous alcoholic group of editors, filmmakers, well-to-do writers and, above all, Milan-style architects', in publisher Carlos Barral's sardonic caricature.[37] Oriol Regàs, the owner of Bocaccio – the *Gauche Divine*'s most iconic hangout – claims the night-club succeeded as it was in tune with Barcelona, 'where not even the upper middle classes fully accepted the Francoist regime': 'It was a more cosmopolitan city, where the fresh air from Perpignan had already begun to filter through.'[38]

David Vilaseca perhaps overstates the case when claiming that 'this deeply subversive movement … produced some of the most innovative films ever made in Spain, let alone under Franco's dictatorship',[39] but the best examples are more engaged and engaging that Barral's quip might suggest. The premiere of *Dante no es únicamente severo* (*Dante Is Not Exclusively Severe*) (Jacinto Esteva and Joaquim Jordá) in Barcelona on 10 November 1966 was a 'happening' that included a jingoistic montage of Spanish historical films saying 'The film you are about to see isn't this kind of thing.'[40] Dominated by a psychedelic-rock soundtrack unheard of in Spanish cinema at the time, and commencing with a group of young adults sitting around a table, self-consciously playing up for the camera, the film uses montage and strong visual imagery to deconstruct the human need to tell stories, ranging from anecdotes to grand socio-political narratives. In one scene, a man reads a newspaper article on what Barcelona will be like in 2000 whilst a voice-over talks of the need for responsible growth and development to ensure their grandchildren inherit a great city; the camera cuts to scenes of chaotic construction under way across a depressed and depressing urban metropolis.

A cosmopolitan desire to look beyond the Pyrenees was similarly a hallmark of the Nova Cançó, the Catalan protest-song movement, first heard on a record released in 1962 of Josep María Espinàs covering five songs originally written and recorded by Georges Brassens,[41] in which the vindication of minority languages and anti-Francoism went hand in hand. Rudimentary musical arrangement was often compensated for by political commitment and lyrical ingenuity, the former instrumental in the popularity enjoyed in non-Catalan-speaking parts of Spain by artists such as Lluís Llach or Raimón (see Chapter 1). The most commercially successful and musically literate exponent of the Nova Cançó was Joan Manuel Serrat, also singled out by his urban proletarian roots. Born in 1943 to an Aragonese mother and a Catalan father, he was raised in Poble Sec – hence his nickname 'el noi del Poble Sec' (the boy from Poble Sec) – the largely immigrant area nestled between the Paral·lel, Barcelona's avenue of popular theatres, and Montjuic. Brought up in a bilingual environment and living alongside revue performers, he first discovered French chanson when he became one of the very few people from his neighbourhood to attend university. Booed at different points in his career for singing in both languages,[42] it was both a shrewd commercial strategy and a reflection of the dual, as opposed to monolingual, neighbourhood in which he was raised. 'El meu carrer' (My road), a song from 1970, nostalgically serenades a childhood home and its human fauna that:

> Is people from all over
> Who work and drink
> Who sweat and eat
> Who rise
> At the break of dawn
> And go to the football
> Every Sunday

The key to what Manuel Vázquez Montalbán refers to as 'Serrat's populist criticism'[43] was the ability to synthesise a university education and personal street experiences in infectious musical fashion to question ingrained hierarchies and counteract prejudices in relation to the linguistic, cultural and class hierarchies ratified by Franco's victory in the Civil War. 'Una muchacha típica' (A typical young girl) ran foul of the censor in 1967 for its depiction of a young woman 'from one of the country's typically respectable families', for whom 'that classic summer in a village by the sea goes without saying … far away from those factories that make it impossible to breathe'.[44] In 'Señora' (Madam), Serrat addresses the well-to-do mother of a girlfriend: 'I know I'm not a good son-in-law, I'm almost a kiss from hell.'

The potential for eroticism to enhance as well as to bridge, albeit temporarily, class divides is also a recurring theme in the novels of Juan Marsé. As Kirsten A. Thorne notes of *Últimas tardes con Teresa* (*Last Evenings with Teresa*), it is 'less concerned with providing a guide for social transformation than it is with creating a new language of erotics grounded in class divisions'.[45] Published by Seix Barral in 1966, the narrative, set a decade earlier, historicises emigration and the interweaving class- and generation-tensions through the relationship between petty criminal Pijoaparte, and the rebellious and beautiful bourgeois Teresa Serrat. The couple meet following the hospitalisation of Maruja, her family servant and his casual girlfriend. According to a review from the time of publication by Mario Vargas Llosa: 'Throughout the novel there is a complicity between the author and Pijoaparte, an unfriendly complicity that, in any case, is unfair to the book's other characters.'[46] The physique of the male protagonist, raised in the slums of Mount Carmelo, which had, since the end of the Civil War, housed many of Barcelona's dispossessed on the city borders beyond Gracia,[47] 'gave away his Andalusian origin – a *charnego*, someone from Murcia (Murcia as a general word for immigrants, not a specific place: another peculiarity of the Catalans), a native of that remote and mysterious Murcia'.[48] Although he hails from Malaga, it is a symptom and cause of the indigenous population's sense of superiority that economic migrants from all over Spain are identified with one particularly poor region. For Teresa's mother, 'Mount Carmelo was somewhat akin to the Congo, a remote and sub-human country with its own laws, different'.[49] By contrast, for the university student, Pijoaparte embodies 'another golden legend of a badly understood progressiveness: collegiality out of solidarity, class barriers removed'.[50]

Adopted after his mother died in child-birth, the largely self-taught Marsé was one of the few Catalan authors of his generation to have worked in manual labour. Although clearly influenced by *Tiempo de silencio*, *Últimas tardes con Teresa* has little of the earlier novel's self-reflective parody – Martín-Santos so effectively mocked his scientist protagonist because he could identify with both his naïveté and his biography. What distinguishes Marsé's work from literature produced in and about Barcelona at the time is, first, the author's biography and, second, the bourgeois characters and intellectuals being objectified and subject(ed) to anthropological dissection at least as much as the city's underclass. This traditional lacuna is manifest in the fact that, as Carles Carreras notes, the Eixample – Ildefons Cerdá's modernist, nineteenth-century expansion project, which extends outwards from what it now the Plaza de Cataluña (and was, under Franco, the Plaza España) – has not figured heavily in literary depictions of Barcelona.[51] Teresa's family lives in Blanes, with its private beaches, but she delights in socialising in working-class areas such as Poble Sec, and the Raval. The latter, also known as the 'barrio chino' (Chinatown) was eulogised by Jean Genet in *The Thief's Journal*. In Carmen Laforet's postwar novel *Nada* – an Ur-text for more overtly politicised female-authored literary depictions of women in the city from the 1960s onwards – the central protagonist, Andrea, is immediately taken aback on inadvertently entering its streets: 'it brought to mind the vivid memory of a carnaval I had seen when young. The people, truth be told, were grotesque: a man passed by me, his eyes bloated by mascara under a broad hat.'[52] Teresa, by contrast, enters the Raval quite deliberately but, to borrow a phrase from Andrew Ross, 'the culture of the highly educated carries insurance for their own safe conduct when they go slumming'.[53]

Marsé's student responds to modernity and modernisation in a manner akin to the nineteenth-century *flâneur* as articulated by Walter Benjamin: 'The deepest fascination of this spectacle lay in the fact that, even as it intoxicated him, it did not blind him to the horrible social reality. He remained conscious of it, though only in the way in which intoxicated people are "still" aware of reality.'[54] She flits between the Raval and the hip hangouts of the upper Avenida Diagonal, what would later be the *Gauche Divine*'s stomping ground. Her social and physical mobility is enabled by the automobile, at this time a luxury item. Pijoaparte, by contrast, is only able to move about the city because of his skill at stealing motorbikes, a criminality that lands him in jail, thereby ending their romantic liaison and dashing his ambitions for social recognition. If Teresa tells her father she does not care if she is thrown out of university, the Murcian quixotically hopes that a couple she introduces him to will provide access to permanent legal employment. They drink with him, but forget him as quickly as Teresa and Pijoaparte do the still infirm Maruja. Increasingly disillusioned with the bluster of casual boyfriend Luis, a doctrinaire Marxist and faculty hero for his imprisonment following student protests, Teresa is less aware than the narrator or the reader of her belonging to a social formation, 'crucified between the marvellous unfurling of history and father's abominable factory',[55] who 'only speak amongst themselves and even then not much because they have urgent and special missions to carry out'.[56]

Status and provenance sutured the socio-cultural and geographical fabrics of Madrid and Barcelona in myriad but distinct fashions. The former's status as Spain's administrative and political capital ensured elites came from multiple and not so readily identifiable backgrounds, whilst fewer business fortunes predated the Civil War. Acknowledging this specificity ought not automatically to overshadow characteristics and challenges Barcelona shared with Madrid and many global cities more broadly. The damage suffered by the Catalan capital, a manifestation of the negative consequences of Francoism's laissez-faire self-interested approach to growth, cannot be solely or even primarily attributed to Spanish antipathy. Situated 30 km outside Madrid, the population of Alcalá de Henares had risen from 30,000 to 150,000 in a decade and, in the words of Manuel Castells:

[the] local government in the hands of a clique of corrupt Falangist officials ignored the new social needs and refused to consider the slightest democratization. On the contrary, most of its members, including planning officials and municipal architects, played an active role in the real estate firms and construction companies that controlled the urban redevelopment.[57]

An editorial from a special issue of *Cuadernos para el diálogo* speaks of how and why the 'right to the city is a basic social demand, a genuine national priority in our case'.[58] Vallecas was the first major stranglehold of local activism. Annexed to Madrid in 1950, this once autonomous muni-cipality had seen its population quadruple over the course of the decade, from 56,530 to 222,602 in 1960.[59] Many inhabitants had previously been evicted from other areas in and around Madrid, and its expansion went largely unregulated. A byword for poverty and urban underdevelop-ment, the proximity of the capital's principal shanty town to the indus-trial belt made it increasingly popular to local developers and, by the end of the 1960s, the local authorities sought to expel some inhabitants in order to tender licences for the construction of permanent residential properties.[60] This led to the creation of a neighbourhood association in 1969, which was largely successful in preventing forced evictions and holding the local administration to account, an impressive logistic and political victory in the context of a highly bureaucratic dictatorial regime. Similar associations were soon established elsewhere both in Madrid and in Barcelona, a veritable 'school of democracy'[61] that became 'a global reference point in the history of social movements'.[62] One of the most remarkable aspects of this phenomenon was the ability to provide a plat-form for activists from different social classes, a cause and consequence of the Spanish Communist Party's achieving what frequently eluded them (see Chapter 1): translating their political programme into tangible improvements in everyday lives.[63]

By the time of Franco's death, the regime was forced into paying lip-service to demands for more equitable housing so as not to under-mine the official ideology of peace and prosperity. A short Government propaganda film titled *Vivienda '73* (*Housing '73*) begins with a panning shot of a recently built housing estate, with children at play under blue skies. Complemented by an uplifting soundtrack, the voiceover speaks of new-builds that are a mixture of private-ownership and social housing. Everything is shown to be ordered and harmonious, with clear signposts to the local church; the viewer is informed of a collective responsibility to provide for the poorest segments of society with less purchasing power.

This sequence paves the way for an itinerant tour of similar developments built throughout Spain, which ends with a reassuring message: 'summing up, more justice, better cities with more and better housing'. *La cabina* (*The Telephone Box*) (Antonio Mecero, 1972) – the first and, at time of writing, only Spanish television programme to win an Emmy award – was shot on location in Madrid: 'Surrounded by a few squalid trees, with only a few benches and bordering some aseptic and utilitarian buildings, it gave from the outset a tone of the cold and dehumanised city that, in reality, is what we were aiming for.'[64] The dominant interpretation of this narrative of an average family man who finds himself locked into a telephone box has been as a metaphor for a human being violently silenced by a totalitarian regime,[65] but the short television film also lends itself to being read as a parody of quixotic vignettes such as *Vivienda '73*. A dystopian image of urban planning informed more by capitalist expediency than human need may have been set in the Spanish capital, but it could in reality have been the outskirts of any major metropolitan centre in which citizens fall victim to the city's pyrrhic utilitarianism: as the protagonist, still imprisoned in the phone box, is transported back to a lorry depot, a similarly faulty replacement phone box is quickly being prepared to be put in its place and capture its next unsuspecting victim/customer.

As Philip Cooke notes: 'Modernity has spatial and temporal coordinates which cannot be reduced simply to the stage of development of the dominant mode of production, but which cannot be entirely divorced from it either.'[66] The ad hoc, inequitable and rapid industrialisation undergone in late Francoism made Spain vulnerable, being particularly badly hit by the international oil crisis of 1973. As in many European countries, birthrates peaked in 1964.[67] By 1975, 61.74 per cent of the population had health cover,[68] but this was often tied up with employment contracts, and was thereby exposed to fluctuations in the market and labour conditions. A demographic boom combined with rising unemployment figures, which rocketed from 4.7 per cent in 1976 to peak at 21.7 per cent in 1985, provided ripe preconditions for juvenile delinquency, already on the rise prior to Franco's death.[69] Of adolescents arrested for the first time, 34 per cent had been physically abused for years; 88 per cent of teenagers with criminal records came from impoverished backgrounds, 75 per cent having spent time in care; and 42 per cent were illiterate.[70] In a survey of under-21 male prisoners in Valencia, 78.7 per cent came from working-class backgrounds, and 59 per cent deemed it acceptable for brothers and sisters to have sexual relations if both were consenting adults, whilst only 42 per cent approved of male homosexuality.[71]

Post-dictatorship, a succession of royal pardons resulted in some common, as opposed to political, criminals being released to roam the streets, but an argument could be made that the distinction does not withstand close scrutiny in the immediate aftermath of a regime that systematically criminalised the poor, failing to address even their most basic needs Throughout the Transition, Eleuturio Sánchez, a.k.a. El Lute, who had been jailed for over two years for stealing hens to eat in 1965 and had gone on to gain celebrity status by virtue of bank robberies and daring prison breaks, was a constant media presence. His memoirs were best-sellers, and he was even the subject of a minor international 1977 hit by Boney M, in which the eponymous protagonist is compared to Robin Hood, his release equated to Spain's democratisation. In 1981, Carlos Saura was presenting his latest film, *Deprisa, deprisa* (*Quickly, Quickly*) (1981), at the Berlin Film Festival, when lead actor, José Antonio Valdelomar, was detained after carrying out a bank robbery.[72] The arresting officer, Juan Antonio González Pacheco, was known amongst his colleagues as Billy el Niño (the Kid), renowned for the vicious torture of suspects. In spite of numerous legal attempts to remove his privileges, at the time of writing he still receives a bonus in addition to his standard police pension thanks to an order of merit awarded in 1977. Valdelomar died in 1992, whilst serving a sentence in Carbanchel prison.

In theory, the 1979 penitentiary act was inspired by Constitutional principles but, according to Mónica Aranda Ocaña and Iñaki Rivera Beiras, 'it did nothing to change the harsh conditions experienced by inmates under regimes which were inherited from the fascist dictatorship'.[73] In spite of the political amnesty, ETA's activities and rising criminality resulted in a record number of inmates. In the 1960s, the novelist Carmen Laforet was shocked on travelling to the USA to hear about levels of violence there in comparison with her city of residence, Madrid, 'where one can go for a walk at midnight with almost the same peace of mind as at midday';[74] her tour guide was reportedly surprised by the young female protagonist of *Nada* being free to roam the streets of Barcelona at night without being bothered. That apologists of the dictatorship so frequently referred to safety as one of its crowning achievements perhaps understandably led many progressive voices to downplay the increase in crime that, albeit exaggerated, was taking place. The unfulfilled challenge was to maintain a serious debate on alarming crime figures without falling into the trap of denying what was taking place on the streets or, alternatively, scapegoating democracy as the culprit.

Belying the more anodyne accounts of the ostensibly peaceful Transition, literary and cinematic images of Barcelona and Madrid made frequent recourse to neon and noir, 'a genre for which there were no significant antecedents in the Spanish literary tradition',[75] to render physically and psychically oppressive dystopian cityscapes, populated with alienated and frequently homicidal protagonists, in which the ills of the Francoist legacy and advanced capitalism collide in a sometimes lethal cocktail. *Bilbao* (Bigas Luna, 1978) is akin to a more perverse Spanish or Catalan variation on *Taxi Driver* (Martin Scorsese, 1976) – seedy nightclubs around the Ramblas offering a correlative to Times Square – lacking the romanticism or redemption of the New York fable. Barcelona is shown to be as claustrophobic as the interiors where dysfunctional sexual and familial relations are the norm. The opening aerial shots of Madrid's Gran Vía in the noir detective thriller *El crack* (José Luis Garci, 1981) dwell on the neon lights of the cinema to foreground a penumbral Spanish Broadway, elements of nostalgia colliding with fear about the present and for the future.

In literature, the most-loved example of a boom in crime fiction was Manuel Vázquez Montalbán's Pepe Carvalho detective series, commencing in 1972 with *Yo maté a Kennedy* (*I Killed Kennedy*). The author, raised in the less disreputable parts of the Raval,[76] was similar to Joan Manuel Serrat, about whom he published the first serious study, in his talent for distilling life experience – including incarceration for anti-Francoist activities where he and his wife annoyed fellow prisoners by playing French chansons[77] – and a university education. In the words of Mari Paz Balibrea:

> in creating the Carvalho saga, Manuel Vázquez Montalbán isn't just chronicling the Transition to democracy from the critical perspective of someone on the left who feels betrayed. He is also creating an alter-ego who faces the reality of his criminal cases in much the same way the intellectual engages with the world he criticises through all his interactions.[78]

In *Los mares del Sur* (*Southern Seas*), first published in 1979, property developer Stuart Pedrell, turns up dead in his car in San Magín, a satellite town he himself constructed for workers coming to work in the recently opened SEAT factories in the late 1950s. Marketed as 'a new city for a new life',[79] San Magín is compared unfavourably by Carvalho with the Raval: 'The ugly poverty of Chinatown had a patina of history. It didn't resemble in the least the poverty prefabricated by prefabricated speculators, the prefabricators of prefabricated neighbourhoods. It is preferable that poverty be sordid as opposed to mediocre.'[80] The narrative is predicated on the investigation of two crimes: the original sin of urban construction, a metaphor for the capitulation of Catalan business interests and Francoism, and the murder of Pedrell presented as a form of repentance and poetic justice when, with a sense of guilt, he returns to the scene of the original crime and begins an affair with Ana Briongos, a factory worker who belongs to the Communist Party. Carvalho encounters a new kind of criminal: knife-wielding second-generation migrants, the unwanted children of Francoism who refuse to be grateful for any crumbs they might be thrown. By 1979, Spain had fourteen youth detention centres,[81] and in that year the police arrested 16,898 minors (defined as those under 21),[82] a high number in relative, albeit not absolute, terms.

The Government began surveying victims in 1978.[83] Crime was encroaching on the respectable parts of the city, with cars stolen and bags snatched, and a rising number of armed bank robberies. In a context where the figure of the *quinqui* was increasingly a source of popular fascination and media concern, *Perros callejeros* (*Street Dogs*) (José

Antonio de la Loma, 1977) capitalised on the phenomenon, heralding the arrival of the most consistently popular cinematic genre of the late 1970s and early 1980s, which would enjoy a healthy afterlife through video piracy and informal, frequently outdoor, screenings. The film opens with a shot of Antoni Gaudí's Sagrada Família. A voiceover informs the audience that Barcelona, like any other city, has emblematic sites, but that rapid urbanisation has resulted in slums and that, yes, justice is required to tackle crimes but so too is compassion. The action takes place in La Mina, a neighbourhood that, since the construction of a theme park on Montjuic in 1966, had become the default choice for relocating slum dwellers.[84]

The *quinqui* films blurred fact and fiction, being stylised biographies of real-life youth delinquents who often appeared as themselves, establishing a precedent for transforming poor and barely pubescent rebels into meta-criminals and cultural archetypes. *Perros callejeros* was inspired by the exploits of José Juan Moreno Cuenca (a.k.a. El Vaquilla – the name for a young bull). Madrid's National Library holds the handwritten manuscript of Moreno Cuenca's prison diaries,[85] which formed the basis of his published memoirs.[86] A keen intellect failed by the school system (there are basic spelling mistakes such as 'avitacion' for *habitación*, or 'trabieso' for *travieso*) emerges alongside savvy self-representation as a modern-day Lazarillo de Tormes, a noble savage persona honed by media appearances. The young criminal was supposed to play himself but his incarceration made this unfeasible.[87] El Torete, another convicted felon, was cast in his place. A generic trait was self-consciously to flag the meta-fictional nature of the films and their characters.

In *Navajeros* (Eloy de la Iglesia, 1980), José Sacristán played a sociologist investigating Madrid's knife-wielding adolescents, whose leader was played by José Luis Manzano, a fourteen-year-old rent boy who learnt of auditions for the film when plying for trade in public toilets.[88] With 'his chiselled features and distinctive curly locks',[89] this native of Vallecas with no formal education (Iglesia, who would become his lover as well as director, was fascinated when he first took him back to his flat and the young lad un-self-consciously used a book on Eurocommunism to light up a spliff[90]) became 'the most striking cover boy for the "quinqui" sub-culture, frequently appearing in the pages of weekly magazines, such as *Fotogramas* and *Interviú*, and even on the cover of *Party*, Spain's first gay magazine'.[91] *Los últimos golpes de Torete* (*The Last Blows of Torete*) (José Antonio de la Loma, 1980) features two investigative journalists, based on radio presenters Encarna Sánchez and Luis del Olmo, who respectively championed empathetic and zero-tolerance approaches to youth criminality in their shows.

The full box-office potential of *Navajeros* was never realised because proprietors of numerous city-centre cinemas, fearful of the audiences it was attracting, prematurely ended its run. At an outdoor showing in Getafe, members of the audience destroyed the screen following a scene of police violence.[92] The incongruous incorporation of funk bass lines into *Perros callejeros* highlights that the *quinqui* genre was the closest Spanish equivalent to the Blaxploitation films that had packed out US cinemas in the early-to-mid 1970s. Numerous follow-ups and sequels relied on the modern Spanish rumba, as popularised by Los Chichos, Los Chunguitos or Los Amaya, 'which combined aspects of traditional flamenco with glossy, disco and pop-inflected production values'.[93] If the success of the *cine quinqui* was most evident in flea-pit cinemas where traditional social realism held little currency, musically literate soundscapes, which provided the soundtrack to real-life slums, constituted a more nihilistic and fatalistic form of protest song than the Nova Cançó. Los Chunguitos had moved from rural Extremadura to Vallecas as youngsters, whilst Los Chichos – whom Moreno Cuenca would play when carrying out robberies in real life[94] – recorded the soundtrack to *Yo, el Vaquilla*, and performed concerts in prisons as an act of solidarity and publicity stunt.[95]

The films were clearly of interest to the public, but to what extent were they in the public interest? When De la Loma first submitted *Perros callejeros* for classification, he attached a carefully worded ten-page document making an ethical case for his project. He claims to have been sensitive to the problems of the young since selflessly accepting a badly paid job as a teacher in the Raval in 1954, and that in making the movie he had been in constant contact with the Guardia Civil who, he claimed, carried out important labour in trying to recuperate these young boys, something he believes he was also doing by providing them with the opportunity to become stars.[96] He says not to pay attention to complaints made by neighbourhood associations, which he dismisses as self-interested and biased; there is a veiled threat in claims that he deliberately excised the sexual abuse of adolescent boys by staff at youth detention centres, or beatings to which they were subjected by the forces of order.[97] Conversely, in a letter dated 20 January 1977, a group of local teachers complained to the Ministry that De la Loma was trading in sensationalism with a crassly anti-Gypsy film (a trader in stolen wares castrates the protagonist for having sex with his niece, and treats her as damaged goods, subsequently prostituting her out) that is, they claim, fostering rather than discouraging criminality amongst young non-professional actors, paid enough to feel stars and neglect their education, but not enough to extricate themselves from their marginal situations. For *Navajeros*, Manzano received 300,000 pesetas to take the lead role; Sacristán was paid 400,000 for little more than a glorified cameo.[98]

Prurience was a generic trait, but the ratio of sociology to exploitation varied, as can be seen in relation to depictions of Barcelona's prolific but precarious sex-trade. Ignacio F. Iquino followed up *Los violadores del amanecer* (see Chapter 5) with *Las que empiezan a los quince años* (*Those who Start at Fifteen*) (1978), which presents young girls as innocents in a corrupt world, but takes sadistic pleasure in multiple rape scenes. *Barcelona sur* (*South Barcelona*) (Jordi Cadena, 1981) privileges American-style modernity over Catalan modernism, dwelling on images of burger bars or pop-punk group Blondie playing on the television. The opening scene depicts a young woman coming out of prison and being met by a girlfriend, whose male companion pimps her out. Physical abuse of prostitutes is depicted as part of everyday life, but a gang rape prompts them to fight back, culminating in a discotheque shoot out.

Extolling violence and crime might not be a constructive response to the challenges of urban malaise, but cinematic pulp fictions affectively communicated the same question articulated by *Los mares al sur* and to which the next two chapters turn: how might it be possible to experience the city in democratic fashion when it has been forged in the likeness of a dictatorial regime?

Chapter 8

The Movida and the reinvention of Madrid

In order to appreciate Madrid's cultural renaissance in the early 1980s, it is first necessary to understand how and why it lagged behind the Catalan capital in the aftermath of Franco's death despite, or perhaps even because of, the fact that, in Joan Ramón Resina's diagnosis, 'Barcelona was structurally unhinged, architecturally disgraced, socially torn apart, and cultural split.'[1] According to Federico Jiménez Losantos: 'At the beginning of the 1970s, thousands and thousands of young people from all over Spain came to Barcelona in search of liberty.'[2] Pepe Ribas, founder of anarchist cultural magazine *Ajoblanco* (named after an Andalusian peasant speciality, garlic and almond soup), speaks of the importance of a King Crimson concert in Granollers, a small city close to Barcelona, that, to his mind, inspired a libertarian parenthesis: 'Without politicians or institutions there were many who for four years – from 1974 to 1977 – nursed the dream of a genuine change in our society.'[3] Run-down housing in Barcelona's old town was far from ideal for families or its many elderly occupants, but offered cheap rents with proximity to both the sea and a plethora of drinking holes for new arrivals in search of adventure.

Comic-book writer Nazario lived in the Plaça Reial, his most famous creation, Anacroma – a transvestite with an extravagant nocturnal social life – first appearing in 1978, a year before homosexuality was decriminalised in Spain, and finding a permanent home in *El Víbora*, an adult comic aimed at young people created in 1979.[4] As Rafael M. Mérida Jiménez notes: 'The Spanish political Transition was very *trans* in Barcelona.'[5] Having tired of Madrid's conservatism, the cross-dressing Ocaña – a native of Andalusia as prone to quoting García Lorca as to exposing his penis on the Ramblas – moved to the Plaça Reial and made Barcelona his own theatrical stage until he died in service, inadvertently setting himself alight when performing as the sun. The cinematic documentary *Ocaña, retrat interminent* (*Ocaña, an Intermittent Portrait*) (Ventura Pons, 1978) was promoted as the first Catalan film to be rendered in Andalusian.[6] In contrast to the first post-Franco films in Catalan – *La nova cançó* (*The New Song*) (Francesc Bellmunt, 1976) and *La ciutat cremada* (*The Burnt City*) (Antoni Ribas, 1976)[7] – responses had focused on its Barcelona-ness as opposed to its Catalan-ness.[8] Featuring a large Catalan ensemble cast including singer-songwriter Joan Manuel Serrat, *La ciutat cremada* charted Barcelona's history from the loss of Spanish colonies in 1898 to the Tragic Week of 1909. With violent clashes between the army and workers, the literary adaptation did not eschew darker aspects of the urban past (exploitation, complicity with the Primo de Rivera dictatorship), but the premiere was a Catalan 'happening'. Attended by politicians, intellectuals and artists, its closing credits were followed by a recital of the Catalan national anthem, 'Els segadors', banned under Franco.[9]

The title and theme of Ribas's film could not have been more apposite. As Ramón Resina surmises: 'To be again someday, Barcelona had to be, in the long decades of the Franco regime, a remembered city.'[10] Rebel city credentials were the product and cause of a burgeoning counter-culture, and yet an ethic and aesthetic rooted in what Andreas Huyssen has in another context termed 'cities and buildings as palimpsests of space' in which the 'strong marks of present space merge in the imaginary with traces of the past, erasures, losses, and heterotopias'[11] did not provide a natural or comfortable habitat for the personal and professional aspirations of its youthful protagonists. In the words of Alberto Mira: 'Whereas for bourgeois intellectuals, nationalist demands were prominent in the early 1970s … a nationalist agenda seems to have been absent in the artistic underground.'[12] These parallel realities cohabited for a time but, in a post-Constitutional landscape – where nationalist aspirations now had a framework, albeit circumscribed (see Part IV), in which to articulate demands – the baton of youthful creative enterprise passed to Madrid.

An iconic photo, which graces the front cover of Germán Labrador Méndez's latest book,[13] featuring two nude adolescents on top of a human statue in the Dos de Mayo Square in Madrid's Malasaña district, has been put to talismanic effect to embody post-Franco liberation. However, as the author reminds us, attention to the context in which it was taken in 1977 tells a different story. The 15-year-old girl fell and broke her arm; police charged and attacked the assembled crowd with tear gas; the May Day civic festivities were cancelled.[14] With the PSOE increasingly able to monopolise the left-wing vote, Tierno Galván agreed to his political formation – the Partido Socialista Popular – being amalgamated into González's party, and set his sights on becoming Mayor of Madrid. His election in 1979 was the first major post-Franco victory for the Spanish left, providing a progressive alternative to his predecessors in office – José Luis Álvarez y Álvarez and Luis María Huete – at a time when dictatorial ghosts took on physical, not just spectral, forms: Blas Piñar's bully-boys from Fuerza Nueva carried out attacks on buildings and people; bombings by extreme right-wing groups were not uncommon (e.g. the Guerrilleros de Cristo Rey blew up counter-cultural hangout La Vaquería on 6 June 1978); and the police continued to act with impunity. During the Transition and beyond, (in)tolerance in Barcelona and Madrid was experienced in different ways. Jiménez Losantos's subsequent reactionary turn can be traced back to his being kidnapped and shot in the knee in 1981 by pro-Catalan independence party Terra Libre for his parliamentary ambitions to represent the interests of all citizens of Catalonia, irrespective of their birthplace. The trajectory of this public intellectual turned media pundit, and such political violence, are atypical, but do illuminate the extent to which nationalism was the major axis of inclusion/exclusion in Barcelona; the correlative in Madrid orientated around the desirability of democracy as a form of civic and national(ist) order.

As both a reaction against the triumphalist discourse of Francoism and an acceptance that the dictatorial city par excellence lacked Barcelona's architecture, mountains and sea views, a new counter-civic pride was articulated in cultural production in relation to the city's human fauna for its inclusivity and conviviality under frequently difficult circumstances. Before providing music for some of the most emblematic films of the Transition, such as *¿Qué hace una chica como tú en un sitio como este?* (*What's a Girl like You Doing in a Place Like This?*) (Fernando Colomo, 1979) and *Navajeros*, the heavy-metal band Burning, from La Elipa (a neighbourhood close to Las Ventas bullring, predominantly consisting of public housing erected in the 1960s), released their breakthrough hit 'Madrid' in 1976. The city is personified as a lover the protagonist cannot live with or without: 'Hey Madrid, I hate you / But what can I do / I can't leave you / and be left without a woman.' If Joan Manuel Serrat's 'Mediterráneo' (Mediterranean) is regularly voted the best popular song in the Castilian language, Joaquín Sabina is the capital's poet laureate and the only living singer-songwriter to rival the musical wordsmanship and commercial appeal of el noi del Poble Sec. The native of Úbeda (Andalusia), born in 1949, penned 'Yo me bajo en Atocha' ('I'm getting off at Atocha) about the experience of rural emigration to an adopted home which, Sabina claims, is a different beast from Barcelona where 'your surname and social background count for a lot';[15] 'I belong to the first generation who use Madrid to make poetry, to turn the city into a myth, to turn it into Babylon.'[16] Released in 1980, 'Pongamos que hablo de Madrid' (Let's say that I'm talking about Madrid) quickly became the city's unofficial anthem, with its artillery of ostensibly negative images – 'girls no longer want to be princesses'; 'birds visit the psychiatrist'; 'the sun is a gas heater' – despite, or perhaps because of, which, the singer, and the complicit listener, love their urban habitat.

Like the other recently elected Socialist mayors, Tierno Galván inherited a dysfunctional city and faced scepticism from large swathes of the population due to the left's purported inability to lead without a descent into chaos. Hamilton Stapell presents the former academic and lawyer, popularly known as the 'Viejo Profesor' (Old Professor), as the chief architect of a Cornucopian revolution in the capital's sense of self and outward image, able 'to transform Madrid from an authoritarian "fortress" to a democratic "plaza"'.[17] Absorbing the dynamism of the neighbourhood associations, Tierno Galván handed over many civic building projects to progressive architects, endeavoured to improve public transport and infrastructure, put the police on retraining schemes, and increased green spaces.[18] He was also careful not to package his progressive agenda in a threatening fashion, the lifelong agnostic making sure to attend the Almudena mass so as to build bridges with the Catholic Church. A less flattering portrait emerges from César Alonso de los Ríos's book-length denunciation of self-interested hypocrisy, 'the creation of a social and political image, some facts invented, others hidden, all deployed for specific political and cultural goals'.[19] The two interpretations are not mutually exclusive; both can be discerned in Tierno Galván's romance with the young people of Madrid. In 1981, over half of Madrid's population were under 30 and only 10 per cent were over the age of 65.[20] Against a backdrop of recession and vertiginous youth unemployment, it made civic and electoral sense for a progressive Mayor to court the 1.1 million inhabitants aged between 15 and 30 dwelling in a compact city.

The Old Professor adopted the paternalistic habit of issuing edicts to the inhabitants of Madrid in which they were instructed in their rights and responsibilities as democratic citizens. An attempt to transcend traditional divisions of left and right to explore more holistic notions of what it means to be a good neighbour were instrumental to cultural production from Madrid, providing an opportunity for revitalising civic pride in a non-chauvinistic and less centralist guise. This is manifest in the production and reception of *Las bicicletas son para el verano* (*Bicycles Are for the Summer*), the first new play to enjoy major commercial and critical success on the post-Franco Spanish stage. Written by Fernando Fernán-Gómez, a popular face from cinema and television, the play depicts the inhabitants of Madrid during the Civil War, irrespective of their political affiliations, as victims of circumstances beyond their control. Born in 1921, Fernán-Gómez was a war child, who has gone on record as claiming he supported the rebels until he saw the consequences of their politics and policies in the postwar period.[21] The play's most devastating line occurs at its close, when Madrid has fallen, and Don Luis responds to a comment about the end of war: 'Peace hasn't arrived Luis: it is the time of victory.'[22] Acerbic social commentary of this kind might not have been allowed only a few years earlier on the mainstream theatrical stage, but the play's presentation of a flattering image of the capital's convivial inhabitants ensured it was a non-threatening interrogation of the past and an example for the present. In the words of Agustín González, a stalwart of Rafael Gil's cinematic adaptations of Fernando Vizcaíno Casas's reactionary best-sellers (see Chapter 2), who played Don Luis on the Madrid stage:

> it didn't directly relate with the situation everyone was going through in Spain at that time but, one way or another, it served to reconcile the opposing feelings of both sides, not only during the war but afterwards, even during the years of the Transition with the incidents that took place in the street. Well, those who found themselves in opposition to each other were reconciled in the theatre and experienced together the performance in a state of ecstasy and overjoyed by the play's humour.[23]

Both the composition of the play (albeit not its most successful theatrical run) and Tierno Galván's election predated the failed coup of 23 February 1981, but the notion of tolerance as a panacea amongst Madrid's inhabitants became hegemonic dogma in the aftermath of Tejero's failed attempt to hold Parliament and, by implication, democracy to ransom.

As the Mayor announced in his message of 1 December 1981: 'It would be an affront to the neighbours of this noble burg not to come together in the legitimate emulation of the other towns, burgs and cities of our country to make a public and pacific demonstration, as good customs and public decorum demand, of love and enthusiasm for our Constitution.'[24] Madrid was shedding traditional inferiority and superiority complexes.

Eduardo Mendicutti's novel *Una mala noche la tiene cualquiera* (*Anyone Can Have a Bad Night*) established a popular trope for the capital as one big party placed under siege.[25] The narrative is told via an inner monologue by La Madelón, a gender-queer country lad from Andalusia locked in his Madrid home on the night of the coup, worried about the fate of their flatmate, the also-transgender La Begum. As they fondly recall shared experiences of the capital, disguising themselves as female members of the Falange to attend fascist rallies, and thinking ahead to growing old together, La Madelón wonders if freedom might have been a personal and political parenthesis: 'I thought about all of this, in that future awaiting us as queens, a vision of us all in the slaughterhouse.'[26]

Self-elected saviours of the *patria* would have had little sympathy for hedonistic transvestites; that said, only a combination of opportunism and tolerance had led arch-homophobe Tierno Galván (see Chapter 5) to become the patron-saint of the Movida, in which 'queer culture took the lead in the lively debates about modernism and postmodernism'.[27] As Peter McDonough, Samuel H. Barnes and Antonio López Pina note: 'The values of the disco left disturb the gothic right. However, they do not necessarily promote ideological consistency or a groundswell of involvement in the traditional parties of labor organization of the left.'[28] Franco was not the sole or even the primary figure by whom the leading lights of the Movida felt silenced; they reacted more against what they perceived to be the excessive politicisation of Spanish society than any particular ideology in and of itself. Alaska, the teenage punk-pop singer and star of Almodóvar's debut feature film *Pepi, Luci, Bom y otras chicas del montón* (*Pepi, Luci, Bom and Other Girls like Mom*) (1980), was born in Mexico in 1963 to a Spanish Republican exile and a mother who had fled Castro's Cuba.[29] Vocally uninterested in politics, she adopted her stage name aged 14 from Lou Reed's 'Caroline says', the lyrics of which she came across in an edition of glam songs translated by Eduardo Haro Ibars (son of journalist Eduardo Haro Tecglen) titled *Gay Rock*. Wearing a Kiss T-shirt her mother had bought in New York, she met band mates Nacho Canut and Carlos Berlanga in Madrid's historic flea market, the Rastro, where they were selling copies of the comic that the child of celebrated filmmaker Luis García Berlanga had set up with one of Vizcaíno Casas's sons.[30]

Almodóvar's early films are the younger, more irreverent siblings of the so-called Madrid comedies – *Tigres de papel* (*Paper Tigers*) (Fernando Colomo, 1977), *Ópera prima* (*Opera Prima*) (Fernando Trueba, 1981) and *Vecinos* (*Neighbours*) (Alberto Bermejo, 1981) – to emerge from a loose network of cinephile ex-students from the Complutense; depicting men in their twenties struggling with adulthood, responsibility and relationships, this genre 'was strikingly akin to Woody Allen's mature comedies of the 1970s',[31] albeit set against the backdrop of a personal and political disillusionment with the path democracy had taken.[32] Almodóvar was, however, older than the rest of the Movida's leading lights, and was also unusual in coming from a humble background in rural La Mancha when most came from well-to-do urban(e) families. Animosity between Nacho Canut, whose father was one of the country's leading dentists, and Mecano, Spain's best-selling pop group of all time, could be traced back to their days as classmates at the same elite schools: Alaska's bandmate believed them to be opportunistically jumping on a bandwagon, as they had never shown much interest in music during their teenage years.

Tierno Galván made an unannounced appearance at the launch, at the five-star Palace Hotel, of Mecano's debut album, and the mainstream media started taking an interest in the Movida.[33] Bullfighting was the Mayor's cultural passion, but he had no compunction in setting a precedent for local authorities to use public money to subsidise pop concerts. If he was unable to offer young people jobs, he could at least facilitate their having a good time, and he was willing to use municipal funds to do so. In a glowing review of a carefully choreographed concert by Tina Turner in Madrid, Andrés Amorós notes how the lights failed at the beginning, prompting the diva to return to her dressing room:

> Widespread disappointment. Patience. That's the moment Don Enrique Tierno exploited to appear down the stairwell next to the stage. The public, bored, awarded him a standing ovation: that's a Socialist Mayor, one who turns up to a 'soul' concert … Signing autographs and shaking hands, like an American candidate … One small detail, that almost nobody noticed: Tina Turner had barely started her first song, whilst her 'fans' were in a trance, and Mayor Tierno quietly slipped out. He had already heard the concert that interested him. José Luis Álvarez, I suppose, wouldn't even have done that.[34]

The most iconic Madrid concert of the early-to-mid 1980s was that given by the Rolling Stones, whose debut Spanish concert, staged in a vastly undersold-out bullring in Barcelona in 1976, had been marred by police violence. Promoter Gay Mercader brought them back to play the country's two biggest cities to coincide with Spain's hosting of the

World Cup. As the poet Luis Cremades notes, two sold-out nights at the Bernabeu Stadium seemed like 'manna from heaven that signalled Madrid as the chosen city',[35] the presence of Socialist politicians at the home of Real Madrid a sign that the times they were a-changing.

Up to the late 1970s, interest and trade in modern art were concentrated in Barcelona;[36] a group of artists and dealers from Seville sought to drum up interest for a commercial art fair in the Catalan capital but obstacles were put in their way. By contrast, as the director of the first edition, Juana de Aizpura, recalls, Tierno Galván could not have been more supportive, 'as he saw the fair as a springboard to turn Madrid into the city that he wanted'.[37] Tax relief was used to entice international dealers to an annual event that continues to the present day; the 25,000 visitors who attended in 1982 increased annually, with 154,000 attending in 1992.

Following Jordi Pujol's election as President of the Catalan Generalitat in 1980, nationalism was privileged at the expense of almost everything else, culture and having a good time included. Philosopher Félix de Azúa famously evoked the image of Barcelona as an asphalt Titanic: 'its nights are getting shorter and shorter', and 'before long this city will resemble a convent school'.[38] Picking up on the image, local rock star Loquillo speaks of wanting to escape the Catalan city walls: 'In Madrid, I forgot all about the political circus that seemed to have taken possession of all of us as if it were the only thing of importance'.[39] Decamping to the Spanish capital made good business-sense for young artists. Slots on TVE such as *Aplauso* (*Applause*) (1978–83), *La edad de oro* (*The Golden Age*) (1983–85) and *La bola de cristal* (*The Crystal Ball*) (1984–88) were instrumental in broadcasting Madrid-based music and pop culture nationally, whilst subsidies acted as a powerful magnet. Early in their careers, many leading Madrid-based graphic artists were dependent on a Barcelona-based publishing industry,[40] but this tendency reversed in the early-to-mid 1980s with a boom in comics, most famously *Madriz*, funded by the city council.[41] This tactic ultimately proved counter-productive, with insufficient demand for a saturated market.[42] Still, it constituted an important manifestation of how and why, in Yaw Agawu-Kakraba's words, '[d]rawing on tendencies in the emerging post-Franco consumer culture that favour the aestheticization of life, postmodernism within the Spanish context emphasizes a continuous pursuit of new experiences, values and vocabularies'.[43] In *El Víbora*, Almodóvar published a photo-novel – later recycled for a scene in sophomore film *Laberinto de pasiones* (*Labyrinth of Passions*) (1982) – titled *Todo tuya* (*All Yours*), starring Fabio McNamara as Patty Diphusa, 'an endearing optimist and megalomaniac' porn star.[44] Diphusa enjoyed a healthy afterlife in the Socialist-endorsed *La luna de Madrid* (*The Moon of Madrid*), designed as a hybrid of New York's *Village Voice* and Andy Warhol's *Interview*. From its inception in November 1983 to its closure five years and forty-eight issues later, the magazine focused on everything on offer in the capital as opposed to Spanish culture per se.

In the November 1984 issue, Paloma Chamorro, presenter of *La edad de oro*, admitted criticism for having favoured Madrid-based musicians and artists but that: 'This is the case for many reasons. First, because the programme is made in Madrid and second because so many things happen here. In Madrid many more things happen – what I'm going to say sounds blasphemous – than in the rest of the Peninsula combined.'[45] *La luna de Madrid* could be the victim of vaulting ambition – see, for example, a cringeworthy interview with French philosopher Jean-François Lyotard about postmodernism[46] – but was instrumental in breaking down barriers between high and popular culture, providing compelling evidence that Chamorro's claim was not merely a reiteration of centralist chauvinism, and that Tierno Galván's Madrid was a global cultural capital. In Maite Usoz de la Fuente's description, *La luna de Madrid* showcased 'an awareness of the all-encompassing nature and generative power of space',[47] privileging a positive reciprocity between city and citizen.

If, as Noël Valis notes, La Movida was 'a paradoxical blend of local themes and postmodern displacement',[48] this is both the product and cause of a performative reiteration of what Susan Larson characterises as 'a micronationalist Madrilenian identity'[49] that gained a new momentum in the wake of the coup. Francisco Umbral, a middle-aged journalist and novelist, reported his fascination with Alaska in his newspaper columns and elsewhere,[50] addressing his readership from the Café Gijón, now familiar to cinema-going audiences through the cinematic adaptation of Camilo José Cela's postwar novel *La colmena* (*The Beehive*) (see Chapter 6). An ostensibly counter-intuitive interest by Umbral in the Movida can be attributed to the shared desires for advocating tolerance and vindicating local urban space that cut across generations and media. His barracks may have been a literary café as opposed to Rock-Ola – the live music venue, which on opening in 1981 had only programmed international acts such as Spandau Ballet on weekends to guarantee full audiences but which changed the policy in 1982 because of the popularity of many Movida bands[51] – but the titling of his column as 'Spleen de Madrid' was an indication that Madrid warranted chronicling in the manner of the French capital in Baudelaire. The nineteenth-century Parisian arcades were now the bars of Malasaña and the terraces of the Castellana Avenue, but there was less of an ambivalent or self-reflective approach to urban consumption than was on display amongst earlier generations of *flâneurs*. The chance encounters and spontaneous exchanges of the realist novels of Benito Pérez Galdós (on which Tierno Galván was a published authority), Marcel Proust or Anthony Powell were less likely to happen in the late twentieth century, but the compact geography and ecumenism of Madrid in the early-to-mid 1980s resulted in a hybrid of premodern sociality and postmodern sensibility, embodying what Alberto Medina defines as 'the authentic character of a new form of democracy that, precisely, demanded the de-politicisation of the population as a basic pre-condition.'[52]

Almodóvar's much repeated quote that he wanted to make films as if Franco had never existed has been contradicted not only by his later cinema, but also by the youthful exuberance of his early work. An adolescent desire to shock implies a desire to express what was previously repressed. The blithe attitude to formal politics reflected in the 'general erections' competition in *Pepi, Luci, Bom* is replicated in the following exchange from a Patty Diphusa strip, which originally appeared in *La luna de Madrid*:

PATTY:	What I am trying to say is that if I am meant to be a Socialist.
PEDRO:	No, but you wouldn't mind sleeping with Felipe González.
PATTY:	Then, to a certain extent I am a socialist. Because with Fraga, for example, I wouldn't have sex. Right?[53]

In real life, Alaska became a celebrity interviewer for *Primera línea* magazine. Marcelino Camacho – the trade unionist whose early release from prison in early 1975 resulted from the political amnesty called for by King Juan Carlos – is her most enthusiastic subject when questioned about reading gossip magazines and playing video-games. Interviewees are asked whom they would like to have sex with out of Dolly Parton, Grace Jones and Ángela Molina: Camacho says 'So that they don't say I'm a racist I'll go for the black girl',[54] Cela says it depends on the time of day,[55] and Manuel Fraga boasts 'with all of them, I say it again, with all of them'.[56]

Artists associated with the Movida pre-existed the PSOE's rise to power, but socio-political patronage imbued them with a collective identity and visibility that would otherwise have been difficult to attain. The General Department of Youth and Socio-Cultural Promotion already existed under the UCD, and a new in-house journal suggested that 'the drop-out or indifferent reactions of young people' were a 'form of response to a hostile society that affords them precious few opportunities'.[57] This was not, however, translated into concrete policies, let alone actions. From the beginning of their time in office, the PSOE were keen that Spain take an active role in the UN's upcoming 'Year of Youth' in 1985; Socialist politicians were also aware that young people were more likely to vote for them than other age-groups, and that they were disproportionately centred in Madrid and Barcelona, where, against a national average of 16.5 per cent, 24 per cent of the population were aged between 16 and 25.[58] A draft policy document dated 2 February 1983 about upcoming cultural events notes that:

> Sería importante extraer de la 'movida' – cultura de los últimos quince años – a todo la 'pléyade' de músicos, actores, animadores, etc. que, a pesar de estar ajenos deliberadamente de los órganos convencionales de información 'olvidados' de cualquier tipo de ayuda, y es más, privándoles

con facilidad de algo tan preciado como la libertad de expresarse, han sido y lo están siendo, el punto de referencia mágico de una gran mayoría de las generaciones contemporáneas.[59]

It will be important to extract from the 'movida' – culture of the last fifteen years – that 'hall of fame' of musicians actors, performers who, in spite of being deliberately distanced from the conventional organs of communication, 'forgotten' by any form of subsidy that can so easily take away from them something as valued as freedom of expression, have and continue to be a magical point of reference for the grand majority of the younger generations.

Often referred to as Spanish punk, the successful co-option of at least some Madrid-based bands was both the cause and consequence of their having less subcultural capital than their British antecedents. The closest Spanish equivalent was La Banda Trapera del Río, from a satellite industrial town outside Barcelona in 1976, whose 'Ciutat podrida' (Rotten City) (with none of the humour or affection of Burning or Sabina) was the first hard-rock song recorded in Catalan. In any case, the less ideological New York punk scene, which mixed street smarts with the snobbery and sophistication of the Warhol art-scene, was a greater influence on the Movida; as Alaska says, for them, photographer Robert Mapplethorpe coming to Madrid was the equivalent to a visit by the Backstreet Boys for a young female fan.[60] From Alaska and Dinarama's '¡A quién le importa!' (What is it to them!) to Mecano's 'Hoy no me puedo levantar' (I can't get out of bed today) via Radio Futura's 'Enamorado de una moda juvenil' (In love with a youthful fashion), the sonic jewels from the Golden Age of Spanish pop privilege personal over parliamentary freedoms.

The Movida's carefully rehearsed flippancy and ostensibly detached aestheticism – what Eduardo Subirats dismisses as corrupt and corrupting consumerism, 'a picaresque version of mercantilism and, on too many occasions, an ancestral pride'[61] – have been diagnosed as a retreat from history and politics, 'the hangover resulting from the utopian content of the superstructure comprising cultural resistance to the dictatorship'[62] Nevertheless, as Paul Julian Smith notes, it 'can be accused of apoliticism only if the political is restricted to formal governance'.[63]

Drawing on empirical research in the USA, political scientist Diana Mutz explores the 'inherent tension between promoting a society with enthusiastically participative citizens and promoting one imbued with tolerance and respect for differences of opinion'.[64] What she terms 'enclave deliberation', characteristic of active politicisation, is both the product and the cause of exclusionary partisan tactics; 'there is no easy answer to the question of how much political inactivity should be accepted in the name of greater tolerance nor, conversely, of how much intolerance of opposition should be accepted in the name of encouraging political activism'.[65] In a more recent polemic, titled *Against Democracy*, Jason Brennan argues that 'decline in political engagement is a *good start*, but we still have a long way to go. We should hope for even less participation, not more.'[66] His rationale is that '[p]olitics tends to make us hate each other, even when it shouldn't. We tend to divide the world into good and bad guys. We tend to view political debate not as reasonable disputes about how to best achieve our shared aims but rather as a battle between the forces of light and darkness.'[67] Brenan's argument stands or falls on our faith in his faith in epistocracy. In what follows, I will make the case that drugs policy in the early democratic period suggests that Spaniards would have been ill-advised to place their trust in the rule of the knowledgeable.

By 1982, more heroin was being consumed in Spain than in the USA.[68] The Guardia Civil had been aware that the drug was being trafficked through Malaga as far back as 1969,[69] but Spaniards as consumers were latecomers to the party, the first registered lethal overdose occurring in 1976,[70] the same year in which Manuel Vázquez Montalbán's *Tatuaje* (*Tattoo*) – featuring references to drugs in Amsterdam and Barcelona, in which heroin was highlighted as a particularly harmful drug – appeared.[71] Rock band Burning befriended heroin addict Haro Ibars around this time, and were impressed by his cosmopolitan experiences.[72] Heroin chic was de rigueur: William Burroughs's *Junkie* came out in Spanish in 1976, and Lou Reed's *Rock 'n' Roll Animal*, released internationally in 1974, arrived in Spain in 1977, a sticker advertising the inclusion of the song 'Heroin'.[73] Scenes of characters shooting up feature in cult film classic

Arrebato (*Rapture*) (Iván Zuleta, 1979), in which Alaska makes an early cameo, heroin and cinephilia depicted as cool and complementary. By the late 1970s, hard drugs were increasingly being consumed by teenagers as young as 13 and 14,[74] often resorting to crime to feed their habits.

A rationale for legalising drugs is the far from implausible claim that providing support for addicts is a more effective cure than custodial sentences. No such logic or commitment was in place in Spain when the winds of change led to decriminalising the possession of heroin and change in the 1983 penal code.[75] Subsequent legislative redresses focused on criminal penalties as opposed to prevention strategies,[76] a kneejerk reaction to public outcry and media hysteria about drug-related crime. Madrid's City Hall had provided all possible facilities for the shooting of *Miedo a salir de noche* (*Fear of Going Out at Night*) (Eloy de la Iglesia, 1980), a parody of the boom in home security and paranoia about personal safety, in which a secretary invents a story of being raped in order to gain the attention of her male boss. In 1984, it became the first of the director's films to be screened by the State broadcaster,[77] at a time when Spain had recently acquired the global record for the highest number of annual bank robberies despite not having a particularly large population.[78] That same year, Tierno Galván seemingly encouraged a young crowd to get drugged up through the use of a colloquialism – 'Rockeros: el que no esté colocado, que se coloque … y al loro' (Rockers, whoever isn't high, time to play catch-up and get high) – at a live music event. This contrasted with the sentiments expressed in one of his regular radio broadcasts, where he instructed listeners not to smoke marijuana on the basis that it is a slippery slope from the consumption of soft to hard drugs.[79] Either the Old Professor was unaware of what he was saying to the assembled adolescent throng or he was irresponsibly willing to adapt his message to suit the audience at hand.

Following the appointment of Joaquín Leguina as the first President of the regional Government in 1983 – a non-historic and artificially created equivalent to the Catalan Generalitat (see Part IV) – all three tiers of political power in the capital came under PSOE control. Different layers of government inherited, collectively and individually, a dysfunctional urban model, with rising youth crime and unemployment, the latter a cause and the former a symptom of the largely undiagnosed drugs epidemic. Protected rents under the dictatorship had led home-owners actively to encourage disrepair, so as to allow them to evict tenants. According to Leguina's calculations, 70 per cent of properties in inner Madrid (calculated as being within the circumference of the M-30 ring-road) were classified as uninhabitable at the time of Franco's death.[80] On the one hand, Madrid's 1985 planning law 'was perhaps Spain's last great attempt at rational modernist urban planning with an emphasis on social justice',[81] an example of the municipal Socialists refusing to kowtow to an increasingly technocratic central Government; conversely, however, the laudable ideals of left-wing architects, frequently with histories of collaborating with neighbourhood associations, have been criticised for causing inflation and speculation when translated into practice.[82] Plans had been left in the pipeline so long that they took insufficient account of new circumstances created by the capital's spiralling crime and addiction rates. Leguina concedes he had no understanding of the drugs problem, let alone a potential solution, and put himself in the hands of Catholic organisation Cáritas.[83]

The first anti-drugs association appeared in 1978,[84] the same year Haro Ibars published an introductory guide to drugs that railed against heroin for reducing addicts to passive, emasculated consumers.[85] It was not, however, until 1986 that the first major national organisation, the Foundation for Help against Drug Addiction, presided over by Queen Sofia, emerged. This was an initiative from civil society, involving leading media figures, such as Jesús de Polanco, and businessmen to offer a free telephone line for addicts and their families, as well as attempting to change public perceptions by fostering the idea of addicts as suffering from an illness as opposed to pariahs who ought to be expelled from the Republic, and privileging prevention over cure with education campaigns for children from primary age upwards.[86] Support from institutions and individuals was widespread, but the Director-General of TVE, Pilar Miró, and Alfonso Guerra were suspicious of a non-public-sector organisation having such prominence, the Vice-President thinking the Red

Cross should deal with the crisis.[87] The intervention of Enrique Sarasola, González's unelected right-hand man (see Chapter 6), who, amongst other things, invited the Colombian narco-politician Pablo Escobar to the PSOE's 1982 victory celebrations,[88] convinced the President to ease tensions over the creation of the Foundation.

Not least amongst the reasons why it is impossible to understand Spain's Transition without reference to heroin is the fact that so many of the country's leading writers, filmmakers, sociologists and politicians have been directly involved with it in their personal and political lives. In 1986, Julio Feo received a phone call from Lola Flores about her son Antonio who, the folkloric singer claimed, was a recovering heroin addict; her immediate concern was that Antonio's ex-girlfriend, whom she held responsible for getting him hooked, was due to fly to Madrid from Argentina – her request (which was denied) was that Felipe González's private secretary block her entry visa.[89] The initial idea for the Foundation for Help against Drug Addiction came from 23-F hero Manuel Gutiérrez Mellado on witnessing the desperation of close personal friend and fellow General, Javier Calderón – former Director of the Spanish secret service – when two of his children became addicted to heroin and eventually died. Other mortal casualties of the Movida included writer Carmen Martín Gaite's daughter, Marta, in 1985; and Eduardo Haro Ibars, who succumbed to AIDS in 1988, the first of four of the children of *El País*'s chief theatre critic to die prematurely. Lola Flores had boasted in 1982 of taking cocaine in *¡Hola!*, but omitted this detail from her memoiris, published in 1992[90] – Antonio's continued debilitating addiction meant he outlived his mother by just two weeks. By 1992, Spain had the highest AIDS rates in Europe: almost two-thirds of the country's sufferers were heroin addicts, and more than forty per cent of heroin users were reckoned to be HIV positive.[91]

González's election programme promised the creation of 800,000 jobs,[92] but structural reforms required a break with the protectionist measures of the Francoist administration, and making Spain's application for EU membership tenable resulted in extensive strike action in 1984 and 1985, alongside the highest unemployment rates in Europe.[93]

On 3 March 1987, the 'Co-ordinador de barrio', a Vallecas community association set up in 1981, presented to the Spanish Parliament a list of places in Madrid they claimed drugs could be bought, alongside the accusation that a number of police officers were involved.[94] Addiction cut across class boundaries, but this does not imply that it affected all classes indiscriminately. As with unemployment, young, working-class men were particularly vulnerable.[95] Belying its bad reputation, crime rates in Vallecas had not traditionally been that high; the arrival of hard drugs changed this and, in the words of local parish priest Enrique Martínez Reguero: 'I never went so many times to the cemetery to bury young boys and men as in the 1980s.'[96] Poli Díaz, nicknamed 'el potro de Vallecas' (the foal from Vallecas), became a Spanish and European featherweight boxing champion. Under the management of Enrique Sarasola, Díaz's seemingly inexorable rise made boxing a fashionable spectator sport for the Socialist elites until his career was scuppered by a debilitating drug addiction that eventually led him to appear in porn films to fund his habit.

The cinematic adaptations of the memoirs of legendary outlaw Eleutorio Sánchez (see Chapter 7) – who was later taken on as an employee of Tierno Galván's law practice in the 1970s – in *El Lute: camina o revienta* (*El Lute: Run for Your Life*) (Vicente Aranda, 1987) and *El Lute II: mañana seré libre* (*El Lute II: Tomorrow I'll Be Free*) (Vicente Aranda, 1988) were an atypical hybrid of the *quinqui* and heritage genres.[97] New arrivals to Vallecas are depicted hastily assembling shacks overnight; in real life, the police could move the homeless on, but not those with a roof, however makeshift, over their heads.[98] As the picaresque narrative depicts, the forces of law nevertheless turned a blind eye to extortionists who demanded protection money. When El Lute refuses, his house is burnt down in front of his young family. Depicting this on-screen a quarter of a century later was less politically charged than *La estanquera de Vallecas* (*The Tobacconist of Vallecas*) (Eloy de la Iglesia, 1987), a cinematic adaptation of a play by José Luis Alonso de Santos in which two desperate thieves hold a widow and granddaughter hostage in a tobacconist's. To a far greater extent than the original play, the film uses the heist as a pretext for political satire and protest. Posters for the upcoming elections, an image of González alongside the real-life slogan 'Por buen camino' (On the right path), form a running motif undercut by scenes of the riot police viciously emptying the square outside the tobacconist. The siege becomes a media-feast, and the civil governor, replete with trademark glasses, was deliberately made to resemble Alfonso Guerra; the quintessentially modern wielder of power makes a rare trip to Vallecas – where the neighbours berate him for failing to tackle unemployment and drugs – to capitalise on the media spotlight. By this time, De la Iglesia and his lover/lead-actor Manzano were heroin addicts. According to screenwriter Gonzalo Goicoechea, the filmmaker both exploited and loved the star: the latter was paid the equivalent of €9,000, €4,800 of which he was convinced to invest in the film, when other actors with his cachet were earning €30,000.[99] Manzano, later imprisoned for assault, died of an overdose aged 29 in 1992, shortly after release from prison.

Tierno Galván's death in 1986 is seen as marking the death-knell of the Movida. The mass-attended funeral of the Old Professor was a major civic and national event; students were given the day off school and university. This act of secular canonisation led to his inheriting Carlos III's title as Madrid's greatest mayor. He would probably not have been remembered so fondly if his term of office had been extended much beyond Spain's European integration. The chief achievements of his municipal policies were to be found in an ephemeral reinvention of city space and urban living, arguably the prime subject-matter and inspiration for Alonso de Santos's most popular play, *Bajarse al moro* (*Going down to Morocco*), which simultaneously celebrates and laments the precariousness of the opportunities for freedom in the capital. The play was staged for four consecutive years with nearly 1,000 performances,[100] a televised version of the Madrid stage production was the third most watched programme in 1986,[101] and the cinematic adaptation (Fernando Colomo, 1989) starring Antonio Banderas remains a popular Christmas film to the present day. In a play about young people searching for their place in the world, Madrid during the Movida is a character in and of itself, an adolescent city with all the charms and problems that entails.

Alonso de Santos, born in Valladolid in 1942, had lived in the capital since his university days and shared with the protagonists of the Movida a desire to combine low and high art, whilst he had access to their world through teaching at the National Drama School and his relationship with his future wife, Margarita Piñero, who worked in the press office of the Mayor's cultural department.

In the play, cousins Chusa and Jaimito live alongside Alberto – a childhood friend of the latter and casual lover of the former – in a small flat in Lavapiés. Located not far from the historic centre, the neighbourhood was a traditional stopping point for recent arrivals to Madrid. It is close to the Rastro market, which, although increasingly regulated, as Tierno Galván used criminality as a pretext to demand for the first time that vendors have licences to hawk their goods,[102] remained a popular hangout for petty criminals and bohemians alike. Chusa returns to the flat with Elena, a middle-class runaway she has just met. Much to Jaimito's consternation, Chusa invites her new friend to move in, and to join the family business by accompanying her on a trip to Morocco where she plans to buy marijuana that she will then sell in Spain. Elena initially appears to be an innocent abroad, but protects her interests like nobody else in the play: after being 'lent' Alberto, who has recently joined the police force, for one night only so that she can lose her virginity and thereby be better equipped to smuggle drugs in her vagina, she not only steals him from Chusa but pulls out of the trip because it is too risky. Elena does, however, invest in the venture and demands her money be returned after Chusa is caught by the police because she and Alberto need it to put towards the deposit for a flat on the outskirts. Alonso de Santos is prescient in documenting a growing gulf between the upwardly mobile and social drop-outs at the individual level that would increasingly divide Spanish society. Rising rents and increased police surveillance would soon expel characters such as Chusa and Jaimito from Madrid's centre, the poorer inhabitants of Lavapiés targeted for eviction by property developers from 1987 onwards.[103]

The Movida – much like the 'swinging sixties' in the UK or Warhol's New York scene – was a combination of unbridled hedonism with economic and symbolic accumulation, an accrual of human casualties and capitalist fortunes. As McNamara, who endured the physical and psychological fall-out of addiction just as Almodóvar was courting international fame, recalls: 'We thought ourselves so clever and that we knew everything when we were also more innocent than Heidi in the mountains.'[104] In *La ley del deseo* (*The Law of Desire*) (Pedro Almodóvar, 1987), designer-clad artists flit between nightclubs, theatres and restaurants; his next film, *Mujeres al borde de un ataque de nervios* (*Women on the Verge of a Nervous Breakdown*) (1988), showcased the capital as a Manhattan-like city-scape in which a luxury flat, self-consciously echoing *How to Marry a Millionaire* (Jean Neguleso, 1953), 'acquires a symbolic centrality'.[105] Any departure from private space in the Oscar-nominated film intimates crisis, most memorably a suicide attempt on a rubbish heap.

The narrative of the slick video-clip to Mecano's 1988 global hit 'La fuerza del destino' (The force of destiny), starring a 15-year-old Penelope Cruz, features her meeting soon-to-be-real-life boyfriend Nacho Cano in a nightclub on the Gran Vía, Madrid's principal thoroughfare. At a time when the areas surrounding the Plaza Mayor had gone from being run-down to no-go areas – cafés drilling holes into teaspoons to avoid their being used to cook heroin – the action then switches to the group drinking and chatting in the capital's most historic square before transcending Madrid's geography to show the nascent lovers on horseback on a beach. Spain's European integration was both the cause and the consequence of the notion of the country's winners and losers being framed in monetary, as opposed to metaphysical, terms, albeit with the children of the vanquished inheriting a systematic set of significant disadvantages frequently concealed by Madrid's (post)modern makeover.

As is mercilessly depicted in *En la lucha final* (*The Fight to the End*), Rafael Chirbes's 1989 novel about a group of back-stabbing members of the cultural glitterati, the creative industries became yet another competitive forum through which to rank status, the display of original paintings by Francis Bacon just one more way of revealing the proud owner as a winner. Amelia, an ex-Communist literary agent, 'still keeps the Revolution card up her sleeve',[106] but lives in the exclusive Moraleja neighbourhood with husband Carlos who, immersed in real-estate fraud, invites his wife's lover, a romantic author, Ricardo, to live with them in their gated community to keep his enemy close at hand. The plan backfires as Carlos is murdered by Santiago, Ricardo's heroin-addict gay lover.

With the mortal casualties of Spain's drugs epidemic receding into the background, a combination of nostalgia and revisionist entrenchment has increasingly transformed the early 1980s into a mythical period, dom-inating the airwaves and concert-stages whilst also providing a unique selling point for the local revellers and tourists attracted to the Movida theme bars that have proliferated in post-Airbnb Malasaña. Alaska and Almodóvar retain properties within walking distance of the neighbour-hood, but tourists on the look-out for Movida veterans are more likely to find them amongst the many AIDS suffers who carry out annual pilgrimages from Madrid care-homes to Lourdes. Partying without a hangover is an attractive proposition for overcoming the schisms of yes-teryear but it is a pipedream: Spain may no longer be divided into the victors and the vanquished of the Civil War, but the power differentials of the past have been imprinted onto an urban fabric. In 1989 Gregorio Peces-Barba, an academic and PSOE politician, who was the Speaker of the Lower House of the Spanish Parliament from 1982 to 1986, left his post at the Complutense University to establish a new higher edu-cation institution for the south of Madrid, the Universidad Carlos III, with campuses in industrial areas such as Leganés and Getafe belonging to what was once known as the 'red belt'.[107] In the twenty-first century, admission to undergraduate courses at the Carlos III for almost all subjects is more competitive than at the Complutense. In terms of pro-gressive social engineering, this is a pyrrhic victory: the Carlos III is often referred to as 'la universidad del sur para los pijos del norte' (the univer-sity in the south for the posh kids from the north). Street-by-street results collated from El País following the 2019 municipal elections revealed the extent to which division between the left- and right-wing vote in the capital mapped almost exactly onto the north–south divide.[108] The legacy of the two Spains remains.

Stapell attributes Madrid's decline to the substitution of cultural with neoliberal goals in the wake of the Old Professor's death: 'After 1986 the capital passed from "punk" to "yuppie", as everyone aspired to be a financier instead of an artist.'[109] Tierno Galván's successor, Juan Barranco, remained in office until 1989, but was voted out in favour of conservative mayors Agustín Rodríguez Sahagún (1989–91) and José María Álvarez del Manzano (1991–2003). In his capacity as a town councillor, the latter had lodged a formal complaint in April 1983 when all-female punk band Las Vulpes had performed, on Easter Sunday, a version in Spanish of Iggy and the Stooges' 'I wanna be your dog' on TVE's *La caja de los ritmos*,[110] with the music programme subsequently being taken off air. On becoming Mayor of Madrid, he was quick to make a symbolic gesture by closing Pacha, as punishment for the iconic nightclub's allowing entry to underage customers.[111] Featuring AC/DC and Metallica, the 1991 Monsters of Rock Tour was scheduled to take place in Madrid; after the Mayor's office systematically refused licences, the concert was moved to Barcelona's Olympic Stadium, and fan-made banners proclaimed 'Manzano, you asshole, Madrid is here'.[112]

In an interview first published in 1991, the incoming Mayor said of the Movida: 'It doesn't need to be buried, because it has petered out, it doesn't even have a body to bury.'[113] At the time, nobody seemed willing to put forward a defence; even its protagonists were disillusioned. Leopoldo Alas's novel *Bochorno* (*Embarrassment*) offers a jaded satire of 'a frayed world determined to exalt the capricious, to celebrate the unconscious and encourage the irresponsible as the most efficient lenitive',[114] lifestyle choices formerly eulogised by *La luna de Madrid* and *Madriz*. It is not necessary to claim the PP had the answers to realise that Stapell's romanticised vision underplays the collateral damage caused by what Joan Ramón Resina terms 'semi-official hedonism',[115] a Socialist doctrine, whose victims were disproportionately poor, that failed to achieve its democratising goals.

Chapter 9

An Olympic renaissance
The Barcelona model

In the manner of the proverbial hare and tortoise, Barcelona was slow to harness the potential of the post-Franco explosion of creativity, but eventually overtook Madrid in the race to become the cultural capital of Spain. The catalyst for this transformation was hosting the Olympic Games, which, initially at least, appeared to constitute a more sustainable cultural revolution than the Movida for four interrelated reasons: (1) the understanding of heroin addiction as a social problem rather than collateral damage; (2) a greater collaboration between the public and private sectors; (3) a privileged natural environment, a city nestled between the mountains and the sea; and (4) better co-ordination between urban renewal and cultural rehabilitation.

Under the chairmanship of Juan Antonio Samaranch, the bad fortunes of both Barcelona and the Olympic Games were seemingly reversed. Described in 1976 as 'the prototype of the perfect Francoist politician',[1] the President of the Provincial Town Council of Barcelona and property developer claims that it was on Juan Carlos's recommendation that he pursued an Olympic, as opposed to a political, post-1975 career.[2] Samaranch turned down a posting in Vienna, biding his time until 1977, when he became the first Spanish ambassador in Moscow following the recommencement of formal diplomatic relations. This was a shrewd move: in a Cold War context, the ability to accrue support from both Hispanic countries and the Eastern Bloc made him a shoe-in for the Presidency of the International Olympics Committee when Lord

Killanin from the UK retired in 1980.[3] The appointment was, however, a poisoned chalice: following the terrorist attacks in Munich in 1972, subsequent Games had run at a financial loss, with reciprocal boycotts by countries either side of the Iron Curtain. Los Angeles was the only candidate bidding to host the games in 1984, delivering a largely unexpected success through spectacle, significantly upping the ante as regards corporate sponsorship and televisual technology, with the local organisers boasting that they did not spend a cent of taxpayers' money. As Barbara Kellerman remarks: 'From being a financial liability that no city other than Los Angeles had been willing to accept, the games had become a highly lucrative business.'[4]

Prior to his appointment as President, Samaranch had already exerted pressure on Narcís Serra, the Socialist Mayor for Barcelona (1979–82), to make an Olympic bid;[5] the decision to go forward with the candidature was agreed in summer 1980 and made public in May 1981.[6] Following the Socialist victory in the 1982 general elections, Serra was appointed as Spanish Minister of Defence. Barcelona's incoming Mayor, Pasqual Maragall, was the grandson of the Catalan poet Joan Maragall, and had completed a doctorate on urban planning in the United States. His vision of the ideal city was much closer to Jane Jacobs's defence of Greenwich Village in *The Death and Life of Great American Cities* (1962) than the largely artificial, car-dominated, sprawling Californian metropolis. As Ferran Mascarell notes of Barcelona in the late 1970s: 'The city belonged more to writers than to urban planners, to poets rather than architects, to citizens not specialists.'[7] Maragall sought to readdress such binaries whilst making sure to give writers, poets and citizens a stake in a new urban project. In a published series of conversations with writer turned politician Maria Aurèlia Capmany, Maragall walked around the city, and discussed its past and his vision for the future. Aurèlia claimed that the Olympics might be a necessary evil, but that she feared it would simply be a repeat of the 1982 World Cup.[8] Barça's Camp Nou Stadium hosted the most games, but the football championship had been a State enterprise marred by corruption scandals and logistical issues.[9] Maragall insisted this would be not the case, and located the candidature within an urban teleology. The capital of a nation without a state, the city did not have the resources available to Madrid or Paris, and macro-events thereby provided the means by which the city could realise its ambitions. He cited as an example the Citadel Park's coming into being as a direct result of Barcelona's hosting the 1888 Universal Exhibition.[10] Furthermore, he argued, the city had 'been a candidate to host the Olympic Games for the last fifty years'.[11] Barcelona had made unsuccessful bids for 1924, 1936, 1940 and 1972.[12] An Olympic Stadium had optimistically been built for the Games that ultimately took place in Berlin during the first year of the Civil War. The President of the Generalitat, Lluís Companys, was executed the following year in Barcelona after being returned to the Francoist authorities by the Gestapo.

As with so much in Catalonia, Barcelona's bid was a matter of historical redress, 'a collective therapy destined to compensate for a historical frustration'.[13] The city had a much needed ally in Samaranch as the Games constituted a last-ditch attempt to salvage a rapidly sinking metropolis. As chief architect Oriol Bohigas – a veteran of the *Gauche Divine* (see Chapter 7) and the neighbourhood associations of the 1970s, eulogised by Maragall in his memoirs as 'a humanist heir to the nineteenth-century tradition'[14] – noted, Barcelona had a lack of monuments in comparison with Paris and Madrid,[15] whilst 'the historic centre – which has the capacity to embody the urban landscape – has lapsed into a state of hygienic decline that makes it uninhabitable; then there are the outskirts – which frequently have a better quality of housing – but, at the end of day, are lacking a truly urban identity'.[16]

Literary depictions of Barcelona in the mid-to-late 1980s do not paint a pretty picture. Félix de Azúa published *Diario de un hombre humillado* (*Diary of a Humiliated Man*), a novel that characterises the Ramblas, a then seemingly unlikely candidate to be a future tourist hotspot, as 'a human drain', 'where the uncivil persists' and in which 'levels of venereal disease are higher than anywhere else in Europe'.[17] Drugs increasingly formed part of the backdrop to a second generation of noir writers such as Andreu Martín and Juan Madrid. In an encyclopedic history of the Raval, Paco Villar refers to heroin as 'the grand protagonist of the process of degradation suffered in the Old Town'.[18] Pasqual Maragall's brother, Pau, a leading light in the vibrant counter-culture of the 1970s, was arrested for drug dealing in 1985, and later died of an overdose after the successful completion of the Games, an investigating judge only returning the body to the family after demanding a promotion from the Mayor.[19] To return to the mid-1980s, rock-star Loquillo recalls the addicts:

> The most picturesque could be found in the Liceu drugstore, next to the theatre of the same name; all of the characters from the songs of Lou Reed or Madrid's Burning resided in this boulevard of lost souls: transvestites, whores, thugs, criminals, rent boys take possession of the place at certain times of the night, making it their own.[20]

In addition to traditional migration flows, Barcelona became home from the 1970s onwards to immigrants from Latin America. Reversing the trend from during and after the Civil War, whereby many Spanish cultural practitioners sought asylum on the other side of the Atlantic, the repressive turn in the Southern Cone made Spain a particularly attractive destination for artists, who were instrumental to post-Franco cultural renaissances.[21]

Before the Andalusian Joaquín Sabina started to poeticise Madrid, the Argentine rocker Moris eulogised his adopted home. Raúl Núñez, another native of Buenos Aires, offered a snapshot of the Raval immediately prior to its gentrification in *Sinatra: novela urbana* (*Sinatra: Urban Novel*), published in 1984 and adapted for the cinema by Francesc Betriu four years later. The eponymous protagonist, nicknamed thus for his physical resemblance to the American crooner (comic actor Alfredo Landa stretches verisimilitude in the film to breaking point in this regard), views the world from his place of residence and work, a pension for the emotionally and economically deprived, alongside the local bars that are his second home:

> He knew all of the old lunatics who passed the night next to his canary bird. He knew all of the petty criminals who sold drugs in the Plaça Reial. He knew all of those lonely guys who washed dishes and jerked off to cheap pornographic magazines. He knew the gloomy and dark Moroccans who headed out to mug people in the night. He knew the police who went

out to look for them. He knew those who had gone mad in their rooms. He knew those who had been saved. He knew them all.[22]

A lonely-hearts club provides a nexus for the running motif of isolation and desire for almost invariably impossible human connection. Amongst the characters Sinatra encounters over the course of the novel are a middle-aged singleton who invites him to lunch at her flat, before he is ejected by her knife-wielding *quinqui* son; a young heroin addict with an imaginary child she believes to be dying; a dwarf who vomits after she consumes alcohol for the first time in preparation for losing her virginity; and an attractive call-girl who homes in on Sinatra after he wins at bingo, but who is the victim, as well as the agent, of sexual exploitation.

At times, there is a Genet-esque romanticisation of poverty – exacerbated in the film adaptation by the contribution of Sabina to the soundtrack – but the overriding tone is crepuscular, desperate lives unfolding in a parochial world that could and should come to an end. This was an exhausted literary and urban model: those who could get out had. By the mid-1980s, the absence of an equivalent to the Movida ensured that middle-class aesthetes were increasingly fixated by interior design, be that in exclusive cocktail bars or their own homes. Artists frequently sought to transcend the city in both physical and imaginative terms, the romantic trope of the city as an extended theatrical space losing its allure. As Sharon G. Feldman notes, in its lunge for cosmopolitanism, Barcelona virtually disappeared from the contemporary Catalan stage.[23] Eduardo Mendoza and Quim Monzó, two expert literary cartographers, both lived and worked abroad. The latter drew especially on time spent in New York, whilst the former transcended the parochialism of proximity by casting a retrospective eye on his native city and the palimpsests of capitalist and urban growth bequeathed by the period between the two Universal Exhibitions, hosted respectively in 1888 and 1929.

La ciudad de los prodigios (*The City of Wonders*) was composed after Mendoza had lived abroad for many years, numerous passages written in hotels and pensions as he travelled in his capacity as a professional interpreter. Proustian recollections of the homeland are mapped onto the genealogy of a city that belongs more to the imagination than to empirical reality, a timeless mythical metropolis that evades the prosaic and petty inconveniences of quotidian existence in the present day: 'the narrator's repeated attempts to defamiliarise the city by undermining mimesis inform readers that Mendoza's Barcelona is a fictional construct, a city of words'.[24] This attempt to transcend space and time does not, however, imply that the novel can be separated from the moment of its creation. As Edgar Illas notes: 'By recalling the historical situation of these past events, *La ciudad de los prodigios* contests the new hegemonic narratives of contemporary Barcelona, namely Maragall's postpolitical call for a "city of the people" and Pujol's nationalist reconstruction of Catalonia'.[25]

When, in November 1986, Barcelona's candidacy was announced as successful, the decision was greeted with euphoria: crowds congregated in the Plaça de Catalunya, and 20,000 volunteers signed up to help in the organisation of the event on the first day alone.[26] There was a performative dimension to the emergence of a nascent identity that, in Mari Paz Balibrea's terms, produced 'a competitive, relentlessly optimistic subject'[27] that would endow 'Barcelona with the means to produce a particular kind of life experience that is unavailable for subjects elsewhere, … defining in this way the city's qualitative advantage'.[28] On re-encountering his city of birth in 1987, Monzó was surprised and perturbed by a renewed civic pride amongst his compatriots, overcoming the previously widespread notion of perpetual decline: 'They are convinced that they are no longer aboard the *Titanic* simply because they can practise the new national sport, which consists in flitting from one *modern* bar to another.'[29] If, in Isabel Coixet's debut film, the critically derided *Demasiado viejo para morir joven* (*Too Old to Die Young*) (1988), both the cinematic aesthetics and the city bear traces of 1950s American kitsch (burger joints, quiffed motorcycle rebels) and the *quinqui* genre, then Ventura Pons's most overtly commercial film, *Què t'hi jueges, Mari Pilli?* (*What do you think, Mari Pilli?*) (1991), is the closest Catalan equivalent to the slick urban female melodrama of Almodóvar's *Mujeres al borde de un ataque de nervios*. An optimism as compulsive as it was compulsory was the symptom and the cause of the fact that, in Daniel Vázquez Sallés's words: 'Barcelona's Olympism managed to convert detractors into bad citizens of Barcelona.'[30]

As Gary McDonogh notes of the 1987 municipal elections, 'the Socialist programs effectively set the stage for all discussions of the city as system, while other parties fought to control it ...During the campaign, Communists even proposed putting aside "the poor" as a political issue, a remarkable acquiescence of the Left to the silences of urban domination.'[31] There were a few relatively isolated voices of dissent to this hegemonic discourse of modernisation: Manuel Vázquez Montalbán's *Barcelonas* (1990) and Manuel Delgado's *La ciudad mentirosa: fraude y miseria del 'modelo Barcelona' (The Fabricated City: The Fraud and Misery of the 'Barcelona Model')* (2007) are bitter laments against ostensibly left-leaning technocrats who, in their view, sacrificed Socialist ideals and the well-being of the working classes through the gentrification of areas such as the Barceloneta and the Raval required to transform the city into a chic global brand. The Olympics may not have been the sole or even the best possible solution, but Barcelona was unquestionably in desperate need of a fix. The iconic centre was, for example, increasingly a no-go area.

From the pages of *Ajoblanco*, Victor Gracia lamented the number of needles left in the Raval, alongside the horrific violence unleashed by drug-trafficking and foreign mafias, before decrying the tendency for Vázquez Montalbán and Juan Goytisolo to exploit the neighbourhood for their own purposes: 'But all of that is nothing more than literature. The reality (so fleeting and subject to change) of "Chinatown" is very different, it is something else.'[32] On 22 February 1988, an explosion of civil unrest followed the death of five people, including two brothers from an important Gypsy family, as a result of heroin overdoses the previous weekend. At around 7.45 p.m., the streets around the Ramblas and Plaça Reial turned into a battleground: marauding groups of Gypsies sought revenge on the Africans suspected of supplying the lethal poison, reputedly pursuing and beating up any black person found with drugs on their person.[33] In a post-heroin landscape, the counter-cultural romance with the city's most historic and literary sites now appeared more dystopian than utopian, but the forward-looking optimistic energy of the 1970s fed into the city's regeneration project at multiple levels. Valencian-born designer Javier Mariscal, who as a young man had lived for many years in the Plaça Reial, became the city's design laureate for the Olympic adventure. In line with the ethos that so often prevailed during Spain's Transition, shared strategic goals laid the groundwork for fragile counter-intuitive alliances. Samaranch effectively redeemed himself for his Francoist past by becoming the first President of the Olympics Committee to see the Games hosted on home turf. He claims that, under the patronage of the Spanish royal family: 'The unity amongst everyone and common sense prevailed: an efficient and innovative formula was found to integrate the always active Catalan civil society into the project; hence, the creation of the Barcelona-92 Association of businessmen.'[34]

If, as Keith Dinnie notes, '[i]nterest in city branding may be seen as part of a wider recognition that places of all kinds can benefit from implementing coherent strategies with respect to managing their resources, reputation and image',[35] Barcelona's hosting of the Olympics – which has arguably been more researched than any other comparable sporting event[36] – is a textbook example of how and why 'global inter-city competition is essentially about a city's ability to attract the highest possible value from global flows of values in order to promote local development'.[37] New public sculptures and art installations alongside green spaces were key to regenerating a city with a privileged location between the sea and the mountains that housed the increasingly fashionable (the Japanese being particular devotees) architecture of Antoni Gaudí. A collaborative exhibition between the Arts Council of Great Britain, the Generalitat and Barcelona Town Hall ran at the Hayward Gallery in London from 14 November 1985 to 23 February 1986 under the title *Homage to Barcelona: The City and Its Art.* In 1988, a show titled *Barcelona, the City and '92* attracted 350,000 visitors before travelling to Rotterdam and other Spanish cities;[38] in 1990, 550,000 people attended an exhibition on modernism housed in Gaudí's Casa Mila, visitors also being directed into the surrounding grid of streets to look at buildings from the turn of the twentieth century;[39] 1991 was declared Year of the Arts. As Dianne Dodd notes: 'Barcelona was launched as a Cultural

City during the Olympics with two principal objectives. First, to promote Catalan regional identity and secondly to move away from the old
"cheap beach holiday image" and promote the business facilities offered
by Barcelona'.[40]

Soprano Montserrat Caballé had joined representatives of the city
council in October 1986 on a last-minute trip to Lausanne to lobby on
behalf of Barcelona's candidacy. Maragall told her that, if successful, he
wanted an official theme tune.[41] This was delivered in the guise of a duet
with rock superstar Freddie Mercury. On tour in Spain, the lead singer
of Queen had said in a televised interview that, of all the great Spanish
institutions, the Barcelona-born Caballé was the greatest and the person he
most longed to meet.[42] Montserrat's brother, Carlos, organised a meeting
between the two stars in February 1987 at Barcelona's Ritz (now Palace)
hotel. Mercury brought with him 'Exercises in free love', a composition he
had written for Caballé that she subsequently brought him out to perform
alongside her when she next returned to play Covent Garden. Accounts
differ as to which of the two stars was keenest to transform this brief
encounter into the more serious collaboration that resulted in an album
and lead single, both titled 'Barcelona'.[43] Mutual professional and personal
admiration aside, the collaboration held strategic advantages for both.
Caballé was no longer capable of taking on the demanding roles and gruel-
ling tours that had established her as the biggest opera star in the world the
previous decade; furthermore, she had fallen out with the Liceu management.[44] Mercury knew he was HIV-positive and would probably never tour
again. Following recording sessions in London, in spring 1987 Mercury
and Caballé headlined the inaugural 'Ibiza '92' event curated to raise funds
for the Olympic city. The broadcast rights for the gala performance, staged
in the island's fashionable Ku nightclub and featuring 200 young attractive
audience members b(r)ought in to maximise the sexiness quotient, were
sold not only to TVE but also to the BBC and other major global players.[45]
Later that same year, Mercury celebrated his forty-first birthday in Ibiza.

'Barcelona' topped the Spanish hit parade and charted well internationally, the music video receiving heavy rotation. What turned out

to be Mercury's final public performance (his deteriorating health forced him and Caballé to lip-synch) provided the centrepiece of 'La nit', a televised spectacle co-ordinated by Italian-born promoter Pino Sagliocco to herald the arrival of the Olympic flag from Seoul in 1988 and to inaugurate the Cultural Olympics. Despite the presence of stars of classical and popular music such as José Carreras and Eddy Grant, the turnout for the free televised performance, staged on the Avinguda de Maria Cristina in front of an audience that included the Spanish royal family, was much lower than anticipated.[46] Sagliocco's bid to organise music-orientated opening and closing ceremonies was unsuccessful.[47] Two other initial proposals failed to go ahead for different reasons: the idea of releasing a bull into the stadium and a dove landing on its head was dismissed amidst safety and security concerns, alongside fears of offending the anti-bullfighting lobby;[48] a stage production of García Lorca's 'Amargo', to feature Miguel Bosé and Antonio Banderas, was deemed inappropriate because of the poem's violent end and homosexual subtext.[49]

The organising committee were keenly aware of not having the financial resources or infrastructure that would be on hand in, say, Los Angeles. The solution sought was to seek the assistance of Els Comediants and La Fura dels Baus, two Catalan performance groups formed in 1979 and 1971 respectively. The latter had travelled to Madrid in 1984 with municipal funds from Tierno Galván's office (prior to ever receiving any Catalan subsidies)[50] to appear on television programme *La edad de oro*, violently smashing a car to pieces in a carefully rehearsed simulacrum of chaos. If this appearance exposed them to a national television audience, an Olympic performance piece titled 'Mediterranean' – which narrated the journey of Jason and the Argonauts to the end of the sea – was set against a more ambitious canvas and, crucially, would be seen by audiences around the world. Some editorialists in Malaysia interpreted the performance as offensively representing 'the defeat of Muslim "evil" in Spain',[51] but 'Mediterranean' was generally applauded as 'folklore harnessed to technology for maximum effect',[52] fusing the past and the present, the local and the cosmopolitan.

La Fura dels Baus were central to the documentary film *Marathon* (Carlos Saura, 1992), which uses montage and carefully composed photography to reinforce yet again the notion of citizenry, sport and culture as a harmonious triptych. Members of what was fast on the road to becoming 'the most important European multinational specialising in *performances*'[53] recall surprise at first seeing queues for their shows after their Olympic Stadium performance.[54]

More generally, in the words of Donald McNeill, Barcelona had 'taken a firm hold on the imagination of *Guardian* readers, clubbers, foodies, and high-disposable-income football followers'.[55] By this stage, Madrid had little to compete with. The opening of the Thyssen Museum in 1990 had shown that the collaboration between the private and public sectors could deliver results, but this was not capitalised upon. Madrid was named European City of Culture for 1992. Joaquín Leguina has referred to this as a consolation prize,[56] mere window-dressing to prevent the capital's being excluded from a jamboree year for Spain, in which Seville also hosted a Universal Exhibition (see Chapter 12). In reality, however, Madrid's budget of €57.9 million made it second only to Glasgow in the scheme's history,[57] with little regeneration or impact gained from this investment.[58]

The Barcelona model was remarkable in many regards, but it was not miraculous, nor did it benefit the city's citizens in equal or universal fashion. Transexual former prostitute Norma Mejía notes, for example, that sex workers were targeted by the authorities in the areas surrounding sports facilities in the build-up to 1992. Designated red-light districts, which they were told would be safer, did not even have street lighting.[59] The last slum in Mount Carmelo was destroyed in 1991 but, in both the short and long term, the Olympics frequently expelled, as opposed to remedying, poverty and drug addiction, as can be gauged from the documentary film *Can Tunis* (José González Morandi, 2007). The narrative conceit of Mendoza's novel *Sin noticas de Gurb* (*No News of Gurb*) – an extra-terrestrial sent to Barcelona to locate the eponymous missing-in-action character – casts a humorous, bemused outsider's eye over the clash between 'an underdeveloped modernism and the rushed *performance* of a postmodernity that had been held back by the last vestiges of Francoism.[60]

The complicity between the narrator, writer and reader in *Sin noticias de Gurb*, originally published in instalments in *El País*, derives, as Julià Guillamon notes, from the fact that the rapid transformation of the city could be disconcerting, often making citizens of Barcelona feel like aliens in their hometown.[61] Conversely, however, its being Mendoza's best-loved novel internationally is attributable to the fashion for all things Barcelona alongside the bemused narrator landscaping a city-scape rendered more legible to non-natives by the Olympic Revolution. The Catalan capital was exotically cultured – although a running gag means the narrator fails ever to enter any museums, which seem perpetually to be closed for refurbishments – but, in taking its (rightful?) place on the global stage, shed idiosyncrasies, albeit retaining injustices: 'It appears that human beings are divided, amongst other categories, between those who are rich and those who are poor. This is a division to which they attach great importance without its being altogether clear why.'[62]

If Spain had traditionally been viewed as a poor nation constantly playing catch-up with its wealthier European neighbours, the 1992 Olympics – in which the host country won a record number of medals – was the first since Tokyo in 1964 not to be directly affected by international unrest and, crucially, the first to take place after the fall of the Berlin Wall. In David Miller's hagiographic biography, it is claimed that, under Samaranch, the International Olympic Committee had become 'the most universal social investment of peace in our time'.[63] If, in 1992, this appeared simplistic and exaggerated, by 2004 – when Barbara Kellerman employed Samaranch as case-study of bad leadership,[64] a toxic combination of a personal need for control and an unreflective genuflexion to corporate interests – it was clearly either fundamentally misguided or misleading. One of the few places where this vision still holds sway is the Juan Antonio Samaranch Olympic and Sports Museum, which opened in 2007 just down the road from the rebaptised (since 2001) Lluís Companys Olympic Stadium, and a few-hundred metres from the Joan Miró museum. For better or worse, the Games not only announced Spain's democratic credentials to the world, but also heralded a new age of peace and optimism in which the Catalan capital became a model for urban(e) control that, in Sharon Zukin's formulation, effectively controlled 'diversity while re-creating a consumable vision of civility'.[65] In a text originally published in 1998, Anthony Giddens noted how the 'debate around New Labour, lively and interesting though it is, has been carried out largely in ignorance of comparable discussions that have been going on in Continental social democracy for some while'.[66] The sociologist, simultaneously a guru to and publicist for the incoming Blair Government, references Spain, but only in relation to the autonomous communities of Catalonia and the Basque Country;[67] Blair himself repeatedly voiced admiration for what Maragall had done for Barcelona.[68]

Margaret Thatcher had been antagonistic to the idea city as a civic unit – dissolving the Greater Metropolitan London Council – and many cultural practitioners and institutions. The reaffirmation by Britpop and the Young British Artists of London's long-lost credentials as a capital of culture in the aftermath of eighteen years of Conservative rule lends itself to comparison with the unleashing of creative energies in the Spanish capital some fifteen years previously. The discrediting of the Movida combined with Madrid's unimaginative approach to urban redevelopment, as well as a sentimental post-Orwell attachment, ensured that the Catalan capital was the chief and generally sole Spanish reference point. It is no coincidence that Almodóvar's breakthrough hit at the British box office, *Todo sobre mi madre* (*All about My Mother*) (1999) – 'a largely atemporal fairytale, simultaneously poeticising the transgressive energy of the past and the cosmopolitan gentrification of the present'[69] – was his first to be set in Barcelona. The Catalan capital had joined forces with mid-sized conurbations such as Birmingham, Frankfurt and Lyon in the mid-1980s as part of the Eurocities project designed to address common problems and form a lobbying group. Having ousted not only the UK's second biggest city, Birmingham, but also Amsterdam and Paris in the competition to host the Olympics, the Catalan capital was then adopted as a model for London to emulate. Maragall was invited to comment on a green paper for planning in the UK capital, which he did with gusto: 'I am convinced that devolving powers to Londoners is better not only for them but for Britain in general ... National governments are not made to run cities, not even capital cities ... The 10 key criteria for the new London government are consistent with the so-called "Barcelona model" which has been so well presented by Richard Rogers and Norman Foster and referred to by Tony Blair.'[70] In less celebratory fashion, the documentary film *En construcción* (*Work in Progress*) (José Luis Guerín, 2002) examined the detrimental effect of gentrification on long-term residences of the Raval.[71] The Catalan bourgeoisie may have returned to Barcelona's old-town in a wave of Olympic euphoria, but they have since retreated beyond the city walls or to the restaurants and bars of the Upper Diagonal, no longer fleeing the poverty of migrants but an out-of-control tourist industry – in a city of fewer than 2 million inhabitants, the number of tourists rocketed from 1.7 million in 1990 to nearly 7.5 million in 2012[72] – which, as documented in *Bye Bye Barcelona* (Eduardo Chibás, 2014), has become intrusive.

In the words of Gyan Prakash: 'If modernity is a Faustian bargain to unleash human potential and subdue nature to culture, then modern cities are its more forceful and enduring "expressions".'[73] As we have seen, this has been brought to the fore in the Spanish context since the advent of mass rural migration. The Olympics and the Movida suggest that peaks in cultural expression coincided with rising wealth and more fluid communications between the capitals of Spain and Catalonia but, to a large extent, both camouflaged the collateral damage of the sprint towards (post)modernity. Madrid and Barcelona have been at the vanguard of this race but offer only a piecemeal vision of the multifaceted realities of Spain and Catalonia in the late twentieth century. Modernity's Faustian bargain might have found its most striking takers in the two major cities but, as I will address in the next section, an accurate cost–benefit analysis demands a more holistic overview of a plural nation state, whose stakeholders arrived at the table with radically uneven cultural and political chips to place.

Part IV

Communities

Introduction

According to José Álvarez Junco: 'Whatever the vicissitudes of Spain in the twentieth century, the Spanish political identity has enjoyed the greatest success of all those that have emerged in the Iberian Peninsula over the last millennium or so, and for this reason alone it merits careful scholarly study.'[1] In this Part, I offer a critical analysis of Spanish community building projects, given that many of its citizens do not identify exclusively or even primarily with the nation state. As Gerald Brenan wrote in the preface to *The Spanish Labyrinth*, first published in 1943: 'Spain is the land of the *patria chica*. Every village, every town is the centre of an intense social and political life. As in classical times, a man's allegiance is first of all to his native place, or to his family or social group in it, and only secondly to his country and government.'[2] A physical and psychic entity forged largely on the basis of exclusion and expansion, Spain did not pre-exist the Spanish empire.

The 1469 marriage of Fernando, King of Aragón, and Isabel, Queen of Castile in Valladolid provided the preconditions for the creation of a centralised nation state, consolidated through the Reconquest of Muslim Spain and Christopher Columbus sailing to the New World under the flag of the Catholic Monarchs. In honour of the first reputed sighting in the Iberian Peninsula of the Virgin Mary, 'Our Lady of the Pillar', in the Cathedral of Zaragoza, the capital of Aragon, the namesake Pilar became the patron-saint of 'Hispanidad', roughly translatable as the Hispanic community. The 1561 establishment of the royal court in Madrid meant the city became at one and the same time the first capital of Spain and of the Spanish empire.

Spain did not have a national constitution until 1808; written and signed in Cadiz, the Andalusian port city that replaced Seville as the gateway to empire, its jurisdiction made little distinction between the metropolis and overseas territories. The expulsion of Napoleonic forces from the Peninsula in the early nineteenth century marks the birth of modern Spanish nationalism. Conversely, however, both the French Enlightenment and the pre-unification rights and traditions of Spain's historic kingdoms and principalities as well as pre-Columbine overseas territories fed into what Brian Hamnett characterises as the 'key issue of investigation during the later eighteenth and early nineteenth centuries': 'first, why, how and when Spanish liberties had been lost and, secondly, how they could be recovered'.[3] Seen in this light, Barcelona arguably has as much in common with a colonial outpost such as Buenos Aires as it does with Madrid. Economic factors had underpinned the first wave of imperial losses that 'stemmed from the metropolitan inability to mobilize sufficient resources to enable the country to continue sustaining the burden of imperial rule'.[4] Following the loss of the last American colonies in 1898, it was unclear if the metropolis could relinquish foreign possessions without incurring losses closer to home.

In the words of philosopher José Ortega y Gasset, the 'history of the decline of a nation is the history of a vast disintegration';[5] 'Castile has made Spain and Castile has unmade it.'[6] As Chapter 10 explores, the political and cultural casualties of Francoism's bellicose centralism are imprinted in Pablo Picasso's *Guernica*, a painting 'widely associated with the transition of a nation from dictatorship to democracy'.[7] If Catalan and Basque nationalists have long claimed that, to borrow a phrase from E. Inman Fox, 'the problem of Spain was founded in Castilian primacy',[8] the 2019 conviction of nine Catalan leaders by the Spanish Supreme Court for sedition has turned them into martyrs and showcased evidence of 'a resurgent Spanish nationalism that has little propensity to recognize or the capacity to accommodate other nationalisms'.[9] It is not necessary to accept the claim that pro-secessionist Catalans orchestrated a coup to recognise that their actions constitute the most significant threat to the constitutional order of 1978 since the military held Spanish democracy to ransom in 1981. Chapters 11 and 12 critically examine the interplay of art, education and politics in negotiating relations between the centre and the periphery in and beyond the historical nationalities to make the case that – as opposed to the dominant discourse now surrounding *Guernica* – culture can be a problem as well as a solution.

Chapter 10

Culture as a democratic weapon

Pablo Picasso's *Guernica*

In *La ciudad no es para mí* (*The City Is Not for Me*) (Pedro Lazaga, 1966), the decade's most successful film at the domestic box office, bumpkin Agustín Valverde is aghast on experiencing city living for the first time when he leaves behind his village in rural Aragon to visit his son and grandchildren in Madrid. The alienation of their urban condominium is epitomised by a Picasso print, which Agustín immediately replaces with a family portrait.

Accepted as a necessary evil, a residual suspicion of modern(ist) art as corrupt and corrupting nevertheless remained at the heart of the regime until the end. As Richard Cleminson and Rosa María Medina-Doménech note of an aggressively marketed real-life pharmaceutical product to treat depression from the time: 'A drawing of a long-haired young woman imitating the languid faces of the avant-garde paintings by Picasso or Modigliani linked the challenges of modern life to the personal failures caused by depression'.[1]

A degree of accommodation with Picasso and his ilk resulted from a growing realisation that autarchy in the cultural, as well as the economic, spheres was unsustainable. By the time of the dictator's death, Picasso was widely considered the twentieth century's greatest artist, and Federico García Lorca ranked as the most translated Spanish playwright. Executed by Falangist thugs shortly after the illegal rebel uprising, Lorca's death alongside *Guernica* were evidence of the regime's violent philistinism, ensuring an indelible link in the international psyche between Franco's victory and a defeat for culture. As numerous studies have shown, the afterlife of *Guernica* is a key barometer for Francoism's socio-political evolution. I will draw upon this scholarship to examine how competing discourses were both constituted by and constitutive of a direct association between culture and democracy, which transformed the former into an increasingly powerful tool of socio-political engineering.

In spite of the reputation he subsequently accrued, Picasso was not ideological by nature. As future friend, biographer and neighbour Patrick O'Brian remarks of the young artist's experiences of Europe's first Great War – in which Spain maintained neutrality – 'even so apolitical an animal as Picasso must have heard the rumbling of guns'.[2] *Guernica* was a commission by elected representatives of the Second Republic who asked Picasso – the acting wartime Director of the Prado – and Joan Miró to brandish their paintbrushes as artillery, to raise awareness about the plight of Spain in advance of the 1937 World Fair in Paris. The first public showing of *Guernica* was part of a satellite cultural battle with clear propagandistic intent. As Gijs van Hensbergen notes: 'Another profoundly moving element of the exhibition was the homage paid to important cultural figures who had already become victims of the war. García Lorca was represented by a photo, and the two realist sculptors, Emiliano Barral and Francisco Pérez Mateo were exhibited in a place of honour.'[3] Across enemy lines, the Vatican allocated space in their pavilion for the Francoists to exhibit works such as Josep Maria Sert's painting *La intercesión de Santa Teresa de Jesús en la Guerra Civil Española* (*Saint Teresa of Jesus's Intercession in the Spanish Civil War*). Picasso's political turn initially failed to make an impact: 'considering the coolness with which it was apparently received, it would have been reasonable to assume that *Guernica* might end up rolled and stored in the back of Picasso's studio'.[4]

Guernica constituted a departure from the 'art for art's sake' ethos that characterised Picasso's earlier output. It is entirely fitting, therefore, that political context as much as artistic quality would be instrumental in the painting's retrospective canonisation. Efforts by Roland Penrose and Herbert Read to exhibit the painting in London's New Burlington Galleries were facilitated by the commercial success at the same space of the International Surrealist Exhibition in 1936 (paintings by Salvador Dalí, Henry Moore and Pablo Picasso, attracting nearly a thousand visits a day).[5] By contrast, an exhibition mounted around *Guernica* with all profits going towards the National Joint Committee for Spanish Relief closed after being seen by a relatively paltry 3,000 visitors.[6] It hit a stronger nerve once transported to the proletarian East End of the capital, with over 15,000 spectators walking past the painting in the Whitechapel Gallery, Picasso asking that people donate a pair of boots to be sent to the front.[7] A subsequent tour of the USA in 1939 generated media interest but failed to attract crowds or urgently needed revenue.[8]

In Aristotelian terms, *Guernica* – 'our culture's Tragic scene', to borrow a phrase from T. J. Clark[9] – generates pity and fear following the collective anagnorisis that there is reason to be afraid for both ourselves and others. As Martin Minchom notes: 'Picasso's art "created reality on its own terms": instead of representing one event literally, the *Guernica* plays on the nightmare of recurring aerial bombardments, in which Gernika is the culmination of a process that had already affected Madrid and Durango.'[10]

In the wake of the Pearl Harbor attacks, the privileged and prescient vision on display in Picasso's canvas attracted more admirers, Basque and Spanish specificity eschewed in a path towards universalism. The painting found a new home in New York's Museum of Modern Art (MoMA) ten years after its opening and, in the words of Gijs van Hensbergen: 'If it had alerted the world to the catastrophic war, it also rang the death knell on a hopelessly exhausted European art. Its showing in New York was in effect a memorial service to a dying continent; its tragic subject matter a eulogy to a vanishing world.'[11] Picasso's stature grew exponentially as new currents such as Abstract Expressionism expanded the genealogies in which *Guernica* could claim pride of place. A new-found ethical and aesthetic universalism came at a political cost: if *Guernica* was about the brutality of modern-day warfare per se, it ceased to be a targeted attack on fascism Spanish-style.

The once apolitical Picasso's conversion to Communism cannot be divorced from his experiences in France or his opposition to Francoism.

That said, occupied Paris was not always inhospitable for ambitious artists and intellectuals. Jean-Paul Sartre was able to leave the Lyceé Pasteur and take up a professorship previously occupied by a Jewish academic at the Lyceé Concordet in the fashionable Opéra district. At a time of food shortages, the business of buying and selling modern art was booming, and Picasso extended his hospitality to Otto Abetz, the German ambassador.[12] In the wake of the Allied victory, that the world's greatest living artist had become a card-carrying Party member did much to boost the association between Communism and intellectuals for sympathisers and detractors alike. Dalí, a panegyrist for Franco, caustically quipped: 'If Picasso is a Communist … neither am I.' Nelson A. Rockefeller, whose parents had been instrumental in the creation of MoMA, for which he was now a board member, declared that Picasso was his favourite of the great European masters – 'an unending source of joy and satisfaction.'[13] The financier and politician's respect for the artist grew as he discovered his formidable business acumen.[14]

The onset and subsequent escalation of the Cold War constituted a fast track to respectability for the Francoist regime, and a public-relations obstacle for Picasso's otherwise rising fortunes. Whilst *Guernica* had been both depoliticised and deterritorialised by MoMA's decision not to make any reference to Spain or the Civil War, Picasso paid a price for his political convictions, as is manifest from the unceremonious removal of his paintings from Dallas Public Library at the height of anti-Communist paranoia.[15] Given this backdrop, it is ironic that, as Paula Barreiro López notes: 'The incorporation of Spain into the western ranks of the Cold War made the regime not only start reconsidering its relation towards modern art but also finally think about the place that Picasso could have in that narrative.'[16] As early as 1951, the first Hispanic-American Biennale was organised by the Francoist authorities under the organisation of the regime's unofficial poet laureate, Luis Rosales. Dalí was an enthusiastic contributor, whilst Picasso rebuffed Rosales's advances.[17] Luis Miguel Dominguín, the bullfighter friend of both Picasso and the dictator, whose brother Domingo recruited intellectuals and artists for the Spanish Communist Party (see Chapter 4), nevertheless claims the former said he would grant permission for *Guernica* to return to Spain were the Francoist authorities to display it in the Prado, and made the following confession: 'Look, Luis Miguel ... I have nothing against Franco, nor am I am so swayed by people as is commonly thought. The thing is that the Communists have shown me more warmth than the Francoists. For that reason they are my friends.'[18]

Irrespective of the veridical status of this anecdotal recollection, relations between Picasso and the regime did begin to thaw. *Guernica* nevertheless presented some very specific challenges, given its counter-narrative to the official line of what had taken place in the Basque Country, the area of Spain most fiercely resistant to centralist control; in a plebiscite conducted in November 1933, a turnout of 87 per cent voted overwhelmingly (83 per cent) in favour of the creation of an independent, autonomous community.[19] The destruction of Gernika, whose symbolic weight in Basque history eclipsed its physical and demographic size, was not the first time aerial bombing had been used during the war. Iconic status derived from the presence of the international press in nearby Bilbao alongside the pedagogical nature of the targeted attack: 'something more than a pretty Basque village was destroyed. A population was terrorised so that it relinquished its resistance.'[20] Following the Republican defeat, prisoners were brought in to assist with the reconstruction of the historic town,[21] recast in the victor's image: the historic central square was given an Andalusian, as opposed to Basque, character, and scarce housing stock was reserved for the Francoist faithful.[22]

Just as war booty was distributed, moral responsibility was transferred. The official line attributed the bombing to Republican forces from the Basque Country and Asturias;[23] apologists for the dictatorship such as future Minister of Culture Ricardo de la Cierva (see Chapter 5) later modified this discredited narrative to claim the German air force had carried out the aerial bombardment, but without informing the Francoists.[24] Another variation was the claim that the scale of 'a unique model for well-carried-out political publicity'[25] had been grossly exaggerated: 'More ink, according to what has been said, has been expended on Guernica than bombs.'[26] The retrospective accommodation and depoliticisation of cultural martyrs were part of Francoist orthodoxy prior to the dictator's death.

As Maria M. Delgado has uncovered, the execution of Lorca – registered as 'war wounds' on a death certificate issued in 1940 – was recast, 'burying the political significance of the atrocities of the Civil War in a fatalistic discourse where such crimes were simply dismissed as the inevitable casualties of a fratricidal conflict'.[27] In this reading, after twenty-five years of peace, Spain now enjoyed a sufficiently mature and tolerant political environment to allow his plays to be staged from the 1960s onwards. More problematic was any attempt to acknowledge – as an internal police report from 1965 did[28] – that Lorca was specifically targeted for his political ideals and sexual inclinations. Ian Gibson's quasi-archaeological reconstruction of the poet's final days was first made available in Spain in 1979, eight years on from its original publication. José Luis Vila-San-Juan's more conciliatory *García Lorca, asesinado: todo la verdad* (*García Lorca, Assassinated: The Whole Truth*) (1975) appeared in the interim, receiving the Espejo de España prize from a jury whose members included Manuel Fraga and De la Cierva.[29]

The ghosts of *Guernica* were harder to put to rest. Franco outlived Picasso by just two-and-a-half years, and the painter constituted a public-relations minefield for the regime and champions of the world's greatest living artist back home alike. In the mid-1950s, a group of artistically minded businessmen established a modest museum in Picasso's native Andalusia. In a letter dated 24 July 1958, sent from the director to Jaime Sabartés, Picasso's secretary and administrator, it is stated that no books on *Guernica* will be put on display 'hasta que todo vuelva a su lógica normalidad' (until everything returns to its logical normality).[30] When the Malaga Museum of Fine Arts opened to the public in April 1961, it contained no paintings by the city's most famous son. In 1962, UNESCO informed the Spanish authorities of plans to stage an exhibition comprising artworks critiquing war, scheduled to include a photograph of *Guernica*. Their response was that the painting had its origins in a specific context, and that exhibiting the image needlessly ran the risk of rekindling hatreds that had been successfully overcome. The director of

UNESCO disagreed, but bowed to the pressures out of respect for Spain's having been a member state since 1952.[31]

The first major space dedicated to Picasso's work was in Barcelona, the Catalan capital in which Picasso lived for many of years and came of age as an artist. Initially consisting of donations from Sabartés and the artist himself, the initiative would probably not have gone ahead if not for the personal intervention of Josep Maria de Porcioles,[32] Barcelona's Mayor from 1957 to 1973. A degree of accommodation is intimated by the Francoist politician and Sabartés often writing to each other in Catalan, but official documents inevitably being rendered in Castilian. An official agreement for the creation of what was initially referred to as the 'Sabartés Collection' (and only later rebaptised at the Picasso Museum) signed on 15 March 1962 pre-empted the twin threats of the regime's centralism and desire to underplay the artist's significance, stipulating that the collection must be on permanent display in its entirety and that it could not be (re) moved.[33] The now almost permanent queues outside Barcelona's Picasso Museum are a far cry from what was once a little-visited space in a neglected area of the old town ignored in almost all tourist guides.

In the twilight years of the dictatorship, *Guernica* constituted a totemic rallying call for the opposition and regime stalwarts alike. Postcard photographic images of the exiled painting were iconic statements of protest and were frequently ripped off walls during police raids. Furthermore, as Paula Barreiro López remarks: 'References to *Guernica* became recurrent iconographic elements of the new artistic languages of the 1960s.'[34] Antonio Saura was, for example, influenced by those North American artists most affected by *Guernica*. His 1963 painting *La gran muchedumbre* (*The Great Crowd*) reinterprets the ethics of Picasso through the aesthetics of Jackson Pollock. Following reports that the regime might be seeking to bring the painting back home, the Valencian-based Equipo Crónica collective created a parodic series titled *Guernica 69*, indicting the very same figures involved in this possible repatriation with the atrocities depicted in the painting.[35]

In October 1971, an exhibition planned to commemorate Picasso's birthday at Madrid's Complutense University was banned by the authorities at the last minute.[36] That same month, canvases of his on display in Madrid's Theo art gallery were attacked by far-right-wing vigilante group the Guerrilleros de Cristo Rey. Although the official line of the fascist *Fuerza Nueva* magazine was that this was the work of Communist agitators, a published letter to the editor claimed of the attack that 'on learning of it I congratulated myself on the fact that there are still Spaniards who don't want the public exposed to such superb filth. Our society still isn't rotten, and we can save if it we put our minds to it.'[37]

Following the artist's death on 1 April 1973, *Fuerza Nueva* featured an atypical obituary, which claimed that 'thirty-seven years after the victory of the national Crusade, Picasso represents personally, ideologically and fundamentally the anti-Spain … He has been a gross servant for the Anti-Christ.'[38] The regime by this time was paying more than lip-service to the artist. Episode 1580A of the State-run newsreel NO-DO from 1973 showered him with posthumous praise, emphasising the quantity of modern art purchased by the Spanish Government for inclusion in the Museum of Contemporary Art since its opening in 1959.[39] Picasso and later his estate were nevertheless clear that two non-negotiable conditions had to be met before *Guernica* could return home from MoMA: Spain had to be a democracy and exhibition space needed to be made available in the Prado so that Picasso's work could be viewed alongside other national treasures such as Goya and Velázquez.

In 1976, Felipe González set a trend amongst Spanish politicians visiting New York by being photographed in front of the painting in MoMA. A lack of political maturity was nevertheless indicated by the fact that historian Herbert Southworth was invited to speak at the international Gernika truth commission in 1977 at a time when his books remained unavailable in Spain. On 26 April, the fortieth anniversary of the bombing, the Picasso family sent a telegram expressing their sympathy and solidarity with the town of Gernika, the inhabitants of which were now publicly able to express their grief for the first time since the end of the Civil War.[40] In front of a chanting crowd, a full-size replica of the painting was unfurled; the local council proposed constructing a museum to house the painting that had made their town a global point of reference.[41]

In a letter dated 11 October 1977 to the Director of Museums, Rosa María Subirana Torrent (the then director of the Picasso Museum) reported multiple anonymous bomb threats, and asked for instructions on the protocol to be adopted in such instances. The following month she wrote to Barcelona's City Hall voicing concerns that the police had suggested the museum be a polling station in the upcoming elections, an option she thought untenable owing to the value of the artworks and a lack of security.[42] During the first six months of 1978, the Picasso Museum averaged around 5,000 visitors a month, an almost identical figure to those recorded at Barcelona's Military Museum, entrance for which was nearly double the price.[43] By this time, Spain was far enough along the route of democratisation for negotiations about the return of *Guernica* to commence, but suffered a setback on 26 April when Paloma Picasso, the artist's daughter, told the Minister of Culture, Pío Cabanillas, that she was suspending all communication in protest against the detention of theatre practitioner Albert Boadella (see Chapter 5). A series of delays effectively served as advance publicity for the painting's eventual return, Picasso being a much bigger household name in Spain in 1981 than he had been just three years previously.

In terms of mainstream appeal for Barcelona's Picasso Museum, the breakthrough was an 'erotic Picasso' exhibition. The inclusion of such artefacts as a feature on the artist from *Playboy* reputedly did not impress the Picasso estate, but it did lead to record attendance figures. In a letter dated 28 March 1979, Subirana Torrent voiced her concern about the lack of adequate security. Over 1,200 visitors had turned up between 11.00 a.m. and 1.30 p.m. the previous Sunday: 'el Museo no sólo no estuvo vigilado sino que además se formaron colas, tumultos, albortos y protestas a la entrada' (not only did the Museum not have any security, but there were also queues, scuffles, disturbances and protests at the entrance).[44] This unprecedented popular appeal did not go unnoticed by Javier Tusell, the recently appointed Director-General of Museums and Artistic Heritage, as well as the chief negotiator for the return of *Guernica*, who enquired about the possibility of bringing the exhibition to Madrid's National Library. In her reply, Subirana Torrent said she would take the request to her board but that she was not personally keen: 'considero que esta exposición tuvo sentido en su día, pero que actualmente debería de pensarse de otra manera' (I think that this exhibition made sense at the time, but would now need to be formulated differently).[45] She also deflected a request to consider collaborating on an exhibition titled '*Guernica* y su entorno' (*Guernica* and its background). A parallel but distinct question was whether, given changes in political rule and the fact that Spain had seemingly amassed sufficient democratic collateral for the painting to return home, more flexibility might be shown in relation to Picasso's stipulation that the museum in his adopted home of Barcelona (some of whose inhabitants and institutions refer to him, albeit anachronistically, as Pau rather than Pablo) should not loan items from its holdings, even on a temporary basis. The eventual return of *Guernica* both reflected and consolidated a specific notion of democracy mapped onto a socio-political climate with over-, albeit not pre-, determined cultural and geographical contours.

On 4 February 1981, King Juan Carlos made his first visit to the town of Gernika, infamously telling hecklers to speak up as he was unable to hear what they were saying. Unrest in the Basque Country was instrumental to the rationale of the failed coup attempt of 23 February 1981 (see Chapter 5). Just over six months later, and a month shy of what would have been Picasso's 100th birthday, MoMA officially signed *Guernica* over to the Spanish State.[46] Right up to the point of its removal, the New York museum had received threats of violence and vandalism. The insurance price quoted for the transfer from the USA to Spain was the highest ever for a work of art, ensuring that *Guernica* travelled without cover on the Lope de Vega aircraft, the company charged with ensuring its safe transfer quoting a value of $15 million for customs purposes.[47] In order to minimise risks, passenger lists were tampered with to ensure that those crossing the Atlantic with Picasso's masterpiece had travelled with Iberia airlines previously.[48]

A 200 peseta stamp was designed to commemorate the homecoming,[49] and *El País* waxed lyrical about the symbolic return: '*Guernica* arriving in Spain ought to signify the total and definite closure of the Civil War and, as such, be a motive for absolute celebration.'[50] A rhetorical sleight of hand typifies such aggressive pacifism: anybody not unconditionally supportive of the painting and the conditions surrounding its repatriation is dismissed for keeping flames of conflict alive. On the same day, the paper's editorial, titled 'La guerra ha terminado' (The war is over), contended it would be regrettable were petty arguments over where *Guernica* was to be exhibited to detract from 'the happiness of this symbolic happening'.[51] The editorial of Basque nationalist paper *Deía* unsurprisingly took a different stance:

> From the propagandistic perspective of centralism the arrival of *Guernica* can be presented as a victory for them: what Francoism wasn't able to achieve, the UCD have managed. It can also be depicted as the intended new page in the pacification of the State with the arrival of the last exile, as *Guernica* has already been termed, when the reality is that many conflicts need to be resolved before any kind of closure is in sight.[52]

Once in Madrid, it was exhibited behind bullet-proof glass in a purpose-built annex of the Prado Museum constructed in the Retiro Park: 'Sidelined in the unfortunate context of the Casón, the painting had the freakish air of an outdated anachronism that no longer played a central role in the history of Spanish art.'[53] The location nonetheless allowed the State technically to respect Picasso's wishes, and provided a bespoke rationale with which to reject appeals on the basis of provenance from the Basque Country and Malaga. Picasso had in fact offered to gift the painting to the Basque Country during the Civil War, but was turned down by José Antonio Aguirre, President of the provisional regional Government. If accepted, it might well have been destroyed, another casualty of war.

More generally, there is a plausible case for *Guernica*'s failure being inscribed in its very material and symbolic survival. Designed as a piece of propaganda, its preservation was initially secondary to proselytising. Only when the painting failed in its military objective to prompt indignation and stop the rebel advance did the aesthetic came to the fore, *Guernica*'s message and canvas becoming a matter of (inter)national concern. A belated arrival in Madrid was testament to the Republican defeat in the Civil War, alongside nearly forty years of dictatorship, and is metonymic of predicating the Transition on understanding Francoist violence as a custodial spectre and not a subject open to new-found democratic interrogation.

Following a press-preview on 23 October 1981, the Spanish public had their first chance to see the painting two days later, as was documented by the State television-channel broadcast at the time and made for posterity.[54] Almost simultaneously, an exhibition opened at the Picasso Museum on the artist's time spent in Barcelona; although nothing on the scale of what was taking place in Madrid, over 20,000 people visited within the first month, including 4,700 schoolchildren.[55] In the post-coup socio-political climate, the return of *Guernica* was seen as evidence of Spain's new-found civility, and the painting itself proof of art's civilising force. The ghosts of the past were indicted by the violent images on the canvas and intimated by the security measures required to protect it. In an acerbic tongue-in-cheek polemic titled *Contra Guernica* (*Against Guernica*), artist Antonio Saura railed against the hyperbole underlying a redemptive narrative of repatriation: 'I scorn the happiness that has invaded Spanish homes, reassured by the magnificent triumph of recuperating the masterpiece *Guernica*, the cultural equivalent of winning the World Cup.'[56] The process was already in motion prior to the PSOE landslide victory, but their term in office consecrated the notion of culture as panacea.

Madrid's original Museum of Modern Art, inaugurated by royal decree, predated MoMA, ominously opening its door to the public in the fateful year of 1898, as Spain lost its final vestiges of empire. This 'unloved and unvisited' institution,[57] situated in the same building as the National Library, fell short of the PSOE's ambitions for showcasing art and democracy. Numerous international experts were invited to the 1984 edition of commercial art fare ARCO (see Chapter 8) to comment on the possibility of converting the San Carlos Hospital into the Spanish equivalent of the Pompidou Centre. Although some were positive about the prospect, others were less convinced. In a letter dated 6 June 1984, R. H. Fuchs from the Van Abbe Museum was particularly scathing about the prospect of providing a Spanish counterpart to the august Parisian institution: 'You cannot give art the flavour of the *Corrida*. You want concentration and some quiet moments. Building a huge centre now in Madrid is like building a Christian Cathedral in Mecca.'[58] Concerns voiced about over-vaulting ambition were disregarded.

The Reina Sofía Centre, later rebranded as a National Museum, made its entry into the State and global art scene in 1986.[59] Madrid's Juan March Foundation had previously carried out important groundwork in developing an audience and taste for international currents in modern art by staging a series of exhibitions dedicated to artists such as Francis Bacon, Roy Lichtenstein and Wassily Kandinsky. Spain now had, for the first time, a large public space capable of hosting major international touring exhibitions. In terms of the permanent collection, Picasso's birthdate of 1881 was taken as the start point for a tour through currents in modern art with a particular emphasis on how these had been construed within a Spanish context. As early as 1989, the director of the Reina Sofía, Tomás Llorens, voiced his desire for *Guernica* to be moved to his centre, which was rebranded as a museum with the arrival of Picasso's masterpiece amongst its somewhat underwhelming holdings.[60] Objections to the move were made for material and ideological motivations. First, a painting that had toured the world was not in great condition and any additional movement, even within the same city, risked damage. Second, if Picasso's wishes to be exhibited in the Prado were to be disregarded, then the de facto argument against cities other than Madrid being granted the opportunity to tender for the right to exhibit *Guernica* vanished. In 1992, the board of the Prado approved the transfer of Picasso's painting (seventeen voted in favour, with four abstentions) in exchange for the Ministry of Culture agreeing to long-overdue extensions to Madrid's oldest National Museum.[61] Looking beyond the time-frame that concerns us here, the Guggenheim Museum in Bilbao would probably not have been built if local politicians and the Foundation itself had not believed it would force *Guernica*'s return to the Basque Country.

The madcap comedy film *El robo más grande jamás contado* (*The Biggest Robbery Never Told*) (Daniel Monzón, 2002) shows a group of hapless criminals attempting to steal *Guernica* from Madrid. When they inadvertently cause damage to the canvas, they wind up being paid more by Government officials, desperate to keep the damage secret, than they would have secured for the painting on the black market. The final satirical scene cuts to news footage reporting that the delicate state of Picasso's masterpiece means it would be impossible to move to the Guggenheim. A regulatory fiction of peace and reconcilement, the *Guernica* effect shows no sign of abating. An international cast starred in the historical epic about the bombing, *Gernika* (Koldo Serra, 2016), whilst the eightieth anniversary of Picasso's painting was represented in television series and documentaries in the USA and Spain,[62] and numerous musicians, including international pop-flamenco sensation Rosalía, were filmed performing in front of the canvas in the Reina Sofía.

Schoolchildren are now more likely to be taken to modern-art museums or Spain's first Museum of Peace, opened in the town of Gernika in 1998, than to Francoist mausoleums. Much as educational curricula often shy away from discussing the Civil War in depth, *Guernica*'s embodiment of reconciliation does not necessarily indicate a broader engagement with history and its victims. Military museums, for example, fail to recognise the complicity of the armed forces with a dictatorial regime. Even in Burgos, the Francoist barracks during the Civil War, reference is made to the city's strategic value but no mention is made of a particular affiliation for the rebels, a portrait of Franco hung next to one of Vicente Rojo Lluch, a devout Catholic General who remained loyal to the Republic. In order to provide space for planned extension works to the Prado, the National Military Museum was moved from Madrid to Toledo,[63] reopened in 2010 by Prince Felipe. As the first city captured from the Moors in the Reconquest, Toledo held a significant place in the Francoist imaginary, subsequently consolidated by a siege in which soldiers led by General Moscardó, and civilians including many children, remained locked in the city fortress where the Military Museum is now housed. When Moscardó died in 1956, a celebratory book was published as part of a series titled 'La epopeya y sus héroes' (The epic and its heroes),[64] and his body was taken from Madrid to Toledo. Until this day, veterans of the siege have the right to be buried there, as was General Milans del Bosch (1915–97), one of the chief architects of the 1981 coup. No mention of this is made in the Military Museum, which claims that, faced with the radical Second Republic, the army was as divided as the rest of Spanish society. The narrative then leaps forward to the Transition, with praise heaped upon General Gutiérrez Mellado, much hated in military circles at the time (see Chapter 5), alongside televised footage of Juan Carlos addressing the nation after the coup in military uniform.

As Spain embarked on its rocky road to democratic normalisation, *Guernica*'s place in MoMA was taken by Jackson Pollock's *One*.[65] There is no obvious replacement were the Reina Sofía to lose its star exhibit. The modern-art museum has the opposite problem to the Prado, which still struggles for space. At any given time, only a fraction of the paintings of Peter Paul Rubens held amongst its permanent collections are on display to the public. Initial expansion plans were put on hold with the creation of the Thyssen Museum, exacerbating pre-existing tensions between the museum's director, Alfonso E. Pérez Sánchez,[66] and the Socialist administration, which culminated in his handing in his letter of resignation after signing a petition against the Gulf War. If he had not done so, he would probably have been dismissed by Jorge Semprún, as were other high-profile signatories such as the Director of the National Library. It is evidence of an unconsolidated pluralistic democratic sphere that the Government was unable to accommodate dissent within its educational and cultural ranks.

Outside Madrid, the Valencian Institute of Modern Art, opened in 1989, in many respects 'stands as the exemplary model for the end-of-the-twentieth-century museum',[67] providing a more satisfying match between space and scope, ambition and reality than the Reina Sofía. The location outside the capital, alongside an initial unwillingness to reach beyond a core demographic of the young and highly educated, nevertheless resulted in this generously funded institution underperforming in terms of visitor-numbers,[68] which were drastically lower than those of, say, the Salvador Dalí museum in Figueres.

A lack of economic and symbolic investment in culture under Franco ensured that Spain's leading contemporary artists often worked and sold their art abroad. Although painters such as Antonio López, Eduardo Chillida and Antonio Saura continued to produce stellar work, as did numerous emerging figures (e.g. Ouka Leele, Javier Mariscal and Miquel Barceló), during the democratic period, there can be no denying that Spanish artists were no longer the trailblazers they had been for much of the century. The country was more visibly represented by architects such as Rafael Moneo – with commissions including the extension to the Prado and Los Angeles Cathedral – and Santiago Calatrava, 'as preoccupied by aesthetics as he is by technology',[69] whose bridges for projects such as the Seville Expo (see Chapter 12) resulted in a 1993 retrospective at the MoMA.

In a somewhat exasperated letter written to the incumbent Spanish Minister of Culture on 19 November 1992, Joseba Arregui Aranburu (Director of Culture for the Basque Country) demanded a response from central Government, which had clearly ignored previous requests, regarding a motion approved by the Basque Parliament to claim rights on *Guernica*.[70] On the logic of the centralist administration this matter had been resolved by the fact that, as a promotional documentary produced by the Ministry of Culture boasted, the Reina Sofía museum was 'a cultural service by the State for the whole State'.[71] *Guernica*, the indictment of fascist violence, now embodies a centralist democratic settlement that relieves those complicit in said aggression of having to take responsibility for their actions like no other work of art.

Chapter 11

The historical nationalities

Culture and community in the Basque Country, Catalonia and Galicia

As Richard Gunther and José Ramón Montero note of the aftermath of Franco's death: 'the legitimacy of the new democratic regime required Basque and Catalan acceptance of the new governmental framework, and this, in turn required a restoration of their self-government rights'.[1] In the popular referendum to ratify the Constitution on 6 December 1978, Basque voters were unique in not endorsing Spain's democratic Magna Carta: 35 per cent of eligible voters voted affirmatively and 11 per cent negatively, with an abstention rate of 50 per cent.[2] As the Basque Country is the most sparsely populated of the historical nationalities, this regional blip mattered little in terms of the overall result of a referendum that covered the whole of Spain, but Basque reluctance nonetheless constituted the most persistent obstacle to the legitimation of the nascent democratic nation state. Prior to Spain's EU membership, Catalan patriotism rarely translated into a widespread desire for independence, whilst nationalism remained comparatively weak in Galicia. Taking, in turn, each of the historical nationalities granted a fast-track route to devolution, this chapter critically interrogates the radically different constellations of political and cultural affect in operation between and within them, so as to understand better the extent to which the centre–periphery relations articulated by the consensus politics of the time were, and remain, fit for purpose.

Violent and exclusionary nationalism: the Spanish State and the Basque Country

On 6 December 1981, municipal councils in the Basque Country and Navarre were unusual in not organising events in celebration of the 1978 Spanish Constitution and flag.[3] This ought not to be taken as proof of overwhelming nationalist sentiment. In the first post-Franco general elections, the PSOE had, for example, emerged as the largest single political force: 'To a major extent the vote for the Socialists was among other things, a rejection of Basque nationalism, although not the notion of Basque autonomy. Its sociological core was the immigrant working class in all four Basque provinces.'[4] Three of these – Vizcaya, Alava, Guipúzcoa – pertained to the administration of the autonomous community of the Basque Country. The fourth, Navarre, opted out of the process towards autonomy under the Second Republic. During the Transition, progressive Basque nationalists – *abertzales* – saw the annexation of Navarre as a priority, whilst for 'the army, the UCD and the Spanish right in general and the Navarese right in particular, it was a bulwark of Spanish unity'.[5]

The emergence of the modern Basque nationalist movement at the end of the nineteenth century had its roots in the division between the rural and the urban alongside the threat (perceived or real) that migrants from the rest of Spain, referred to pejoratively as *maketos*, posed to identity and community. In the nineteenth century, the Carlist Wars were effectively a Basque Civil War, pitching the liberal urban centres against rural, staunchly religious elites that championed economic autarchy as ratified through the *fueros*, rights whose origins could be traced back to the Middle Ages. A non-romance language with obscure roots and lacking a systematised grammar or strong literary tradition, Basque presented self-evident challenges if it were to be employed as part of an assimilation programme. Sabino Arana – the founder of the Partido Nacionalista Vasco (Basque Nationalist Party; PNV) in 1895 – argued, 'drawing on pre-existing memories of what the foreign invader had been', that *maketos* were their Moors.[6] He thereby privileged race over culture: 'citizens who wanted to become members of the party had to prove their Basque origins by demonstrating that their first four surnames, later only one of the four, were etymologically Basque.[7] Having studied in Catalonia, Arana opposed what he believed to be Catalans' diluted aspirations and instead championed autonomy. As Stanley Payne remarks, the PNV's founding principles were 'at one and the same time racist (positioning a distinct and superior Basque race), reactionary, segregationist, intolerant, ultra-clerical and in [their] own way quite radical.[8] Basque nationalism was less mainstream or widely accepted in the early twentieth century than in Catalonia. From the outset of the Civil War, the rebels faced fierce opposition in the Basque Country but could also count on support.

Following the Francoist victory, Vizcaya and Guipúzcoa were divested of their relative economic independence, unlike Alava and Navarre, which were rewarded for their loyalty. As Paloma Aguilar notes: 'contrary to what Basque nationalism has maintained, first in clandestinity and then in democracy, the overall situation in the Basque Country (at least during the war years and immediately after) was not clearly worse than in the rest of Spain.[9] Picasso's *Guernica* did much to foster this image, but more decisive was the fertile breeding ground for a retrospective narrative of martyrdom created by the Francoist State's systematic policy of repression, as opposed to concession, in response to the actions of ETA from the 1960s onwards. The organisation was formed by young militants in 1959. Despite its creation being announced on the same symbolic date, 31 July (St Ignatius Day, named after the founder of the Jesuits born in the Basque town of Azpeitia), that Arana had chosen to launch the PNV some sixty-four years previously, the younger organisation 'broke with the religious traditionalism in Basque politics and declared itself non-confessional',[10] 'ETA's ideology was a combination of traditional Basque nationalism and Marxism with influences from Third World revolutionary struggles.[11] Frustrated with the inability of the PNV to offer any meaningful resistance to the dictatorship, ETA did not initially carry out violent attacks, which only began to rise in the late 1960s,[12] provoking a disproportionate response from the dictatorial State. In the build-up to the Burgos trials, a state of emergency was declared in the rest of Spain. International opinion rallied around the tortured Basque prisoners facing the genuine prospect of being garrotted. Jean-Paul Sartre described ETA as an admirable combination of anti-German resistance movements from the Second World War and more recent anticolonial struggles.[13]

The credibility of ETA's predominantly Marxist critical doctrine would have been undermined if the largely non-Basque working class had been excluded from the struggle to overthrow the exploitative colonial State. Language and culture, as opposed to race, thereby became the cornerstone of the Basque struggle. In a context where host communities were often far from welcoming, the attraction of a Che Guevara-style revolutionary chic for dispossessed youth was self-evident. Following a similar pattern to Madrid and Barcelona, a new town consisting of State housing, Ocharcoaga (or Otxarkoaga in Basque), was inaugurated on the outskirts of Bilbao in 1961. The authorities were alerted to the fact that poor living conditions had converted it and surrounding shanty towns into a recruitment ground for separatist movements.[14] Another symptom and cause of 'a changing society in which the classical alliances and loyalties disappeared'[15] was the fact that many 'Basque priests considered it their duty as Christians and priests, as well as citizens, to take on the role of modern prophets and fearlessly denounce injustice and corruption'.[16] Under the influence of the Second Vatican Council, the Spanish Church had entered into a period of self-reflection about its traditionally non-critical support of the regime; this took on accented resonances in the Basque Country as a result of an atypical ecclesiastical resistance to the regime dating back to the complex alliances of the Civil War and the intensification of repression during the 1960s.

In the words of Pamela Beth Radcliff: 'the forced demobilization of other kinds of associationism after the Civil War only further enhanced the parish's role as primary locus of local sociability in the 1940s and 1950s'.[17] As opposed to the role of the centrally appointed civil governor – 'a "viceroy" in the provinces and a "servant" in Madrid'[18] – priests had the authority to privilege the interests of their parishioners over those of an increasingly discredited State. In the Basque context, this was exacerbated by the fact that, until the late 1970s, the Jesuit Deusto University had an almost exclusive monopoly on higher education. By the late 1960s, an ecclesiastical monopoly was turning against the regime in which it had been nurtured, the authorities finding it increasingly challenging to honour the so-called 'clergy charter' (laid down in the 1953 concordat with the Vatican) that meant priests could not be charged with criminal offences unless a bishop concurred with the judgment. In July 1968, the dictatorial regime reinterpreted the charter and opened a prison for rebel priests in Zamora.[19] The inmates were predominantly Basque.

Across wide swathes of progressive society, ETA had successfully established a link between the right to self-determination and democratisation. By the time of Franco's death, however, the Basque-speaking population was down to 25 per cent, and only 10 per cent of those speakers were literate in the language.[20] There was therefore a cultural as well as a political battle to be fought. As Rob Stone and María Pilar Rodríguez note of the period between 1975 and 1980: 'At no other time has Basque cinema been marked by such a forceful and radical ideological vindication of the Basque language and the role of Basque cinema in the cause of self-determination and ultimate independence.'[21] Following the national general elections of 1977, the Socialist Ramón Rubén Cavia, a local metal-worker who had been a political prisoner under Franco, became the first democratically elected post-Franco President (Lehendakari) of the Basque Parliament. Although the PSOE received the largest number of votes, they still required the support of nationalist parties to govern effectively, and Cavia's non-Basque heritage made him an unacceptable candidate to them. His term was short-lived, and the PNV occupied the presidency until 2009, resulting in unprecedented largesse for cultural production: 'Basque government grants and subsidies were crucial in developing the Basque publishing industry, and were based on agreeing to buy around three hundred copies of every book published in Euskera.'[22]

In the first democratic municipal elections in 1979, Jon Castañeres from the PNV was elected Mayor of Bilbao, replacing José Luis Berasetegui Goicoechea – a local man from the Francoist rank and file – who had occupied the role since July 1975. Otxarkoaga quickly became the source of political debate as the city council demanded both autonomy from the State and compensation for having inherited a defective housing estate in urgent need of repair. At a municipal meeting on 20 December 1979, topics for debate included a forty-eight-page report that claimed: 'El Barrio es viejo a los quince años, está lleno de un conjunto de taras y son directamente consecuencia de la actuación del creador que fue el Ministerio de Vivienda' (The neighbourhood is old at fifteen, full of defects, and these are the direct result of those who created it, the Ministry of Housing).[23] The claim that they had willingly taken on responsibility as part of increased devolution was given short shrift:

> era un Ayuntamiento no democrático, un Ayuntamiento que era prolongación directa de la Administración central, un Ayuntamiento sin independencia ninguna de criterio para decidir y de hecho venía a aceptar – como su propio Alcalde – las implicaciones y direcciones de la Administración Central. Este Ayuntamiento se encuentra en una situación diametralmente opuesta.[24]

> this was a non-democratic City Hall, a City Hall that was a direct extension of the central administration, a City Hall with no decision-making powers and that in fact came to accept – like its own Mayor – the repercussions and directives from Central Administration. This City Hall finds itself in a diametrically opposed situation.

The conflict continued and the terms of democratic participation were debated in a meeting on 8 January 1981, when there was general consent over the need to send a delegation to Madrid to demand payment of contractors hired by the Town Hall to carry out repairs in Otxarkoaga, but disagreements about how many local residents should be funded to attend.

Throughout the democratic period, the PNV fought for Basque independence through parliamentary, as opposed to violent, means. For their detractors, however, their contextualisation of the actions of ETA frequently crossed the lines into justification, and the spectre of terrorist violence often, although not always, strengthened their position at the negotiating table. The traditional buoyancy of the Basque economy was also under threat as the global recession impacted negatively on manufacturing centred in and around Bilbao. Public unrest and violence had an adverse effect on the tourist industry in San Sebastian, the coastal capital of Guipúzcoa;[25] the entry of armed police into the bullring in Pamplona in 1978 was not the kind of danger welcomed by the foreigners increasingly drawn to the San Fermín celebrations, allured by the romance of Ernest Hemingway and the bulls.

From 1953 onwards, San Sebastian had hosted an International Film Festival that had helped extend the traditional summer season of this coastal resort into September. As Mar Diestro-Dópido notes, local folklore – with events such as the *tamborada* (drum playing), dance and bullfights – featured heavily in the first decade, sometimes at the expense of the films themselves.[26] By the late 1960s, however, it had become a key forum for oppositional cinema, and a conduit for Basque and Spanish filmmakers to connect with the outside world. A letter sent to the nascent Minister of Culture by the office of the Civil Governor in San Sebastian in the early 1980s made a case for funding on the basis that it provided an ideal forum to carry out surveillance on suspected members of ETA.[27]

Minutes from local town council meetings suggest strong inter-party support for showcase ventures such as the Film Festival and the International Jazz Festival, which had run since 1966. The only reservations came from Herri Batasuna, the political arm of ETA's military wing, focused more single-mindedly on Basque culture. A proposal for improved municipal libraries dated 6 February 1984 lamented: 'Nuestra lengua en una situación de supervivencia, nuestras relaciones humanas, artísticas, creativas, participativas … con unos niveles de alineación que no ayudan nada al reencuentro y avance que debemos desarrollar como seres libres en un Pueblo en Libertad' (Our language fighting for survival, our human, artistic, creative, participatory relations … with a degree of alienation that hardly aids our coming together or the advances we should nurture as free beings in a Land of Freedom).[28]

Moving away from rural settings long depicted as synecdochal of Basque identity, in the cinema of the time, 'Bilbao became Scorsesian with its mean streets of rain, rust and neon providing the dystopian setting for films dealings [sic] with terrorist pasts, drug addiction, corruption, juvenile delinquency and disruptive sexualities.'[29] *El pico*

(*The Hit*) (Eloy de la Iglesia, 1983), a relatively late entry into the *quinqui* genre (see Chapter 7), depicts the homoerotic friendship between two junkies, one the son of a Guardia Civil officer and the other of an *abertzale* politician. A recurring theme in films such as *La muerte de Mikel* (*The Death of Mikel*) (Imanol Uribe, 1984) and *La blanca paloma* (*The White Dove*) (Juan Miñón, 1989) is the tragic consequences of love and desire colliding with nationalist sentiment. The poverty of human possibilities is contrasted with the beauty of the natural landscape in *27 Hours* (Montxo Armendáriz, 1984), exposing the underbelly of San Sebastian. A young woman overdoses whilst caught up in a police riot. Extra-diegetic music tends to be classical, but the characters listen almost exclusively to punk and metal. This was the era of pro-nationalist radical Basque rock music – far more hard-hitting than what was contemporary in Madrid – spearheaded by La Polla Records and Barricada, who nevertheless tended to sing in Castilian, the language of the occupier.[30]

Dominant languages invariably have an unfair advantage in bilingual contexts but it would be quixotic to insist on mono-lingualism in the majority of Basque cultural and institutional settings. That not even all PNV MPs have sufficient level to formulate their interventions in the vernacular requires the presence of simultaneous interpreters in the Basque Parliament, whilst most university courses offered in Basque are also run in Castilian.[31] As Joseba Gabilondo notes: 'Basque language and its speakers have always lived in various, heterogeneous, political formations where other languages were used as State languages.'[32] This is both the cause and consequence of the fact that:

> the continental and diasporic Basque Country cannot be described by the model following the model of the (post)imperialist nation state. The Basque historian must also account for the fact that most Basque institutions have been developed in a marginal, symbiotic, or even parasitic relation to those of the (post)imperialist nation-state, mainly France and Spain.[33]

Translated into twenty-five languages, Bernardo Atxaga's *Obabakoak* – which appeared in 1988 in Basque, in 1989 in Castilian and in 1992 in English – marked the point when 'Basque literature became a first-world minority language celebrated by the media all over the world'.[34] Set on at least four continents and unfolding from the Middle Ages to the present day, the book's magic-realist style simultaneously embraces and jocularly mocks exoticised rural identities. Reviewers homed in on comparisons with texts such as Salmon Rushdie's *Midnight's Children* in what has become the most canonical of postcolonial Spanish texts.

In a prologue written especially for the English-language edition, Atxaga claims the Basque language 'survived, this stubborn language, by withdrawing, by hiding away like a hedgehog in a place, which, thanks to the traces it left behind there, the world named the Basque Country or *Euskal Herria*'.[35]

Proud Catalonia: a cultural reality

What Tom Lewis refers to as 'the multifaceted array of discursive transactions that comprise "Spanish" literary history'[36] played out very differently in Catalonia, where there is a strong tradition of letters, with attempts to systematise the grammar taking place in the early twentieth century. In spite, or more likely because, of this, Catalan under Franco was considered a hill-billy dialect of Spanish, 'a source of internal division, a useless linguistic fossil'.[37] In 1968, singer-songwriter Joan Manuel Serrat was poised to represent Spain in Eurovision with 'La, la, la'. When he placed as a condition on his taking part that he be allowed to perform the song in Catalan, he recalls that the television executive asked him if he wanted to be a provincial or a universal singer, thereby relegating any non-Castilian language spoken in Spain to a non-cosmopolitan secondary status.[38] From the 1960s onwards, a national literature prize in Spain for works published in Catalan was introduced, albeit with the hierarchical stipulation that the covering letter must be written in Castilian.[39]

By the time of Franco's death, 'the majority of Catalans had a general sense that language and culture were the main markers of Catalan identity'.[40] In the 1974–75 academic year, 66,000 students took Catalan courses in over 300 Catalan schools, the majority of those enrolled in

Barcelona coming from Spanish-speaking families.[41] On 4 March 1975, a proposal advanced by Jacint Soler Padró at a Barcelona City Hall meeting for a relatively small subsidy of 50 million pesetas to support teaching in Catalan was rejected, a symbolic demonstration of loyalty to the regime by rejecting any threat to the hegemony of Castilian. This was a pyrrhic victory: individuals and corporations immediately offered donations to support the cause.[42] On 21 June 1975, the minutes of the meeting of FC Barcelona's junta of directors were recorded in Catalan for the first time since the Civil War.[43] *Avui*, the first newspaper to be written entirely in Catalan since 1939, was launched in 1976 with a print run of 120,000 copies on 11 September, the Diada – Catalonia's National Day.[44]

The Diada pays tribute to the defeat of the Catalan armies who backed the Habsburg claim to the Spanish throne at the hands of supporters of the Bourbon dynasty. In the words of Eduardo Mendoza: 'It doesn't commemorate the defeat suffered in 1714. Year by year, it simply recalls the lost opportunity.'[45] The despotism of the Bourbons did, however, hold some benefits for Catalonia, which experienced an economic and cultural boom in the late eighteenth and nineteenth centuries. As Franco's chosen heir and a Bourbon, Catalan nationalists might not be expected to warm to Juan Carlos, but he was quick to turn on the charm. The King's first official tour as Head of State was to Catalonia, where he famously switched from Castilian to Catalan in a televised broadcast from Barcelona.[46] This could be seen as a democratic attempt to construe Catalan-speakers as citizens rather than subjects or, alternatively, a cynical concession to linguistic plurality in place of a genuine redistribution of power. In any case, he showed more political sensitivity and *seny* (the Catalan word for common-sense pragmatism) than his son some four decades later. In his first real test as the latest Bourbon monarch, Felipe VI was either provocative or unaware in a televised address to the nation on 3 October 2017: filmed in front of a portrait of Carlos III – his forefather popularly known as 'el mejor alcalde de Madrid' (Madrid's best Mayor) for the regeneration of the capital during his centralist reign (1759–88)[47] – Felipe employed rhetoric that appeared to deny citizenship to any inhabitant of Spain not fully committed to the post-Franco Constitution.

The 1979 statute of autonomy transferred eighty-nine competencies to Catalonia. This was more than those allocated to any other autonomous communities, the Basque Country included. By the time of the unconstitutional referendum of 2017, the number of competencies had increased to 274.[48] Juan Carlos and Adolfo Suárez negotiated the return of Josep Tarradellas, the President of the Generalitat in exile. The three men were committed to the principle that the interests of Catalonia would be best protected within the framework of the Spanish nation state. Autonomous tax-raising powers in the Basque Country were a historic right ratified by the Constitution. Negotiators from the PNV have often suggested that their Catalan counterparts did not seek fiscal autonomy in the late 1970s, fearful of the logistic challenges it might pose as well as preferring to devolve unpopular decisions to the State apparatus.[49] The turnout for the referendum to approve the Constitution in Catalonia was marginally above the national average, with a higher percentage voting affirmatively.[50] Tarradellas self-styled himself as the embodiment of Catalan interests – hence, for example, his mythical phrase, 'Ja sóc aquí' (I have returned), as he addressed adoring crowds on his return to Barcelona.

In his memoirs, the first Catalan President of the democratic period claims he never believed in the model of Spain being divided into multiple autonomous communities, arguing that there should have been two or three at the absolute maximum.[51] As Diego Muro notes, the Constitution never adequately resolved two conflicting models of autonomy: 'the constitutional framework based on symmetrical federation' versus 'a more flexible confederate system'.[52] Tarradellas advocated for the latter, establishing a strict hierarchy, claiming that Catalonia ought not to be treated like La Mancha or Murcia.[53] On the one hand, it is clear that one way of diluting the aspirations of the historical nationalities was to roll out the autonomous communities across the Peninsula; if powers are devolved everywhere, then said devolution ceases to have such symbolic and political power. Conversely, however, Tarradellas's comments are symptomatic of the same sense of political and cultural entitlement that had led many bourgeois Catalans to label all Spanish workers living in Catalonia as being from Murcia irrespective of their place of origin (see Chapter 7). The long-term effects of the Francoist infantilisation of Catalan culture are more diffuse and harder to register, let alone remedy, than straightforward prohibition, but so too are the vectors of class inscribed in the socio-geographical fabric of Catalonia itself.

In the aftermath of the 1 October referendum, social media was quick to pick up on video images of the Guardia Civil from Murcia (a region in which the far-right Vox was the most voted-for political party in the November 2019 general elections) being applauded by local residents as they prepared to restore 'law and order' in Catalonia. Conversely, a comment by journalist Toni Soler on Catalan television that, had it been left to Ciudadanos, Catalonia would have ended up being like Murcia, went viral. It is no coincidence that Vox has its most loyal voters in Almeria and Murcia, two regions that have traditionally exported migrants to Catalonia, which have unemployment levels amongst the highest in Spain and local businesses quick to exploit non-Spanish immigrant manual labour to maximise profits.

Since the Transition, the Catalan regional Government has adopted the twin strategies of utilising popular culture to reach the masses, and showcasing high culture to foreground its status as a major European and global player. One of the first acts of the Generalitat following its re-establishment in 1980 was to come to the aid of Barcelona's ailing Liceu, effectively bringing Catalonia's bourgeois temple and Spain's only opera house for most of the twentieth century into the public domain.[54] Back in 1976, Lluís Pasqual and Fabià Puigsever had established the Teatre Lliure, which quickly became Barcelona's leading repertory theatre in Catalan at a time when, as lead actor Lluís Homar recalls: 'It's not a question of whether there was a good or bad tradition, there simply wasn't one.'[55] Since its initial publication in 1974, Manuel de Pedrolo's *Mecanoscrit del segon origen* (*Manuscript of the Second Origins*) has been canonised as a foundational text in Catalan children's literature, despite the author's fascination with the pubescent body and desires of Alba, his female protagonist, who is stranded in a post-apocalyptic landscape with a young black boy, Dídac. The proto-ecological novel shows the two young friends rediscovering Catalonia and looking for ways to ensure the survival of the human race. Between 1978 and 1980, the Instituto Nacional del Libro Español (National Institute for Spanish Books) invested over 8 million pesetas in publishing books in Catalan, with a special emphasis on children's literature.[56]

In 1980, the first democratic elections since before the Civil War for the Catalan Parliament were held. Jordi Pujol led the Convèrgencia i Unió (Convergence and Union; CiU) to victory, and the conservative Catholic banker began a twenty-three year consecutive term as President of the Generalitat. On the Armed Forces Day held on 30 and 31 May 1981, Pujol declared that the programme for the two days embodied the Catalan desire to construct a Constitutional Spain: 'Barcelona was garlanded with both Spanish banners and Catalan *senyeras* and the presence of the king and queen was applauded by large crowds, associating together the parliamentary monarchy, the cultural diversity of Spain and the constitutional flag.'[57] Pujol continued with the accommodationist tactic piloted by Tarradellas, but was more aggressive in his negotiating tactics and promotion of Catalan culture. Quick to realise the potential of television, he took advantage of Spanish television's dropping Texan soap-opera *Dallas* from its schedules just before the infamous 'Who shot J. R.?' storyline to ensure that a dubbed version was part of the Catalan-language TVE3's first-day broadcast.[58] From 1980 onwards, the amount and range of the already obligatory teaching of Catalan at primary and secondary level was increased. In 1983, the Catalan language became a component part of the university entrance exam.[59] What was nevertheless 'still missing for a great number of young Castilian speakers in Barcelona [was] the opportunity to use Catalan with native speakers, particularly peers, in everyday interactions'.[60] This was important in socio-linguistic terms, but also in relation to equal opportunities, given the rising perception since the arrival of Pujol that Catalan was more elegant than Castilian.[61]

Catalan politicians frequently complain that the idiosyncrasies of the Spanish electoral rules, a 'strange mixture of proportional and majority systems designed to strengthen the representation of less populated provinces',[62] favours the conservative tendencies of the Castilian heartlands. Conversely, however, within Catalonia it similarly plays in favour of nationalist parties. In the 1987 regional elections, the Socialists held on to Barcelona City Council but CiU strengthened its control of the prosperous rural vote. At the time, Susan M. DiGiacomo understood this as both cause and consequence of an involution in political campaigning of the previous decade, which had at least paid lip-service 'to dissolving the twin boundaries of culture and class that divide Catalan society'.[63] Across the towns and villages of Catalonia, there are a huge variety of traditional festivities that were actively promoted during the late 1970s and 1980s.[64] In 1978, an impromptu Holy Week parade took place in L'Hospitalet de Llobregat, part of Barcelona's industrial belt. Since then, more ambitious Easter celebrations modelled on Seville's April Fair have proved especially popular amongst first- and second-generation immigrants from Andalusia. Lovers of flamenco claim their culture is ghettoised and undervalued by the Catalan authorities, whilst associations of the Catalan *sardanista* dance critique any public subsidy from the Generalitat to 'these "foreign" forms of culture to the culture of "indigenous" traditions'.[65] The latter include *castells* – human towers, a very literal example of community-building – 'a clear symbolic representation of the people, of popular democracy' that have enjoyed a popular renaissance in recent decades.[66]

Citizens of Catalonia with one parent born there and one from abroad tend to show similar levels of support for independence to those of the overall population, but those with both parents born outside the autonomous community have significantly lower levels of support than those with both born in Catalonia.[67] What Miranda Joseph terms the 'implicitly exclusionary deployments of community'[68] frequently go unchallenged. The difference between Barça football club, which recruits its players from around the world, and Athletic Bilbao, 'a unique case in the world of postmodern football, a pocket of resistance in the new global order',[69] which has traditionally only recruited bona fide Basque players, is symptomatic of an ostensibly more accommodating approach to integration. In her novelistic memoirs, Najat El Hachmi writes: 'I became an unconditional fan of Barça without having any idea of what an off-side or a penalty was. It didn't matter. The issue was combating an oppressive enemy.[70] The Moroccan-born writer nevertheless observes how Catalan intellectuals often switch to Castilian when addressing her because of an automatic assumption based on her skin colour that she is not conversant in the language of a land she has called home since childhood, even doing the same with her son, born in Vic, a traditional stronghold of Catalan nationalism.[71] As Sarah Gore has shown, 'language is a means of excluding non-EU immigrants from key areas of membership of Catalan society'.[72] Basque politicians typically mirror the electorate in terms of their linguistic capabilities and usage, but a far higher percentage of Catalan MPs have Catalan as their mother tongue than their voters.[73]

A shared aspiration for EU membership smoothed over ideological and territorial divides during the Transition, providing the promise of the end to a curse by which, in the words uttered in the midst of a Madrid bar crawl by lead character, Max Estrella, in the Galician-born Ramón del Valle-Inclán's early-twentieth-century classic *Luces be bohemia* (*Bohemian Lights*): 'Spain is a grotesque deformation of European civilisation'.[74] From the Catalan perspective, EU membership also made secession a more viable prospect. Industry became less reliant on domestic Spanish markets for its goods, and the regional Government intensified efforts to import and export cultural goods to Europe, often without the mediation of the Madrid-based State administration. In the twenty-first century, only seven non-Catalan Spanish universities offer courses in Catalan culture and language, which can be studied in twenty-seven German institutions of higher learning.[75]

Prior to 1986, even the most hardline of Catalan nationalists rarely saw independence as a tenable goal. Whilst the Basque Government opened an office in Brussels before the Constitutional Court deemed it illegal, Pujol never made any such attempt, despite, or perhaps because of, the fact that more trips were made abroad by officials from Catalonia than from any other autonomous community.[76] Catalonia, a prosperous region in an impoverished European State, was disadvantaged by being rich and poor in relative but not absolute terms: that Catalan GDP exceeds 75 per cent of the EU average ensures it does not have access to the subsidies available to the richest regions of Greece and Portugal,[77] whilst the fiscal equalisation mechanism naturally draws resources from the richer areas in an attempt to reduce the unequal social and economic geography of the Spanish nation state. By 1993, Catalan gross income per capita was 22.7 per cent above the Spanish average, but disposable income was only 17.8 per cent higher.[78]

Between 1987 and 1997, public-sector theatres in Madrid received 69.5 per cent of the total State budget for theatre, leaving just over 30.5 per cent for the rest of the autonomous communities and the private sector.[79] In addition to housing a disproportionate number of State companies, such as the Compañía Nacional de Teatro Clásico (National Classical Theatre Company) – created in 1986 as the Spanish equivalent to the UK's Royal Shakespeare Company and France's Comédie Française – Madrid now also had devolved funds at its disposal. Hence, for example, the Festival de Otoño (October Festival) was established in 1984 to bring works from the North American and European high-art tradition, as well as selected experimental works, to the capital and surrounding satellite towns.[80] Theatre practitioners such as Peter Brook were brought, often at considerable expense to the Spanish tax-payer, to perform in Madrid, with the expectation that they would provide a model of good practice for local practitioners. In spite, or perhaps even because, of this tendency, Barcelona was generally considered 'as the theatrical capital of the Spanish State, next to which Madrid was perceived as obsolete and conservative'.[81]

As early as 1972, there were calls for Catalan theatre to transcend textual hegemony.[82] This has become a trademark of the (post)modern stage, with La Fura dels Baus and Els Comediants at the vanguard. Whilst the employment of non-verbal communication allowed Catalan culture to travel, translation into the vernacular showcased prestige. A paradigm 'such that anything English was perhaps over-respected or treated with awe'[83] played into a vogue for Shakespeare. The English bard is performed more regularly in post-Franco Spain than the leading dramatists of the Spanish Golden Age – Calderón de la Barca, Lope de Vega and Tirso de Molina[84] – but the tendency is particularly blatant in Catalonia. As part of an exercise in historical redress from the Spanish chauvinism of the Francoist period, the Lliure, in its first three decades, staged eleven Shakespeare productions, three by Molière and none by the three afore-mentioned Spanish playwrights.[85] Productions typically highlight cultural and political aspirations alongside 'the identification through Shakespeare with some of the issues (both aesthetic and moral) affecting other citizens of the European Community'.[86]

In the vein of Norway, whose National Theatre predates its independence, the return of Josep Maria Flotats, the Generalitat's golden boy, to Catalonia in 1983 from France, made the prospect of Catalonia having its own State auditorium a real prospect. In 1989, Flotats stated: 'A city and a country that don't have their own great theatre produced locally and in their own language are as bereft as a school that doesn't have its own basic resources'.[87] This fits with the general principles according to which such institutions first came into being elsewhere in Europe: 'connected to nation-states (or desired nation-states) was an actor–audience relationship in which both parties could be perceived as representative of the nation'.[88] The Catalan National Theatre eventually opened its door in 1996 and, as Marvin Carlson notes, '[i]ts detractors were quick to compare it to a mausoleum, a Catalan Valley of the Fallen'.[89] That same year, the PSOE were ousted from national government.

The PP's incoming President, José María Aznar, required the support of parties from the Basque Country, Catalonia and the Canary Islands to form a government. An initial honeymoon period between the centralist Spanish State and Catalonia contrasted with the hardline approach adopted by the PP in relation to the Basque Country. The refusal to bestow legitimacy upon moderate nationalists, let alone ETA, increased divisions within Basque society, which resulted in the PP increasing its representation in the Basque Country, but exacerbated pre-existing tensions.[90] Relations in Catalonia were relatively stable in comparison, but Pujol no longer enjoyed the popular support he had once had. Following a landslide victory in the 2000 elections, Aznar no longer had to pay lip-service to regional nationalists. The PP President initially conceded far more than González ever did, but Aznar's Government also resurrected Spanish nationalism, which up until then had been considered by many to be 'virtually a non-existent phenomenon, dissolved at the end of Francoism'.[91] After twenty-three years in power, Pujol lost the 2003 Presidential elections, voters losing faith in him but not in a narrative of cultural superiority and victimhood that had added credence given an increasingly intransigent, cocksure central Government. Aznar lost the 2004 general elections, having misled the electorate, attributing the Islamic terrorist bombings of trains heading to Madrid's Atocha railway station to ETA. Montserrat Guibernau was already predicting 'a radical-ization of Catalan nationalism in the near future'.[92] The CiU had asserted the right to self-determination in party documents during the 1990s, but it first became an election pledge in 2010 under the leadership of Artur Mas.[93] He now needed to contend with the rising nationalist sentiment of both the Spanish State and the pro-secessionist lobby. Pujol's rhetoric, once an effective negotiating tool, was being adapted for increasingly destructive ends. What was once the most culturally rich area of the Spanish State has become an echo chamber, arguably more parochial than it was during Francoism.

The management of the august Liceu have been reduced to handing out flyers on the Ramblas, artistic director Joan Matabosch jumping ship to the Teatro Real in 2013. Building on the momentum of the dir-ectorship of the Belgian Gerard Mortier (2008–13) – with the pedi-gree of having run Salzburg's Grosses Festspielhaus and able to attract heavyweights to perform, conduct and direct – Madrid, for the first time, can lay claim to having Spain's finest opera house. Internationally fêted filmmaker Isabel Coixet, resident of Barcelona's staunchly nation-alist Gracia neighbourhood, has complained that many artists remained silent in their opposition to the referendum out of fear of being branded fascists.[94] Lluís Pasqual was ousted from the directorship of the Lliure after Andrea Ros accused him of bullying behaviour. His supporters claim the young actress was put up to this when the veteran director refused to align himself with separatists. Irrespective of the truth of such (counter-)claims, practitioners not unequivocally aligned with the pro-secessionist movement have increasingly sought employment outside Catalonia. In spite of having little experience with the Spanish Golden

Age, Lluís Homar was, for example, appointed in 2019 as Director of the Compañía Nacional de Teatro Clásico.

Galicia is different: poverty, folklore and tourism

The Spanish State has long accommodated individuals and communities from plural and diverse backgrounds on the condition that local variations be formulated as component parts of the organic whole. At Christmas 1964, the Ministry of Information and Tourism launched a propaganda campaign to commemorate '25 años de paz' (25 years of peace) with materials in both Basque and Catalan.[95] Fraga's famous 'Spain is different' slogan has been understood primarily in relation to 'identity differentiation on the basis of an orientalist approach that made the notion of difference its core appeal in tourist marketing'.[96] Hence, for example, flamenco became a metonym for Spain, a folklorised version of Gypsy culture that showcased the exoticism of Spanish difference. However, attention to primary documents from the period suggests that another sense of 'difference' was also being articulated. In a Ministry-produced tourist guide for the Anglophone market, *Spain at a Glance*, the different regions and varying climates are described thus: 'Multiform in every aspect, Spain is truly a land of contrasts. Indeed, it is quite evident that SPAIN IS DIFFERENT.'[97]

As Begoña Barrera notes of the Falangist Sección Femenina (Women's Section), they sought 'to convert regionalism into an aesthetic and emotional element, in such a way that regional diversity ceased to be a problematic aspect in the composition of the general picture of the nation'.[98] In a letter dated 2 February 1967 from Emilio Otero Val, Director of the Centro Gallego de Santander (Galician Centre in Santander), he proposes that the travel expenses of their music-and-dance troupe be covered to allow them to perform in Bilbao's summer festivities: 'Su "Sección de gaitas" a cargo de un grupo de jóvenes y simpáticas señoritas, procedidas de un magnífico cuadro de baile, harán vibrar de emoción a la numerosa colonia gallega radicada en esa maravilloso capital, y al público en general' (organised by a group of nice young women, who belong to an excellent dance team, their 'bagpipes sections' will make the large Galician community resident in your great capital, as well as the general public, quiver with excitement).[99] The request was successful.

Poverty, Ortega y Gasset suggested, stirred Galicia, 'populated by surrendered, suspicious souls, lacking confidence in themselves', to apathy rather than action.[100] Under Franco, the anti-Galicianist stance of the clergy contrasted with that adopted by their counterparts in Catalonia and the Basque Country.[101] Amidst the bars and restaurants that now populate the largely postindustrial city of Vigo can be found a statue of a human figure with a suitcase in hand, known as the 'Monumento al emigrante' (Monument to the emigrant), constructed in 1971 by Camilo Nogueira Martínez. In the 120 years between 1853 and 1973, at least 1.3 million (some say closer to 2 million) Galicians emigrated, around half of them during the dictatorship period.[102] In the early twenty-first century, around 6 per cent of the national population are from this autonomous community and yet 'Galicia is the public face of Spain: today, more than 27 per cent of Spaniards registered overseas are Galicians.'[103] Inhabitants who have stayed put have not usually preserved the same myths of intermittent heroics and martyrdom as in the Basque Country and Catalonia: 'Galicians who have lived in the present democracy believe our past to be one of social, political, economic, and cultural backwardness: they are convinced, in other words, that we come from a country dominated by misery and poverty.'[104]

Between the twelfth and fifteenth centuries, the importance of Santiago de Compostela as a major pilgrim destination resulted in a significant corpus of literature, above all lyric poetry, being produced in Galician.[105] That hardly any literature was produced in the language between the fifteenth and nineteenth centuries was both a symptom and a cause of Galician losing its prestige: the nobles from the metropolis became increasingly dominant in urban centres, and the replacement of local clergy by Castilian-speaking abbots and priests 'served to enhance the subaltern status of Galician' and even infiltrated more isolated communities.[106] Rosalía de Castro's poetry collection *Os cantares gallegos*

(*Galician Songs*) of 1863, the first modern work in Galician, marked the onset of an unlikely literary renaissance that did not translate into a nationalist legacy: 'In the years following her death and for the length of the twentieth century, the equation between Rosalía de Castro and Galician sentimentality acted as a highly serviceable ruse geared towards the feminization of Galicia and, thus, its political demobilisation.'[107] Given such associations, dissident works logically sought to de-sentimentalise the rural idyll. Manuel María's 1970 poem *Remol* (*Embers*), for example, closes with the following lines:

> The farmers' children are sad,
> their childhood a kind of prison.
> Does the sight of life sadden them?
> The sight of the land give them pain?
> Has nostalgia taken possession of their souls?
> Do they know, perhaps, foresee
> the emigrants' bread they will eat?[108]

This provides an ill fit with the folklorism cultivated by the Franco regime, and belongs to a literary tradition that hones in on the darkness conjured by poverty and ancestral forces alike.

Eduardo Blanco Amor's 1959 novel *A esmorga* (*On a Bender*), featuring a twenty-four-hour drinking spree that ends violently, was set in 1934 in an attempt to make it less of an obvious affront to the current regime, although the Galician-language film adaptation (Ignacio Vilar, 2014) set the action in the 1950s against the backdrop of Franco's inauguration of a new building and the local madam holding back the best prostitutes for the visiting bigwigs.

Novel and film alike draw inspiration from Ramón del Valle-Inclán, who was born in Galicia but wrote in Castilian and maintained an ambivalent relationship with his homeland.[109] *Divinas palabras* (*Divine Words*), subtitled *Tragicomedia de aldea* (*A Village Tragedy*), is, to borrow a phrase from Roberto Lima, a 'semi-classic interpretation of rural Galicia's reality (sorrow, drudgery, death)' that 'encompasses the grotesque both in characterisation and in situation'.[110] Pedro Gailo, a 'drunk, lecherous and would-be incestuous sacristan',[111] lives with his wife, Mari, and daughter. Their family unit is augmented when Pedro's sister dies and her dwarf son, whose family members make money out of by exhibiting him as a freak show in village fêtes, comes to live with them. The barbarity of the rural peasantry comes to the fore when they inadvertently murder the dwarf by forcing him to drink alcohol. On being caught with her lover, an itinerant huckster, Mari is subjected to public humiliation, with the locals calling for her death. She is only saved by the intervention of the cuckold husband, who is able to evoke the power of the Church and scripture to keep the mob at bay. Given its 'anticlerical tone, Biblical parodies, irreverent language, and unmitigated exposition of hypocrisy and avarice',[112] it is not altogether surprising that *Divinas palabras* had only one major production in Spain during the Franco dictatorship. It was then staged in 1975,[113] and was intended to be the inaugural production at the Centro Dramático Galego (Galician Dramatic Centre), but Valle-Inclán's estate withheld permission for it to be translated into Galician. Its place was taken by Georg Büchner's *Woyzeck*.[114]

Valle-Inclán is Lorca's only serious rival for the title of Spain's greatest playwright of the early twentieth century. His friend, the future Nobel Prize-winning poet Juan Ramón Jiménez, sent a copy of *Divinas palabras* to a director of Dublin's Abbey Theatre in an attempt to have the play staged there, as he believed it shared concerns with works of Irish theatre by the likes of W. B. Yeats, Augusta, Lady Gregory and John Millington Synge. The petition was unsuccessful, but the parallels between Galicia and a similarly sentimentalised Ireland in relation to landscape, culture and folklore are frequently remarked upon. Yeats was staged in Galician in the 1920s, and the boom of Irish drama translated into the vernacular in the 1970s was part of an endeavour to showcase the literary possibilities of the language of Rosalía de Castro.[115] According to the novelist Gonzalo Torrente Ballester, like Franco a native of Ferrol, there is nevertheless a crucial difference: 'Galicia is a maritime country that doesn't have maritime myths. It's a Celtic country that doesn't have Celtic myths.'[116] Valle-Inclán, who negotiates myths and superstitions aplenty in his work, may very well disagree, but the lesser claim can nevertheless be made that they have not had so great an effect in the formation of a national canon.

Torrente Ballester's most acclaimed novel, *La saga/fuga de J. B.* (*The Saga/Escape of J. B.*), first published in 1974 and written during his Visiting Fellowship at New York's Albany University, where he first encountered nostalgia – the classic Galician emigrant's 'morriña' for the homeland – was designed to settle this deficit. Inspired in equal measure by the narrative palimpsests of Miguel Cervantes's *Don Quixote*, arguably western literature's first novel, and the modernist prose of James Joyce's Dublin, Torrente Ballester treats mythical characters such as Merlin[117] and historical figures such as Valle-Inclán[118] as largely interchangeable, neither the real nor the fantastical providing the key to unlocking the mysteries of over 600 pages of uncanny prose: 'I was not called to the Council of Orense where the bishops of Galicia and Portugal examined my doctrine and my conduct, but I am sure they wouldn't have understood me anyway because they are sticklers for the word in whose name they judge me.'[119] Drawing on characters he met in his youth in the Galician city of Pontevedra,[120] Torrente Ballester – a former Falangist[121] who throughout his later life displayed a critical sympathy towards Galician regionalism[122] – employed the secessionist aspirations of Castroforte from Spain and Galicia alike to downplay genuine regional nationalism, which is taken to an absurdist extreme: 'Spanish particularism reaches its paroxysm.'[123]

A specificity of post-Franco Galician society, 'in which bilingualism may be widespread but does not imply allegiance to the state-sponsored language',[124] are the phonetic and philological overlaps between the local vernacular and Portuguese and Castilian alike. The facility of the local language allows the Castilian-language newspaper *La voz de Galicia* sometimes to include quotations in Galician without translation in a way that would not occur in Catalonia or the Basque Country. As a result, there is a very real danger of Galician losing its specificity because of the repeated and constant linguistic interference from Spanish. The so-called 'lusistas' believe a solution to the relegation of Galician to the status of a dialect of Spanish lies in forging closer links with Portugal, effectively advancing the Iberianism long championed by Portuguese Nobel Prize winner José Saramago who, disillusioned with his own country, went to live in semi-exile in Lanzarote.[125] By contrast, the 'autonomistas' see no advantage in becoming subservient to another nation-state that, in any case, has not shown great interest in the Galician national(ist) project.[126] Further divisions ensued from competition between North and South Galicia to house the administrative seat of the recently baptised autonomous community. In the end, it was situated in the more centrally located Santiago de Compostela, resulting in mass protests in A Coruña.[127]

Fraga has proved as central to the Galician regional Government as it has to the longevity of this veteran politician. This self-proclaimed 'don Quijote de Villalaba' (don Quixote from Villalba) is committed not to return 'to the situation prior to the Catholic Monarchs, with Christian and Muslim kingdoms, placing the Peninsula's equilibrium in jeopardy'.[128] In the first post-Franco general elections, his Alianza Popular (People's Alliance; AP) did not achieve good results in Galicia, and their first breakthrough at the polls was in the 1981 inaugural elections for the regional Government, when they put forward local, well-respected political figures on their list of candidates.[129] The first President of the newly inaugurated Galician Government (the Xunta) was the AP's affable intellectual Gerardo Fernández Albor, a champion of Galician letters who had carried out training as a Luftwaffe pilot in Nazi Germany shortly before the onset of the Second World War. Clientelism and personal charisma often prevailed at the ballot box, perpetuating the quasi-feudal relations of the Franco regime in one of Europe's poorest regions. Smugglers had long provided essential goods such as penicillin, and increasingly professionalised networks for bringing tobacco across the border gave job opportunities and buoyed local economies.[130]

In the early-to-mid 1980s, the counterfeit tobacco with which, by tradition, guests would be regaled at Galician weddings, was replaced, amongst younger attendees, with white powder. The widespread tolerance amongst the local authorities and communities alike turned the coastal region into the principal entry of cocaine into Europe, Colombian drugs lords such as Pablo Escobar and the Ochoa brothers striking deals with local clans experienced at navigating the challenges presented by the Atlantic Ocean and local politicians alike. As investigative journalist Nacho Carretero remarks: 'Never had Galicia exported a product with such success. Not even seafood.'[131] If, in Madrid, the market value of a gram of cocaine was 10,000 pesetas, in Vilagarcia the same quantity could be bought for 6,000.[132] A ring of family-run drugs cartels constituted a loose confederation, regularly meeting in the Parador of Albariño,[133] a State-run hotel inaugurated by Fraga in 1966 in his capacity as Minister of Tourism and Information in an area renowned for its white wines. At a time when the Catalan Miquel Roca was about the only leading politician to talk publicly of the need to take urgent action over the ticking time-bomb of widespread drug consumption,[134] Mariano Rajoy committed what seemed like career suicide as president of the district council of Pontevedra by raising concerns about Fraga's contacts with drugs lords: lucrative party donors and folk heroes to much of the electorate. The leader of the AP effectively sent the future Prime Minister into exile in Madrid just as the charismatic Sito Miñanco, Galicia's answer to Pablo Escobar, bought the local football club in Cambados in 1986. It is not necessary to believe accusations made by Escobar's associates that the equivalent of £5 million was paid towards the PSOE's 1986 election campaign in exchange for not extraditing Colombian prisoners to stand trial in North America to appreciate that their hands were also far from clean.[135]

Just as heroin was claiming its first wave of casualties in the Spanish capital (see Chapter 8), Manuel Soto, the Socialist Mayor of Vigo (1979–91), became obsessed with turning Vigo into 'the capital of the Atlantic Movida'.[136] He capitalised on the city's burgeoning reputation as a hotbed of youth and a cultural hotspot[137] to organise a publicly funded cultural exchange between artists and hangers-on from the two destinations to have an alcohol- and chemically infused dialogue as opposed to, say, investing in local libraries.[138] Greeting the visiting dignitaries in a suit by Adolfo Domínguez – the Galician-born designer who, on moving to Madrid, was at the vanguard of 1980s Spanish fashion[139] – the plan was derailed when a civil servant was hit by a flying bottle at the official closing reception.[140] By 1990, Soto had not desisted in his populist patronage of popular culture but, with a new, determinedly anti-pharmaceutical message, spent 170 million pesetas (equivalent to over €1 million) on bringing Madonna to play Galicia on her debut Spanish tour, alongside Galician punk-rockers Siniestro Total as the opening act. Profits were to be donated to drugs charities, with full-page advertisements claiming it was a civic responsibility to attend: 'Hoxe tódo los vigueses estaremos con Madonna e Siniestro Total contra la a droga' (Today all the citizens of Vigo are with Madonna and Siniestro Total in the fight against drugs). With a repertoire including songs such as the sardonic reworking of Lynyrd Skynyrd's 'Sweet Home Alabama' as 'Miña terra gallega' – with the refrain 'Donde el cielo el cielo es siempre gris' (Where the sky is always grey) – Siniestro Total's lead singer Julián Hernández asked from the stage, 'Where is Sito Miñanco?'[141] The drugs kingpin was at the time a fugitive, a warrant having been issued for his arrest. Arriving by private plane, the Queen of Pop spent less than eight hours in Vigo and was faced with a half-empty stadium. Costly promotional campaigns were carried out in Galicia and neighbouring Portugal, but local authorities could not genuinely have believed this benefit concert was ever going to make a profit with the 40,0000 tickets priced at 1,200 pesetas (a third of the cost for Madonna's sold-out dates at London's much larger Wembley Stadium).[142] Soto blamed Galician television for bypassing Vigo's initiative: the exclusive television rights for Madonna's Spanish tour had been sold to TVE, which broadcast her concert from Barcelona's Olympic Stadium, but the Socialist Mayor claimed they could have filmed a documentary. The Xunta-controlled television channel had its loyalties elsewhere, opting to broadcast a concert by megastar Prince. The singer had, in an act of inter-town rivalry taken to ridiculous extremes, been booked to play outside a Jesuit school in A Coruña on the same night. The concerts exacerbated pre-existing tensions between the Socialist-controlled Vigo and the more politically and socially conservative A Coruña, which, until 2015, had streets named after the generals who rose up against the Second Republic, as well as the founder of the Spanish Legion, José Millán Astray.

Following a brief two-and-a-half-year period in which the Xunta had been run by the PSOE alongside the nationalist Coalición Galega, the PP regained control in February 1990, Fraga himself occupying the presidency. His populist inauguration ceremony was a portent of things to come: accompanied by 200 bagpipers, it was followed by a popular feast with traditional Galician dishes.[143] If, as Xosé Manoel Núñez Seixas notes, Fraga sought 'to combine Spanish constitutional loyalty with a reinforced regional identity',[144] the incoming President clearly felt most at home in the realm of popular, Galician culture 'presented as something harmless and decorative, existing peacefully within the Spanish state'.[145] Carlos Núñez, a leading Galician bagpiper and staple of the international world-music scene, notes how his Breton colleagues were surprised to learn that the Francoist regime supported Galician music.[146] As Javier Campos Calvo-Sotelo notes, 'Celtic music dismantles the ability for real action of Galician nationalism', as can be seen 'in the substitution of certain symbols and images associated with pro-Galician claims for others related to the Celtic world'.[147] Official patronage, which Núñez at least claims to equate to clientelistic favouritism and to be detrimental to quality in relation to the commercially minded Celtic music scene in Brittany,[148] is manifest in the fact that a third of Celtic music events are financial losses, with only a tenth making a profit; 70 per cent of them are retransmitted on Galician radio stations and one out of three is partially televised.[149] When Núñez opened for Julio Iglesias at the Royal Albert Hall in 2014, he spoke to the London audience of his collaborations with Irish group The Chieftains, and was invited out by the headliner to perform a rousing rendition of 'Un canto a Galicia' (A song for Galicia), one of very few Spanish-language songs to be performed in the Latin lover's set. Fraga has been similarly adept at promoting Galicia on (inter)national stages. He sought to strengthen links with Madrid, opening, for example, the Casa de Galicia in a building just behind the Prado Museum;[150] has invested culturally and institutionally in diaspora communities, especially in Latin America, the number of registered voters overseas rising from 6,000 to over 300,000 between 1989 and 2005;[151] and 'has ardently pursued the idea of a Europe of the Regions, espousing the idea of three levels of government, subsidiarity, and the need for a Galician presence in Brussels'.[152] Unlike the more prosperous Basque Country and Catalonia, Galicia is a significant recipient of European Structural Funds.[153]

The pilgrimage to Santiago de Compostela is the most successful manifestation of Fraga's exploitation of his community's mythologised rural past; according to an official tourist brochure, 'Galicia is not only the land of St James, but also the gateway to Heaven.'[154] During the time of Muslim rule in the Southern Iberian Peninsula, pilgrims from the international community of Christendom were called upon to make a pilgrimage and thereby protect the remains of St James from the infidel. In the words of Hispanist and founder of the British Council School in Madrid, Walter Starkie: 'The growth of Santiago de Compostela in size and power became a great menace to Moslem power in Spain and excited the envy and fear of Córdoba.'[155] A less spiritual interpretation is offered by Tubby, the TV scriptwriter protagonist of David Lodge's novel *Therapy*: 'Christian Spain badly needed some relics and a shrine to boost its campaign to drive out the Moors.'[156] He asks Maureen, an ex-girlfriend mourning the loss of a son who had been volunteering in Africa after a Cambridge degree, 'Doesn't it bother you that millions of people may have been coming here for centuries all because of a misprint?'[157]

Starkie's travelogue did much to promote the Way of St James as an adventurous tourist attraction. Fraga's Ministry utilised the full repertoire of 'Spain is different' imagery to promote multiple routes to Santiago, principally but not exclusively from France, Portugal and the Basque Country. According to a tourist guide describing different towns that pilgrims could pass through: 'Perhaps it might be difficult for many to begin the route by foot or on horseback and the "seventies" style will take over: the motor vehicle, the expedition by bus, train or even by plane.'[158] Although pilgrims use transport of all kinds, this prophecy never came to pass. As René Freund wrote of his experiences of walking the Way in 1998 with his wife: 'that walking is a luxury for the privileged hasn't yet been fully understood because there are still too many people who have to walk because they have no other choice'.[159]

Freund's theory that its being an 'entirely unintellectual experience' provides an explanation for 'why it has come back into fashion in our brain-focussed society'[160] is played out in *The Way* (2010), an English-language film directed by Emilio Estevez, the Hollywood actor of

Galician descent, and starring his real-life father, Martin Sheen, as a renowned eye surgeon who takes time out from his professional life (perhaps for the first time) when he embarks on the pilgrimage to scatter the ashes of his son, who died in the Pyrenees. Contrasted with the Canary Islands (as one character in Lodge's *Therapy* says, 'given a choice between the Siberian salt mines and a four-star hotel in Playa de las Americas, I'd choose Siberia any day'[161]), even the novel's sceptical protagonist succumbs to the therapeutic values of the Way: 'The pilgrimage, even in the bastardized, motorized form in which I was doing it, had begun to lay its spell on me.'[162] The route to Santiago as the repository of archaic forces facilitating a retreat from the mechanised modern world constitutes a conflation of the twin notions of Spain remaining different. Galicia is an outlier as regards the other historical autonomous communities in terms of nationalism and economic wealth. Updating and transferring the Francoist model of folklorising Andalusia, it nevertheless provides an archetypal model for 'a long-standing recognition-deficit that is rooted in the denial of the Spanish state to acknowledge its multinational character'.[163] In the next chapter, I unpack the myriad guises by which the said pact has been articulated and contested through culture during the dictatorship and the democratic period.

Chapter 12

What qualifies as Spanish culture?

The State, autonomous communities
and the culture wars

What is the relationship between culture, the State and democratisation during and after the Franco regime? The various sections of this book have responded to this question in different ways and reveal, both individually and collectively, how, in a radically divided society, one of the few things almost everyone in Spain is in agreement about is the civilising force of art and knowledge. In this final chapter, my aim is to unpick the ideological stakes at play in competing definitions of culture, as well as to establish genealogies to understand better how and why the toxic philanthropy of the late dictatorship period bequeathed a heuristic legacy of ideological and aesthetic veneration. Predicated on what Germán Labrador characterises as the 'national determination in the blind execution of an unlimited programme of normalisation',[1] such processes, I suggest, ostensibly champion democracy and culture whilst limiting the parameters by which they can be conceptualised.

Francoism was prone to nurturing a culture of non-inquisitiveness at home whilst putting dissident culture to work to whitewash its image abroad. As Chapter 1 documented, 'the Adornian vision of popular culture as a debased and debasing mass culture'[2] prevailed amongst the Marxist-inflected opposition to the dictatorship, who called upon the healing powers of education and culture as an antidote to the opium of the people. Voices from popular culture and the regime did not, however, uniformly advocate maintaining the status quo, with concern raised about cultural development lagging behind advances in the socio-economic realm. Ensuring adequate access in rural areas was costly and challenging. A census from 1966 shows more money was spent on culture per capita in the province of Soria, which also had the third highest ranking in health (behind Avila and Huelva),[3] but its ageing population could hardly be considered amongst the healthiest and most cultured in Spain. In 1970, 70 per cent of Madrid homes were equipped with television sets, but only 11 per cent had them in the province of Soria.[4]

By 1971, there were over 4,000 official television clubs dotted around the Peninsula, often in small localities that had not traditionally had a cinema.[5] These top-down enterprises encouraged continuing education and social gatherings, reformist sections of the regime becoming increasingly alive to the possibilities of popular culture for positive, as well as nefarious, ends. In 1969, the Ministry of Information and Tourism sought tenders from publishers to produce mass editions of literary classics from Spain and Latin America to be sold in street kiosks at reduced prices. These were heavily advertised, and the first in the collection – Miguel de Unamuno's *La tía Tula* (*Aunt Tula*), with a new introduction by Julián Marías – was bought by over a million Spaniards;[6] subsequent editions of highbrow novels from the Latin American boom by Mario Vargas Llosa and Carlos Fuentes sold over 300,000 a piece.[7]

If audiences had increasing access to culture, practitioners began to have more resources to access. In possession of one of the finest private antique collections in Spain,[8] Juan March opened a Foundation bearing his name in 1955, which provided both a home and a source of funding for artists and intellectuals. As José Manuel Sánchez Ron notes: 'the list of those who received grants from the Foundation is almost a *Who's Who* or, better still, a *Who Will Be Who* of Spanish scientific and humanistic culture as much then as in the years that followed.'[9] In 1981, Cuenca's Museum of Abstract Art came under the aegis of the Foundation, having been established in 1966 by Fernando Zóbel – whose family fortune, made in Manila, the capital of the Spanish colony of the Philippines, had allowed him to pursue his artistic vocation and attend Harvard, where he had carried out research and written about Federico García Lorca – in this off-the-beaten-track town, located between Madrid and Valencia, in which artists such as Gustavo Torner and Antonio Saura had studios. Featuring works by the crème de la crème of Spanish abstract art, the collection was curated so as to complement the design and landscape surrounding the so-called 'hanging houses' (thus described for their position on the edge of a cliff) in which it was located.[10] In 1967, Alfred Barr, the first Director of New York's MoMA, referred to it as 'the most beautiful small museum in the world'.[11] Spain could no longer be seen as a cultural backwater.

Disillusioned with the cut-throat competitiveness of the capital of modern art, César Manrique, 'fleeing from a conflictive, aggressive and mass-produced world', returned to his native Lanzarote in 1966.[12] Adopting a paternalistic approach to his fellow inhabitants, Manrique – alarmed by the architectural and ecological effects of mass tourism on Gran Canaria and Tenerife – dedicated himself to preserving the volcanic island's unique geography and celebrating its nature and inhabitants through bespoke modernist sculpture and architectural design. Fraga lent his support,[13] as did Pepín Ramírez, the shy and retiring Mayor of Lanzarote.[14] This island became Manrique's personal playground and portfolio, leading to commissions elsewhere in the Canaries and the Peninsula, as well as the maritime park in Ceuta, a Spanish enclave in Morocco.[15] With Manrique now widely heralded as a hero back home for defending Lanzarote from the ravages of mass tourism, a letter to the local newspaper about a public sculpture inaugurated by Fraga in the 1960s suggests his work was not always so well received: 'speaking to many farmers about what their thoughts were on the monument to the peasant, they seemed somewhat annoyed as they said that only some-body who didn't know our countryside could have come up with such a thing'.[16] The impoverished Lanzarote and Cuenca were at the vanguard of modern art alongside Barcelona and Madrid, Government officials decamping to the island to inaugurate a new showcase of plastic arts, featuring works by Picasso and Francis Bacon (the British painter who would not receive his first Spanish retrospective until 1978 at the Juan March Foundation).

A positivist association of art with democratisation was most expli-citly formulated in relation to the Joan Miró Foundation, modelled on the

Institute of Contemporary Arts in London. In a letter dated 27 November 1968, the artist wrote to the architect Josep Lluís Sert: 'I have great faith in these people who are full of youth and can set new paths for the future world in the making. It's very good that we are also contributing to it with our own effort.'[17] When the Foundation eventually opened its doors to the public in summer 1975, a few short months prior to Franco's death, critic Alexandre Cirici enthused: 'If we know how to work in freedom, I think we have a beautiful path ahead of us. We can't sign off without praising Joan Miró as an example of generosity and civic responsibility. Joan Miró, many thanks.'[18] This was a concrete example of museums as what Tony Bennett terms 'civic laboratories',[19] as opposed to mausoleums, a harbinger of culture embodying and catalysing change in the Transition.

In 1976, Oviedo hosted the inaugural edition of its Biennale of Visual Arts. Controversy surrounded the town council's decision to collect funds by popular subscription to commission Juan de Avales to create a sculpture in honour of Franco,[20] but over 50,000 people reputedly attended. Amongst those were 5,000 students from across the region, who completed surveys that suggested they were often lacking in knowledge but keen to learn more: 'it brings to the fore the need for a total overhaul of teaching in this discipline, to be supported in tandem by acts of diffusion by Asturian institutions responsible for culture.'[21] Such initiatives paved the way for the opening of the Fine Arts Museum in Oviedo in 1980. Relatively weak regional nationalism compounded by the lack of major-name local artists ensured that it was always envisaged as a home for art from across the Peninsula and not just Asturias. Considered 'one of the most complete, museologically sound, self-confident, and successful regional museums in all of Spain', the Fine Arts Museum shone in an increasingly stagnated cultural and educational landscape.[22]

Since the mid-1960s, teachers had self-organised summer camps to improve pedagogical practice. These became increasingly politicised around the time of Franco's death, leading, for example to, the order of the civil governors of Ourense (Galicia) and Valencia to cancel events days before they were due to take place. Between 1975 and 1980, around 25,000 teachers participated annually in such laboratories for pedagogical professionalisation, also serving as pressure groups against the often dire working and learning conditions in Spanish schools.[23] Andrés Amorós, a professor from the Complutense University and commissioner for the Juan March Foundation complained of the state of Madrid's National Library, queues often resulting from the lack of neighbourhood libraries, and the discovery of an unpublished Leonardo da Vinci manuscript indicative of the lack of professionalisation as regards the holdings.[24] Even the Prado was in a precarious state in the 1970s, lacking the space or climatological conditions necessary to safeguard its artistic patrimony, as was documented in a book for the Juan March Foundation published by Alfonso E. Pérez Sánchez, the Deputy (and future) Director of Spain's flagship museum.[25] The board of the Friends of the Prado was created in 1980 as a response to the lack of virtually any outreach or educational programmes, only later coming into competition with the institution.[26]

When incoming President Leopoldo Calvo was asked by journalists about his new life in the Moncloa Palace, he infamously responded: 'Here, one doesn't live well. There are many telephones and few books.' As Calvo notes in his memoirs, the comment was taken as a slight by his predecessor, Adolfo Suárez, who employed intuition and charisma as an effective substitute for erudition: 'Not least amongst my political disadvantages has been having learnt almost everthing from books. But the temptation of culture is huge for pragmatic politicians: remember the not always accurate quotations that [Alfonso] Guerra would use for decorative purposes.'[27] Following the PSOE's landslide in the 1982 general elections, Guerra, the country's new Vice-President, recalls being greeted by military portraits on first entering his new workspace:

> I made a mental note to contact the Museum of Contemporary Art so that they would change those visual impulses for something current and in line with modern power. It was not long before a magnificent large canvas by the painter [Joan] Hernández Pijuan was hung, an area covered in blue with slight pinkish touches that emanated calm and serenity; it was a genuine rainbow of peace.[28]

As Eric Storm notes, 'an emphatically modern design by Joan Miró' was soon chosen 'as a standard logo for all the tourism promotion of the state, the famous semi-abstract sun in red, yellow and black, with the single word *España* beneath it.[29] On the one hand, a concerted effort to patent associations of culture and democratisation that predated the arrival of Guerra's party to government was clearly taking place. Conversely, this was not mere window dressing: the PSOE's investment in culture and education was unprecedented.

Over the course of their fourteen years in government, the country went from having sixteen universities to sixty,[30] the number of undergraduates doubling from 669,848 to 1,295,585 in the decade between 1982 and 1992.[31] The proportion of the State budget allocated to the Ministry of Culture rose from 0.74 per cent in 1983 to 0.95 per cent in 1985.[32] This was still lower than in neighbouring France, but far eclipsed the UK, which did not even have a Ministry of Culture at the time. The annual 688 million pesetas invested in library buildings in 1982 had risen to 1,400 pesetas in 1985, democratising access to culture across the Peninsula.[33] An internal 1986 Ministry of Culture report on corporate sponsorship drew on surveys to conclude that positive PR was a far greater motivation for businesses than fiscal relief when it came to sponsoring the arts.[34] The UCD's former Minister of Culture, Ricardo de la Cierva, wrote with concern to the AP's Vice-President Alfonso Osorio, asking him to communicate to Fraga that, in his opinion, the party's unwill-ingness to take culture seriously was doing them political harm.[35] When Juan March died in a car crash in 1962, the most commonly used epitaph for the Mallorcan businessman, who had both invested in and reaped the rewards of the illegal Francoist uprising against the Second Republic, was 'the great philanthropist'.[36] Nowadays, Juan de la Cierva (Ricardo's uncle) is best known for bequests that fund major university research posts, but his legacy comes from being the engineer who arranged for a plane to be sent from England to Tenerife in 1936 to transport the future Caudillo to orchestrate the coup.

As can be seen by the case of Salvador Dalí – not inaccurately described by Antoni Tàpies as 'the most scandalous example of mutual profit between painting and politics (of the ultra-conservative) kind in history'[37] – a fast track to democratic respectability was facilitated by a

269

landscape in which the notion of a non-democratic patron or practitioner of the arts simply did not compute. In opposition to local opinion, which considered the town's most famous son an unreliable, tiresome clown, local Mayor Ramón Guardiola Rovira sought Fraga's support to open the Salvador Dalí Museum in Figueres in December 1969.[38] Franco reputedly told the painter that 'You will turn Figueras into the Mecca of contemporary art'.[39] Failing to provide explanation for his gift of a portrait of Carmen Franco to the Caudillo family, a hagiographic biography of Dalí suggests that the 'Spain of General Franco took a dim if not hostile view of this exhibitionist's character'.[40] Unlike folkloric singer Lola Flores (see Chapter 2), Dalí retained artistic immunity in fiscal affairs, indulged under democracy and dictatorship alike. Having flouted French and US laws, he became a Spanish resident for tax purposes in 1985, but the surrealist genius did not demean himself by filling in a mundane tax return.[41]

In December 1983, keynote speeches at a symposium on culture and society were delivered by incoming Minister of Culture, Javier Solana, and the Director of the Juan March Foundation, José Luis Yuste. The latter spoke with evangelical zeal of how '[t]o admit freedom of culture means disseminating a tolerant mentality amongst the citizenry'.[42] Between 1983 and 1986, the Foundation, in collaboration with the Ministry, piloted a new initiative, 'Cultural Albacete' (Culture in Albacete), which in its first years brought over 142 cultural acts to a city 'particularly forgotten about when it came to promoting culture'.[43] Relative proximity to Madrid was another reason for Albacete's being chosen, although invitations were conditional on all visiting speakers having to spend at least one night in the region that gave birth to Don Quixote, the idea being that this would forge genuine relations with institutions, cultural practitioners and audiences. Being on the periphery entails not only exclusion from the culture and politics of the metropolis, but often being left out of official narratives. Talking of a workers' strike in Albacete, for example, Óscar J. Martín García notes: 'it is surprising that the historiography has hardly bothered to assess the political implications of the collective action that took place in that area with the socio-economic conditions least suited to it'.[44]

What qualifies as Spanish culture?

The wider Madrid regional Government owes its existence in part to Albacete. Originally, it was intended to incorporate the Spanish capital into the makeshift autonomous community of the largely rural Castile La Mancha, which in its final configuration represented 16 per cent of Spain's landmass and 4 per cent of its population. According to the first President of the Madrid regional Government, Joaquín Leguina, this proposal was deemed unacceptable for two reasons: first, suspicion that the city of Madrid would reserve all of the regional power and resources for itself; and second, that incorporating into the land mass of Castile La Mancha would require relinquishing Albacete to the regional Government of Murcia. As the new President of Castile La Mancha, the Socialist José Bono, said of the inauguration of the only autonomous community not to have a university at the time of its creation: 'there were no demonstrations of joy; I'd even go as far as saying that the date went unnoticed'.[45] Castile La Mancha was home to some of Spain's greatest artistic patrimony; its tent at the 1992 Universal Exhibition was the most visited of the autonomous communities, with nine El Greco portraits on display.[46] Beginning in 1979, Almagro – the rural town in which Almodóvar shot the semi-autobiographical *Volver* (*Return*) (2006), and the location of Spain's only original seventeenth-century theatre – hosted a modest classical theatre festival. From 1983 onwards, it grew in size and scope thanks to support from the newly created autonomous community,[47] and an attempt at the State level to diversify tourism beyond the traditional beach holiday.[48]

Following his death in Mexico in 1983, Luis Buñuel was much more celebrated in Calanda, the small town of his birth in Aragon, than he had been during his lifetime, culminating in the opening of a cultural centre bearing his name in 2000. The devolution of political and administrative responsibilities to the newly created autonomous communities has been replicated in the cultural sphere, but is limited by issues of feasibility as well as ideology. In 1983, the seat of the regional Government of Aragon was inaugurated in the restored seventeenth-century Pignatelli Building in Zaragoza. On 16 March 1986 the Fundación Museo Pablo Serrano (Pablo Serrano Museum Foundation) was created and declared in the public interest. The private collection of Aragon's leading modern sculptor was initially housed and made available to the public in the government building, before forming the basis of the region's first major contemporary art museum, which eventually opened its doors in 1994, following major financial problems, in a specially commissioned modernist space constructed alongside the Pignatelli Building.[49] Francisco de Goya's birthplace in Fuendetodos, alongside the scattering of a few generally minor or preparatory works in and around Zaragoza, has been sufficient for the Government of Aragon to promote a route dedicated to the painter,[50] but for reasons of conservation and dissemination there are clear justifications for the bulk of his artistic patrimony remaining in Madrid. The Spanish capital's film archives also retain much of the primary material corresponding to Buñuel. As Román Gubern notes, more generally, a proliferation of often duplicated efforts in regional activities reflects a heritage 'in which the cultural diversity of Spain's regions plays a major role', but can serve to camouflage the extent to which 'costly activities such as recuperation and restoration remain largely centralized in the national archives in Madrid which are integrated into the central state apparatus'.[51]

An association by which, in the words of Luisa Elena Delgado, 'in Spain, culture is understood as providing the passageway to citizenship',[52] resulted in a situation described as follows by playwright Paloma Pedrero: 'we have just been reborn as Europeans; the party in power, Socialist they say, doesn't stop talking about culture even in brothels'.[53] The fact that Spain traditionally had a cultural deficit did not mean (over) compensating in the present was invariably the solution. Amongst the population of Font de la Pólvora – a poor and badly connected largely Romani enclave built as an overspill to the prosperous Catalan town of Gerona in 1974 – 66.2 per cent of the population were unable to read in 1980; school drop-out rates were over 80 per cent.[54] By comparison, 90 per cent of homes in the autonomous community of Madrid had books,[55] with its citizens having the most highbrow cultural tastes in the State, the difference from national averages being most pronounced in relation to visiting museums.[56] It might have been nice for the young people in Font de la Pólvora – whose favourite, and often sole, cultural activities were clubbing (46.5 per cent) and cinema (21 per cent)[57] – to have access to a broader range of art-forms, especially given the relation between the lower level of educational studies and the greater disparity between men and women in terms of access to culture.[58] However, the drugs epidemic, the onset of AIDS and rising unemployment ensured that worrying about the lack of variety in their leisure activities was not a concern that individuals or the State could necessarily afford to prioritise.

As Raquel Medina notes, the institutionalisation of poetry at the level of regional autonomies and the State resulted in a proliferation of opportunities,[59] with an almost carnivalesque proliferation of prizes making it virtually impossible to find a community in Spain without a poet or a writer with a prize to his or her name. In *Kika* (Pedro Almodóvar, 1993), Almodóvar mocked the craze for all things cultural by casting his own mother as the presenter of a spoof television programme titled 'Hay que leer' (One must read). Adopting a stylised version of her real-life persona as a woman who has always lived in a La Mancha village, she offers that week's guest, a highbrow author, local delicacies. Indeed, she shows more interest in the intricacies of his personal life than his latest novel, which she says she will not be able to read as she has a cataract. Almodóvar employs satire to make a similar point to one articulated in more serious fashion by David Looseley as follows:

> To assume that *la culture cultivée*, whether traditional or avant-garde, is immediately accessible to all, that cultural deprivation can therefore be remedied by the statistical measurement of 'cultural needs' and a techno-cratic adjustment of provision, is to ignore the fact that these needs are socially and historically determined and only occur in those who already have the codes required to satisfy them.[60]

Hence, for example, in 1989, the PSOE-controlled Madrid local authorities drew inspiration from Lorca's *Romancero gitano* (*Gypsy Ballads*) to baptise street names of a neighbourhood specially constructed to absorb Gypsy communities outside Villaverde Alto. The new inhabitants 'who had never heard of Lorca complained that they had been granted housing in a backwater neighbourhood with ludicrous street names'.[61] Tensions between Gypsy and non-Gypsy communities were, if anything, on the rise since the PSOE's arrival in central government. The most vociferous complaints by the residents of Bilbao's impoverished San Francisco area (see Chapter 11) were about the presence of Gypsy neighbours – many of whom had been relocated there following the city's devastating floods of 1983 – who, it was complained, were far more problematic neighbours than recently arrived African migrants.[62] Cosmopolitan, democratic Spaniards are more prone to critique Gypsy communities for a reputed lack of culture and unwillingness to send their children to school rather than on racial grounds, although that is not to say that such critiques are not frequently racialised. When a social worker put up a placard at the entrance to the Villaverde estate saying 'Colonía para población marginal' (Neighbourhood for a marginal population), annoyed inhabitants ripped it down.[63] In the early 1990s, press coverage of Gypsy communities increased, focusing almost exclusively on rising levels of drugs and crime.[64]

As Tony Bennett remarks: 'to suggest that some societies lack culture, understood, in its restrictive definition, as a set of higher intellectual and cultural forms, has been a means of exorcising colonial power'.[65] This dynamic is further complicated by Spain's status as a 'nation that is at once Orientalized and Orientalizing',[66] also comprising, to borrow a phrase from Ian Gibson, a 'fascinating mini-continent',[67] the socio-economic terrain of which is far from homogeneous. In contrast to what had been the case under dictatorship, flamenco constitutes a more challenging aspect of Spain's artistic patrimony in democracy than Federico García Lorca, around whose figure a veritable heritage industry has emerged. As Maria M. Delgado notes, this cult figure 'now functions as part of the mystery of Granada; his homes, haunts and supposed burial grounds as much part of the city-scape as the Alhambra, Albaycín and Sacramento caves'.[68] The belated Spanish cultural turn was rendered somewhat anachronistic by changes elsewhere, through which 'the image of the taste-*exclusive* highbrow, along with the ranking from "snob" to "slob", is obsolete';[69] '[b]ecause status is gained by knowing about, and participating in (that is to say, by consuming) many if not all forms, the term "omnivore" seems appropriate for those at the top of the emerging status hierarchy'.[70] That the omnivorous cultural disposition was greater amongst young people in post-dictatorship Portugal than Spain has been interpreted by Robert M. Fishman and Omar Lizado as the result of the revolutionary nature of its road to democracy, which led to 'a situation in which hierarchies of all sorts, including aesthetic ones, came into question from an egalitarian perspective'.[71] Shortly after the creation of the Andalusian regional Government, attempts were made to make teaching flamenco in schools obligatory, but it was never properly embedded in the curriculum as many teachers felt, in the words of William Washabaugh, 'that flamenco's values seem to run contrary to those of the dignified culture they feel obligated to cultivate in their teaching'.[72]

Following the reconquest of Granada, the Spanish Crown expanded further south in the fifteenth century, with the incorporation of the Canary Islands, 100 km off the African coast, into a nascent nation-state. As Pedro Fernaud notes: 'The Canaries were not land incorporated into Spain but were rather an integral part of the decisive factor – Castile – in the forging of Spanish unity from the outset'.[73] Whilst constituting both an antecedent for and antechamber to colonial adventures in the New World, Spanish expansion southwards came to a halt with Columbus's arrival in America. In her will, Isabel the Catholic Queen nevertheless requested that Spain keep imperial adventures in Africa going.[74] Following the loss of Spain's final American colonies in 1898, renewed interest was taken in Africa, with colonial wars in Morocco not only occupying the professional army, but also prompting protests back home as a result of forced conscription from which the privileged elites were generally exempt. General Franco forged his reputation and brutal wartime tactics in Africa.[75] In 1937, he attempted to organise a sea pilgrimage to Mecca for Moroccan Muslims, a venture aborted following an aerial bombing attack by Republican forces. As Ignacio Tofiño-Quesada has analysed, 'Francoist propaganda used the incident to highlight the antireligious zeal of the "red government paid by Moscow" and the need to strengthen the links between Spanish rebels and Moroccan armies in order to fight a common cause against Communism and atheism.'[76] This rhetorical sleight of hand was an attempt to evade what Helen Graham refers to as 'the enormous and evident contradiction of a latter-day Catholic crusade whose front-line troops were Islamic mercenaries'.[77]

Franco's anti-Communist credentials were instrumental to Spain's admission into the United Nations in 1955, at a time when the international organisation was committed to decolonisation, Morocco gaining its independence in 1956. This posed a challenge to the aggressive expansionism of the regime's Africanist discourse,[78] in which the ostensibly civilising forces of Christianity and education were used to justify the forging of an international community united by the Spanish language in the Western Sahara and what Benita Sampedro Vizcaya terms 'this artificial and unbounded construct that we have come to call Equatorial Guinea'.[79] In a manner akin to arguments wielded by the Salazar regime in Portugal, the Franco dictatorship contended its African territories were not colonial outposts, but rather integral components of the Spanish nation-state. As a result of 'the politics and economics of autonomous federalism in the late 1960s, Equatorial Guinea had a high per-capita income in comparison to other African areas, along with one of the continent's highest literacy rates'.[80] From 1964 onwards, the Sección Femenina began to train young women in Equatorial Guinea and to organise exchanges by which they could be sent to be educated in Spain; in a striking example of the colonial pedagogy of subservience, the Francoist organisation was increasingly vexed about former charges not always bowing to rule as the decade progressed.[81]

In Donato Ndongo's debut novel, *Shadows of Your Black Memory*, a largely autobiographical narrator, who has 'learned much from Father Ortiz, but above all to be like the whites, educated, well-mannered, and distant',[82] recalls receiving lessons over which an image of Franco presided: 'your eyes met the direct gaze of the Youngest of Generals in Europe, the Invincible Leader of Spain by the Grace of God, by whose blessing all of you were allowed to break ranks just before and after going into the classroom'.[83] Shortly before the regime bowed to international pressure to hold a referendum amongst the population of

Equatorial Guinea on their future, the Spanish film *Cristo negro* (*Black Christ*) (Ramón Torrado, 1963) cast doubt, in the words of Susan Martin-Márquez, on their 'readiness for independence, highlighting their vulnerability in the hands of foreign interests and a small group of ruthless nationalists, while foregrounding Spaniards' selfless dedication to the betterment of their African "brothers"'.[84] Violence against the native population is attributed exclusively to Northern European colonisers.

In 1966, the Francoist Government invited representatives of the United Nations to Equatorial Guinea in the hope of persuading them of the economic and cultural benefits of the territory's remaining part of Spain.[85] The initiative was counter-productive, as it further prompted the international community to weigh in behind nationalist demands to end what was increasingly seen as an anachronistic colonial state. Owing to pressures for decolonisation to be carried out according to the rules of the United Nations, not the Spanish dictatorship, more political freedoms and parties were paradoxically allowed in Spain's southernmost region than back on the mainland. In 1968, on the symbolically loaded date of 12 October – known at the time as the 'día de la Raza' (Race Day) – marking Columbus's arrival in the New World, Fraga represented the Spanish Government in officially transferring powers to the newly independent state. As Alicia Campos Serrano notes, in order to save face, 'decolonisation had to be presented by the westerners as the culmination of the colonial period and not as the culmination if its decline'.[86] The positive spin of this emancipatory narrative were undermined by the actions of the former colonised and colonisers alike. Francisco Macías, the first leader of the newly independent country, rose to power largely because he appealed to the young, and his rhetoric and actions stressed a future free of Spanish influence.[87] His regime became increasingly repressive, unleashing, for example, a vicious campaign against colonial residents and Nigerian guest workers in the aftermath of a failed coup attempt in 1969 in which members of the Spanish Guardia Civil who had remained in Equatorial Guinea participated.[88] The once relatively prosperous, oil-rich African nation quickly descended into being amongst the poorest in the world. A telex dated 14 July 1976 sent to regional media outlets communicated that the order dating from 22 August the previous year, for all references to what was taking place in the former colony to remain classified, had been extended for a further six months.[89] In contrast to, say, the Iranian Revolution (see Chapter 5), the Spanish media paid virtually no attention to the 1979 coup of Teodoro Obiang, trained like King Juan Carlos in the elite Zaragoza military school, or the human-rights abuses of his regime, which he continues to rule to the present day.

Silence surrounding Equatorial Guinea is in marked contrast to the Western Sahara,[90] an area equivalent to nearly 60 per cent of the Iberian Peninsula simply handed over to Morocco on 27 February 1976.[91] The Spanish authorities failed to honour their pledge to the United Nations to carry out first a referendum amongst the population of what was known as Spain's fifty-third province about their future and the aspirations of the armed resistance group, the POLISARIO Front, for the creation of a new autonomous nation.[92] Even prior to withdrawal, the bully-boy tactics of Morocco's King Hassan II raised fears amongst Spanish political elites that the army might be humiliated.[93] An additional reason that Madrid acquiesced to Moroccan demands was concern that an independent Western Sahara would support the burgeoning pro-independence movement in the Canary Islands,[94] which had already established close ties with the Organization of African Unity (OAU) and the Angolan Government. Since the early 1960s, Canarian nationalists identified as colonised Africans on geographical grounds and on the basis that the islands' native Guanches were ethnically and linguistically Berbers.[95] In 1969, radical pro-independence movements planted a bomb in Las Palmas airport whilst, according to Carlos Robles Piquer, he accompanied Adolfo Suárez and Juan Carlos to a meeting with the OUA's President, Edem Kodjo, and Canarian nationalists, at which the latter expressed their regret at not being able to rip off their white skins.[96]

The Francoist rhetoric of its African territories being provinces of Spain, as opposed to colonial possessions, was coming home to roost: their independence offered a precedent to regional nationalisms. In 1977, the Spanish Government took the unusual decision to appoint the career diplomat Antonio de Oyarzábal as the Civil Governor of Tenerife (a position that stood him in good stead to be transferred to the even more conflictual Basque province of Guipúzcoa in 1979), where he sought to combine the navigation of local unrest and negotiating with foreign powers (e.g. Libya, Angola, Venezuela, Cuba and Puerto Rico) to persuade them to desist in their support of the pro-independence movement in the archipelago.[97] Sabino Arana, the father of Basque nationalism, had attempted to write a telegraph to Washington to congratulate the US President on liberating Cuba in 1898.[98] The rhetoric of ETA located its struggle within a wider matrix of anticolonial discourse, but the case for the Spanish State's occupation of the peripheral nationalities was complicated by the latter's resilient contribution to the Spanish empire. The Catalan bourgeoisie had defended slavery long after it had become obsolete in most of the rest of Spain.[99] When preparing their inaugural tour of Equatorial Guinea in 1954, the Sección Femenina were very aware that the colonial population comprised predominantly Basques and Catalans.[100] Most Spanish citizens resident in the Western Sahara were repatriated to the Canary Islands causing, for example, the population of Fuerteventura to spike from 17,957 in 1970 to 27,104 in 1980.[101]

Santa Cruz de Tenerife and Cadiz, not coincidentally two gateways to the New World, are home to Spain's two most important carnivals, which largely went underground during the Franco dictatorship.[102] When future President Carlos Arias Navarro was Civil Governor of Tenerife, he reputedly ordered a no-tolerance prohibition of the celebration of the carnival after his car was hit by an egg.[103] The carnival was resurrected surreptitiously during the 1960s as the tourist-friendly 'fiestas del invierno' (winter festivities), with local groups, *murgas*, composing and performing humorous songs that provided caustic social commentary. In 1966, for example, one performed a ditty titled 'Verdades verdaderas' (Truthful truths),[104] which lamented that the town council showed no concern about the perilous state of Baltasar Núñez Street, filled as it was with potholes. In 1977, the carnival was officially resurrected, becoming the first to be authorised in post-Franco Spain.[105] In one song, 'El voto' ('The vote'), a local *murga* held the distant young President to account:

Tú querías que votáramos por ti,
y lo conseguiste,
después de pasarnos las noches enteras
sin saber qué hacer.
Ay Suárez,
que después de haber votado
todo se te ha olvidado
y no quieres de aquí más saber.

You wanted us to vote for you,
and you got your way,
after we spent whole nights
not knowing what to do.
Oh, Suárez,
now that we've voted for you,
you have forgotten about everything,
and you don't want to know anything more about us here.

Voters from the Canary Islands may have lent the UCD their vote but, as the chorus reminds its leader: 'algún día volverán las elecciones' (elections will be held again one day).

A disillusioned electorate ended their contractual arrangement with Suárez in the 1979 general elections, the left-wing, fiercely nationalist coalition group the Unión del Pueblo Canario taking control of the archipelago. In the wake of the 1982 elections, however, the Europeanist promise of modernisation relegated the pan-African discourse to the status of historical curiosity, the PSOE governing in coalition with the newly formed Agrupaciones de Independientes de Canarias, which absorbed many ex-members of the UCD and whose 'mix of populism and island mentality'[106] provided a conducive environment for the carnival to expand, with its beauty pageants and floats becoming mass-televised spectacles by the end of the decade.

If, under Franco, folklore provided the acceptable face of regional heterogeneity, festivities took on this role during the years of PSOE hegemony. Switching between the sacrilegious and the sanctimonious, a two-tier system came into operation whereby the State took charge of culture in the narrow aesthetic sense of the word, and the amorphous anthropological notion is seemingly perpetually on display in the main squares throughout the land. As the novelist Antonio Muñoz Molina criticises, 'if there is something in Spain that is immune from criticism it is the totalitarianism of the *fiesta*, something with which the left and right get equally confused';[107] '[y]ou can be anything other than a party-pooper'.[108] In Tordesillas, a small town outside Valladolid where the Spanish and Portuguese signed a treatise in 1494 to divide their colonial possessions in Latin America, a medieval tradition by which the villagers, mounted on horseback, lance a bull until it falls to its death, was resurrected, having being celebrated clandestinely after Fraga had prohibited it in fear of offending tourists in the late 1960s. Against the backdrop of declining birth rates and an increase in only children, a network of festivals has been instrumental in preserving extended kinship structures, youngsters often travelling to the villages of their grandparents or cousins for the festivities surrounding the local patron-saint.

In the words of Terry Eagleton: '[o]nce power has been alchemised into culture, dissolved into the texture of our everyday conduct, we can all come to be pleasantly oblivious of the coercive instruments it holds in reserve'.[109] The State's cultural artillery, as earnest as it is epicurean, was deployed in the quincentenary celebrations of Columbus's voyage to the Americas and the hosting of a Universal Exhibition in Andalusia's capital. Juan Carlos had first had the idea of enhancing the colonial commemorations through an Expo in 1976,[110] and a commission for the quincentenary celebrations existed before the PSOE came to power. The arrival in government of González and Guerra, native sons of Seville, in 1982 nevertheless gave a new impetus and importance.[111] During their mandate, 12 October – the date that Columbus became the first European to set foot on American soil – was declared a national bank holiday. With neo-colonial overtones, the quincentenary year provided a focal point for meshing economic muscle with soft power. A letter dated 12 January 1987 from the Ministry of Culture to the Presidential Office, titled 'Objectivo: el Estado Cultural' (Objective: the Cultural State), declared:

Sin duda, el 1992 será una cita cultural de carácter extraordinario. Si algo es la Comunidad de los pueblos hispanos, es un hecho cultural: la historia, la lengua son esa casa común en la que lo europeo y lo americano encuentran una forma original de ser. Este hecho cultural es la que da a España una posición privilegiada como interlocutora entre los dos mundos.[112]

Without a doubt, 1992 will be a cultural date of an extraordinary nature. If the Community of Hispanic people can be said to exist, then it is a cultural reality: history and language are what we have in common, through which the European and the American find an original way of being. This cultural reality is what gives Spain a privileged position between two worlds.

This is a more measured exaltation of a revisionist historical summary offered by the future President José María Aznar in his memoirs: 'Iberia-America, Latin America, Hispanic America, this is our great historical gesture and our perpetual opportunity.'[113] In this process, economic muscle and soft power frequently collude. As Stephanie Dennison, for example, observes: '"Spanish" culture is aggressively marketed through the world, by the Instituto Cervantes, a Spanish public institution founded in 1991 to promote Spanish language teaching and knowledge of the cultures of Spanish-speaking countries.'[114] In her memoirs, the popular Seville-based former Minister of Culture and Spanish ombuds(wo)man Soledad Becerril writes: 'There was an argument over whether what was being commemorated was the Discovery, or whether we were dealing, as some claimed, with an "encounter between two worlds". The term Discovery, as the majority of historians have always referred to it, prevailed.'[115] As Alastair Reid, the Scottish English-language translator of Borges and Neruda, noted in an essay originally published in the *New Yorker*, these discoveries were given no choice about being discovered, and a year of mourning, not celebration, might have been in order.[116]

Over 14 million people, including sixty-nine heads of state or government and countless celebrities, visited Seville,[117] at the time the smallest city to have hosted an Expo. Not all of the publicity generated was positive. There was a mutiny outside Puerto Rico amongst the Spanish crew of a ship retracing Columbus's voyage.[118] In 1991, Guerra resigned as

Vice-President (although not as Vice-Secretary of the PSOE or as an MP) because his brother, Juan Guerra, had taken bribes and kickbacks from a government office he ran in Seville, a city newly flush thanks to Socialist patronage. In relation to the Expo displays, the Andalusian press praised exhibits featuring high and difficult pieces of art,[119] but a lack of co-ordination and forward-planning ensured that the City's Museum of Fine Arts, containing key works by Murillo and Zurbaran, was closed for refurbishments from April to October.[120] Most visitors from the north of Spain left with the impression that the lack of organisation was typical of southern frivolities.[121] Jesús Aguirre, a native of Cantabria coerced into living in Andalusia as the Duchess of Alba's consort (see Chapter 2), resigned from the organising committee: 'In Seville are to be found all sorts of flights of imagination, weird and lacking in imagination, but never administrators.'[122] This impression is not altogether false, but neither is it entirely fair.

By the time of Franco's death, the challenge of decaying historic centres was already being discussed with, for example, Soledad Becerril collaborating with a new magazine, *La ilustración regional* (*Regional Enlightenment*) on thoughtful and realistic opinions about the limits and possibilities of regeneration.[123] By the late 1970s, city councils such as Gerona and Seville were looking to apply for competitive government funds to make their old towns more attractive for tourists and local residents alike.[124] This task was further complicated and delayed by the drugs epidemic of the 1980s, which increasingly turned windy, picturesque streets into seedy and dangerous no-go areas. The Olympics and Expo allowed Barcelona and Seville to lead the pack, not so much by solving the drug problem, but by displacing it with police squads – much as had happened in the Soviet Union in advance of the 1980 Moscow Olympics – created to clear the Andalusian city of dealers and addicts alike.[125] With the ready-made excuse of keeping the public safe against potential ETA attacks, the police used excessive force against anybody who got in their way, firing rubber bullets at anti-Expo demonstrators.[126] If the Expo was designed as 'an occasion to celebrate cosmopolitanism and pluralism',[127] it and the year's other mega-events carried unfortunate echoes of the Franco regime's attempts to utilise culture to whitewash less pleasant socio-political realities.

In 1990, the priest Enrique de Castro organised the '1992: 500 años de mendicidad' (1992: 500 years of begging) events with talks and conferences aimed at improving social care; there were over 3,000 attendees, events culminating with a mass-demonstration outside Carabanchel prison demanding better conditions.[128] A rare dissenting critical voice to a 1992 retrospective of Tàpies's work, staged with the Catalan artist's blessing at London's Serpentine Gallery, was Giles Auty, who asked: 'If Spain is genuinely a happier and free country now, where one stands a greater chance of being mugged but less of being beaten, might not Tàpies find some way to celebrate the fact?'[129] It is not necessary to subscribe to the politics of the critic from the *Spectator* to recognise that violent social antagonisms hovered not far from the surface of Spain's remarkable but nonetheless largely cosmetic (post)modern makeover. Although democratic Spaniards often showcased a rightly celebrated tolerance in their attitudes and behaviour, violence against the 'other' was not an unheard-of phenomenon. In September 1991, for example, the show-house of a housing estate designed for Gypsies was burnt down in Villaverde Bajo.[130] The following year, military and police artillery was employed by the perpetrator of the racially motivated murder of a young Dominican woman in the Madrid suburb of Aravaca.[131] As documented in the five-part Netflix documentary series, *El caso Alcásser* (*The Alcásser Murders*) (Elias León, 2019), the crime that obsessed Spain as 1992 came to an end involved the kidnapping, rape and brutal killing of three teenage girls – Míriam, Toñi and Desirée – from a small town in the region of Valencia.[132] The case was sensationalised to an irresponsible degree, live television shows broadcast from the village hall featuring interviews with devastated friends and family.

The three underage victims had hitchhiked their way to a night-club that formed part of the 'ruta de bakalao', an informal network of once underground and now increasingly mainstream nightclubs dotted along the Valencian highways: 'thousands of young people – no longer hundreds, as in the beginning – considered "partying" and pills to be their universal 1992.'[133] In the early-to-mid 1980s, Ibiza and Valencia had two of the most vibrant DJ cultures in Europe. Whilst MDMA and ecstasy were the favoured disco pills in the former, back on the mainland, mescaline was the drug of choice. In the words of journalist Rafa Cervera: 'It's a drug that characterised Valencia, which became horchata, fallas, paella and mescaline.'[134]

Across the Mediterranean, the licensed hedonism of Ibiza was kept partly in check by local club-owners, who knew to keep residents and local authorities on side. In the early 1970s, Abel Matutes, who had studied law and business at the University of Barcelona, and played professional football as part of the first team of RCD Español, the city's 'other' team, returned home to be named Mayor of Ibiza. Over the coming decades, he combined a political career, which culminated in his becoming Foreign Minister in 1996 in Aznar's first Government, with developing a multi-million-pound local family business with interests in the island's hotel, leisure and banking industries.[135] In Valencia, by contrast, clubs often sprang up on disused industrial sites, and promoters exploited legal loopholes and blind spots in the passage of licensing jurisdiction from the State to the autonomous communities to enable revellers to travel between clubs – hence the term 'route' – and keep the partying going for up to seventy-two hours around weekends.[136] By the turn of the decade, there were imitation routes in other autonomous communities of Andalusia, Galicia, Catalonia and Asturias.[137] This was reflected alongside Spain's entangled temporalities and hybrid geographies in the club scene in *Jamón, jamón* (*A Tale of Ham and Passion*) (Bigas Luna, 1992), a film set in the arid rural Monegros area outside Zaragoza – 'the Spain of brothels, old age pensioners, highways and dust'[138] – and featuring a fifteen-year-old Penelope Cruz dancing to 'Así me gusta a mí', a million-copy-selling crossover hit – that also topped the Japanese and Israeli singles charts – by Chimo Bayo, a latecomer to the Valencian club scene. Synthetic drugs and the dancing arguably kept at least some clubbers away from heroin, but their party lifestyle also racked up casualties: a 1993 Canal Plus documentary that provoked panic and excitement in viewers was sensationalist, although there could be no denying hard statistics such as the 15,043 road accidents in Spain during 1992 that involved drivers aged between 18 and 24.[139]

For many young Spaniards, women and girls especially, the Alcásser murders had a much more significant effect on their lives than the Barcelona Olympics or the Seville Expo. In addition to the fear and pity the case inspired, many parents became much stricter about allowing their children to go out, with the imposition of a gendered pedagogy by which hedonistic activities were declared off limits to girls for fear of their ending up like Míriam, Toñi and Desirée.[140] At its worst, the Spanish State adopted an authoritarian role that wanted power but refused to accept responsibility; the structures had not been in place to ensure the safety of its youngest citizens, and this was instrumental in prompting a conservative socio-political turn. Nowhere was this more in evidence than in the city and region of Valencia, a traditional left-wing stronghold, whose regional Government came under PP control in 1995, a year before the Party displaced the PSOE from State power.

In his memoirs, José María Aznar writes:

> Valencia had a special significance for us … The link between Madrid and Valencia would generate for reasons of geographical proximity some very important synergies in the region of Valencia, which would help to consolidate a position there able to stand up to radical Catalan nationalism, and nationalism within Valencia itself.[141]

Josep Tarradellas, the first post-Franco President of Catalonia, maintained that Valencia and the Balearic Islands had a completely different history, and it made little sense therefore to group together the struggle of Catalan-speaking countries.[142] Left-wing parties in Valencia were nevertheless criticised by the right for advocating pan-Catalanism, and dispensing with a specifically regional identity.[143] As a result, Catalan, as opposed to Spanish, nationalism was often seen as a greater threat to Valencian identity, and the right exploited folklore and local patrimony to consolidate their own position, taking, for example, legal action to prevent reconstruction works initiated by the PSOE on the Roman amphitheatre in the village of Sagunto from continuing, based on the reputed inauthenticity of the materials being used.[144]

In a published conversation between the writer Fernando Sánchez Dragó and leader of Vox, Santiago Abascal, the latter says he would not like it if his son were gay, an atheist or left-wing, but that he would accept it. What he could not bear would be an heir who turned his back on Spain.[145] This is because it would fracture his sense of individual identity and community. A decade earlier, the future leader of the far-right start-up claimed: 'Spain is, above all, the carrying out of that great imperial adventure'.[146] It is (too) easy to laugh at Vox promotional clips featuring Abascal on horseback and the message that the Reconquest will begin in Andalusia, but the unconstitutional Catalan referendum has served to push epic intransigence back into the mainstream. In 2017, a polemic by a secondary-school teacher from Murcia with tenuous links to the University of Harvard titled *Imperiofobia* (*Phobia of Empire*) became a surprise best-seller,[147] championed by, amongst others, the Instituto Cervantes. That same year, the lead story of the State television news on 11 October featured bullfighter Cayetano Rivera – orphaned as a child following his father Paquirri's death in the ring (see Chapter 3) – refusing to surrender after being badly gored in a *corrida* taking place as part of the *fiestas de Pilar* in Zaragoza, where Spanish and Latin American flags decorate the baroque basilica of the cathedral, to which families continue to take their children to receive the blessing of the Virgin prior to their First Communion.

Ten days after the referendum in Catalonia, where the 2011 prohibition on professional bullfights had more to do with rejecting the 'national *fiesta*' than animal rights (worse happens to animals in many local festivities), and on the eve of the 'día de la Hispanidad', the bloodied face of a matador provided a potent visual metaphor for how and why the ostensibly civilising mission of Spanish normalisation – what Juan Pablo Fusi triumphalistically characterised as 'the culture of the Transition'[148] – will remain incomplete until its citizens both individually and collectively acquire a greater critical awareness of the symbolic and real violence underpinning the communities on which it rests.

Anti-bullfighting protestors have adopted as a rallying call 'No es cultura, es tortura' (It's not culture, it's torture) as if anything categorised as culture were somehow immune from censure. Spaniards invest heavily both emotionally and financially in culture: at a time when budgets are being cut in France, in 2019 the PSOE increased cultural spending by nearly 10 per cent,[149] overtaking the United Kingdom in absolute terms both in relation to per capita investment and as a percentage of overall government spending.[150] This will not necessarily be money well spent as long as the excessive politicisation of cultural institutions replicates the fissures along which Spanish society operates, thereby undermining the supposed democratising and civilising function of the arts whilst also acting as an obstacle to long-term and strategic planning. The ethos of having to pledge allegiance to rival gangs in the sphere of governance equates to the State retaining control of the message.

Conclusion

In July 2019, I took a break from revising the manuscript of this book to eat in Avila's Parador Hotel. None of my luncheon companions was willing to accompany me afterwards to Casa Eladio, one of several Francoist bars to have popped up across Spain. I took a solitary walk beyond the walls of this traditional Castilian town, going for a pre-emptive drink in a medieval-themed bar located next door. Procrastination over, I was initially taken aback on entering the self-proclaimed 'zona nacional' (national zone) to hear 'Sweet child of mine' by Guns N' Roses blasting out of the speakers and to see Paul Preston's far-from-hagiographical biography of Franco occupying pride of place behind the bar. Military hats and paraphernalia provided more predictable ambience. Tickets for upcoming bullfighting events were advertised, alongside a range of kitsch merchandise including T-shirts, wine and cigarette lighters. Framed photos of the Caudillo next to El Cordobés, and Juan Carlos with Sofia, as well as Adolfo Suárez, adorned the walls. The PP's Esperanza Aguirre was the only active politician to be celebrated in this visual hall of fame. Heroes and villains were clearly distinguished. A photo of leading lights from Podemos in casual clothes was accompanied by a caption asking patrons to imagine the chaos if this motley crew were to be voted into government. A 'comic' quip next to an image of a Guardia Civil officer brandishing a pistol proclaimed: 'There was a time in which separatism was resolved in minutes ... and at a much lower price.' I paid for my beer (10 cents more than in the medieval hangout) and left behind a group of domino-playing pensioners and an uninterested barmaid to return to neutral territory.

One of the great myths of Francoism was that Spaniards required a strong hand to avoid descending into tragic chaos. The Transition proved this not to be the case, a necessary but not a sufficient condition for the establishment of a mature democracy. In the words of Chantal Mouffe: 'Antagonism is struggle between enemies, while agonism is struggle between adversaries.'[1] Shared goals such as modernisation and joining the European Union served for an extended period to camouflage the antagonistic nature of personal and political relations in Spain, but avoiding conflict is no substitute for developing means by which to negotiate between adversarial positions. A solution to the constitutional crisis in Catalonia has been made irrecoverably more challenging by the reciprocal intransigence of the Spanish State and the pro-independence lobby, any attempt to understand – let alone sympathise with – the opponent's position construed as a form of capitulation.

In the heady early days of Podemos, rallies concluded with a communal singalong to a 1968 protest song by Lluís Llach – who, from 2015 to 2017, was also a pro-Catalan-independence MP for Gerona – titled 'L'Estaca' (The stake). The lyrics, about an oppressive stake, refer to an exhausted regime, weighing its citizens down personally and politically. In addition to connecting nostalgically with the spirit of popular opposition, the connotations were clear: the 'regime of '78' was as past its sell-by date in the twenty-first century as Francoism had been by the late 1960s. Podemos are rightly circumspect in their appropriation of oppositional music. There has, for example, been no attempt to resurrect 'Yup lala', a staple of popular Basque festivities of the 1970s,[2] featuring the refrain: 'We praise you ETA / because you are the staff of the people / and because the strength is great / The people are happy for you.' 'Yup lala' is a comic exaltation of the assassination of Admiral Carrero Blanco, a milestone in the Transition to democracy. Casa Eladio pays tribute to Franco's martyred right-hand man with a photo of him in military uniform, stating alongside it the date when he was assassinated by the terrorist organisation ETA.

Conclusion

The regulatory fictions by which Spain understands its recent past are in flux, and for the first time in decades there is a lack of consensus over what took place during the Transition. As José Ignacio Torreblanco notes, Podemos have effectively updated the romantic narrative of 1808 by which a popular revolt in Madrid served to oust the French invaders to contend that the masses were responsible for the return of democracy, a democracy then hijacked by the elites.[3] Given a twenty-first-century post-financial-crash context, in which the gulf between the rich and poor has increased more than in other European countries,[4] the appeal of this vision is clear. The case against the 'regime of '78' is not, however, as robust or romantic as it may initially appear. It is, for example, true that the first appeals to disinter the crimes of Francoism came largely from civil society, but there was no popular clamour to explore the past in the 1980s: always attentive to opinion polls and sociological data, the PSOE Government of Felipe González and Alfonso Guerra would probably have commemorated the fiftieth anniversary of the Civil War differently if there had been. Attempts by the recently legalised Communist Party in the 1970s to domesticate the affiliated Comisiones Obreras trade union admittedly led to mutually disadvantageous conflict,[5] but industrial action of the democratic period has typically been kept in check by wage earners: 'the moderation or caution of the rank-and-file base, far from being forced on them by the labour leadership, instead emerges as the most broadly shared motivation for the leaders' restraint'.[6]

As Jordi Gracia notes: 'To turn the Transition into something sacred infantilises that process as much as denigrating it. Both behaviours reduce political debate to partisan munition and deactivate the best arguments to be made against the heroic Transition and the Socialist decade.'[7] It is unfortunate, for example, that a historian of Santos Juliá's calibre has responded to what he clearly perceives to be Podemos's affront to his and his generation's authority with disdain, speaking of their 'disposable narratives'.[8] When I asked Felipe González about calls to revise the Constitution, he responded that it would at least mean these kids might take the time to read it.[9] The tightrope political situation of the 1970s complicates the task of judging the actions of others with hindsight, but the following decade is arguably richer in terms of ethical analysis. It is in the 1980s that Spanish politicians and people are free to make decisions, principal amongst them to take pride in the Transition.

Smugness and self-satisfaction are saboteurs of development. Jazmín Beirak, a former employee of Madrid's National Library, claims not to have been interested in actively participating in parliamentary politics until the emergence of Podemos. She was elected an MP and became the cultural spokes(wo)man in the Madrid Assembly, joining Íñigo Errejón in splinter group Más Madrid after he broke away from Podemos. Beirak respects the labour carried out by the PSOE in relation to the institutionalisation of the Ministry, but contends that neither this nor the PP's more financially utilitarian approach envisages access to culture as a basic human right. Her understanding of the role of politicians is that they provide infrastructure and resources to enable cultural activities, but that they themselves ought to remain at arm's length, leaving the labour itself to practitioners. She regrets her efforts were initially too concentrated in the centre of the Spanish capital, reflecting the culture familiar to herself and her circle.[10] Beirak is unusually self-reflective about her practices and background, a welcome exception to a wider tendency that has, to my mind, always blighted Podemos: the parochialism of its university-dominated elites. Más Madrid lost control of the City Hall because of a low turnout in poorer southern districts, which had been increasingly sidelined from the party's urban project.

The rise of the new political parties has often gone in tandem with an increasingly mainstream feminist movement, another sign that the social contract of the Transition is in the process of renegotiation. Spain's leading sociologist of the democratic period, Amando de Miguel, proclaimed it an injustice that 'being macho has negative connotations, and feminism the reverse'.[11] Given that Alfonso Guerra publicly ridiculed what he considered to be 'a kind of folkloric feminism', which advocated such stupidities as feminine versions of male professions,[12] the social legitimation of the feminist movement is far from clear. One can only imagine what the PSOE's former Vice-President must think of the decision of Unidos Podemos to use the feminine form of its name – Unidas

Conclusion

Podemos – from April 2019 onwards. The only positive thing to emerge from the tragic gang-rape of an 18-year-old woman during the 2016 San Fermín festivities in Pamplona was that it brought to popular attention Spain's antiquated laws and corresponding attitudes of some members of the judiciary.[13] When Carmen Maura spoke in 1991 of being raped five days prior to Franco's death by a soldier before being insulted by the military judge for not forgiving her assailant,[14] the experiences of an actress 'comically' violated in Almodóvar's debut film went largely unnoticed. When I spoke in 2018 to Mertxe Leránoz, the Director of the Navarrese Institute for Equality, she said she thought that Pamplona was no worse than other festivities such as Valencia's Festival of Fire, Las Fallas, and that she had dealt with women in previous years who had endured similar experiences to those of the 2016 victim, but without the same media exposure.[15] Following mass protests and multiple prosecutions, in June 2019 the Spanish Supreme Court increased the sentences of the five men who formed the self-monikered 'manada' (wolf pack), imprisoning them for rape, and not the lesser charge of sexual abuse for which they were first charged.

Back in 2014, Bryan Cameron asked the question of the 15-M: 'is the movement a precursor to the systematic overhaul of Spanish parliamentary politics or merely an ephemeral expression of indignation doomed to fade away?'[16] If Podemos promised a 'new Transition', the jury is out on whether this has been delivered, but there has undoubtedly been a new *desencanto* (disenchantment). At a time when thousands of Spaniards were evicted from their homes, Iglesias's public image was irrecoverably damaged when it was revealed he was seeking a preferential mortgage deal for a chalet in the prosperous mountainous area in outer Madrid. His becoming the leader of Podemos was initially presented as a means to an end, allowing the 15-M movement to have electoral representation. It now appears as if it may have been the other way around: the 15-M was the means by which an ambitious, untenured university academic ended up at the forefront of national politics. As Podemos consolidated into a major political force, Iglesias struggled to maintain control over the party, and did so largely by discrediting his rival, Errejón, accusing him of capitulating to the system. A drama played out on Twitter, and Iglesias maintained his primacy by having doctrinaire anticapitalist factions control the party, thereby breaking with the ethos enshrined in the 15-M movement of transcending traditional left–right dichotomies. As a disillusioned former Podemos MP said to me in a follow-up email to a conversation in the cafeteria of the Complutense University: 'To paraphrase the replicant from *Blade Runner*, I've seen things you people wouldn't believe. You cannot imagine the piggish behaviour, disgusting stuff and filthy backstabbing I've witnessed.'[17] As I put the final polishes on this book, Spain has experienced a month of its first coalition Government, Iglesias one of four Vice-Presidents.

It is difficult to predict where Spain will go from here, but what is self-evident is that the Transition will continue to underpin culture and politics for at least the immediate future. Illustrative parallels can be established between present-day Spain and the UK of the late 1970s, 'an age of resurgent environmentalism, economic decline and cultural nostalgia'[18] in which secessionist movements in Ireland, Scotland and Wales gathered momentum. The International Monetary Fund had lost confidence in the British economy, forcing Labour Prime Minister James Callaghan and Chancellor Denis Healey to abandon a post-Second World War 'consensus built on deficit spending and full employment'.[19] The choice for many between the two major parties increasingly appeared to be like picking being Pepsi and Coca-Cola. When punks began brandishing swastikas, it was not usually because they were Nazi sympathisers (although a minority were), but because they were challenging the complacency associated with the defeat of fascism and the 1977 celebrations for Queen Elizabeth II's Silver Jubilee. If, forty years on, the Transition is a source of nostalgic re-entrenchment and critical disdain alike, it is in no small measure because it is Spain's D-Day.

Notes

Introduction

1 Tobias Buck, *After the Fall: Crisis, Recovery and the Making of a New Spain* (London: Weidenfeld and Nicolson, 2019), p. 2.

2 James A. Bernal, Antonio Gasparrini, Carlos M. Artundo and Martin McKee, 'The effect of the late 2000s financial crisis on suicides in Spain: An interrupted time-series analysis', *European Journal of Public Health*, 23.5 (2013): 732–6 (pp. 732, 734).

3 Buck, *After the Fall*, pp. 102–3.

4 Kostis Kornetis, '"Is there a future in this past?" Analyzing 15M's intricate relationship to the *Transición*', *Journal of Spanish Cultural Studies*, 15.1–2 (2014): 83–98 (p. 86).

5 Pablo Iglesias and Enric Juliana, *Nudo España* (Barcelona: Arpa & Alfil, 2018), p. 125.

6 Sarah Thomas, *Inhabiting the In-Between: Childhood and Cinema in Spain's Long Transition* (Toronto: University of Toronto Press, 2019), p. 9.

7 Marvin D'Lugo, *Carlos Saura: The Practice of Seeing* (Princeton: Princeton University Press, 1991), p. 228.

8 Cited in Antonio Guerra, *Felipe González: socialismo es libertad* (Barcelona: Galba, 1978), p. 60. For a documentary film that charts the discrimination and prejudice endured by many Spanish migrants, see *El tren de la memoria* (*The Memory Train*) (Marta Arribas and Ana Pérez, 2005).

9 James Mark, Bogdan C. Jacob, Tobias Dupprecht and Ljubica Spaskovska, *1989: A Global History of Eastern Europe* (Cambridge: Cambridge University Press, 2019), p. 17.

10 *Ibid.*, p. 272.

11 Pamela Beth Radcliff, *Modern Spain: 1808 to the Present* (Chichester: Wiley-Blackwell, 2017), p. 251.

12 Clive Barnett, *Culture and Democracy: Media, Space and Representation* (Edinburgh: Edinburgh University Press, 2003), p. 2.

13 Pablo Iglesias, *Una nueva Transición: materiales del año del cambio* (Madrid: Akal, 2015), p. 64.

14 Juan Carlos Monedero, *La Transición contada a nuestros padres: nocturno de la democracia española* (Madrid: Catarata, 2013), p. 29.

15 CIS, *La opinión pública española y la integración europea* (Madrid: CIS, 1995), p. 62.

16 *Ibid.*, pp. 64–5.

17 Concepción Cascajosa Virino and Vicente Rodríguez Ortega, 'Daenerys Targaryen will save Spain: *Games of Thrones*, politics and the public sphere', *Television and New Media*, 20.5 (2018): 423–42 (p. 427).

18 Neil Blain and Hugh O'Donnell, *Media, Monarchy and Power* (Bristol: Intellect, 2003), p. 91.

19 Amadeo Martínez Inglés, *Juan Carlos I: el rey de las cinco mil amantes* (Barcelona: Chiado, 2017), p. 323.

20 See Jaume Muñoz Jofre, *La España corrupta* (Granada: Comares, 2016), p. 110.

21 Joan Ramón Resina, 'The weight of memory and the lightness of oblivion: The dead of the Spanish Civil War', in Carlos Jeréz-Farrán and Samuel Amago (eds), *Unearthing Franco's Legacy: Mass Graves and the Recovery of Historical Memory in Spain* (Notre Dame: University of Notre Dame Press, 2010), pp. 221–42 (p. 227).

22 See Guillem Colom-Montero, 'Quim Monzó' (2018), *The Literary Encyclopedia*, http://staging.litencyc.com/php/speople.php?rec=true&UID=14103 (accessed 29 April 2020).

23 See Ignacio Sánchez Cuenca, *La desfachatez intelectual: escritores e intelectuales ante la política* (Madrid: Catarata, 2016).

24 Laura Desfor Edles, *Symbol and Ritual in the New Spain: The Transition to Democracy after Franco* (Cambridge: Cambridge University Press, 1998), pp. 22, 56.

25 In the words of Gregorio Morán: 'In our recent history never has the state dedicated so many funds and means for an ideological-advertising campaign such as that of those for "25 Years of Peace"'. *El cura y los mandarines: historia no oficial del bosque de los letrados* (Madrid: Akal, 2014), p. 253. Fraga's brother-in-law, Carlos Robles Piquer, was the chief architect of this exercise in soft-power designed to showcase that the prosperity and stability of the Franco regime had allowed the wounds of the Civil War to heal. See Carsten Humlebaek, *Inventing the Nation* (London: Bloomsbury, 2015),

pp. 72–4; Carlos Robles Piquer, *Memoria de cuatro Españas: República, guerra, franquismo y democracia* (Barcelona: Planeta, 2011), pp. 251–62.

26 Michel-Rolph Trouillot, *Silencing the Past: Power and the Production of History* (Boston, MA: Beacon Press, 1995), p. 118.

27 Helen Graham, 'Writing Spain's twentieth century in(to) Europe', in Helen Graham (ed.), *Interrogating Francoism: History and Dictatorship in Twentieth-Century Spain* (London: Bloomsbury, 2016), pp. 1–25 (p. 6).

28 See Pedro Pintado Quintana, *El ferrocarril Valladolid a Ariza, 1895–1995* (Barcelona: Lluis Prieto, 1995).

29 La Numancia: La Voz de Soria ¡Ya!, '¡Otra vez elecciones!', *La Numancia: La Voz de Soria ¡Ya!* (2016), unpaginated.

30 Sebastian Balfour and Alejandro Quiroga, *The Reinvention of Spain: Nation and Identity since Democracy* (Oxford: Oxford Unviersity Press, 2007), p. 69.

31 Jesús López-Peláez Casellas, 'The politics of flamenco: *La leyenda del tiempo* and ideology', *Popular Music*, 36.2 (2017): 196–215 (p. 203).

32 Lourdes Orozco, 'Performing the local/performing the state', in Maria M. Delgado and David T. Gies (eds), *A History of Theatre in Spain* (Cambridge: Cambridge University Press, 2012), pp. 372–90 (p. 376).

33 Matthew Machin-Autenrieth, *Flamenco, Regionalism and Musical Heritage in Southern Spain* (London: Routledge, 2016), p. 57.

34 Omar G. Encarnación, *Spanish Politics: Democracy after Dictatorship* (Cambridge: Polity Press, 2008), p. 92.

35 Diego Muro, 'When do countries recentralize? Ideology and party politics in the age of austerity', *Nationalism and Ethnic Politics*, 21:1 (2015): 24–43 (p. 33).

36 Ludger Mees, 'Nationalist politics at the crossroads: The Basque Nationalist Party and the challenge of sovereignty (1998–2014)', *Nationalism and Ethnic Politics*, 21:1 (2015): 44–62 (p. 51).

37 Helena Miguélez-Carballeira, '*Ocho apellidos vascos* and the poetics of post-ETA Spain', *International Journal of Iberian Studies*, 30.3 (2017): 165–82.

38 Carlos Closa and Paul M. Heywood, *Spain and the European Union* (Houndmills: Palgrave Macmillan, 2004), p. 79.

39 David Rieff, *In Praise of Forgetting: Historical Memory and Its Ironies* (New Haven: Yale University Press, 2016), pp. 24, 36.

40 *Ibid.*, p. 63.

41 Ignacio Fernández de Mata, 'Rude awakening: Franco's mass graves and the decomposition of the Spanish Transition', in Ofelia Ferrán and Lisa Hilbink (eds), *Legacies of Violence in Contemporary Spain: Exhuming the Past, Understanding the Present* (New York: Routledge, 2017), pp. 121–47 (p. 121).

42 Henry Kissinger, *Years of Renewal* (New York: Simon and Schuster, 1999), p. 632.

43 Santos Juliá, *Historia de las dos Españas* (Madrid: Taurus, 2004), p. 288.

44 Laurie Lee, *Cider with Rosie/As I Walked Out One Midsummer Morning* (London: Penguin, 1990), p. 366.

45 Rieff, *In Praise of Forgetting*, p. 41.

46 Not all family requests for the bodies of Republicans to be taken to the Valle were accepted (see Daniel Sueiro, *El valle de los caídos: los secretos de la cripta franquista* (Madrid: La esfera de los libros, 2006), p. 260). In reality it was limited to 'a few Catholic Republicans, considerably restricting the range of victims incorporated from the losing side, and confirming yet again the arbitrary nature of the choice – even this small concession encountered a certain degree of opposition on the part of the staunchest section of the regime' (Paloma Aguilar, *Memory and Amnesia: The Role of the Spanish Civil War in the Transition to Democracy* (New York: Berghahn, 2002), p. 80).

47 See Ramón Cué, *El Valle de los Caídos, reconciliación de España* (El Escorial: Plataforma, 2012).

48 Editorial Patrimonio Nacional, *Santa Cruz del Valle de los Caídos* (Madrid: Editorial Patrimonio Nacional, 1984), p. 5.

49 It is often claimed that prisoners were given the choice and paid to work on the construction project. In reality, however, they often had little option, this providing the only way to pass some money to their frequently starving families. For a first-person account of someone who worked there, see Tário Rubio, *El valle de los caídos y la represión franquista* (Tarragona: Arola, 2011).

50 Aguilar, *Memory and Amnesia*, p. 80.

51 Slavoj Žižek *The Plague of Fantasies* (London: Verso, 1997), p. 4.

52 Francisco Ferrandiz, 'Guerras sin fin: guías para descifrar el Valle de los Caídos en la España contemporánea', *Política y sociedad*, 48.3 (2011): 481–500 (490).

53 The Socialist Ministry of Culture decided to take the ex-President of Kenya but not the French Minister for women's rights to the Valle in 1983. Information taken from Box no. 60361 at the Ministry of Culture Archive.

54 Judith Butler, *Precarious Life: The Power of Meaning and Violence* (London: Verso, 2004), p. 148.

55 Angel Smith, *Historical Dictionary of Spain*, 3rd edn (Lanham, MD: Rowman & Littlefield, 2018), p. 263.

56 Alan O'Leary and Neelam Srivastava, 'Violence and the wretched: The cinema of Gill Pontecorvo', *Italianist*, 29 (2009): 249–64 (p. 261).

Notes

57 Bonnie N. Field, 'Transition modes and post-transition interparty politics: Evidence from Spain (1977–82) and Argentina (1983–89)', *Democratization*, 13.2 (2006): 205–26 (p. 215).

58 Bonnie N. Field, 'From consensual to complex multi-level democracy: The contours of contestation and collaboration in Spain', *Comillas Journal of International Relations*, 1 (2014): 41–52 (p. 45).

59 Alfonso Sastre, '¿Dónde estoy?', *El País*, 24 February 1977, https://elpais.com/diario/1977/02/24/opinion/225586801_850215.html (accessed 29 April 2020).

60 Rosa Montero, *Cinco años de país* (Madrid: Debate, 1982), pp. 81–2.

61 Rosa Montero, *Crónica del desamor* (Madrid: Santillana, 2011), p. 66.

62 See Sally Faulkner, *A Cinema of Contradiction: Spanish Film in the 1960s* (Edinburgh: Edinburgh University Press, 2006), pp. 145–73.

63 Anny Brooksbank Jones, *Women in Contemporary Spain* (Manchester: Manchester University Press, 1997), p. 48.

64 David Serafin, *Madrid Underground* (London: Collins St James Place, 2011), p. 24.

65 Chris Grocott and Gareth Stockey, *Gibraltar: A Modern History* (Cardiff: University of Wales Press, 2012), p. 124.

66 Jorge de Esteban and Lluis López Guerra, 'Electoral rules and candidate selection', in Howard R. Penniman and Eusebio M. Mujal-León (eds), *Spain at the Polls, 1977, 1979, and 1982* (Durham, NC: Duke University Press, 1985), pp. 48–72 (p. 66).

67 Jordi Cornella-Detrell, 'The afterlife of Francoist cultural politics: Censorship and translation in the Catalan and Spanish literary market', *Hispanic Research Journal*, 14.2 (2013): 129–43 (p. 130).

68 Shirly Mangini, *Rojos y rebeldes: la cultura de la disidencia durante el franquismo* (Barcelona: Anthropos, 1987), p. 11.

69 E.g. Luis Pérez Bastías and Fernando Alonso Barahona, *Las mentiras sobre el cine español* (Barcelona: Royal, 1995).

70 Francisco Franco Foundation, File 311.

71 See Jordi Amat, *La primavera de Múnich* (Barcelona: Tusquets, 2016).

72 See Mariano de Mazo, José Luis Muniain and Alberto Otaño, *Los cenocentristas: radiografía política de unas cenas* (Madrid: Ellacuría, 1970).

73 Available for consultation at the Fundación Pablo Iglesias.

74 Joaquín Satrústegui (ed.), *Cuando la Transición se hizo posible: el contubernio de Munich* (Madrid: Tecnos, 1993).

75 Júlia Navarro, *Nosotros, la Transición* (Madrid: Temas de hoy, 1995).

76 Victoria Prego, *Así se hizo la Transición* (Barcelona: Plaza & Janes, 1995). For more on the television series, see Manuel Palacio, 'La televisión constructora de símbolos culturales para el espacio público: La Transición

y la modernidad de los años ochenta', in Carmen Peña Ardid (ed.), *Historia cultural de la Transición: pensamiento crítico y ficciones en literatura, cine y televisión* (Madrid: Catarata, 2019), pp. 193–206 (pp. 201–2).

77 Esther Pérez Villalba, *How Political Singers Facilitated the Spanish Transition to Democracy, 1960–1982: The Cultural Construction of a New Identity* (Lewiston: Edwin Mellon Press, 2007), p. 7.

78 Ben Highmore, *Ordinary Lives: Studies in the Everyday* (London: Routledge, 2011), p. 168.

79 Raymond Williams, *On Culture and Society*, ed. Jim McGuigan (London: Sage, 2014), p. 36.

80 John Hooper, *The Spaniards* (London: Penguin, 1986); John Hooper, *The New Spaniards* (London: Penguin, 1995); John Hooper, *The New Spaniards*, 2nd edn (London: Penguin, 2006).

81 Alan Rusbridger, *Breaking News: The Remaking of Journalism and Why It Matters Now* (Edinburgh: Canongate, 2018), p. 170. Information taken from a telephone interview between John Hooper and Duncan Wheeler conducted on 22 July 2013.

82 Joseph Harrison, *The Spanish Economy: From the Civil War to the European Community* (Cambridge: Cambridge University Press, 1995), p. 13.

83 Sasha D. Pack, 'Tourism and political change in Franco's Spain', in Nigel Townson (ed.), *Spain Transformed: The Late Franco Dictatorship, 1959–75* (Houndmills: Palgrave Macmillan, 2007), pp. 47–66 (p. 54).

84 Geoffrey Huard, *Los antisociales: historia de la homosexualidad en Barcelona y París, 1945–1975* (Madrid: Marical Pons, 2014), pp. 169–70.

85 *Ibid.*, p. 184.

86 José M. Magone, *Contemporary Spanish Politics*, 2nd edn (London: Routledge, 2009), p. 260.

87 See María Ascensión Cerezo Gallegos, *40 años de la primera Asociación de Consumidores de España* (Madrid: Dirección General de Salud Público, Alimentación y Consumo, 2004).

88 E.g. A. Martínez Olmedilla, 'Consejos para la mujer', *Boletín de Galerías Preciados* (January 1962): 15.

89 Emeterio Diez Puertas, 'Estudio preliminar: cuatro dictadores frente al cine', in José María Caparrós and Magí Crusells, *Las películas que vio Franco (y que no todos pudieron disfrutar): cine en El Pardo, 1946–1975* (Madrid: Cátedra, 2018), p. 64.

90 *Ibid.*, p. 66.

Notes

91 Carlos Abella, *Adolfo Suárez: el hombre clave de la Transición* (Madrid: Espasa Calpe, 2006), p. 20.

92 Helen Graham and Jo Labanyi, 'Introduction', in Helen Graham and Jo Labanyi (eds), *Spanish Cultural Studies: An Introduction. The Struggle for Modernity* (Oxford: Oxford University Press, 1995), pp. 1–19 (p. 3).

93 Jacques Derrida, *Spectres of Marx* (Newark: Routledge Classics, 2012), p. 60.

94 Jo Labanyi, 'Introduction: Engaging with ghosts; or, theorizing culture in modern Spain', in Jo Labanyi (ed.), *Constructing Identity in Contemporary Spain* (Oxford: Oxford University Press, 2002), pp. 1–14 (p. 1).

95 *Ibid.*, pp. 1–2.

96 Email to the author sent on 9 October 2017.

97 Richard Lehan, *The City in Literature: An Intellectual and Cultural History* (Berkeley: University of California Press, 1998), p. 291.

98 David Chaney, *Cultural Change and Everyday Life* (Houndmills: Palgrave, 2002), p. 7.

Part I: Celebrity

Introduction

1 Lucia Graves, *A Woman Unknown: Voices from a Spanish Life* (London: Verso, 1999), p. 139.

2 Joke Hermes, *Re-Reading Popular Culture* (Oxford: Blackwell, 2003), p. 11.

3 Tatjana Pavlović, *The Mobile Nation: España cambia de piel* (Bristol: Intellect, 2011), p. 15.

4 Pilar Falcón Osorio, *El imperio rosa: poder e influencia de la prensa del corazón* (Barcelona: CIMS, 1998), p. 17.

5 IOP, *Estudio sobre los medios de comunicación de masas en España: Primera Parte, Prensa* (Madrid: IOP, 1964), p. 5.

6 *Ibid.*, pp. 14, 73.

7 Mary Vincent, *Spain, 1833–2002: People and State* (Oxford: Oxford University Press, 2007), p. 180

8 Stephanie Sieburth, 'The conversation I never had with Carmen Martín Gaite', *Revista de estudios hispánicos*, 36 (2002): 227–39 (p. 235).

9 Nigel Townson, 'Introduction', in Nigel Townson (ed.), *Spain Transformed: The Late Franco Dictatorship, 1959–1975* (Basingstoke: Palgrave Macmillan, 2007), pp. 1–29 (p. 25).

Chapter 1 Fandom and mass-culture in late-Francoist Spain: Manuel Benítez 'El Cordobés' and Raphael

1   Sharon Marcus, *The Drama of Celebrity* (Princeton: Princeton University Press, 2019), p. 9.

2   Tara Zanardi, 'National heroics: Bullfighters, machismo and the cult of celebrity', *Journal for Eighteenth-Century Studies*, 35.2 (2012): 199–221 (p. 206).

3   Justin Crumbaugh, *Destination Dictatorship: The Spectacle of Spain's Tourist Boom and the Reinvention of Difference* (Albany: State University of New York Press, 2009), p. 42.

4   Joseph Harrison, *The Spanish Economy: From the Civil War to the European Community* (Cambridge: Cambridge University Press, 1995), p. 13.

5   Larry Collins and Dominique Lapierre, *Or I'll Dress You in Mourning: The Story of El Cordobés and the New Spain He Stands For* (London: Simon & Schuster, 1968), p. 24.

6   Demeterio Gutiérrez Alarcón, *Los toros de la Guerra y del franquismo* (Barcelona: Caralt, 1978), p. 188.

7   José Méndez Santamaría, *La centenaria plaza de toros de Santa Cruz de Tenerife* (Madrid: Egotarre, 2001), p. 82.

8   Antonio Burgos, *Curro Romero: la esencia* (Barcelona: Planeta, 2000), p. 237.

9   Collins and Lapierre, *Or I'll Dress you in Mourning*, pp. 248–9.

10 E.g. Manuel Davilla, *Manuel Benítez El Cordobés: su leyenda, su arte, sus películas* (Barcelona: Editorial Alas, 1965); and Jarcho, *El Cordobés: su vida, sus películas* (Mallorca: Cort, 1961).

11 See Duncan Wheeler, 'Los toreros estrellas del desarrollismo: Manuel Benítez *El Cordobés* y Sebastián Palomo *Linares*', *Revista de estudios taurinos*, 41 (2017): 43–69.

12 Muriel Feiner, *¡Torero! Los toros en el cine* (Madrid: Alianza, 2004), p. 116.

13 Cited in Santiago Córdoba, 'Los toros en el mundo', *El ruedo* (18 January 1962): 3–4 (p. 3).

14 Clement Díaz Ruiz, *Fuengirola: de pueblo a ciudad* (Malaga: Imprenta del Meditérraneo, 1995), pp. 235–6.

15 Norberto Alcover, *La cultura española durante el franquismo* (Bilbao: Ediciones Mensajero, 1977), p. 213.

16 María Verónica de Haro de San Mateo, 'Bullfighting as television entertainment during the Franco regime', *Communication & Society*, 29.3 (2016): 69–85 (p. 70).

17 Pilar Toboso, *Pepín Fernández, 1891–1982. Galerías Preciados: El pionero de las grandes almacenes* (Madrid: CIP, 2001), p. 323.

Notes

18 Kenneth Tynan, '*El Cordobes* – and tremendismo', in Peter Haining (ed.), *A Thousand Afternoons: An Anthology of Bullfighting* (London: Peter Owne, 1970), pp. 98–108 (pp. 98–9).

19 Peter Brown cited in Deborah Geller, *The Brian Epstein Story*, ed. Anthony Wall (London: Faber & Faber, 2000), p. 86.

20 Nat Weiss cited in *ibid.*, p. 87.

21 *Ibid.*, p. 116.

22 Frank 'El Inglés' Evans, *The Last British Bullfighter* (London: Pan Macmillan, 2009), p. 30.

23 Kostis Kornetis, '"Let's get laid because it's the end of the world!": Sexuality, gender and the Spanish Left in late Francoism and the *Transición*', *European Review of History: Revue européenne d'histoire*, 22.1 (2015): 176–98 (p. 177).

24 See Eider de Dios Fernández, '*Las que tienes que servir* y las servidas: La evolución del servicio doméstico en el franquismo y la construcción de la subjetividad femenina', *Revista historia autónoma*, 3 (2013): 97–111.

25 The archives of the letters sent to Elena Francis are housed in the Arxiu Comarcal del Baix Llobregat, in this case, in File ACBL50-19-T2-630201.

26 See Juan Soto Viñolo, *Querida Elena Francis* (Barcelona: Grijalba, 1995), pp. 143–52.

27 *Ibid.*, p. 146.

28 The most exhaustive but hardly impartial account of Manuel Benítez's brief liaison with the young María Dolores is to be found in Manuel Díaz's autobiography, *De frente y por derecho* (Madrid: Martínez Roca, 2012), pp. 35–55.

29 Gutiérrez Alarcón, *Los toros de la Guerra*, p. 197.

30 Benjamín Bentura Remacha, 'Editorial: la protesta en el ruedo y de paisano', *Fiesta nacional*, 21 May 1968, 3.

31 Rafael Núñez Florenciano, 'Bullfights as a national festivity', in Javier Moreno-Luzón and Xosé M. Núñez Seixas (eds), *Metaphors of Spain: Representations of Spanish National Identity in the Twentieth Century* (New York: Berghahn, 2017), pp. 181–97 (p. 185).

32 Juan Francisco Gutiérrez Lozano, 'Football and bullfighting on television: Spectacle and Spanish identity during Franco's dictatorship', in Peter Goddard (ed.), *Popular Television in Authoritarian Europe* (Manchester: Manchester University Press, 2013), pp. 17–35 (p. 31).

33 Haro de San Mateo, 'Bullfighting as television entertainment': 76.

34 José María Maravall, *Dictadura y disentimiento político: obreros y estudiantes bajo el franquismo* (Madrid: Alfaguera, 1978), pp. 169–73.

35 Miguel Gómez Oliver, 'El movimiento estudiantil español durante el franquismo (1965–1975)', *Revista crítica de ciencias sociales*, 81 (2008): 93–110 (p. 105).

Notes

36 Jaume Ayats and Maria Salicrú-Maltas, 'Singing against the dictatorship (1959–1975): The *nova cançó*', in Sílvia Martínez and Héctor Fouce (eds), *Made in Spain: Studies in Popular Music* (New York: Routledge, 2013), pp. 28–41 (p. 33).

37 José Álvarez Cabelas, *Envenenados en cuerpo y alma: la oposición universitaria al franquismo en Madrid* (Madrid: Siglo XXI Editores, 2004), p. 215.

38 *Ibid.*, pp. 117–18.

39 Gregorio Valdelvira, *La oposición estudiantil al franquismo* (Madrid: Síntesis, 2006), p. 132.

40 Álvarez Cabelas, *Envenenados en cuerpo y alma*, pp. 213–42.

41 Álvaro Fleites Marcos, '¿Retirarse a tiempo? La visión del mayo de 1968 francés en la España contemporánea', *Historia actual online*, 19 (2009): 163–76 (pp. 166–7).

42 *Ibid.*, pp. 171–2.

43 Paul Preston, *El zorro rojo: la vida de Santiago Carrillo* (Barcelona: Debate, 2013), p. 224.

44 Joaquín Arbide, *Sevilla en los 60* (Seville: RD Editores, 2002), p. 169.

45 Alberto Romero Ferrer, *Lola Flores: cultura popular, memoria sentimental e historia del espectáculo* (Seville: Fundación José Manuel Lara, 2016), p. 13.

46 In the words of Sílvia Martínez: '*Copla* could also be called "classic Spanish song". Just as one could talk of a classic American song, here we allude to a class of songs that have certain common features but differing forms of interpretation in actual practice. These modes of interpretation have varied substantially throughout the twentieth century.' Sílvia Martínez, 'Stick to the *copla!* Recovering old Spanish popular songs', in Martínez and Fouce, *Made in Spain*, pp. 90–100 (p. 90).

47 Lola Flores cited in G. Orfila, 'Entrevista: Lola Flores', *Fotogramas*, 17 December 1965, 22.

48 Alejandro Yarza, *The Making and Unmaking of Francoist Kitsch: From 'Raza' to 'Pan's Labyrinth'* (Edinburgh: Edinburgh University Press, 2018), p. 141.

49 Kostis Kornetis, Eirini Kotsovili and Nikolaos Papadogiannis, 'Introduction', in Kostis Kornetis, Eirini Kotsovili and Nikolaos Papadogiannis (eds), *Consumption and Gender in Southern Europe since the Long 1960s* (London: Bloomsbury, 2016), pp. 1–26 (p. 16).

50 Hilario López Millán, *Crónica rosa de España: de la Collares a Rociito* (Barcelona: Planeta, 2001), p. 38.

51 Raphael Gil and Alfonso Gil, *¿Y mañana qué?* (Barcelona: Plaza & Janes, 1998), p. 66.

52 See Duncan Wheeler, 'At the crossroads of tradition and modernity: Raphael and the politics of popular music in Spain', *Journal of European Popular Culture*, 4.1 (2013): 55–70 (p. 59).

Notes

53 Raphael and Gil, *¿Y mañana qué?*, p. 330.

54 Ivan Raykoff and Robert Deam Tobin, 'Introduction', in Ivan Raykoff and Robert Deam Tobin (eds), *Song for Europe: Popular Music and Politics in the Eurovision Song Contest* (Aldershot: Ashgate, 2007), pp. xvii–xxi (p. xviii). See also Paul Allatson, ' "Antes cursi que sencilla": Eurovision song contests and the kitsch-drive to Euro-unity', *Culture, Theory and Critique*, 48.1 (2007): 87–98.

55 This document, dated 21 January 1966, is contained in the papers of Licinio de la Fuente, who would go on to become Minister of Employment. University of Navarra, File 101, Box 98.

56 Juan Luis Ayllón *et al.*, *Eurovisión, un fenómeno paranormal* (Madrid: AlfasSur, 2004), p. 29.

57 Carles Gámez, *Cuando todo era ye-yé* (Valencia: Midas, 1997), p. 32.

58 See, for example, the Spanish television programme broadcast by Channel 6 in May 2008 titled *1968: I Lived through Spanish May*.

59 Juan Francisco Gutiérrez Lozano, 'Spain was not living a celebration: TVE and the Eurovision Song Contest during the years of Franco's dictatorship', *Journal of European Television History and Culture*, 1.2 (2012): 11–17 (p. 15).

60 Benny Pollock and Graham Hunter, *The Paradox of Spanish Foreign Policy: Spain's International Relations from Franco to Democracy* (London: Pinter, 1987), p. 55.

61 See Jorge Semprún, *Autobiografía de Federico Sánchez* (Barcelona: Planeta, 1977), p. 69.

62 Gregorio López Bravo de Castro cited in Ángel Bayod, *Franco visto por sus ministros* (Barcelona: Planeta, 1981), p. 120.

63 Preston, *El zorro rojo*, p. 26.

64 Bayod, *Franco visto por sus ministros*, p. 122.

65 See Veronika Ryjik, *'La bella España': el teatro de Lope de Vega en la Rusia soviética y postsoviética* (Madrid: Iberoamericana Vervuert, 2019).

66 José Luis Sánchez Noriega, *Mario Camus* (Madrid: Cátedra, 1998), p. 142.

67 Email sent to the author on 23 November 2011.

68 Hence, for example, Anna Basmanova very kindly sent me a copy of a course-book she has designed for intermediate-level university students of Spanish based around the film *Digan lo que digan*.

69 See, for example, www.raphaelfans.com (accessed 30 April 2020); or https://es-la.facebook.com/pages/category/Artist/Club-Raphael-Santo-Domingo-Oficial-132848503546182/ (accessed 11 May 2020).

70 Lawrence Grossberg, 'Is there a fan in the house? The affective sensibility of fandom', in Lisa L. Lewis (ed.), *The Adoring Audience: Fan Culture and Popular Media* (London: Routledge, 1992), pp. 50–65 (p. 63).

Notes

71 As Anthony V. H. Fung, for example, argues: 'the rise of fandom in mainland China is situated at a crossroads where capitalism cuts across dogmatic ideology after China's entry to the World Trade Organization'. Anthony V. H. Fung, 'Fandom, youth and consumption in China', *European Journal of Cultural Studies*, 12.3 (2009): 285–303 (p. 286).

72 Gerardo Irles, *¡Sólo para fans! La música ye-yé y pop española de los años 60* (Madrid: Alianza, 1997), pp. 19–20.

73 El Cordobés reportedly received around seventy letters a day. Marino Gómez Santos, *El Cordobés y su gente* (Madrid: Escelier, 1965), p. 79.

74 The unpaginated issues of this bulletin are available for consultation in the reading rooms of Spain's National Library in Madrid.

75 Rosario Coca Hernando, 'Towards a new image of women under Franco: The role of *Sección femenina*', *International Journal of Iberian Studies*, 11.1 (1998): 5–13 (p. 13).

76 Maribel Andujar, 'A Doña Raphaelita', *Club Raphael*, issue 10.

77 See n. 69.

78 See Joaquín de Aguilera, *Televisión y acción cultural* (Madrid: Ediciones de la Junta Central de Información, Turismo y Educación Popular, 1971).

79 Theodor Adorno, 'On popular music', in Simon Frith and Andrew Goodwin (eds), *On Record* (London: Routledge, 1990), pp. 301–14 (p. 305).

80 Tania Modleski, *Loving with a Vengeance: Mass-Produced Fantasies for Women*, 2nd edn (New York: Routledge, 2008), p. 17.

81 Raymond Williams, *On Culture and Society*, ed. Jim McGuigan (London: Sage, 2014), p. 10.

82 William W. Kelly, 'Introduction: Locating the fans', in William W. Kelly (ed.), *Fanning the Flames: Fans and Consumer Culture in Contemporary Japan* (Albany: State University of New York Press, 2004), pp. 1–16 (p. 1).

83 Francisco Umbral, 'Crónicas de Madrid: Raphael', *Destino*, 8 May 1971, 19.

84 Antonio Isasi-Isamendi, *Memorias tras la cámara: cincuenta años de un cine español* (Madrid: Ocho y medio, 2004), p. 335.

85 Arxiu Comarcal del Baix Llobregat, File ACBL50-19-T2-68001.

86 See Duncan Wheeler, 'Raphael and Spanish popular song: A master entertainer and/or music for maids', *Arizona Journal of Hispanic Cultural Studies*, 16 (2012): 11–29 (pp. 18–20).

87 Raphael and Natalia's wedding was shrouded in secrecy as they attempted to escape the media glare by marrying in Venice; this only served to intensify interest, and a book was even published that compiled different press clippings and detailed one journalist's attempts to cover the event. Yale, *Raphael y Natalia: la boda del silencio* (Madrid: Publicaciones Controladas, 1972).

88 Raphael cited in Baltasar Porcel, 'Raphael, o el ídolo', *Destino* (September 1968): 22–3 (p. 23).

89 Carmen Sevilla and Paco Rabal, *Aquella España dulce y amargura: la historia de un país contada a dos voces* (Barcelona: Grijalba, 1999), p. 62.

Chapter 2 Aristocracy and generational change: The houses of Alba, Franco and Bourbon

1 Alberto Oliva and Noberto Angletti, *Revistas que hacen e hicieron historia* (Barcelona: Sol 90, 2002), p. 357.

2 Mary Vincent, *Spain, 1833–2002: People and State* (Oxford: Oxford University Press, 2007), p. 180.

3 Paul Preston, *Juan Carlos: A People's King* (London: HarperCollins, 2004), p. 81.

4 Oliva and Angletti, *Revistas que hacen e hicieron historia*, p. 338.

5 See Duncan Wheeler, 'All of her friends call her Alaska: The cultural politics of locating Olvido Gara in and beyond Madrid's Movida', *Journal of Spanish Cultural Studies*, 17.4 (2016): 361–83 (pp. 364–5).

6 Abbas Milaní, *The Shah* (New York: St Martin's Press, 2011), p. v.

7 Benny Pollock and Graham Hunter, *The Paradox of Spanish Foreign Policy: Spain's International Relations from Franco to Democracy* (London: Pinter, 1987), p. 27.

8 'Vida social: el alma de la fiesta', *¡Hola! Número extraordinario. Duquesa de Alba: una mujer única protagonista de una vida irrepetible* (2014), 46–65 (p. 48).

9 Tico Medina, *Cayetana, Duquesa de Alba* (Barcelona: Nuestros Contemporáneos, 1972), p. 20.

10 *Ibid.*, p. 60.

11 Charles Powell, *Juan Carlos of Spain. Self-Made Monarch* (Houndmills: Macmillan, 1996), p. 3.

12 Preston, *Juan Carlos*, pp. 6–7.

13 Cited in *ibid.*, p. 40.

14 *Ibid.*, p. 134.

15 *Ibid.*, p. 136.

16 Powell, *Juan Carlos of Spain*, p. 17.

17 José María Pemán, *Mis encuentros con Franco* (Barcelona: Dopesa, 1976), p. 186.

18 Francisco Franco Salgado-Araujo, *Mis conversaciones privadas con Franco* (Barcelona: Planeta, 1975), p. 431.

19 Preston, *Juan Carlos*, p. 169.

20 Jaime Peñafiel, *La nieta y el general: tres bodas y un funeral* (Madrid: Temas de hoy, 2007), p. 131.

21 Andrew Morton, *Ladies of Spain: Sofía, Elena, Cristina y Letizia. Entre el deber y el amor*, trans. Alejandro Pradera (Madrid: La esfera de los libros, 2013), p. 54.

22 Lorenzo Díaz, *La televisión en España, 1949–1995* (Madrid: Alianza, 1994), pp. 111–12.

23 Jaime Peñafiel, *La historia de '¡Hola!'* (Madrid: Temas de hoy, 1995), p. 91.

24 Preston, *Juan Carlos*, p. 173.

25 Cited in Pilar Urbano, *La Reina* (Barcelona: Plaza and Janés, 2003), p. 154.

26 Anon., 'Hemos entrado en casa de los príncipes Juan Carlos y Sofía', *Garbo*, 18 July 1964: 32–5.

27 Preston, *Juan Carlos*, p. 216.

28 See Teresa M. Vilarós, 'El baño del ministro y el embajador: Fraga y Duke en Palomares, 1966', *Res publica: revista de historia de las ideas políticas*, 13–14 (2004): 247–62.

29 Juan Francisco Fuentes, *Adolfo Suárez: biografía política* (Barcelona: Planeta, 2011), p. 208.

30 See Carlos Abella, *Adolfo Suárez: el hombre clave de la Transición* (Madrid: Espasa Calpe, 2006), pp. 25–9.

31 Fuentes, *Adolfo Suárez*, p. 74.

32 Cited in José Luis Navas-Migueloa, *La generación del príncipe* (Madrid: G. del Toro, 1972), unpaginated.

33 Javier Memba, 'El <<si, quiero>> ...', in Juan Carlos Laviana (ed.), *1976: las cortes franquistas se hacen el harakiri* (Madrid: Biblioteca El Mundo, 2006), pp. 140–9 (p. 142).

34 Paloma Barrientos, *Carmen Martínez Bordiú: a mi manera* (Barcelona: Ediciones B, 2006), p. 19.

35 José María Bayona, *Alfonso de Borbón, María del Carmen Martínez Bordiú* (Barcelona: Dopesa, 1971), p. 71.

36 *Ibid.*, p. 71.

37 Jaime Peñafiel, ' "Por mí me casaría ahora mismo", nos declaró Don Alfonso de Borbón en su primera entrevista después del anuncio oficial de su compromiso', *¡Hola!*, 25 December 1971, 4–5, 27 (pp. 4–5).

38 Pilar Cernuda, 'Carmen Martínez-Bordiú, unos días antes de su boda', *Teresa* (March 1972): 7–12 (p. 10).

39 Pilar Urbano, *El precio del trono* (Barcelona: Ciudad de lectores, 2011), p. 409.

40 Barrientos, *Carmen Martínez Bordiú*, p. 53.

Notes

41 José Apezarena, *Luis Alfonso de Borbón: un príncipe a la espera* (Barcelona: Plaza & Janes, 2007), p. 228.

42 Juan Luis Cebrián, *Primera página: vida de un periodista (1944–1988)* (Barcelona: Random House, 2016), p. 123.

43 Javier Tusell, *Juan Carlos I: la restauración de la monarquía* (Madrid: Temas de hoy, 1995), p. 557.

44 Morton, *Ladies of Spain*, p. 54.

45 Cited in Urbano, *La Reina*, p. 286.

46 Powell, *Juan Carlos of Spain*, p. 84.

47 Pollock and Hunter, *The Paradox of Spanish Foreign Policy*, pp. 82–3.

48 Preston, *Juan Carlos*, p. 318.

49 Powell, *Juan Carlos of Spain*, p. 84.

50 *Ibid.*, p. 143.

51 Mary Vincent, 'Religion: The idea of Catholic Spain', in Javier Moreno-Luzón and Xosé M. Núñez Seixas (eds), *Metaphors of Spain: Representations of Spanish National Identity in the Twentieth Century* (New York: Berghahn, 2017), pp. 122–41 (p. 137).

52 Cited in Pilar Urbano, *La gran desmemoria: lo que Suárez olvidó y el Rey prefiere no recordar* (Barcelona: Planeta, 2014), p. 271.

53 Manuel Fraga, *En busca del tiempo servido* (Barcelona: Planeta, 1987), p. 220.

54 Paul Preston, *The Triumph of Democracy in Spain* (London: Methuen, 1986), p. 118.

55 Sara Ahmed, *The Cultural Politics of Emotion* (Edinburgh: Edinburgh University Press, 2004), p. 12.

56 Peter Brook, *The Melodramatic Imagination: Balzac, Henry James, Melodrama and the Mode of Excess* (New Haven: Yale University Press, 1976), p. 20.

57 Fernando Vizcaíno Casas, *Hijos de papá* (Barcelona: Planeta, 1979), p. 10.

58 CIS, *Pareja humana: Estudio No. 1.234* (Madrid: CIS, 1980).

59 Gérard Imbert, *Elena Francis, un consultorio para la transición* (Barcelona: Península, 1982), p. 54.

60 Ahmed, *The Cultural Politics of Emotion*, p. 8.

61 Kathleen Doyle, 'The gothic in Martín Gaite's *El cuarto de atrás*: Destabilizing the Sección Femenina's myth of *la mujer muy mujer*', in Marian Womack and Jennifer Wood (eds), *Beyond the Black Room: New Perspectives on Carmen Martín Gaite* (Oxford: Peter Lang, 2011), pp. 173–88 (p. 174).

62 Samuel O'Donoghue, *Rewriting Franco's Spain: Marcel Proust and the Dissident Novelists of Memory* (Lewisburg: Bucknell University Press, 2018), p. 135.

63 Catherine O'Leary and Alison Ribeiro, *A Companion to Carmen Martín Gaite* (Woodbridge: Tamesis, 2008), p. 105.

64 Carmen Martín Gaite, *El cuarto de atrás* (Barcelona: Destino, 1978), p. 64.

65 See Duncan Wheeler and Diana Holmes, 'Introduction', in Corín Tellado, *Thursdays with Leila* (Cambridge: MHRA, 2016), pp. 1–19 (pp. 7–8).

66 Andrés Amorós, *Sociología de una novela rosa* (Madrid: Taurus, 1968), pp. 73–4.

67 Diana Holmes, *Romance and Readership in Twentieth-Century France: Love Stories* (Oxford: Oxford University Press, 2006), p. 18.

68 Amorós, *Sociología de una novela rosa*, p. 35.

69 Corín Tellado, *Déjanos vivir* (Barcelona: Bruguera, 1976), p. 10.

70 Corín Tellado, *El pasota* (Barcelona: Bruguera, 1979), p. 57.

71 *Ibid.*, p. 84.

72 Pablo Sánchez León, 'Radicalism without representation: On the character of social movements in the Spanish Transition to democracy', in Gregorio Alonso and Diego Muro (eds), *The Politics and Memory of Democratic Transition: The Spanish Model* (New York: Routledge, 2011), pp. 95–112 (p. 108).

73 Terence Cave, *Thinking Literature* (Oxford: Oxford University Press, 2016), pp. 4–5.

74 Ahmed, *The Cultural Politics of Emotion*, p. 172.

75 Peñafiel, *La historia de '¡Hola!'*, p. 75.

76 Paloma Aguilar, untitled article, in Fundación Pablo Iglesias, *Tiempo de Transición* (Madrid: Fundación Pablo Iglesias, 2007), pp. 81–116 (p. 99).

77 See Duncan Wheeler, 'In conversation with Gay Mercader, the man who brought rock and roll to Spain', *Arizona Journal of Hispanic Cultural Studies*, 18 (2014): 181–96 (p. 184).

78 Apezarena, *Luis Alfonso de Borbón*, p. 254.

79 Barrientos, *Carmen Martínez Bordiú*, p. 14.

80 *Ibid.*, p. 130.

81 Alfonso de Borbón, *Las memorias de Alfonso de Borbón* (Barcelona: Ediciones B, 1990), p. 160.

82 Apezarena, *Luis Alfonso de Borbón*, p. 236.

83 Carmen Martínez-Bordiú, *La mujer invisible: disfrutar la madurez* (Barcelona: Martínez Roca, 2001), p. 12.

84 Manuel Vicent, *Aguirre, el magnífico* (Madrid: Santillana, 2012), p. 26.

85 *Ibid.*, p. 142.

86 Jesús Aguirre (ed.), *Cristianos y marxistas: los problemas de un diálogo* (Madrid: Alianza, 1969).

87 Letter sent from Sabino Alonso-Pueyo to Fraga, dated 6 December 1968. Contained in the Fundación Pablo Iglesias, ref. no. C 1143, D41.

Notes

88 Cayetana Stuart y Silva, *Yo, Cayetana: Cayetana Stuart y Silva* (Barcelona: Espasa, 2013), p. 200.

89 Cebrián, *Primera página*, p. 256.

90 José Cavero, *El político: biografía de Francisco Fernández Ordóñez* (Madrid: Ediciones de las Ciencias Sociales, 1990), p. 42.

91 María Eugenia Yagüe, *La duquesa de Alba: la última diva de la nobleza* (Madrid: La esfera de los libros, 2009), p. 170.

92 Pablo Martín Acaña and Elena Martínez Ruiz, 'The Golden Age of Spanish capitalism: Economic growth without political freedom', in Nigel Townson (ed.), *Spain Transformed: The Late Franco Dictatorship, 1959–75* (Houndmills: Palgrave Macmillan, 2007), pp. 30–46 (p. 41).

93 Santiago Pérez Díaz, *Francisco Fernández Ordóñez* (Madrid: Cambio 16, 1977), p. 17.

94 Franisco Fernández Ordóñez, 'Epílogo para españoles', in C. H. Cadyn and J. Delepierres, *¿Defraudar o pagar sus impuestos?* (Madrid: Edición Católica, 1969), pp. 223–9 (p. 228).

95 Michael Feenay Callan, *Sean Connery* (London: Virgin, 2002), p. 182.

96 William Chislett, *Spain: What Everyone Needs to Know* (Oxford: Oxford University Press, 2013), p. 92. See also Dionisio Martínez Martínez, *La reforma de la imposición sobre la renta: un informe de 1976* (Madrid: Instituto de estudios fiscales, 1979). Footballer Johan Cruyuff cites the major motivation for his moving in the early 1970s from his home country to Catalonia as economic: 'At Ajax in those days I was earning a million guilders, on which I paid 72 per cent tax. At Barcelona, not only would I get twice as much, but I'd be paying only 30 or 35 per cent to the Spanish taxman.' Johan Cruyuff, *My Turn: The Autobiography* (London: Macmillan, 2016), p. 39.

97 Francisco Fernández Ordóñez, *La España necesaria* (Madrid: Taurus, 1980), p. 194.

98 *Ibid.*, p. 187. See also 'Palabras de Francisco Fernández Ordóñez', in Fundación para la promoción de los estudios financieros, *Semana de estudios de derecho financiero* (Madrid: Fundación para la promoción de los estudios financieros, 1978), pp. 53–65; *Palabras en libertad: conversaciones con Eduardo G. Rico* (Barcelona: Argos Vergara, 1982), pp. 61–72; Santiago Delgado Fernández and Pilar Sánchez Millás, *Francisco Fernández Ordóñez: un político para la España necesaria, 1930–1992* (Madrid: Biblioteca Nueva, 1997), pp. 187–207.

99 Cayetano Martínez Irujo, *De Cayetana a Cayetano* (Madrid: La esfera de los libros, 2019).

100 Bradley S. Epps, 'To be (a part) of a whole: Constitutional patriotism and the paradox of democracy in the wake of the Spanish constitution of 1978', *Revista de estudios hispánicos*, 44.3 (2010): 545–68.

Notes

101 Juan Francisco Fuentes, *Con el Rey y contra el Rey: los socialistas y la monarquía de la Restauración canovista a la abdicación de Juan Carlos I (1879–2014)* (Madrid: La esfera de los libros, 2016), p. 360.

102 Pilar Urbano, *La Reina muy de cerca* (Barcelona: Planeta, 2009), p. 188.

103 See Duncan Wheeler, 'Letter from Madrid: A conversation with Alfonso Guerra', *Political Quarterly*, 87.3 (2016): 312–17.

104 Anon., 'Después de ganar las elecciones', *¡Hola!*, 13 November 1982, 84–6 (p. 84).

105 José Antonio Olivar, 'Carmen Romero', *¡Hola!*, 13 November 1982, 76–8.

106 Anon., 'Después de ganar las elecciones', p. 84.

107 Jaime Peñafiel, 'Don Felipe González y doña Carmen Romero, comunicativos y confidenciales', *¡Hola!*, 25 December 1982, 50–8 (p. 58).

108 *Ibid.*, p. 56.

Chapter 3   *¡Hola!* in the age of champagne socialism: Isabel Preysler, Miguel Boyer, Julio Iglesias, Francisco Rivera 'Paquirri' and Isabel Pantoja

1 Andrés López Martínez, *Julio Iglesias: cuando vuelva a amanecer* (Lleida: Milenio, 2013), p. 208.

2 E. P., 'La mujer de España, la más famosa de España', *Diario 16*, 31 July 1992, 15.

3 Magel García and Julia Higueras, *Voluntad de hierro: memorias autorizadas del Doctor Iglesias* (Madrid: Martínez Roca, 2004), pp. 137–8, 143.

4 Alfredo Fraile, *Secretos confesables* (Barcelona: Península, 2014), p. 43.

5 López Martínez, *Julio Iglesias*, p. 55.

6 On 12 June 1975, Suárez was watching a charity bullfight at Las Ventas when he was informed that Herrero Tejedor had died in a car crash. Suárez's friend Luis Ángel de la Viuda is reputed to have said: 'That's the end of Adolfo's career'. Cited in Gregorio Morán, *Adolfo Suárez: historia de una ambición* (Barcelona: Planeta, 1979), p. 293.

7 Fraile, *Secretos confesables*, p. 52.

8 Julio Iglesias, *Entre el cielo y el infierno* (Barcelona: Planeta, 1981), p. 221.

9 See Katia Chornik, 'When Julio Iglesias played Pinochet's prison', *Guardian*, 15 May 2014, www.theguardian.com/music/2014/may/15/julio-iglesias-valparaiso-pinochet-chile (accessed 1 May 2020).

10 Iglesias, *Entre el cielo y el infierno*, pp. 127, 221.

11 Cited in López Martínez, *Julio Iglesias*, p. 106.

12 Antonio del Valle, *Julio Iglesias ¿truhán o señor? Secretos íntimos desvelados por su mayordomo* (Madrid: Royper, 1986), p. 196.

Notes

13 Assumpta Roura, *Isabel Preysler: el triunfo de una mujer* (Barcelona: Plaza & Janes, 1986), p. 134.

14 López Martínez, *Julio Iglesias*, p. 145.

15 Jaime Peñafiel, 'Final feliz en Miami', *¡Hola!* (6 February 1982): 49–59 (p. 59).

16 López Martínez, *Julio Iglesias*, p. 153.

17 *Ibid.*, pp. 162–5.

18 For more details, see Marina Pérez de Arcos, 'Redefining Leadership in International Relations: Spain, the EEC and NATO (1982–1986)', unpublished D.Phil. thesis, University of Oxford, 2016, pp. 294–9.

19 Manuel Fraga, *En busca del tiempo servido* (Barcelona: Planeta, 1987), p. 388.

20 For the most detailed and impartial account of Reagan's visit to Spain, see Charles Powell, *El amigo americano: España y Estados Unidos de la dictadura a la democracia* (Madrid: Galaxia Gutenberg, 2011), pp. 608–16.

21 See Karen DeYoung, *et al.*, 'Reagan begins visit to Spain', *New York Times*, 7 May 1985, available at www.nytimes.com/1985/05/10/world/remark-by-reagan-on-lincoln-brigade-prompts-ire-in-spain.html (accessed 1 May 2020).

22 Pilar Urbano, *La Reina muy de cerca* (Barcelona: Planeta, 2009), p. 66.

23 Fraile, *Secretos confesables*, pp. 67–8.

24 Lluis Fernández, *Isabel Preysler: la divertida biografía de una santa filipina* (Madrid: Temas de hoy, 1991), p. 180.

25 R. I. M. Dunbar, 'Gossip in evolutionary perspective', *Review of General Psychology*, 8.2 (2004): 100–10 (p. 100).

26 Francisco Umbral, *Crónica de esa guapa gente: memorias de la jet* (Barcelona: Planeta, 1991), p. 309.

27 Roy F. Baumeister, Liqing Zhang and Kathleen D. Vohs, 'Gossip as cultural learning', *Review of General Psychology*, 8.2 (2004): 111–21 (p. 120).

28 Bernard Crick, *Democracy: A Very Short Introduction* (Oxford: Oxford University Press, 2002), p. 11.

29 Juan Luis Galiacho, *Isabel y Miguel: 50 años de historia de España* (Madrid: La esfera de los libros, 2014), p. 48.

30 Salvador Arancibia, *De crisis en crisis: La modernización y la lucha por el poder en la banca* (Madrid: Pirámide, 2011), p. 12.

31 Jordi Pujol, *Memòries: temps de construir (1980–1993)* (Barcelona: Proa, 2012), p. 99.

32 Rosa Montero, *Cinco años de país* (Madrid: Debate, 1982), p. 63.

33 Ernesto Ekaizer, *José María Ruiz Mateos, el último magnate* (Barcelona: Plaza & Janes, 1985), p. 721.

34 Cass Mudde and Cristóbal Rovira Kaltwasser, *Populism: A Very Short Introduction* (Oxford: Oxford University Press, 2017), p. 75.

35 See Pablo Martín Aceña and Begoña Moreno, 'Miguel Boyer Salvador', in Enrique Fuentes Quintana (ed.), *La Hacienda en sus ministros: Franquismo y democracia* (Zaragoza: Prensas Universitarias de Zaragoza, 1997), pp. 205–27 (pp. 218–21).

36 Carmen Martínez Bordiú, 'A partir de esta semana Carmen Martínez-Bordiú escribe para ¡Hola! desde París', ¡Hola! (March 1985): 78–81 (p. 80).

37 The Spanish Finance Minister has always insisted that what he said was taken out of context, and that he was simply referring to the fact that Spain had one of Europe's largest growing economies at the time. See María Antonia Iglesias, *La memoria recuperada: lo que nunca han contado Felipe González y los dirigentes socialistas* (Madrid: Santillana, 2003), p. 201.

38 Isidro López and Emmanuel Rodríguez, 'The Spanish model', *New Left Review* (May–June 2011): 5–28 (p. 8).

39 Gregorio Rodríguez Cabrero, 'El Estado del bienestar en España (1982–1996): entre la universalización y la reestructuración', in Álvaro Soto Carmona and Abdón Mateos López (eds), *Historia de la época socialista en España, 1982–1996* (Madrid: Silex, 2013), pp. 147–67 (p. 159).

40 Richard Maxwell, *The Spectacle of Democracy: Spanish Television, Nationalism and Political Transition* (Minneapolis: University of Minnesota Press, 1995), pp. 19–20.

41 Jordi Roca Jusmet, 'La distribución de la renta entre las clases sociales', in Miren Etxezarreta (ed.), *La reestructuración del capitalismo en España, 1970–1990* (Barcelona: Icaria, 1991), pp. 595–645 (p. 622).

42 *Ibid.*, pp. 630, 632.

43 Galiacho, *Isabel y Miguel*, p. 284.

44 Mario Conde, *Los días de gloria* (Madrid: Planeta, 2010), p. 862.

45 José María Aznar, *Memorias 1* (Barcelona: Planeta, 2012).

46 Ramón Reig, 'Comunicación masiva e industria culturales', in Jordi Gracia and Domingo Ródenas de Moya (eds), *Más es más: sociedad y cultura en la España democrática, 1986–2008* (Madrid: Vervuert: Iberoamericana, 2009), pp. 71–92 (p. 77).

47 In this programme, aired between 1976 and 1985, a film was broadcast to introduce a theme that was then debated by an expert panel.

48 See Emilio Lahera and Antonio Pérez Vargas, 'La mafia de los toros', *Interviú*, 2 November 1978, 71–3; Joaquín Vida, 'La fiesta, bajo el "trust": ¿Quién mata los toros?', *Interviú*, 27 May 1978, 28–31.

49 Documentation contained in File 945.1 at the Municipal Archive in Fuengirola.

50 Carrie B. Douglass, *Bulls, Bullfighting and Spanish Identities* (Tucson: University of Arizona Press, 1997), p. 19.

Notes

51 A treatise he wrote on the bulls written in 1951 was reissued with a prologue by Jesús Aguirre, the Duke of Alba, in 1989. Enrique Tierno Galván, *Los toros, acontecimiento nacional* (Madrid: Turner, 1989).

52 Cathryn Bailey, '"Africa begins at the Pyrenees": Moral outrage, hypocrisy, and the Spanish bullfight', *Ethics & the Environment*, 12.1 (2007): 23–37 (p. 26).

53 Julian Pitt-Rivers, 'The Spanish bull-fight and kindred activities', *Anthropology Today*, 9.4 (1993): 11–15 (p. 14). The celebrated anthropologist overstated his case: according to a poll conducted in June 1991, 62 per cent of Spaniards believed that bullfighting was a national tradition that ought to be preserved, with 54.3 per cent considering it an art-form. A hardly negligible 32 per cent believed it ought to be banned, although this was significantly lower than the 43.5 per cent who suggested that any spectacle involving the suffering of animals ought to be automatically prohibited. Information taken from the archive of the Centro de Investigaciones Sociológicas (study no. 1961).

54 Adrian Shubert, *Death and Money in the Afternoon: A History of the Spanish Bullfight* (Oxford: Oxford University Press, 1999), p. 170.

55 *El País, Libro de estilo* (Madrid: El País, 2002), p. 26.

56 Raúl Pozo del and Diego Bardón, *El ataúd del astracán: el regreso de El Cordobés* (Barcelona: Ediciones Zeta, 1980), p. 79.

57 Correspondence contained in File SF/C02744-30 at the Municipal Archive in Cordoba.

58 José Carlos Arévalo and José Antonio del Moral, *Nacido para morir* (Madrid: Espasa-Calpe, 1985), p. 103.

59 Pantoja was often asked about performing an outdated style of music.

60 Arévalo and del Moral, *Nacido para morir*, p. 103.

61 Ana Baeza, *Isabel Pantoja, 'La Princesa de Triana': marcada por el destino* (Barcelona: Lecturas, 1992), p. 37.

62 See Timothy J. Mitchell, *Blood Sport: A Social History of Spanish Bullfighting* (Philadelphia: University of Pennsylvania Press, 1991), p. 94.

63 Carlos Monegro, 'Sevilla se desbordó en el adiós final a Paquirri', *Diario 16*, 29 September 1984, 29–32.

64 Baeza, *Isabel Pantoja*, p. 6.

65 Francisco Correal, 'Isabel Pantoja lloró ante la tumba de Paquirri mientras repetía <<Te quiero, mi vida, te quiero>>', *Diario 16*, 27 September 1985, 34.

66 See Luis Arechederra, 'The death of a bullfighter: Spanish law on privacy and the right to name and likeness', *International and Comparative Law Quarterly*, 40 (1991): 442–5.

67 Francisco Umbral, 'Las semanas de Oro: Isabel Pantoja', *Interviú*, 3 December 1986, 80.

68 Simon Frith, *Performing Rites: On the Value of Popular Music* (Cambridge, MA: Harvard University Press, 1996), p. 212.

69 Baeza, *Isabel Pantoja*, p. 6.

70 Stephanie Sieburth, *Survival Songs: Conchita Piquer's 'Coplas' and Franco's Regime of Terror* (Toronto: University of Toronto Press, 2014), p. 3.

71 Chris Perriam, *Stars and Masculinities in Spanish Cinema* (Oxford: Oxford University Press, 2003), p. 201.

72 Terenci Moix, *Suspiros de España: la copla y el cine de nuestro recuerdo* (Barcelona: Plaza & Janes, 1993), p. 316.

73 Available on TVE's website. See www.rtve.es/alacarta/videos/en-la-tuya-o-en-la-mia/tu-casa-mia-071015-2220/3315342/ (accessed 31 July 2018).

74 Ricardo Mateos Sáinz de Medrano, *Nobleza obliga* (Madrid: La esfera de los libros, 2006), p. 525.

75 Rodrigo Fresán, 'El extraño caso del doctor Raphael & Mr. Raphael', in *Mierda de música: un debate sobre clasismo, amor, odio y buen gusto en la música pop* (Barcelona: Blackie, 2017), pp. 13–27 (p. 23).

Part II: Censorship
Introduction

1 Jeremy Treglown, *Franco's Crypt: Spanish Culture and Memory since 1936* (London: Chatto & Windus, 2014), p. 97.

2 Helen Graham, review of Jeremy Treglown, *Franco's Crypt: Spanish Culture and Memory since 1936*, *Guardian*, 21 March 2014, www.theguardian.com/books/2014/mar/21/francos-crypt-spanish-culture-memory-since-1936-review-jeremy-treglown (accessed 1 May 2020).

3 Steven Lukes, *Power: A Radical View*, 2nd edn (London: Palgrave Macmillan, 2005), p. 12.

4 Michel Foucault, *The Archaeology of Knowledge* (London: Routledge, 2002), p. 146.

5 Paul Allain, 'The archive', *Contemporary Theatre Review*, 25.1 (2015): 32–5 (p. 35).

6 Timothy Garton Ash, *The File: A Personal History* (London: Atlantic, 1997), p. 96.

Chapter 4 The regulation of cultural production during and after Manuel Fraga (1962–75)

1 Pamela Beth Radcliff, *Modern Spain: 1808 to the Present* (Chichester: Wiley-Blackwell, 2017), p. 221.

Notes

2   See Ignacio Fernández Sarasola, 'Viñetas truncadas: el control sobre las historietas durante el franquismo', *International Journal of Iberian Studies*, 30.1 (2017): 41–57 (pp. 44, 47, 48).

3   See Keith Sutton, 'Round the London art galleries', *Listener* (18 January 1962): 13.

4   Broadcast script sent by producer George MacBath for Edward Lucie-Smith speaking on new Spanish painting sent to the Tate Gallery. Tate Archives, File T992/165/1.

5   *Ibid.*

6   *Ibid.* For the artist's retrospective account of the incident, see Antoni Tàpies, *A Personal Memoir: Fragments for an Autobiography* (Barcelona: Fundació Antoni Tàpies and Indiana University Press, 2009), p. 342.

7   Rosalía Torrent, *España en la Bienal de Valencia: 1895–1997* (Castellón: Diputación de Castellón, 1997), p. 228.

8   Letter contained in Box 10, File 6, General Archive, University of Navarra.

9   José María García Escudero, *La primera apertura: diario de un director general* (Barcelona: Planeta, 1978), p. 256.

10 Virginia Higginbotham, *Spanish Film under Franco* (Austin: University of Texas Press, 1988), p. 62.

11 Letter contained in Box 10, File 1, General Archive, University of Navarra.

12 In a letter to General Franco dated 11 October 1962, the Spanish ambassador wrote the following:

> The principle of 'freedom' is like a second religion in this country, even for Catholics … I always make the point here that Spain has not been, is not, and will never be a totalitarian country. It is, rather, a country in search of and trying to establish, as has been said before, its own sense and form of liberty.

> Cited in Jesús Palacios, *Las cartas de Franco* (Madrid: La esfera de los libros, 2005), pp. 430–1.

13 Javier Muñoz Soro, *Cuadernos para el diálogo (1963–1976): una historia cultural del segundo franquismo* (Madrid: Marcial Pons, 2005), p. 226.

14 Cited in Antonio Beneyto, *Censura y política en los escritores españoles* (Barcelona: Plaza & Janes, 1977), p. 415.

15 Ricardo Martín de la Guardia, *Cuestión de tijeras: la censura en la Transición a la democracia* (Madrid: Síntesis, 2008), p. 75.

16 *Ibid.*, p. 77.

17 *Ibid.*, p. 98.

18 Cited in Beneyto, *Censura y política*, p. 259.

Notes

19   Patricia O'Connor, 'Between the silence of submission and the challenges of authenticity: Theatrical censorship in Franco's Spain', in Catherine O'Leary, Diego Santos Sánchez and Michael Thompson (eds), *Global Insights on Theatre Censorship* (New York: Routledge, 2016), pp. 58–67 (p. 60).

20   *Ibid.*, p. 62.

21   These documents are contained in the Archivo Julián Borderas Pallaruelo held at the Fundación Pablo Iglesias, Box no. AJBP-481-15.

22   O'Connor, 'Between the silence of submission', p. 62.

23   Undated, although similar claims are also made in a letter dated 7 July 1972. File T-AE-Arr-3.

24   Diego Santos Sánchez, *El teatro pánico de Fernando Arrabal* (Woodbridge: Tamesis, 2014).

25   For a summary of these disputes, see Kessell Schwartz, 'Posibilismo and imposibilismo: The Buero Vallejo–Sastre polemic', *Revista hispánica moderna*, 34.1–2 (1968): 436–45.

26   Cited in Beneyto, *Censura y política*, p. 22.

27   T. Avril Bryan, *Censorship and Social Conflict in the Spanish Theater: The Case of Alfonso Sastre* (Washington: University Press of America, 1982), p. 9.

28   File T-AE-Bue-33.

29   Guido Bonsaver, *Censorship and Literature in Fascist Italy* (Toronto: University of Toronto Press, 2007), p. 3.

30   In File 318, Box 1, cuts are made in this respect to *Un matrimonio muy … muy … muy feliz* (*A Very … Very … Very Happy Marriage*) in a report dated 4 September 1968.

31   In File 318, Box 1, a report dated 7 August 1968 on *No somos ni Romeo ni Julieta* (*We're Hardly Romeo and Juliet*) cuts references to prostitution in Madrid's Casa del Campo.

32   In File 318, Box 1, a report dated 6 August 1968 on *El armario* (*The Wardrobe*) insists the following line by Elisa be excised: 'No sé por qué en España no está permitido el striptease' (I don't know why striptease isn't allowed in Spain).

33   The correspondence on *Enseñar a un sinvergüenza* (*To Teach a Shameless Individual*), dated 27 September 1967, demands the following cuts: 'Viva el Plan de Desarrollo y dos otras tonterías más' (Long live the Development Plan, and a couple of other idiocies) and '¿El ministro? … ¿Le llaman el ministro porque se queda con todo?' (The minister? … Do they call him the minister becomes he keeps everything for himself?). File 318, Box 1.

34   File 218, Box 1. For more information on the emerging field of scholarship on the historical 'care' of Republican children, see Mirta Núñez Díaz-Balart, 'La

infancia "redimida": el último eslabón del sistema penitenciario franquista', *Historia y comunicación social*, 6 (2001): 137–48; Lorrain Ryan, 'The sins of the father: The destruction of the Republican family in Franco's Spain', *History of the Family*, 14.3 (2009): 245–52; and Ricardo Vinyes, 'Las desapariciones infantiles durante el franquismo y sus consecuencias', *International Journal of Iberian Studies*, 19.1 (2006): 53–73.

35 See, especially, Manuel L. Abellán, *Censura y creación literaria en España* (Barcelona: Península, 1980); Alejandro Ávila, *La censura del doblaje cinematográfico en España* (Barcelona: CIMS, 1996); María del Camino Gutiérrez Lanza, *Traducción y censura de textos cinematográficos en la España de Franco: doblaje y subtitulado inglés–español*, unpublished Ph.D. thesis, University of León, 1999; Alberto Gil, *La censura cinematográfica en España* (Barcelona: Ediciones B, 2009); Román Gubern, *La censura: función política y ordenamiento jurídico bajo el franquismo (1936–1975)* (Barcelona: Península, 1981); Román Gubern and Domènec Font, *Un cine para el cadalso (40 años de censura cinematográfica en España)* (Barcelona: Euros, 1975); Berta Muñoz Cáliz, *Expedientes de la censura teatral franquista*, 2 vols (Madrid: Fundación Universitaria Española, 2006); Hans Jörg Neuschäfer, *Adiós a la España eterna: la dialéctica de la censura. Novela, teatro y cine bajo el franquismo* (Barcelona: Anthrophos, 1994).

36 Raquel Merino-Álvarez, 'Mapping translated theatre in Spain through censorship archives', in Catherine O'Leary, Diego Santos Sánchez and Michael Thompson (eds), *Global Insights on Theatre Censorship* (New York: Routledge, 2016), pp. 176–90 (p. 177).

37 Raquel Merino-Álvarez, 'A historical approach to Spanish theatre translations from censorship archives', in Isabel García-Izquierdo and Esther Monzó (eds), *Iberian Studies on Translation and Interpreting* (Oxford: Peter Lang, 2012), pp. 123–40 (p. 125).

38 Marianne Hirsch, 'Feminist archive of possibility', *differences: A Journal of Feminist Cultural Studies*, 29.1 (2018): 173–88 (p. 174).

39 Jacques Derrida, *Archive Fever: A Freudian Impression* (Chicago: Chicago University Press, 1996).

40 *Ibid.*, p. 17.

41 *Ibid.*, p. 36.

42 Luis Vaquerizo García, *La censura y el Nuevo Cine Español: cuadros de realidad de los años sesenta* (Alicante: Publicaciones de la Universidad de Alicante, 2014).

43 Xavier Valiño, *Veneno en dosis camufladas: la censura en los discos de pop rock durante el franquismo* (Lleida: Milenio, 2012), p. 55.

44 *Ibid.*, p. 120.

45 *Ibid.*, p. 141.

46 *Ibid.*, p. 142.

47 E.g. Carlos Geli, 'Naipes por pezones y vinilos rayados', *El País*, Catalan edn, 25 May 2016, https://elpais.com/ccaa/2016/05/24/catalunya/1464123584_153366.html (accessed 1 May 2020).

48 Songs banned by Radio 1 in the UK include: The Beatles, 'A Day in the life' (1967); Donna Summer, 'Love to love you baby' (1976); the Sex Pistols, 'God save the Queen' (1977); Frankie Goes to Hollywood, 'Relax' (1984); George Michael, 'I want your sex' (1987); and the Shamen's 'Ebeneezer Goode' (1992). Sarah Thornton, *Club Cultures: Music, Media and Subcultural Capital* (Cambridge: Polity Press, 1995), p. 130.

49 Valiño, *Veneno en dosis camufladas*, p. 244.

50 AGA, Box 67385.

51 AGA, Box 04093.

52 Patricia O'Connor, 'Government censorship in the contemporary Spanish theatre', *Education Theatre Journal*, 18.4 (1966): 443–9 (p. 444).

53 Cited in Adolfo Marsillach, *Tan lejos, tan cerca* (Barcelona: Tusquets, 1998), p. 311.

54 *Ibid.*, p. 312.

55 *Ibid.*, p. 316.

56 Joan Estruch, *Saints and Schemers: Opus Dei and Its Paradoxes* (Oxford: Oxford University Press, 1995), p. 227.

57 Cited in Marsillach, *Tan lejos, tan cerca*, p. 317.

58 See Mercedes Cabrera and Fernando del Rey, *The Power of Entrepreneurs: Politics and Economy in Contemporary Spain* (New York: Berghahn, 2007), pp. 118–20; and Javier Tusell, *Juan Carlos I: La restauración de la monarquía* (Madrid: Temas de hoy, 1995), pp. 217–21.

59 Marsillach, *Tan lejos, tan cerca*, p. 321.

60 See Andrés Amorós, Marina Mayorall and Francisco Nieva, *Análisis de cinco comedias* (Madrid: Castalia, 1977), pp. 189–93.

61 For press reactions, see Francisco Álvaro (ed.), *El espectador y la crítica: el teatro en España, 1970* (Madrid: Prensa Española, 1971), pp. 95–7.

62 Santiago Trancón, *Castañuela 70: esto era España, señor* (Madrid: Rama Lama Music, 2006), p. 319.

63 Circular found in Box 2568 in the Municipal Archive of Almeria.

64 See Víctor Manuel, *Antes de que sea tarde: memorias descosidas* (Barcelona: Penguin Random House, 2015), pp. 71–3.

65 Carlos Barral, *Memorias*, ed. Andreu Jaume (Barcelona: Lumen, 2015), p. 453.

66 Cited in Duncan Wheeler, 'In conversation with Gay Mercader, the man who brought rock and roll to Spain', *Arizona Journal of Hispanic Cultural Studies*, 18 (2014): 181–96 (p. 183).

67 Antonio Cazorla Sánchez, *Fear and Progress: Ordinary Lives in Franco's Spain, 1939–1975* (Malden: Wiley-Blackwell, 2010), p. 11.

68 Juan Cobos Arévalo, *La vida privada de Franco: confesiones del monaguillo del Palacio de El Pardo* (Córdoba: Almuzara, 2009), p. 228.

69 General Archive, University of Navarra, File 016, Box 021.

70 *Ibid.*

71 Cited in Emilio Romero, *Papeles reservados: volúmen II* (Barcelona: Plaza & Janes, 1986), p. 517.

72 Catherine O'Leary, '"Irrepresentable en España": Fernando Arrabal and the Spanish censors', *Journal of Iberian and Latin American Research*, 14.2 (2008): 29–52 (p. 30).

73 Taken from the Archive of future Vice-President Alfonso Osorio, housed at the Fundación de la Transición, File 4, 'Correspondencia'.

74 Bryan, *Censorship and Social Conflict*, p. 1.

75 Alberto Vassallo de Mumbert, 'Alfonso Paso, un legionario de honor', *La legion: revista de los tercios* (September 1978): 18–19.

76 Natalia Figueroa, 'Alfonso Paso', *ABC*, 16 July 1978, 19.

77 This correspondence is held at the Juan March Foundation. The letters referred to correspond to Files LAP-Cor-051 and Lap-Cor-007 respectively

78 Hence, for example, Teatro Candilejas's 1972 production of Sastre's *Escuadra hacia la muerte* (*Condemned Squad*) was approved for over-18s subject to any parallels with the current situation in Spain or references to the army being evaded in references to a hypothetical Third World War. Character surnames were to be foreign as opposed to Spanish. The practitioners are warned that performances will be monitored. Document dated 29 September 1972 in File 318, Box 1.

79 Michael Thompson, 'Conclusion: The power of theatre', in Catherine O'Leary, Diego Santos Sánchez and Michael Thompson (eds), *Global Insights on Theatre Censorship* (New York: Routledge, 2016), pp. 259–67 (p. 261).

80 File 322.

81 See Paul Preston, *Franco* (London: Fontana Press, 1995), pp. 252–70.

82 See Maximiano García Venero, *La Falange en la guerra de España: la unificación y Hedilla* (Paris: Ruedo Ibérico, 1967), p. 575.

83 Cited in Carlos Aguilar and Francisco Llinás, 'Visceralidad y autoría: entrevista con Eloy de la Iglesia', in Carlos Aguilar, Dolores Devesa, Carlos Losilla, Francisco Llinás, José Luis Marqués *et al.*, *Conocer a Eloy de la Iglesia* (San Sebastián: Filmoteca Vasca, 1996), pp. 97–173 (p. 111).

84 Luis Martín-Santos, *Tiempo de silencio* (Barcelona: Seix Barral, 1978), p. 61.

85 Andrea Bresadola, 'Luis Martín-Santos ante la censura: las vicisitudes editoriales de *Tiempo de silencio*', *Creneida*, 2 (2014): 258–96 (pp. 275–7).

86 See José Luis Castro de Paz, *Fernando Fernán-Gómez* (Madrid: Cátedra, 2010), pp. 180–219.

87 Catherine O'Leary, *The Theatre of Antonio Buero Vallejo: Identity, Politics and Censorship* (Woodbridge: Tamesis, 2005), p. 85.

88 Esteve Riambau, *Ricardo Muñoz Suay: una vida en sombras* (Barcelona: Tusquets, 2007), pp. 417–18.

89 García Escudero, *La primera apertura*, p. 269.

90 Javier Muñoz Soro, *Cuadernos para el diálogo (1963–1976): una historia cultural del segundo franquismo* (Madrid: Marcial Pons, 2005), p. 231.

91 This information has been taken from AGA, Box 36/04307.

92 See Duncan Wheeler, 'Los toreros estrellas del desarrollismo: Manuel Benítez *El Cordobés* y Sebastián Palomo *Linares*', *Revista de estudios taurinos*, 41 (2017): 43–69.

93 Domingo Dominguín, *Dominguínes contra Dominguínes* (Madrid: Espasa-Calpe, 2008), pp. 156–7.

94 Fernando Vizcaíno Casas, *Suma de la legislación del espectáculo* (Madrid: Santillana, 1962), p. 346.

95 *Ibid.*, p. 380.

96 William Viestenz, *By the Grace of God: Francoist Spain and the Sacred Roots of Political Imagination* (Toronto: University of Toronto Press, 2014), p. 3.

97 Cited in Pilar Urbano, *España cambia la piel: entrevistas políticas* (Madrid: Sedma y Ediciones, 1976), p. 216.

Chapter 5 Key performance indicators: Democratisation and freedom of speech (1975–81)

1 Paul Rae, 'Freedom of repression', *Theatre Research International*, 36.2 (2011): 117–32 (p. 117).

2 Cited in Philip Ziegler, *Wilson: The Authorised Life of Lord Wilson of Rievaulx* (London: Weidenfeld & Nicolson, 1993), p. 464.

3 Javier Tusell, *Juan Carlos I: la restauración de la monarquía* (Madrid: Temas de hoy, 1995), pp. 620–2.

4 Juan Francisco Fuentes, *Adolfo Suárez: biografía política* (Barcelona: Planeta, 2011), p. 118.

5 Walther L. Bernecker, 'Monarchy and democracy: The political role of King Juan in the Spanish *Transición*', *Journal of Contemporary History*, 33.1 (1998): 65–84 (p. 72).

Notes

6   Bonnie N. Field, 'A "Second Transition" in Spain? Policy, institutions and
     interparty politics under Zapatero (2004–2008)', in Bonnie N. Field (ed.),
     *Spain's Second Transition? The Socialist Government of José Luis Rodríguez
     Zapatero* (Abingdon: Routledge, 2011), pp. 1–19 (p. 2).

7   Document contained in the Archivo Osorio titled 'Instrucción del Ministerio
     de Gobernación a los gobernadores civiles en materia de orden público', not
     indexed at time of writing.

8   James Burns, 'The wrinkled new face of Spain', *Index on Censorship*, 6.3
     (1977): 3–8 (p. 3).

9   *Ibid.*

10   José A. Mondría Beltrán, 'Reflexiones ante un 20 de septiembre', *La Legión:
     revista de los tercios* (October 1977): 18–19 (p. 19).

11   The best source of information on these strikes is two documentary films:
     Llach: la revolta permanent (*Llach: The Permanent Revolt*) (Lluís Danés,
     2006) – which focuses on singer Lluís Llach returning to Vitoria to per-
     form the protest song he wrote about the events in the Basque town – and
     Sanfermines '78 (Juan Gautier and José Ángel Jiménez, 2005).

12   Ignacio Sánchez Cuenca, 'Consenso y conflicto en la Transición española
     a la democracia', in Adam Przeworski and Ignacio Sánchez-Cuenca
     (eds), *Democracia y social democracia: homenaje a José María Maravall*
     (Madrid: Centro de estudios políticos y constitucionales, 2012), pp. 153–
     91 (p. 154).

13   *Ibid.*, p. 177.

14   Ricardo Martín de la Guardia, *Cuestión de tijeras: la censura en la Transición
     a la democracia* (Madrid: Síntesis, 2008), pp. 250–1.

15   See Rhiannon McGlade, *Catalan Cartoons: A Cultural and Political History*
     (Cardiff: University of Wales Press, 2016), pp. 210–14.

16   Carme Molinero and Pere Ysás, *La Transición: historia y relatos* (Madrid:
     Siglo XXI, 2018), p. 128.

17   Pilar Ortuño Anaya, *European Socialists and Spain: The Transition to
     Democracy, 1959–77* (New York: Palgrave, 2002), p. 42.

18   Jaume Claret, *Por favor: una historia de la Transición* (Barcelona: Crítica,
     2000), p. 133.

19   Juan Roldán Ros, 'The media and the elections', in Howard R. Penniman
     and Eusebio M. Mujal-León (eds), *Spain at the Polls, 1977, 1979, and 1982*
     (Durham, NC: Duke University Press, 1985), pp. 253–73 (p. 265).

20   In the second edition of *El precio de la Transición* (*The Price of the Transition*),
     Gregorio Morán claims that the publishers of the first edition had insisted on
     replacing 'Here we have a King conspiring against his President' with '…

trying to free himself of ...'. Gregorio Morán, *El precio de la Transición*, 2nd edn (Madrid: Akal, 2015), p. 156.

21 See Richard Gunther, 'The Spanish model revisited', in Gregorio Alonso and Diego Muro (eds), *The Politics and Memory of Democratic Transition: The Spanish Model* (New York: Routledge, 2011), pp. 17–40 (p. 23).

22 Asadollah Alam, *The Shah and I: The Confidential Diaries of Iran's Royal Court, 1969–1977* (London: I.B. Tauris, 1991), pp. 552–4.

23 Chris Perriam, Michael Thompson, Susan Frenk and Vanessa Knights, *A New History of Spanish Writing, 1939 to the 1990s* (Oxford: Oxford University Press, 2000), p. 21.

24 Antonio Álvarez Solís, 'Editorial: caídas pero importantes', *Interviú*, 10 (1976): 4.

25 See Peter W. Evans, 'Marisol: The Spanish Cinderella', in Antonio Lázaro Reboll and Andrew Willis (eds), *Spanish Popular Cinema* (Manchester: Manchester University Press, 2004), pp. 129–51; Sarah Wright, *The Child in Spanish Cinema* (Manchester: Manchester University Press, 2013), pp. 59–88.

26 Javier Barreiro, *Marisol frente a Pepa Flores* (Barcelona: Plaza & Janes, 1999), p. 139.

27 Paloma San Basilio, *La niña que bailaba bajo la lluvia* (Barcelona: Penguin Random House, 2014), p. 122.

28 *Ibid.*, p. 123.

29 Carmen Sevilla and Carlos Herrera, *Memorias* (Barcelona: Belarcqua, 2005), p. 145.

30 Andrés Amorós, *Luis Miguel Dominguín: el número uno* (Madrid: La esfera de los libros, 2008), p. 335.

31 Isabel Carabantes de las Heras, 'La transición de la literatura erótica (del auge a la normalización)', in José Luis Calvo Carilla, Carmen Peña Ardid, María Ángeles Naval, Juan Carlos Ara Torralba and Antonio Ansón (eds), *El relato de la Transición/La Transición como relato* (Zaragoza: Prensa de la Universidad de Zaragoza, 2013), pp. 179–94 (p. 181).

32 Santiago Fouz-Hernández, 'Introduction: One hundred years of sex', in Santiago Fouz-Hernández (ed.), *Spanish Erotic Cinema* (Edinburgh: Edinburgh University Press, 2017), pp. 1–18 (p. 5).

33 See Duncan Wheeler, 'Las relaciones trilaterales entre la legislación sobre la violencia de género, la pornografía y el cine español', *Secuencias*, 2015, https://revistas.uam.es/secuencias (accessed 2 May 2020).

34 E.g. Montserrat Roig, 'Mi sexo ante la pornografía', *Vindicación femenina* (July 1979): 8–13.

35 Ursula Tidd, *Jorge Semprún: Writing the European Other* (London: MHRA, Maney & Legenda, 2014), p. 162.

Notes

36 Alberto Mira, *De Sodoma a Chueca: una historia cultural de la homosexualidad en España en el siglo XX* (Barcelona: Egales, 2004), p. 451.

37 Alejandro Melero, *Placeres ocultos: gays y lesbianas en el cine español de la Transición* (Madrid: Notorious, 2010), p. 35.

38 See Duncan Wheeler, 'All of her friends call her Alaska: The cultural politics of locating Olvido Gara in and beyond Madrid's Movida', *Journal of Spanish Cultural Studies*, 17.4 (2016): 361–83 (p. 371).

39 Carlos Aguilar and Francisco Llinás, 'Visceralidad y autoría: entrevista con Eloy de la Iglesia', in Carlos Aguilar, Dolores Devesa, Carlos Losilla, Francisco Llinás, José Luis Marqués *et al.*, *Conocer a Eloy de la Iglesia* (San Sebastián: Filmoteca Vasca, 1996), pp. 97–173 (pp. 140–1).

40 Melero, *Placeres ocultos*, p. 247.

41 Simon David Breden, *The Creative Process of Els Joglars and Teatro de la Abadía: Beyond the Playwright* (Woodbridge: Tamesis, 2014), p. 60.

42 Rosa Díaz and Mont Carvajal (eds), *Joglars 77, del escenario al trullo: libertad de expresión y creación colectiva 1968/1977* (Barcelona: Icaria, 2006), p. 76.

43 *Ibid.*, p. 78.

44 Albert Boadella, *Memorias de un bufón* (Madrid: Espasa-Calpe, 2001), p. 270.

45 *Ibid.*, p. 282.

46 Gonzalo Pérez de Olaguer, *Els anys difícils del teatre català: memoria crítica* (Tarragona: Arola Editors, 2008), p. 152.

47 Anon., 'Doce mil manifestantes piden amnistía para Els Joglars', *ABC* (16 March 1978): 15.

48 Pepe Ribas, 'Por el ajo de la cerradura: del muermo al boom nuclear', *Ajoblanco* (April 1978): 4–5 (p. 4).

49 Unless otherwise noted, all information about Boadella's thoughts and recollections is taken from an interview conducted with the author in Madrid on 20 September 2017.

50 Cortes Generales, *Juan Carlos I: discursos (1975–1995)* (Madrid: Congreso de los Diputados y Senado, 1996), p. 137.

51 Antonio Alférez, 'Los dueños del mundo: Jomeini, la espiral del poder islámico', *Los domingos de ABC*, 21 October 1979, 15–18 (p. 17).

52 Janet Afary and Kevin B. Anderson, *Foucault and the Iranian Revolution: Gender and the Seductions of Islam* (Chicago: University of Chicago Press, 2005), p. 118.

53 Jesús López-Pacheco, 'La ira de Irán, ironía del imperialismo', *Tiempo de historia*, 63 (1980): 5–21 (p. 21).

54 Dick Howard, *The Specter of Democracy* (New York: Columbia University Press, 2002), p. viii.

55   Fernando Vizcaíno Casas, *Un año menos* (Barcelona: Planeta, 1979), p. 152.

56   Benny Pollock and Graham Hunter, *The Paradox of Spanish Foreign Policy: Spain's International Relations from Franco to Democracy* (London: Pinter, 1987), p. 61.

57   US President Jimmy Carter began his career in his family's peanut-growing business.

58   Pedro Rodrigo, 'Otra lección histórica', *Fuerza nueva* (24 February 1979): 3.

59   Stanley G. Payne, *Fascism in Spain, 1923–1977* (Madison: University of Wisconsin Press, 1999), p. 457.

60   Sebastian Balfour and Alejandro Quiroga, *The Reinvention of Spain: Nation and Identity since Democracy* (Oxford: Oxford University Press, 2007), p. 44.

61   Paloma Aguilar, untitled article, in Fundación Pablo Iglesias, *Tiempo de Transición* (Madrid: Fundación Pablo Iglesias, 2007), pp. 81–116 (p. 98).

62   Jo Labanyi, 'The language of silence: Historical memory, generational transmission and witnessing in contemporary Spain', *Journal of Romance Studies*, 9.3 (2009): 23–35 (p. 27).

63   Amando de Miguel, *El final del franquismo: testimonio personal* (Madrid: Marcial Pons, 2003), p. 160.

64   Christopher Tulloch, 'Vigilados: Surveillance of foreign press correspondents during the Spanish Transition to democracy', *International Journal of Iberian Studies*, 28.1 (2015): 5–17 (p. 11).

65   Eva Forest, *Testimonias de lucha y resistencia: en la prisión de Yeserías* (Hendaye: Mugalde, 1977), pp. 49–59.

66   *Ibid.*, p. 39.

67   AGA, Box 36/05269. The board also approved it for international distribution, a freedom not granted to all films.

68   Timothy Garton Ash, *Free Speech: Ten Principles for a Connected World* (London: Atlantic, 2016), p. 128.

69   Cited in José Luis Díaz Echegaray, *Regulación del juego del bingo: comentarios y textos legales* (Madrid: Técnicos Asesores del Juego, 1979), p. 67.

70   See Jerónimo Rullán, *Legislación del juego de bingo* (Madrid: Asociación Empresarial de Juegos Autorizados, 1979); José María Neila, *Legislación sobre el juego del bingo* (Barcelona: Editoriales de derechos reunido, 1979).

71   Susana Díaz, *Modos de mostrar: encuentros con Lola Salvador* (Madrid: TECMERIN, 2012), p. 74.

72   Sally Faulkner, 'Rehearsing for democracy in dictatorship Spain: Middlebrow period drama, 1970–1977', in Sally Faulkner (ed.), *Middlebrow Cinema* (London: Routledge, 2016), pp. 88–106 (pp. 97–9).

73   Emeterio Díez Puertas, *Golpe a la Transición: El secuestro de 'El crimen de Cuenca' (1978–1981)* (Barcelona: Laertes, 2012), p. 61.

74 Marcos Ordóñez, *Alfredo el grande. Vida de un cómico: Landa lo cuenta todo* (Madrid: Aguila, 2008), p. 219.

75 AGA, Box 42/0342.

76 Interview with the author on 21 September 2018 in the offices in Madrid of the family law firm, which continues to this day.

77 Juan Pérez Millán, *Pilar Miró, directora de cine* (Madrid: Calamar, 2007), p. 112.

78 Díaz, *Modos de mostrar*, p. 83.

79 Díez Puertas, *Golpe a la Transición*, p. 137.

80 Luis Ortega and Miguel Sánchez Morón, 'El derecho al juez ordinario', *El País*, 29 April 1980, 11–12.

81 Díez Puertas, *Golpe a la Transición*, p. 163.

82 AGA, Box 42/03432.

83 Díez Puertas, *Golpe a la Transición*, p. 293.

84 Rafael López Pintor, *La opinión política española: del franquismo a la democracia* (Madrid: CIS, 1982), pp. 107, 26.

85 Juan Francisco Fuentes, *Con el Rey y contra el Rey: los socialistas y la monarquía de la Restauración canovista a la abdicación de Juan Carlos I (1879-2014)* (Madrid: La esfera de los libros, 2016), p. 288.

86 See Duncan Wheeler, 'Letter from Madrid: A conversation with Alfonso Guerra', *Political Quarterly*, 87.3 (2016): 312–17.

87 Javier Cercas, *Anatomía de un instante* (Barcelona: Random House Mondadori, 2009), p. 37.

88 *Ibid.*, pp. 62–6, 278–9.

89 See Morton Heiberg, *US–Spanish Relations after Franco, 1975–1989* (Lanham, MD: Lexington, 2018), pp. 115–18.

90 Santiago Carrillo, *Memorias* (Barcelona: Planeta, 2008), p. 886.

91 Cercas, *Anatomía de un instante*, pp. 160–1.

92 Hayley Rabanal, '"Pacto de olvido", "dolor diferido": Javier Cercas's affective recuperation of the transition in *Anatomía de un instante*', *Modern Language Review*, 111.3 (2016): 727–53 (p. 753).

93 Díez Puertas, *Golpe a la Transición*, p. 309.

94 *Ibid.*, p. 343.

95 *Ibid.*, pp. 336–7.

96 A. A., 'Protestan por el <<especial calidad>> dado a *El crimen de Cuenca*', *Ya*, 24 July 1982.

Chapter 6 The regime of '81: Patronage and permissiveness

1 Charles Tilly, *Democracy* (Cambridge: Cambridge University Press, 2007), p. 94.

Notes

2 Roger Simon, *Gramsci's Political Thought: An Introduction* (London: Lawrence & Wishart, 1991), p. 22.

3 Information taken from Box 213, titled 'Ferias y fiestas', held in Valencia Municipal Archive.

4 Manuel Fraga, *En busca del tiempo servido* (Barcelona: Planeta, 1987), p. 191.

5 Carlos Robles Piquer, *Memoria de cuatro Españas: República, guerra, franquismo y democracia* (Barcelona: Planeta, 2011), p. 22.

6 Enrique Bustamante, *Radio y televisión en España: historia de una asignatura pendiente de la democracia* (Barcelona: Gedisa, 2006), p. 84.

7 José María Álvarez Monzoncillo and Juan Menor Sendra, 'La estructura del audiovisual en la Transición', in Manuel Palacio (ed.), *Las imágenes del cambio: medios audiovisuales en las transiciones a la democracia* (Madrid: Biblioteca Nueva, 2013), pp. 15–34 (p. 21).

8 Cited in Miguel Fernández Braso, *Conversaciones con Alfonso Guerra* (Barcelona: Planeta, 1983), p. 82.

9 Carsten Humlebaek, *Inventing the Nation* (London: Bloomsbury, 2015), p. 121.

10 *La enseñanza de la Constitución: quinto concurso experiencias escolares* (Madrid: Santillana, 1983).

11 Josep Martí i Ferrando and Josep Montesinos i Martínez, *10 anys de convivència democràtica: la Constitució de 1978* (Valencia: Generalitat Valenciana, Conselleria de Cultura, Educació i Ciència, 1988).

12 Miguel Ángel Torremocha, *La Constitución: juego y aprendo* (Madrid: Editorial Popular, 1985.

13 *LODE: Aprender en libertad* (Madrid: PSOE, 1983), p. 2. For objections to the LODE and this approach, see Óscar Alzaga, José Manuel Otero, Javier Tusell and Ricardo Jérez, *La LODE: un obstáculo para la libertad de enseñanza* (Madrid: Fundación Humanismo y Democracia, 1984); and Jesús López Medel, *Libertad de enseñanza: derecho a la educación y autogestión* (Madrid: Fundación Humanismo y Democracia, 1984).

14 Alessandro Pellegata, 'Constraining political corruption: An empirical analysis of the impact of democracy', *Democratization*, 20.7 (2013): 1195–218 (pp. 1196, 1199).

15 Ministry of Culture Archive, Box 67337.

16 *Ibid.*

17 Ministry of Culture Archive, Box 89921.

18 Ministry of Culture Archive, Box 67343.

19 Agnes Cornell and Victor Lapuente, 'Meritocratic administration and democratic stability', *Democratization*, 21.7 (2014): 1286–304 (p. 1292).

20 See Fernando Lara, '¡En qué país vivimos!', *La calle* (3–9 February 1981); and Francisco Espinosa Mestre, *Shoot the Messenger: Spanish Democracy*

and the Crimes of Fascism (Brighton: Sussex University Press, 2013), pp. 8–9.

21 AGA, Box 42/03419.

22 Peter Besas, *Behind the Spanish Lens: Spanish Cinema under Fascism and Democracy* (Denver: Arden Press, 1985), p. 254.

23 John Hopewell, *Out of the Past: Spanish Literature after Franco* (London: BFI, 1986), p. 227.

24 Mari Paz Balibrea, *Tiempo de exilio: una mirada crítica a la modernidad española desde el pensamiento republicano en el exilio* (Barcelona: Montesinos, 2007), p. 15.

25 Sarah Bowskill, 'Politics and literary prizes: A case study of Spanish America and the Premio Cervantes', *Hispanic Review*, 80.2 (2012): 289–311 (p. 296).

26 *Ibid.*, p. 294.

27 James F. English, *The Economy of Prestige: Prizes, Awards and the Circulation of Cultural Value* (Cambridge, MA: Harvard University Press, 2005), p. 7.

28 Juan Marsé, *Las muchacha de las bragas de oro* (Barcelona: Planeta, 1993), p. 177.

29 Santos Juliá, *Elogio de historia en tiempo de memoria* (Madrid: Fundación Alfonso Martín Escudero & Marcial Pons, 2011), p. 27. For details of the decision-making process behind the award of the Planeta prize during the Transition, see Rafael Borrás Betriu, *La guerra de los planetas: memorias de un editor* (Barcelona: Ediciones B, 2005), pp. 255–85, 311–45, 353–79.

30 English, *The Economy of Prestige*, p. 25.

31 Enrique Sacau-Ferreira, 'Performing a Political Shift: Avant-Garde Music in Cold War Spain', unpublished D.Phil. thesis, University of Oxford, 2011, pp. 177–8.

32 Jesús Aguirre, *Memorias del cumplimiento 4: crónica de una dirección general* (Madrid: Alianza, 1988), pp. 72–3.

33 See Igor Contreras, '*El Concierto de la Paz* (1964): Three commissions to celebrate 25 years of Francoism', in Esteban Buch, Igor Contreras Zubillaga and Manuel Deniz Silva (eds), *Composing for the State: Music in Twentieth Century Dictatorships* (Abingdon: Routledge, 2016), pp. 168–86; Arthur Custer, 'Contemporary music in Spain', *Music Quarterly*, 48.1 (1962), 1–18.

34 Sacau-Ferreira, 'Performing a Political Shift', p. 184.

35 See Gareth J. Wood, *Javier Marías's Debt to Translation: Sterne, Browne, Nabokov* (Oxford: Oxford University Press, 2012), pp. 169–70.

36 Javier Marías, *Así empieza lo malo* (Barcelona: Penguin Random House, 2016), p. 442.

37 Felipe González and Juan Luis Cebrián, *El futuro no es lo que era: una conversación* (Barcelona: Alfaguara, 2001), pp. 30, 35–6.

Notes

38 Paul Preston, *The Triumph of Democracy in Spain* (London: Methuen, 1986), p. 205.

39 Cortes Generales, *Juan Carlos I: Discursos (1975–1995)* (Madrid: Congreso de los Diputados y Senado, 1996), p. 290.

40 Ministry of Culture Archive, Box 62283.

41 Felipe González, 'Introducción', in Rafael Ballesteros (ed.), *Propuestas culturales PSOE* (Madrid: Mañana, 1976), pp. 1–5 (p. 2).

42 Ministry of Culture Archive, Box 67352.

43 Manuel Palacio, *La televisión durante la Transición española* (Madrid: Cátedra, 2012), p. 218.

44 Bustamante, *Radio y televisión en España*, p. 60.

45 Alfonso Guerra, *Dejando atrás los vientos: memorias, 1982–1991* (Madrid: Espasa Calpe, 2006), p. 74.

46 Information taken from an internal report dated 8 June 1981, Ministry of Culture Archive, Box 89225.

47 Palacio, *La televisión durante la Transición*, p. 210.

48 José Carlos Rueda Laffond and María del Mar Chicharro Merayo, *La televisión en España (1956–2006): Política, cultura y consumo televisiva* (Madrid: Fragua, 2006), p. 289.

49 José Miguel Contreras and Manuel Palacio, *La programación de televisión* (Madrid: Síntesis, 2010), p. 93.

50 See Lourdes Orozco, *Teatro y política: Barcelona (1980–2000)* (Madrid: Publicaciones de la Asociación de Directores de Escena en España, 2007), pp. 45–7, 80–1, 131.

51 Information taken from interview with the author conducted in Madrid on 20 September 2017.

52 David Mariezkurrena Iturmendi and Fernando E. Garayoa, *Barricada: ElectricAos* (Panplona: Pamiela, 2010), pp. 131, 138. For a good overview of the censorship of music in the democratic period, see Robin Ragan, 'Censorship in political music lyrics and concerts during the Transition to democracy and the 1980s in Spain', *Hispanic Journal*, 38.1 (2017): 29–43.

53 María-José Ragué-Árias, *El teatro de fin de milenio en España (de 1975 hasta hoy)* (Barcelona: Ariel, 1996), p. 114.

54 Jonathan Mayhew, 'Poetry, politics, and power', *Journal of Spanish Cultural Studies*, 3.2 (2002): 237–48 (p. 240).

55 *Ibid.*, p. 244.

56 Nuria Triana-Toribio, *Spanish Film Cultures: The Making and Unmaking of Spanish Cinema* (London: BFI Palgrave, 2016), p. 30.

57 Jesús Franco, *Memorias del tío Jess* (Madrid: Santillana, 2005), p. 386.

58   Mariano Ozores, *Respetable público: cómo hice casi cien películas* (Barcelona: Planeta, 2002), pp. 142, 278.

59   Sally Faulkner, *A History of Spanish Film: Cinema and Society, 1910–2010* (London: Bloomsbury, 2013), pp. 197–217.

60   Monzoncillo and Sendra, 'La estructura del audiovisual en la Transición'.

61   Ministry of Culture Archive, Box 62262.

62   Anthony Mughan and Richard Gunther, 'The media in democratic and non-democratic regimes: A multilevel perspective', in Anthony Mughan and Richard Gunther (eds), *Democracy and the Media: A Comparative Perspective* (Cambridge: Cambridge University Press, 2000), pp. 1–27 (p. 1).

63   Javier Callejo Gallego, *La audiencia activa. El consumo televisivo: discursos y estrategias* (Madrid: CIS, 1995), p. xiii.

64   Francisco Umbral was one of the few to pick up on this (deliberate?) ambiguity. Francisco Umbral, *La década roja* (Barcelona: Planeta, 1993), p. 124.

65   See Giulia Quaggio, 'Social movements and participatory democracy: Spanish protests for peace during the last decade of the Cold War', *Archiv für Sozialgeschichte*, 58 (2018): 279–302.

66   See Carlos Closa and Paul M. Heywood, *Spain and the European Union* (Houndmills: Palgrave Macmillan, 2004), p. 19.

67   Ángeles García, 'TVE no emitió anoche la canción "Cuervo ingenuo" de Javier Krahe', *El País*, 24 February 1986, https://elpais.com/diario/1986/02/24/radiotv/509583603_850215.html (accessed 2 May 2020).

68   Richard Maxwell, *The Spectacle of Democracy: Spanish Television, Nationalism and Political Transition* (Minneapolis: University of Minnesota Press, 1995), p. 86.

69   Consuelo del Val Cid, *Opinión pública y opinión publicada: los españoles y el referéndum de la OTAN* (Madrid: CIS, 1996), p. 315.

70   See Carlos Gómez, 'Fracaso la ofensiva "guerrista" contra el nombramiento de Pilar Miró para RTVE', *El País*, 19 October 1986, https://elpais.com/diario/1986/10/19/espana/530060403_850215.html (accessed 2 May 2020).

71   Concepción Cascajosa Virino, 'Introduction: A review of the history of women creators of film and TV in Spain', in Concepción Cascajosa Virino (ed.), *A New Gaze: Women Creators of Film and Television in Democratic Spain* (Newcastle: Cambridge Scholars, 2015), pp. xv–xxxi (p. xxi).

72   Cited in Vicente Rodríguez Ortega, 'Matilde Fernández: Directing television', in Virino, *A New Gaze*, pp. 181–8 (p. 185).

73   Lolo Rico, *El libro de 'La bola de cristal'* (Barcelona: Plaza & Janes, 2003), p. 118.

74   Carlos Solchaga, *Las cosas como son: diarios de un político socialista (1980–1994)* (Barcelona: Galaxia Gutenberg, 2017), p. 461.

Notes

75 See Sergio Gálvez Biesca, *La gran huelga general: el sindicalismo contra la <<modernización socialista>>* (Madrid: Siglo XXI Editores, 2017), pp. 590–7.

76 Richard Gunther, José Ramón Montero and José Ignacio Wert, 'The media and politics in Spain: From dictatorship to democracy', in Gunther and Mughan, *Democracy and the Media*, pp. 28–84 (p. 50).

77 Maxwell, *The Spectacle of Democracy*, p. 50.

78 Julián Fernández Cruz, *Encarna Sánchez. Ahora es mi turno: mentirosas sinvergüenzas* (Madrid: Akal, 2009), p. 8.

79 See 'The Andalusian gulf', *Economist*, 1–7 September 1984, 44.

80 González and Cebrián, *El futuro no es lo que era*, p. 158.

81 José Barrionuevo, *2001 días en Interior* (Barcelona: Ediciones B, 1997), p. 319.

82 Paddy Woodworth, 'The war against terrorism: The Spanish experience from ETA to al-Qaeda', *International Journal of Iberian Studies*, 17.3 (2004): 169–82 (p. 171).

83 Fernando Savater and Gonzalo Martínez-Fresneda, *Teoría y presencia de tortura en España* (Barcelona: Anagrama, 1982), p. 57.

84 Luis Martín-Estudillo, 'The culture of democratic Spain and the issue of torture', *Hispanic Issues On-Line*, 14 (2014): 138–60 (p. 143).

85 *Ibid.*, p. 144.

86 *Ibid.*, p. 143.

87 As Paul Preston notes of the trial of the chief architects of the 23-F: 'In court, the defendants revealed themselves to be ill-mannered bullies. The extent of their arrogance, disloyalty – even to one another – petty-mindedness and moral bankruptcy was to have an enormous and unexpected impact on civil–military relations'. Preston, *The Triumph of Democracy*, p. 218.

88 Lorenzo Silva, Manuel Sánchez and Gonzalo Araluce, *Sangre, sudor y paz: La Guardia Civil contra ETA* (Barcelona: Península, 2017), p. 112.

89 See Paddy Woodworth, *Dirty War, Clean Hands: ETA, the GAL and Spanish Democracy* (Cork: Cork University Press, 2001), p. 291.

90 Robert T. Clark, *Negotiating with ETA: Obstacles to Peace in the Basque Country, 1975–1988* (Reno: University of Nevada Press, 1990), p. 3.

91 *Ibid.*, p. 4.

92 Barrionuevo, *2001 días en Interior*, p. 62.

93 Joaquín Leguina, *El camino de vuelta: del triunfo de Felipe González a la crisis del PSOE* (Madrid: La esfera de los libros, 2012), pp. 286–93.

94 Woodworth, 'The war against terrorism', p. 172.

95 Jeremy Harris told me this over lunch at New College, Oxford, on 24 June 2014.

96 John Hooper told me this as part of a telephone interview conducted on 22 July 2013.

97 Samuel P. Huntington, 'Democracy's third wave', *Journal of Democracy*, 2.2 (1991): 12–34 (pp. 12–13).

98 Juan Carlos Revilla, 'Milicios al poder en Argentina', in Juan Carlos Laviana (ed.), *1962: Del Contubernio de Munich a la huelga minera* (Madrid: Biblioteca El Mundo, 2006), pp. 74–89 (p. 77).

99 See Cortes Generales, *Juan Carlos I*, pp. 170–1.

100 Richard H. Immerman, *The Hidden Hand: A Brief History of the CIA* (Chichester: Wiley-Blackwell, 2014), pp. 108–12.

101 In his diary entry commenting upon his meeting with Suárez on 9 January 1980, the US President writes: 'We have underestimated Spain's importance both in Latin America and in the Middle East. He described some of the Islamic nations as "Allah above, oil below, nothing in between". To a remarkable degree, [the] Afghanistan, Iran, and Palestinian problems are interrelated.' Jimmy Carter, *White House Diary* (New York: Ferrar, Straus & Giroux, 2010), pp. 391–2. The minutes made by the British of a meeting held at the Spanish Embassy in London on 7 May 1980 between Suárez and Thatcher focus almost exclusively on the Spanish President's recent tour of Middle Eastern countries. The British Prime Minister expresses her gratitude for efforts to improve relations between the UK and Saudi Arabia before noting how, in mediating between the West and Arab states, Spain was 'probably able to play a part which no other country could'. Document contained in the online archives of the Margaret Thatcher Foundation, available at https://c59574e9047e61130f13-3f71d0fe2b653c4f00f32175760e96e7.ssl. cf1.rackcdn.com/C07E0CA0BA544DCE871140D9CBE21D96.pdf (accessed 10 August 2018).

102 See Ana María Córdoba Hernández, 'España, Israel y Palestina: pasado y presente de sus relaciones diplomáticas', *Historia y política*, 26 (2011): 291–323.

103 See Santiago Delgado Fernández and Pilar Sánchez Millás, *Francisco Fernández Ordóñez: un político para la España necesaria, 1930–1992* (Madrid: Biblioteca Nueva, 1997), pp. 339–41.

104 See Humlebaek, *Inventing the Nation*, pp. 117–27.

105 See Manuel de Paz Sánchez, *Franco y Cuba: estudios sobre España y la Revolución* (Gran Canaria: Ideas, 2006), p. 375.

106 Charles Powell, *El amigo americano: España y Estados Unidos de la dictadura a la democracia* (Madrid: Galaxia Gutenberg, 2011), p. 513.

107 Manuel Castells, Jordi Borja and Felipe González, 'Europa, España y América Latina: una nueva dimensión en las relaciones atlánticas', in Sociedad Estatal para la ejecución de programa del Quinto Centenario, *Encuentros América Latina-Europa en la perspectiva de 1992*, Vol. I (Madrid: Sociedad

Estatal para la ejecución de programa del Quinto Centenario, 1990), pp. 15–37 (p. 31).

108   See José Cavero, *El político: biografía de Francisco Fernández Ordóñez* (Madrid: Ediciones de las Ciencias Sociales, 1990), pp. 280–2.

109   In his autobiography, F. W. de Klerk writes:

> Prime Minister Gonzales [*sic*] of Spain provided me with a useful insight into the thought processes of revolutionary organizations, which greatly helped me throughout the negotiations. With his own background and experiences of resistance, he warned me that I should prepare myself for a great deal of mass action and protest during the negotiations with the ANC. I should also expect that they would say one thing at the negotiating table one day, and something completely contradictory the next day in public. (F.W. de Klerk, *The Last Trek: A New Beginning. The Autobiography* (London: Macmillan, 1998), p. 185)

110   Archie Brown, *The Gorbachev Factor* (Oxford: Oxford University Press, 1996), p. 116.

111   Soledad Fox Maura, *Ida y vuelta: la vida de Jorge Semprún* (Barcelona: Debate, 2016), p. 61.

112   Jorge Semprún, *Federico Sánchez se despide de ustedes* (Barcelona: Fabula Tusquets, 1996), pp. 252–5.

113   Salman Rushdie, *Los versos satánicos* (Barcelona: Círculo de lectores, 1989).

114   See Rosa Mora, 'No podemos perder esta batalla', *El País*, 31 July 1992, https://elpais.com/diario/1992/07/31/cultura/712533610_850215.html (accessed 2 May 2020).

115   Kenan Malik, 'Shadow of the Fatwa', *Index on Censorship*, 37.4 (2008): 112–20 (p. 112).

116   Cited in Pepe Ribas, '¿Es peligroso escribir?', *Ajoblanco* (May 1989): 64–73 (p. 67).

117   See Simon Lee, *The Cost of Free Speech* (London: Faber & Faber, 1990), pp. 76–93.

118   *Ibid.*, p. 25.

Part III: Cities
Introduction

1   CIS, *Ancianos* (Madrid: CIS, 1982).

2   Pamela Beth Radcliff, *Modern Spain: 1808 to the Present* (Chichester: Wiley-Blackwell, 2017), p. 235.

Notes

3 Antonio Cazorla Sánchez, *Fear and Progress: Ordinary Lives in Franco's Spain, 1939–1975* (Malden: Wiley-Blackwell, 2010), p. 96.

4 James Burns, *Barça: A People's Passion* (London: Bloomsbury, 1999), p. 9.

5 Eugenio Trías, *El pensamiento cívico de Joan Maragall* (Barcelona: Ediciones 62, 1985), p. 172.

6 William Genieys, *Las élites españolas ante el cambio de régimen político* (Madrid: CIS, 2004), pp. 182–3.

7 Eulàlia Solé, *SEAT (1950–1993)* (Barcelona: Ediciones de la Tempestad, 1994), p. 35.

8 *Ibid.*, p. 45.

9 Diego Armando Maradona, *El Diego* (London: Yellow Jersey, 2004), p. 73.

Chapter 7 Urbanisation and development: Class, gender and race

1 George Orwell, *Homage to Catalonia* (London: Penguin, 2000), p. 3.

2 *Ibid.*, p. 48.

3 Jaime Gil de Biedma, *Diarios, 1956–1985*, ed. Andreu Jaume (Barcelona: Penguin Random House, 2016), p. 416.

4 Barry Jordan, *Writing and Politics in Franco's Spain* (London: Routledge, 1990), p. 178.

5 Alfonso Sastre, *La taberna fantástica/Tragedia fantástica de la gitana Celestina*, ed. Mariano de Paco (Madrid: Cátedra, 1995), p. 125.

6 Francisco Caudet, *Crónica de una marginación: conversaciones con Alfonso Sastre* (Madrid: Ediciones de la Torre, 1984), p. 122.

7 Julien Agirre, *Operación Ogro: cómo y por qué ejecutamos a Carrero Blanco* (San Sebastián: Hordago, 1978), pp. 77–9.

8 Teresa San Román, *La diferéncia inquietant: velles i noves estratègies culturals dels gitanos* (Barcelona: Fundació Serveis de Cultura Popular & Alta Fulla, 1994), p. 46.

9 *Ibid.*, p. 71.

10 *Ibid.*, p. 47.

11 In 2015, the television programme 'Ochentame otra vez' (Take me back to the 1980s) centred on his political career and advocacy for the Gypsy community. Available at www.rtve.es/alacarta/videos/ochentame-otra-vez/ochentame-otra-vez-soy-gitano/2983558 (accessed 3 May 2020).

12 San Román, *La diferéncia inquietant*, p. 72; see also Aurelio Cebrián Abellán, *Marginalidad de la población gitana española* (Murcia: Universidad de Murcia, 1992), pp. 39, 89.

Notes

13 Lou Charnon-Deutsch, *The Spanish Gyspy: The History of a European Obsession* (Philadelphia: Pennsylvania State University Press, 2004), p. 10.

14 Lidia Merás, 'The gypsies according to NO-DO: The image of the Spanish Roma from dictatorship to democracy', in Stuart Davies and Maite Usoz de la Fuente (eds), *The Modern Spanish Canon: Visibility, Cultural Capital and the Academy* (Cambridge: MHRA, 2018), pp. 136–47 (p. 136). For a good overview of on-screen depiction of Gypsies in Spain, see Isabel Santaolalla, '*Los otros': entnicidades y <<raza>> en el cine español contemporánea* (Zaragoza: Prensas Universitarias de Zaragoza, 2005), pp. 85–117.

15 Antonio Sabater, *Gamberros, homosexuales, vagos y maleantes* (Barcelona: Hispano-Europea, 1962), p. 73.

16 David Harvey, *Rebel Cities: From the Right to the City to the Urban Revolution* (London: Verso, 2012), p. 5.

17 Carlota Solé, Faustino Miguélez, Rosa Junyent and Antonio Izquierdo, *Aproximación al problema de la integración sociocultural de los inmigrantes en Cataluña* (Madrid: Fundación Juan March Working Papers, 1977), p. 5.

18 Manuel Castells, *The City and the Grass Roots: A Cross-Cultural Theory of Urban Space* (London: Edward Arnold, 1983), p. 220.

19 Agirre, *Operación Ogre*, p. 25.

20 Castells, *The City and the Grass Roots*, p. 217.

21 Gil de Biedma, *Diarios*, p. 523.

22 Juan Goytisolo, *Autobiografía* (Barcelona: Galaxia Gutenberg, 2017), p. 181.

23 *Ibid.*, p. 208.

24 Montserrat Roig, *Tiempo de cerezas* (Barcelona: Plaza & Janes, 1986), p. 117.

25 Catherine Davies, *Contemporary Feminist Fiction in Spain: The Work of Montserrat Roig and Rosa Montero* (Oxford: Berg, 1994), pp. 35–6.

26 Doreen Massey, *Space, Place and Gender* (Cambridge: Polity Press, 1994), p. 179.

27 Mercè Clarasó, 'The two worlds of Mercè Rodoreda', in Catherine Davies (ed.), *Women Writers in Twentieth-Century Spain and Spanish America* (Lewiston: Edwin Mellon Press, 1993), pp. 43–54 (p. 44).

28 Deborah L. Parsons, *Streetwalking the Metropolis: Women, the City and Modernity* (Oxford: Oxford University Press, 2003), p. 4.

29 Mercè Rodoreda, *La calle de las Camelias* (Barcelona: Bruguera, 1983), p. 114.

30 Esther Tusquets, *Correspondencia privada* (Barcelona: Anagrama, 2001), p. 122.

31 Roger Alier i Aixalà and Francesc X. Mata, *El gran teatro del Liceo* (Barcelona: Edicions Francesc X. Mata, 1991), p. 338.

32 Jean-Louis Guereña, *La prostitución en la España contemporánea* (Madrid: Marcial Pons, 2003), p. 442.

Notes

33   Amadeo Clave, 'Gente marginada: las bar-girls', *Cuadernos para el diálogo* (June 1972): 26–7 (p. 26).

34   Jaume Martí-Olivella, 'Catalan cinema: An uncanny transnational performance', in Dominic Keown (ed.), *A Companion to Catalan Culture* (Woodbridge: Tamesis, 2011), pp. 185–205 (pp. 185–6).

35   See Teresa M. Vilarós, 'Barcelona como piedras: la impolítica mirada de Jacinto Esteva y Joaquim Jordà en *Dante no es únicamente severo*', *Hispanic Review*, 78.4 (2010): 513–28.

36   Sara Nadal-Melsió, 'Editor's preface. The invisible tradition: Avant-garde Catalan cinema under late Francoism', *Hispanic Review*, 78.4 (2010): 465–8 (p. 467).

37   Carlos Barral, *Memorias*, ed. Andreu Jaume (Barcelona: Lumen, 2015), p. 711.

38   Oriol Regàs, *Los años divinos* (Barcelona: Destino, 2010), p. 247.

39   David Vilaseca, *Queer Events: Post-Deconstructive Subjectivities in Spanish Writing and Film, 1960s to 1990s* (Liverpool: Liverpool University Press, 2010), p. 129.

40   Cited in *ibid.*, p. 165.

41   Silvia Martínez, 'Judges, guitars, freedom and the mainstream: Problematizing the early *cantautor* in Spain', in Isabelle Marc and Stuart Green (eds), *The Singer-Songwriter in Europe: Paradigms, Politics and Place* (Abingdon, Routledge, 2016), pp. 123–35 (p. 126).

42   Luis García Gil, *Serrat y Sabina: a vista de pájaro* (Madrid: T & B, 2012), p. 186.

43   Manuel Vázquez Montalbán, *Serrat* (Gijáon: Júcar, 1972), p. 197.

44   Alcalá de Henares, AGA, Box 67385. According to the censor: 'La nota "típica" de esta canción es la mordacidad y aunque corregida, mantiene su carga satírica, pero en mi opinión puede aceptarse' (The 'typical' reference is where this song has its bite and, although amended, it retains a satirical charge. I nevertheless think it can now be accepted').

45   Kirsten A. Thorne, 'The revolution that wasn't: Sexual and political decay in Marsé's *Últimas tardes con Teresa*', *Hispanic Review*, 65.1 (1997): 93–105 (p. 104).

46   Mario Vargas Llosa, 'Una explosión sarcástica en la novela española moderna', *Ínsula* (April 1966): 1, 12 (p. 1).

47   See M. Custodia Moreno, 'Les lluites veinals: el barri del Carmel', in Mercé Tatjer and Cristina Carrea (eds), *Barraques i la Barcelona informal del segle XX* (Barcelona: Ajuntament de Barcelona i museo d'história de Barcelona, 2010), pp. 167–76; Maximiliano Díaz Molinaro, 'L'ocupació, la construcció i la vida a les barraques', in Tatjer and Carrea, *Barraques i la Barcelona informal*, pp. 83–106.

48 Juan Marsé, *Últimas tardes con Teresa* (Barcelona: Penguin Random House, 2015), p. 23.

49 *Ibid.*, p. 198.

50 *Ibid.*, p. 177.

51 Carles Carreras, *La Barcelona literària: una introducció geográfica* (Barcelona: Proa, 2003), p. 152.

52 Carmen Laforet, *Nada*, ed. Rosa Navarro Durán (Barcelona: Planeta, 2016), p. 204.

53 Andrew Ross, *No Respect: Intellectuals and Popular Culture* (New York: Routledge, 1989), p. 5.

54 Walter Benjamin, *The Writer of Modern Life: Essays on Charles Baudelaire* (Cambridge, MA: Belknap Press of Harvard University Press, 2006), p. 89.

55 Marsé, *Últimas tardes con Teresa*, p. 324.

56 *Ibid.*, p. 325.

57 Castells, *The City and the Grass Roots*, p. 247.

58 'Editorial: proceso al urbanismo', *Cuadernos para el diálogo* (April 1970): 3.

59 Carlos Colorado and Luis H. Castellanos, *Madrid, villa y puente: historia de Vallecas* (Madrid: Ediciones La Librería, 2015), p. 127.

60 Elisabeth Lorenzi, 'Vallecas y la construcción de la identidad barrial', in Vicente Pérez Quintana and Pablo Sánchez León (eds), *Memoria ciudadana y movimiento vecinal: Madrid, 1968–2008* (Madrid: Catarata, 2008), pp. 79–98 (p. 84).

61 Georgina Blakeley, *Building Local Democracy in Barcelona* (Lewiston: Edwin Mellon Press, 2004), p. 114.

62 Castells, *The City and the Grass Roots*, p. 21.

63 In the first post-Franco democratic elections, the Communist vote was atypically strong in those areas of metropolitan Madrid where their political programme had a proven track record of delivering concrete results in local neighbourhoods. See Marcelo Caparella and Fanny Hernández Brotons, 'La lucha por la ciudad: vecinos-trabajadores en las periferias de Madrid, 1968–1982', in Quintana and Sánchez León, *Memoria ciudadana y movimiento vecinal*, pp. 33–52 (pp. 49–50).

64 Antonio Mercero, 'Notas a un corto: un cálido rodaje', in Antonio Mercero and José Luis Garci, *La cabina* (Madrid: Helios, 1973), pp. 27–32 (p. 27).

65 See Juan Martín, Eric Garn and Kristine Rohrer, '*La cabina* o el horror del absurdo', *Hispania*, 98.4 (2015): 701–13 (p. 703).

66 Philip Cooke, 'Modernity, postmodernity and the city', *Theory, Culture and Society*, 5 (1988): 475–92 (p. 490).

67 Enrique Gil, 'Cultura del trabajo y sociedad del ocio: la medida del valor de la juventud', *Revista de estudios de la juventud*, 15 (1984): 87–103 (p. 100).

Notes

68 Margarita Vilar-Rodríguez and Jerónima Pons-Pons, 'El triunfo del modelo hospitalario público sobre lo privado', in Margarita Vilar-Rodríguez and Jerónima Pons-Pons (eds), *Un siglo de hospitales entre lo público y lo privado (1886–1986)* (Madrid: Marcial Pons, 2018), pp, 263–321 (p. 273).

69 See José Félix Tezanos, '¿Por qué crece la delincuencia juvenil?', *Cuadernos para el diálogo* (June 1973): 18–20.

70 Enrique Martínez Reguera, *La calle es de todos: ¿de quién es la violencia?* (Madrid: Editorial Popular, 1982), p. 6.

71 Dirección General de Bienestar de la Consellería de Transporte, *Delincuencia juvenil en el país valenciano* (Valencia: Consellería de Transporte i Binestar Social, 1980), pp. 41–2 (p. 49).

72 'Valdelomar se drogaba con heroína en *Deprisa, deprisa*', *El País*, 15 March 1981, https://elpais.com/diario/1981/03/15/madrid/353507058_850215.html (accessed 3 May 2020).

73 Mónica Aranda Ocaña and Iñaki Rivera Beiras, 'The Spanish penal and penitentiary system: From the re-socialising objective to the internal governance of prisons', in Vincenzo Ruggeiro and Mick Ryan (eds), *Punishment in Europe: A Critical Anatomy of Penal Systems* (Houndmills: Palgrave Macmillan, 2013), pp. 245–62 (p. 247).

74 Carmen Laforet, *Paralelo 35* (Barcelona: Planeta, 1967), p. 15.

75 John Macklin, 'Realism revisited – myth, mimesis and the *novela negra* in Spain', in Rob Rix (ed.), *Leeds Papers on Thrillers in the Transition: 'Novela negra' and Political Change in Spain* (Leeds: Trinity & All Saints, 1992), pp. 49–73 (p. 49). There was a limited tradition of noir writing prior to the Civil War. See Joan Ramón Resina, *El cadáver en la cocina: la novela criminal en la cultura del desencanto* (Barcelona: Anthropos, 1997), pp. 11–42.

76 George Tyras, *Geometrías de la memoria: conversaciones con Manuel Vázquez Montalbán* (Granada: Zoela, 2003), p. 18.

77 José V. Saval, *Manuel Vázquez Montalbán: el triunfo de un luchador incansable* (Madrid: Síntesis, 2004), p. 87.

78 Mari Paz Balibrea, *En la tierra baldía: Manuel Vázquez Montalbán y la izquierda española en la postmodernidad* (Barcelona: El Viejo Topo, 1999), p. 70.

79 Manuel Vázquez Montalbán, *Los mares del Sur* (Barcelona: Planeta, 2003), p. 134.

80 *Ibid.*, p. 137.

81 Amanda Cuesta, 'Els quinquis del barri', in Amanda Cuesta and Mery Cuesta (dirs), *Quinquis del 80: cinema, premsa i carrer* (Barcelona: Diputació de Barcelona y Centre de Cultura Contemporània de Barcelona, 2009), pp. 14–47 (p. 37).

Notes

82 Juan A. Ríos Carratalá, *Quinquis, maderos y picoletos: memoria y ficción* (Seville: Renacimiento, 2014), p. 35.

83 Francisco Alvira Martín and Andrés Canteras Murillo, *Delincuencia y marginación juvenil* (Barcelona: Publicaciones de Juventud y Sociedad, 1986), p. 20.

84 Mercé Tatjer, 'Barraques i projectes de remodelació urbana a Barcelona, de l'Eixample al litoral (1922–1966)', in Tatjer and Carrea, *Barraques i la Barcelona informal*, pp. 37–60 (p. 59).

85 Juan José Moreno Cuenca, *Le llamaban el Vaquilla* (Barcelona: Juan Moreno Cuenca, 1983).

86 Juan José Moreno Cuenca, *Yo 'El Vaquilla': memorias recopiladas por José Antonio de la Loma* (Barcelona: Seix Barral, 1985).

87 Juan José Moreno Cuenca, *Hasta la libertad* (Barcelona: Ediciones B, 2001), p. 40.

88 Eduardo Fuembuena, *Lejos de aquí: José Luis Manzano* (Albacete: Uno editorial, 2017), p. 140.

89 Tom Whittaker, 'Sonorous flesh: The visual and the aural erotics of skin in Eloy de la Iglesia's *quinqui* films', in Santiago Fouz-Hernández (ed.), *Spanish Erotic Cinema* (Edinburgh: Edinburgh University Press, 2017), pp. 154–68 (p. 154).

90 Fuembuena, *Lejos de aquí*, p. 146.

91 Tom Whittaker, 'Sonorous flesh', p. 154.

92 Fuembuena, *Lejos de aquí*, p. 216.

93 Tom Whittaker. 'Mobile soundscapes in the *quinqui* film', in Lisa Shaw and Rob Stone (eds), *Screening Songs in Hispanic and Lusophone Cinema* (Manchester: Manchester University Press, 2018), pp. 98–113 (p. 100).

94 Moreno Cuenca, *Hasta la libertad*, p. 270.

95 See Rosa Peña and J. A. Valderrama, *Nosotros, los Chichos* (Barcelona: Ediciones B, 2005).

96 AGA, Box 36/05243.

97 All of this document is contained in Box 36/05243. Although he is an unreliable narrator, it does seem likely that De la Loma was accurate in this description. There are multiple references to such incidents in Moreno Cuenca's memoirs: Moreno Cuenca, *Hasta la libertad*, pp. 190, 306. Furthermore, in 1979, the journalist Xavier Viander was handed down a prison sentence for his reports on far-right groups in the Basque Country and accused of slander by the Guardia Civil for publishing comments made by the Vaquilla. Cuesta, 'Els quinquis del barri', p. 95.

98 Fuembuena, *Lejos de aquí*, p. 144.

Chapter 8 The Movida and the reinvention of Madrid

1 Joan Ramón Resina, *Barcelona's Vocation of Modernity: Rise and Decline of an Urban Image* (Stanford: Stanford University Press, 2008), p. 178.

2 Federico Jiménez Losantos, *La ciudad que fue Barcelona, años 70* (Madrid: Temas de hoy, 2007), p. 11.

3 Pepe Ribas, *Los 70 a destajo: Ajoblanco y libertad* (Barcelona: Destino, 2007), p. 171.

4 Ana Merino, *El cómic hispánico* (Madrid: Cátedra, 2003), p. 142.

5 Rafael M. Mérida Jiménez, *Transbarcelonas: cultura, género y sexualidad en la España del siglo XX* (Barcelona: Ediciones Bellaterra, 2016), p. 10.

6 Alberto Mira, 'Ocaña, retrat intermitent/Ocaña, an Intermittent Portrait (Ventura Pons, 1977): The Mediterranean *movida* and the passing away of Francoist Barcelona', in Maria M. Delgado and Robin Fiddian (eds), *Spanish Cinema, 1973–2010: Auteurism, Politics, Landscape and Memory* (Manchester: Manchester University Press, 2013), pp. 49–63 (p. 54).

7 See Laura Gómez Vaquero, 'De la reivindicación política a la industrial: la cultura en la Transición a través de tres documentales musicales', *Kamchatka*, 4 (2014): 147–64 (p. 156).

8 Mira, 'Ocaña', p. 50.

9 See Pere Alberó, 'El cine histórico en Cataluña tras la muerte de Franco: una noche de pasión y 25 años de espera', in José Enrique Monterde (ed.), *Ficciones históricas* (Madrid: Academia de las artes y las ciencias cinematográficas de España, 1999), pp. 91–100 (pp. 91–2).

10 Ramón Resina, *Barcelona's Vocation*, pp. 7–8.

11 Andreas Huyssen, *Present Pasts: Urban Palimpsests and the Politics of Memory* (Stanford: Stanford University Press, 2003), p. 7.

12 Mira, 'Ocaña', p. 55.

13 Germán Labrador Méndez, *Culpables por la literatura: imaginación política y contracultura en la Transición española, 1968–1986* (Madrid: Akal, 2017).

14 *Ibid.*, pp. 305–6.

15 Javier Menéndez Flores and Joaquín Sabina, *Sabina: En carne viva* (Barcelona: Random House Mandadori, 2006), p. 88.

16 *Ibid.*, p. 85.

17 Hamilton M. Stapell, *Remaking Madrid: Culture, Politics, and Identity after Franco* (New York: Palgrave Macmillan, 2010), p. 45.

18 *Ibid.*, pp. 49–67.

19 César Alonso de los Ríos, *La verdad sobre Tierno Galván* (Madrid: Anaya & Maria Muchnik, 1997), p. 20.

20 Stapell, *Remaking Madrid*, p. 87.

21 See, for example, his comments in the documentary film *La silla de Fernando* (*Fernando's Chair*) (Luis Alegre and David Trueba, 2006).

22 Fernando Fernán-Gómez, *Las bicicletas son para el verano*, ed. Eduardo Haro Tecglen (Madrid: Espasa-Calpe, 2009), p. 220.

23 Cited in Lola Millás, *Agustín González: entre la conversación y la memoria* (Madrid: Ocho y medio, 2005), p. 92.

24 Enrique Tierno Galván, *Bandos del alcalde* (Madrid: Tecnos, 1986), p. 62.

25 See, for example, the film *El calentito* (Chus Gutiérrez, 2005); and *Hoy no me puedo levantar*, a theatrical musical based on the Mecano songbook.

26 Eduardo Mendicutti, *Una mala noche la tiene cualquiera* (Barcelona: Tusquets, 1988), p. 34.

27 Gema Pérez-Sánchez, *Queer Transitions in Contemporary Spanish Culture* (Albany: State University of Albany Press, 2007), p. 187.

28 Peter McDonough, Samuel H. Barnes and Antonio López Pina, 'Authority and association: Spanish democracy in comparative perspective', *Journal of Politics*, 46.3 (1984): 652–88 (p. 665).

29 All information about Alaska unless otherwise noted is taken from a conversation with the author that took place in her home in Madrid on 8 April 2008.

30 Silvia Grijalba, *Dios salve a La Movida* (Madrid: Espejo de tinta, 2006), p. 93.

31 Marvin D'Lugo, *Guide to the Cinema of Spain* (London: Greenwood Press, 1997), p. 24.

32 See Juan Carlos Ibáñez and Paula Iglesias, 'Comedia sentimental y postmodernidad en el cine español de la Transición a la democracia', in Manuel Palacio (ed.), *El cine y la Transición política en España* (Madrid: Biblioteca Nueva, 2011), pp. 103–25.

33 Javier Adrados, *Los tesoros de Mecano* (Barcelona: Cúpula, 2011), pp. 26–7.

34 Andrés Amorós, *Diario cultural* (Madrid: Espasa-Calpe, 1983), pp. 123–4. When the UCD controlled the town hall, the first municipal talent show for aspiring rock bands had been launched in 1978, with Álvarez present to hand out the awards. The audience was not impressed by either his presence, the choice of winners, or the ceremony itself, with multiple scuffles and protests taking place. See Jesús Ordovás, *La revolución pop* (Madrid: Celeste, 2002), pp. 38–9.

35 Vicente Molina Foix and Luis Cremades, *El invitado amargo* (Barcelona: Anagrama, 2014), p. 171.

36 See Julián Díaz Sánchez, *La idea de arte abstracto en la España de Franco* (Madrid: Cátedra, 2013), pp. 303–4; Narcís Selles, 'De transiciones, desplazamientos y reformulaciones: Arte, derogación del franquismo y

mutación capitalista', in Juan Albarrán (ed.), *Arte y Transición* (Madrid: Budmaria, 2012), pp. 17–40.

37 Cited in Paloma Primo de Rivera García-Lomas, *Arco '82, génesis de una feria* (Madrid: Ministerio de Educación, Cultura y Deporte, 2015), p. 104.

38 Félix de Azúa, 'Barcelona es el *Titanic*', *El País*, 14 May 1982, https://elpais.com/diario/1982/05/14/opinion/390175205_850215.html (accessed 4 May 2020).

39 Loquillo, *En las calles de Madrid* (Barcelona: Penguin Random House, 2018), p. 142.

40 Pedro Pérez del Solar, 'From *Carajillo* to *Madrid*: Comics of the Movida', in William J. Nichols and H. Rosi Song (eds), *Toward a Cultural Archive of 'La Movida': Back to the Future* (Madison: Fairleigh Dickinson University Press, 2014), pp. 251–71 (p. 255).

41 See Mario López González, 'Joy transition: Consensual fun in La Movida's *Madriz* magazine', *Bulletin of Hispanic Studies*, 92.2 (2015): 155–70.

42 See Antonio Altarribia Ordóñez, *La España del tebeo* (Madrid: Espasa-Calpe, 2001).

43 Yaw Agawu-Kakraba, *Postmodernism in Spanish Fiction and Culture* (Cardiff: University of Wales Press, 2010), p. 12.

44 Maite Usoz de la Fuente, *Urban Space, Identity and Postmodernity in 1980s Spain* (Cambridge: Legenda, 2015), p. 85. See also Pedro Pérez del Solar, 'From *Carajillo*', p. 255.

45 Cited in Borja Casani and Juan Carlos de Laiglesia: 'Paloma Chamorro: "Intento contagiar mi fascinación"', *La luna de Madrid*, 12 (1984): 42–45 (p. 45).

46 For a snapshot of his and other Spaniards views of post-modernism at the time, see José Tono Martínez (ed.), *La polémica de la posmodernidad* (Madrid: Libertarias, 1986).

47 Usoz de la Fuente, *Urban Space*, p. 107.

48 Noël Valis, *The Culture of Cursilería: Bad Taste, Kitsch and Class in Modern Spain* (Durham, NC: Duke University Press, 2002), p. 29.

49 Susan Larson, 'Shifting modern identities in Madrid's recent urban planning, architecture and narrative', *Cities*, 20.6 (2003): 395–402 (p. 396).

50 E.g. Francisco Umbral, *Diccionario cheli* (Madrid: Ediciones Grijalbo, 1983), p. 180.

51 Antonio de Prada, *Rock-Ola: Templo de la Movida* (Madrid: Amargord, 2010), p. 52.

52 Alberto Medina, *Exorcismos de la memoria: política y poéticas de la melancolía en la España de la transición* (Madrid: Ediciones Libertarias, 2001), p. 72.

53 Pedro Almodóvar, *Patty Diphusa y otros textos* (Barcelona: Anagrama, 1991), p. 95.

54 Alaska, 'Comida de coco: Marcelino Camacho', *Primera línea*, 8 (1985): 64–9 (p. 66).

55 Alaska, 'El testamento de Don Camilo', *Primera línea*, 6 (1985): 10–15 (p. 15).

56 Alaska, 'Alaska versus Fraga', *Primera línea*, 7 (1985): 54–9 (p. 56).

57 Elena Bordón Fernández, 'Algunos indicadores de la actual crisis juvenil', *De juventud: revista de estudios e investigaciones*, 1 (1980): 49–99 (p. 98). For an excellent overview of publications on youth culture in Spain, see Carles Feixa and Laura Porzio, 'Los estudios sobre culturas juveniles en España (1960–2003)', *Revista de estudios de juventud*, 64 (2004): 9–28.

58 Information taken from files contained in the Ministry of Culture Archive, Box 62269.

59 *Ibid.*

60 Mario Vaquerizo, *Alaska* (Valencia: La Máscara, 2001), p. 121.

61 Eduardo Subirats, *Después de la lluvia: sobre la ambigua modernidad española* (Madrid: Temas de hoy, 1993), p. 111.

62 Teresa M. Vilarós, *El mono del desencanto: la crítica cultural de la transición española (1973–1993)* (Madrid: Siglo Veintiuno de España, 1998), p. 35.

63 Paul Julian Smith, *Spanish Visual Culture: Cinema, Television, Internet* (Manchester: Manchester University Press, 2006), p. 65.

64 Diana C. Mutz, *Hearing the Other Side: Deliberative versus Participatory Democracy* (Cambridge: Cambridge University Press, 2006), p. 3.

65 *Ibid.*, p. 133.

66 Jason Brennan, *Against Democracy* (Princeton: Princeton University Press, 2016), p. 3.

67 *Ibid.*, pp. 231–2.

68 Juan Carlos Usó, *¿Nos matan con heroína? Sobre la intoxicación farmacológica como arma de estado* (Biscay: Libros crudos, 2015), p. 127.

69 José María Mato Reboredo, 'Problemática de las drogas nocivas', in Dirección General de la Guardia Civil, *Curso monográfico sobre drogas nocivas* (Madrid: Dirección General de la Guardia Civil, 1969), pp. 11–48 (p. 40).

70 Juan Carlos Usó, *Drogas y cultura de masas: España (1855–1995)* (Madrid: Taurus, 1996), p. 308.

71 Manuel Vázquez Montalbán, *Tatuaje* (Barcelona: Planeta, 1998), p. 127.

72 Alfredo Crespo, *Burning Madrid* (Barcelona: 66rpm, 2012), p. 53.

73 Usó, *¿Nos matan con heroína?*, pp. 76–7.

74 José A. Sainz Cantero, 'Realidad social y política criminal en la España de la Transición', *Cuadernos de política criminal*, 21 (1983): 745–60 (p. 751).

75 Robert J. MacCoun and Peter Reuter, *Drug War Heresies: Learning from Other Vices, Times and Places* (Cambridge: Cambridge University Press, 2001), p. 96.

Notes

76 *Ibid.*, p. 208. For a well-informed, albeit clumsily expressed, overview of Spanish legislation on drugs in English, see Carlos González Zorrilla, 'Drugs and criminal policy in Spain (1982–1992)', *European Journal of Criminal Policy and Research*, 1.2 (1993): 76–95.

77 Diego Galán, 'Un autor desconocido en televisión', *El País*, 25 November 1984, https://elpais.com/diario/1984/11/25/radiotv/470185203_850215.html (accessed 4 May 2020).

78 Usó, *¿Nos matan con heroína?*, p. 100.

79 Enrique Tierno Galván, *Charlas de radio pronunciadas por el alcalde D. Enrique Tierno Galván: Madrid, 1979–1980* (Madrid: Ayuntamiento de Madrid, 1981), pp. 45–6.

80 Interview with the author in Madrid on 22 May 2018.

81 Malcolm Alan Compitello, 'Designing Madrid, 1985–1997', *Cities*, 20.6 (2003): 403–11 (p. 403).

82 Manuel Ayllón, *La dictadura de los urbanistas: un manifiesto por una ciudad libre* (Madrid: Temas de hoy, 1995), pp. 216–17.

83 Interview with the author in Madrid on 22 May 2018.

84 Domingo Comas, *El uso de drogas en la juventud* (Madrid: Ministerio de Cultura, Instituto de la Juventud, 1985), p. 71.

85 Eduardo Haro Ibars, *De que van las drogas* (Madrid: Ediciones de la Piqueta, 1978), pp. 63–6.

86 Unless otherwise noted, information about the creation of the Foundation comes from an interview carried out with former President and current Vice-President Ignacio Calderón in Madrid on 29 August 2018. For a good potted history of the Foundation, see Abel Hernández, *La sombre de la fiera: veinte años frente a las drogas* (Madrid: Fundación de ayuda contra la drogadicción, 2007).

87 *Ibid.*, pp. 25–6.

88 In his biography of Escobar, Alonso Salazar Jr notes: 'Pablo admired the popularity of González who, at the time, was Spain's great hero and emanated both power and glory.' Alonso Salazar Jr., *Pablo Escobar: el patrón del mal* (Doral: Prisa Ediciones, 2001), p. 97.

89 Julio Feo, *Aquellos años* (Barcelona: Ediciones B, 1993), p. 496.

90 Usó, *Drogas y cultura de masas*, p. 351.

91 John Hooper, *The New Spaniards*, 2nd edn (London: Penguin, 2006), p. 153.

92 'El PSOE promete crear 800,000 empleos en los próximos cuatro años', *El País*, 17 September 1982, https://elpais.com/diario/1982/09/17/portada/401061601_850215.amp.html (accessed 11 May 2020).

93 Nancy Bermeo, 'Sacrifice, sequence, and strength in successful dual transitions: Lessons from Spain', *Journal of Politics*, 56.3 (1994): 601–27 (pp. 604–5).

Notes

94 Marçal Sarrats, *Así en la tierra: Enrique de Castro y la Iglesias de los que no se callan* (Barcelona: Lectio, 2013), pp. 121–5.

95 Juan F. Gamella, 'Heroína en España (1977–1996): balance de una crisis de drogas', *Claves de razón práctica* (May 1997): 20–9 (p. 23).

96 Cited in Sarrats, *Así en la tierra*, p. 85.

97 See Roberto Robles Valencia, 'El Lute: primer y último quinqui. Cierre e historización de lo quinqui', in Joaquín Florido Berrocal, Luis Martín-Cabrera, Eduardo Matos-Martín and Roberto Robles Valencia (eds), *Fuera de la ley: asedios al fenómeno quinqui en la Transición española* (Granada: Comares, 2015), pp. 197–212.

98 Matilde Fernández Montes, 'Vallecas, identidades compartidas, identidades enfrentadas: la ciudad, el pueblo y el campo, el suburbio y el barrio', *Revista de dialectología y tradiciones populares*, 62.1 (2007): 33–83 (p. 57).

99 Alejandro Melero, *La noche inmensa: la palabra de Gonzalo Goicoechea* (Madrid: TECMERIN, 2013), p. 99.

100 Margarita Piñero, *La creación teatral en José Luis Alonso de Santos* (Madrid: Fundamentos, 2005), p. 399.

101 Lorenzo Díaz, *La televisión en España, 1949–1995* (Madrid: Alianza, 1994), p. 709.

102 Andrés Trapiello, *El Rastro: historia, teoría y práctica* (Barcelona: Destino, 2018), p. 111.

103 María Roces, 'De las ruinas a la rehabilitación: el caso de Lavapiés', in Vicente Pérez Quintana and Pablo Sánchez León (eds), *Memoria ciudadana y movimiento vecinal: Madrid, 1968–2008* (Madrid: Catarata, 2008), pp. 183–96. For photographic documentation of the neighbourhood during this period of flux alongside the battle against gentrification, see Marivi Ibarrola, *De Lavapiés a la cabeza* (Madrid: Marivi Ibarrola, 2018).

104 Fabio McNamara and Mario Vaquerizo, *Fabiografía* (Barcelona: Espasa, 2014), p. 98.

105 Peter W. Evans, *Women on the Verge of a Nervous Breakdown* (London: BFI, 1996), p. 28.

106 Rafael Chirbes, *En la lucha final* (Barcelona: Anagrama, 1991), p. 31.

107 See Gregorio Peces-Barba, *La democracia en España: experiencias y reflexiones* (Madrid: Temas de hoy, 1996), p. 330.

108 Borja Andrino, Kiko Llaneras, Daniele Grasso and Elena G. Sevillano, 'El mapa del voto en toda España, calle a calle', *El País*, 3 May 2019: https://elpais.com/politica/2019/05/01/actualidad/1556730293_254945.html (accessed 4 May 2020).

109 Stapell, *Remaking Madrid*, p. 171.

110 'TVE considera "hipócritas" las críticas a la canción de Las Vulpes', *El País*, 28 April 1983: https://elpais.com/diario/1983/04/28/radiotv/420328803_850215.html (accessed 4 May 2020).

111 Toni Riera (ed.), *40 años de historia* (*40 years of Pacha*) (Barcelona: Lunwerg, 2008), p. 82.

112 Mariano Muniesa, *AC/DC en España* (Barcelona: Quarentena Ediciones, 2015), pp. 83–4.

113 Cited in Rafa Cervera, *Alaska y otras historias de la movida* (Barcelona: Random House Mandadori, 2003), p. 335.

114 Leopoldo Alas, *Bochorno* (Barcelona: Versal, 1991), p. 110. In an article discussing the book, the author referred to the Movida as 'an ephemeral invention that nobody can now remember without a degree of shame'. Leopoldo Alas, 'Madrid, cuna del requiebro y del chotis', *Ajoblanco* (April 1991): 60–4 (p. 60).

115 Joan Ramón Resina, 'Short of memory: The reclamation of the past since the Spanish Transition to democracy', in Joan Ramón Resina (ed.), *Disremembering the Dictatorship: The Politics of Memory in the Spanish Transition to Democracy* (Amsterdam: Rodopi, 2000), pp. 83–125 (p. 95).

Chapter 9 An Olympic renaissance: The Barcelona model

1 Ramón Chao, *Después de Franco: España* (Madrid: Ediciones Felmar, 1976), p. 34. Samaranch had been a member of the Francoist Parliament from 1964 onwards, and had combined being the Spanish undersecretary for sport with working his way up the International Olympics Committee.

2 Juan Antonio Samaranch, *Memorias olímpicas* (Barcelona: Planeta, 2002), p. 51.

3 Barbara Kellerman, *Bad Leadership: What It Is, How It Happens, Why It Matters* (Boston, MA· Harvard Business School Press, 2004), p. 62.

4 *Ibid.*, p. 60; see also Greg Andranovich, Matthew J. Burbank and Charles H. Heying, 'Olympic cities: Lessons learned from mega-event politics', *Journal of Urban Affairs*, 23.2 (2001): 113–31.

5 Christopher Kennett and Miquel de Moragas, 'Barcelona, 1992: Evaluating the Olympic legacy', in Alan Tomlinson and Christopher Young (eds), *National Identity and Global Sports Events: Culture, Politics and Spectacle in the Olympics and the Football World Cup* (New York: State University of New York Press, 2006), pp. 177–98 (p. 179).

6 Donald McNeill, *Urban Change and the European Left: Tales from the New Barcelona* (London: Routledge, 1999), p. 41.

Notes

7 Ferran Mascarell, *Barcelona y la modernidad: la ciudad como proyecto de cultura* (Barcelona: Gedisa, 2007), p. 31.

8 María Aurèlia Capmany and Pasqual Maragall, *Caminant yunts per la ciutat*, ed. X Febrès (Barcelona: Laia, 1984), p. 81.

9 Alejandro Quiroga, *Football and National Identities in Spain: The Strange Death of Don Quixote* (New York: Palgrave Macmillan, 2013), pp. 61–2.

10 Capmany and Maragall, *Caminant yunts*, p. 81.

11 *Ibid.*, p. 83.

12 Kennett and de Moragas, 'Barcelona, 1992', p. 179.

13 Pasqual Maragall, *Oda inacabada* (Barcelona: RBA, 2008), p. 161.

14 *Ibid.*, p. 158.

15 Oriol Bohigas, *Reconstrucció de Barcelona* (Barcelona: Ediciones 62, 1985), p. 152.

16 *Ibid.*, pp. 34–5.

17 Félix de Azúa, *Idiotas y humillados* (Barcelona: Anagrama, 2010), pp. 139, 206.

18 Paco Villar, *Historia y leyenda del barrio chino: crónica y documentos de los bajos fondos de Barcelona, 1900–1992*, 3rd edn (Barcelona: Ediciones de la Campana and Ajuntament de Barcelona, 2009), p. 283.

19 Maragall, *Oda inacabada*, pp. 62–4.

20 Loquillo, *Barcelona, ciudad* (Barcelona: Ediciones B, 2010), p. 119.

21 See, for example, Carmen Ciller, 'The influence of Argentinian acting schools in Spain from the 1980s', in Dean Allbritton, Alejandro Melero and Tom Whittaker (eds), *Performance and Spanish Film* (Manchester: Manchester University Press, 2016), pp. 110–21.

22 Raúl Núñez, *Sinatra: novela urbana* (Barcelona: Anagrama, 1988), p. 12.

23 Sharon G. Feldman, *In the Eye of the Storm: Contemporary Theater in Barcelona* (Lewisburg: Bucknell University Press, 2009), p. 41.

24 Caragh Wells, 'The city of words: Eduardo Mendoza's *La ciudad y los prodigios*', *Modern Language Review*, 96.3 (2001): 715–22 (p. 717).

25 Edgar Illas, *Thinking Barcelona: Ideologies of a Global City* (Liverpool: Liverpool University Press, 2012), p. 59.

26 McNeill, *Urban Change*, p. 410.

27 Mari Paz Balibrea, *The Global Cultural Capital: Addressing the Citizen and Producing the City in Barcelona.* (London: Palgrave Macmillan, 2017), pp. 165–6.

28 *Ibid.*, p. 212.

29 Quim Monzó, *Zzzzzzzz …* (Barcelona: Quaderns Crema, 1987), p. 146.

30 Daniel Vázquez Sallés, *Recuerdos sin retorno: para Manuel Vázquez Montalbán* (Barcelona: Península, 2013), p. 102.

Notes

31 Gary McDonogh, 'Discourses of the city: Policy and response in post-transitional Barcelona', in Setha M. Low (ed.), *Theorizing the City: The New Urban Anthropology Reader* (New Brunswick: Rutgers University Press, 2003), pp. 342–76 (p. 354).

32 Victor Gracia, '"El chino": los chorizos autóctonos desbancados por los grupos extranjeros', *Ajoblanco*, 2 (1987): 52–61 (p. 54).

33 McNeill, *Urban Change*, p. 35.

34 Samaranch, *Memorias olímpicas*, p. 241.

35 Keith Dinnie, 'Introduction to the theory of city branding', in Keith Dinnie (ed.), *City Branding: Theory and Cases* (Basingstoke: Palgrave Macmillan, 2011), pp. 3–7 (p. 3).

36 See Alan Tomlinson and Christopher Young, 'Culture, politics, and spectacle in the global sports event: An introduction', in Tomlinson and Young, *National Identity and Global Sports Events*, pp. 1–14 (p. 10).

37 Ari-Veikko Anttiroiko, *The Political Economy of City Branding* (London: Routledge, 2014), p. 1.

38 John R. Gold and Margaret M. Gold, *Cities of Culture: Staging International Festivals and the Urban Agenda, 1851–2000* (Aldershot: Ashgate, 2005), p. 209.

39 *Ibid.*

40 Dianne Dodd, 'Barcelona, the making of a cultural city', in Diane Dodd and Annemoon van Hemel (eds), *Planning Cultural Tourism in Europe: A Presentation of Theories and Cases* (Amsterdam: Boekman Foundation and Ministry of Education, Culture & Sport, 1999), pp. 53–63 (p. 58).

41 Robert Pullen and Stephen Taylor, *Montserrat Caballé: Casta Diva* (London: Victor Gallancz, 1994), p. 304.

42 *Ibid.*, p. 289.

43 See Greg Brooks and Simon Lupton, *Freddie Mercury: His Own Life in His Own Words* (London: Omnibus, 2008), pp. 93–7; Laura Jackson, *Freddie Mercury: The Biography*, 2nd edn (London: Piatkus, 2011), pp. 206–14; Pullen and Taylor, *Montserrat Caballé*, pp. 289–319; Rick Sky, *The Show Must Go On: The Life of Freddie Mercury* (London: HarperCollins, 1994), p. 138.

44 Pullen and Taylor, *Montserrat Caballé*, pp. 257–8.

45 Juan Suárez, 'Ibiza '92: Hollywood en el Mediterráneo', *Diario de Ibiza*, 29 May 1987, p. 19.

46 '"La nit" de la Olimpiada Cultural', *El País*, 10 October 1988, https://elpais.com/diario/1988/10/10/cultura/592441212_850215.html (accessed 4 May 2020).

47 See Duncan Wheeler, 'Barcelona, a musical olympus? Live concerts, club cultures, television and city branding', *Journal of Spanish Cultural Studies*, 21 (2020): 79–96.

48 Josep Roca, 'Ceremonies in the organisation of the games: The experience of COOB '92', in Miquel de Moragas, John MacAloon and Montserrat Llinés (eds), *Olympic Ceremonies: Historical Continuities and Cultural Exchange* (Lausanne: International Olympics Committee, 1995), pp. 227–40 (p. 240).

49 Manuel Huerga, 'Ceremonies production: The Barcelona '92 experience', in De Moragas, MacAloon and Llinés, *Olympic Ceremonies*, pp. 251–55 (p. 253).

50 Feldman, *In the Eye of the Storm*, p. 57.

51 John MacAloon, 'Olympic ceremonies as a setting for intercultural exchange', in De Moragas, MacAloon and Llinés, *Olympic Ceremonies*, pp. 29–43 (p. 41).

52 James Riordan, 'Olympic ceremonies in history (1980–1994): A pilgrimage to the past and a gesture of faith in the future', in De Moragas, MacAloon and Llinés, *Olympic Ceremonies*, pp. 147–56 (p. 148).

53 Albert Boadella, *Memorias de un bufón* (Madrid: Espasa-Calpe, 2001), p. 343.

54 Conversation with the author at the International Theatre Federation conference held in Barcelona in July 2013.

55 McNeill, *Urban Change*, p. 9.

56 Interview with the author held in Madrid on 22 May 2018.

57 Gold and Gold, *Cities of Culture*, p. 232.

58 *Ibid.*

59 Norma Mejía, *Transgenerismos: una experiencia transexual desde la perspectiva antropológica* (Barcelona: Bellaterra, 2006), p. 88.

60 Eduardo Barros Grela, 'Modernidades tru(n)cadas: parodia de la Razón en la obra de Eduardo Mendoza', *Bulletin of Hispanic Studies*, 90.6 (2013): 697–711 (p. 715).

61 Julià Guillamon, *La ciutat interrompuda: de la contra cultura a la Barcelona postolímpica* (Barcelona: Magrana, 2001), pp. 228–9.

62 Eduardo Mendoza, *Sin noticias de Gurb* (Barcelona: Seix Barral, 1992), p. 20.

63 David Miller, *Olympic Revolution: The Olympic Biography of Juan Antonio Samaranch* (London: Pavilion, 1992), p. 258.

64 Kellerman, *Bad Leadership*, p. 64.

65 Sharon Zukin, *The Culture of Cities* (Oxford: Blackwell, 1995), p. 31.

66 Anthony Giddens, *The Third Way: The Renewal of Social Democracy* (Cambridge: Polity Press, 1998), p. viii.

67 *Ibid.*, pp. 32, 134.

68 McNeill, *Urban Change*, p. 7.

69 Duncan Wheeler, '(Dis)locating Spain: Performance intertextualities in *Todo sobre mi madre*', *JCMS: Journal of Cinema and Media Studies*, 58.1 (2018): 91–117 (p. 101).

70 Pasqual Maragall, 'London's green paper: The view from Barcelona', *Planning in London* (1997), 5–7 (p. 5).

71 See Natalia Nuñez, 'Whose vanguardist city? The Barcelona urban model as seen from the periphery in José Luis Guerín's *En construcción*', in Helena Buffery and Carlota Caulfield (eds), *Barcelona: Visual Culture, Space and Power* (Cardiff: University of Wales Press, 2012), pp. 89–103.

72 Ashifa Kassam, 'Barcelona's tourism booms, swelling its coffers and littering its beaches', *Guardian*, 15 June 2014, www.theguardian.com/travel/2014/jun/15/barcelona-tourism-boom-economy-residents (accessed 4 May 2020).

73 Gyan Prakash, 'Introduction', in Gyan Prakash and Kevin M. Kruse (eds), *The Spaces of the Modern City: Imaginaries, Politics and Everyday Life* (Princeton: Princeton University Press, 2008), pp. 1–20 (1).

Part IV: Communities
Introduction

1 José Álvarez Junco, *Spanish Identity in the Age of Nations* (Manchester: Manchester University Press, 2011), p. 3.

2 Gerald Brenan, *The Spanish Labyrinth: The Social and Political Background of the Spanish Civil War* (Cambridge: Cambridge University Press, 2006), p. xv.

3 Brian Hamnett, *The Enlightenment in Iberia and Ibero-America* (Cardiff: University of Wales Press, 2017), p. 211.

4 Brian Hamnett, *The End of Iberian Rule on the American Continent, 1770–1830* (Cambridge: Cambridge University Press, 2017), pp. 315–16.

5 José Ortega y Gasset, *España invertebrada* (Madrid: Revista de occidente, 1955), p. 26.

6 *Ibid.*, p. 58.

7 James Attlee, *'Guernica': Painting the End of the World* (London: Head of Zeus, 2017), p. 10.

8 E. Inman Fox, 'Spain as Castile: Nationalism and national identity', in David Thatcher Gies (ed.), *The Cambridge Companion to Modern Spanish Culture* (Cambridge, Cambridge University Press, 1999), pp. 21–36 (p. 22).

9 Richard Gillespie, 'Between accommodation and contestation: The political evolution of Basque and Catalan nationalism', *Nationalism and Ethnic Politics*, 21.1 (2015): 3–23 (p. 15).

Notes

Chapter 10 Culture as a democratic weapon: Pablo Picasso's *Guernica*

1   Rosa María Medina Doménech and Richard Cleminson, 'Consumerism, gender diversity and moralization of sexuality in the Iberian 1960s', in Kostis Kornetis, Eirini Kotsovili and Nikolaos Papadogiannis (eds), *Consumption and Gender in Southern Europe since the Long 1960s* (London: Bloomsbury, 2016), pp. 59–84 (p. 68).

2   Patrick O'Brian, *Picasso: A Biography* (London: HarperCollins, 2010), p. 207.

3   Gijs Van Hensbergen, *'Guernica': The Biography of a Twentieth-Century Icon* (London: Bloomsbury, 2005), p. 68.

4   *Ibid.*, p. 5.

5   James Attlee, *'Guernica': Painting the End of the World* (London: Head of Zeus, 2017), p. 131.

6   *Ibid.*, p. 133.

7   *Ibid.*, p. 141.

8   *Ibid.*, p. 163.

9   T. J. Clark, 'Picasso and tragedy', in Museo Nacional Centro de Arte Reina Sofía, *Pity and Terror: Picasso's Path to Guernica* (Madrid: Museo Nacional Centro de Arte Reina Sofía, 2017), pp. 19–56 (p. 20).

10 Martin Minchom, *Spain's Martyred Cities: From the Battle of Madrid to Picasso's 'Guernica'* (Brighton: Sussex Academic Press, 2015), p. 216.

11 Van Hensbergen, *Guernica*, p. 153.

12 See Jonathan Rée, 'Peas in a matchbox', *London Review of Books*, 18 April 2019, www.lrb.co.uk/the-paper/v41/n08/jonathan-ree/peas-in-a-matchbox (accessed 6 May 2020).

13 Nelson A. Rockefeller, 'Introduction', in Dorothy Canning Miller (ed.), *The Masterpieces of Modern Art: The Nelson A. Rockefeller Collection* (London: Orbis, 1982), pp. 17–19 (p. 17).

14 Joseph A. Persico, *The Imperial Rockefeller: A Biography of Nelson A. Rockefeller* (New York: Simon & Schuster, 1982), pp. 178–9.

15 Van Hensbergen, *Guernica*, p. 193.

16 Paula Barreiro López, 'Classified files: Picasso, the regime and the avant-garde in Francoist Spain', in Jonathan Harris and Richard Koeck (eds), *Picasso and the Politics of Visual Representation: War and Peace in the Era of the Cold War and Since* (Liverpool: Liverpool University Press, 2013), pp. 89–107 (p. 90).

17 Genoveva Tusell, *El 'Guernica' recobrado: Picasso, el franquismo y la llegada de la obra a España* (Madrid: Cátedra, 2017), p. 95.

Notes

18 Cited in Carlos Abella, *Luis Miguel Dominguín* (Madrid: Espasa-Calpe, 2005), p. 152.

19 Alberto Reig Tapia, '*Guernica* como símbolo', in Carmelo Garitaonandía and José Luis de la Granja (eds), *La Guerra Civil en el País Vasco: 50 años después* (Bilbao: Servicio Editorial Universidad del País Vasco, 1987), pp. 123–55 (p. 131).

20 Alberto Reig Tapia, *Violencia y terror: estudios sobre la guerra civil española* (Torrejón de Ardoz: Akal, 1990), p. 166.

21 Dacia Viejo-Rose, *Reconstructing Spain: Cultural Heritage and Memory after Civil War* (Brighton: Sussex University Press, 2011), p. 132. For a discussion of the town's role within the Basque imagination in relation to the Civil War see Euskal Arkeologia, Etnografia ETA Kondairi Museoa and Musée Basque et de l'histoire de Bayonne, *Gernika: de icono vasco a símbolo universal* (Bilbao and Bayonne: Euskal Arkeologia, Etnografia ETA Kondairi Museoa and Musée Basque et de l'histoire de Bayonne, 2007), pp. 2–11.

22 Viejo-Rose, *Reconstructing Spain*, p. 131.

23 Walther L. Bernecker, 'Cincuenta años de historiografía sobre el bombardeo de Gernika', in Manuel Tuñón de Lara (ed.), *Gernika: 50 años después (1937–1987). Nacionalismo, República, Guerra Civil* (Bilbao: Servicio Editorial Universidad del País Vasco, 2012), pp. 219–42 (pp. 221–2).

24 *Ibid.*, p. 222. Reactionary populist historians such as Pio Moa have succeeded in keeping completely discredited visions, such as that of Jesús Salas Larrazábal, *Guernica: el bombardeo. La historia frente al mito* (Madrid: Galland, 2012), in the public domain.

25 Vicente Talón, *Arde Guernica* (Madrid: G. del Toro, 1973), p. 287.

26 *Ibid.*

27 Maria M. Delgado, 'Memory, silence and democracy in Spain: Federico García Lorca, the Spanish Civil War, and the law of historical memory', *Theatre Journal*, 67.2 (2015): 177–96 (p. 180).

28 *Ibid.*

29 *Ibid.*, p. 183.

30 Barcelona, Archive of the Museu Picasso, File FJS/TEX/3162.

31 Tusell, *El 'Guernica' recobrado*, pp. 81–3.

32 See Sílvia Domènech, *El Museu Picasso, 50 anys a Barcelona: Els orígens* (Barcelona: Museu Picasso, 2013).

33 Barcelona, Archive of the Museu Picasso, File FJS/TEX/3/45.

34 Barreiro López, 'Classified files', p. 100.

35 Tusell, *El 'Guernica' recobrado*, p. 129.

36 Barreiro López, 'Classified files', p. 101.

Notes

37 Manuel Maysounave, 'Cartas al director: a propósito de Picasso', *Fuerza Nueva* (8 January 1972): 5.

38 Jaime Tarraga, 'Picasso o la anti-España', *Fuerza Nueva*, 5 May 1973, 20–3 (p. 20).

39 For a history of the representation of Picasso in the NO-DO newsreel, see Lidia Merás, 'Picasso al alcance de todos los españoles: Picasso en el noticiario NO-DO', *Ayer: Revista de historia contemporánea*, forthcoming. I would like to thank Lidia for sending me a copy of this article prior to publication.

40 Van Hensbergen, *Guernica*, p. 282.

41 Attlee, *Guernica*, p. 197.

42 Arxiu Municipal de Barcelona, Box 60106.

43 Arxiu Municipal de Barcelona, File 6004, titled 'Museus gestió'.

44 Arxiu Municipal de Barcelona, Box 60106.

45 *Ibid.*

46 Tusell, *El 'Guernica' recobrado*, pp. 269.

47 See the Archive of the SIT Transporte Internacionales, Serie Informe *Guernica*, available for consulation in the library of the Reina Sofía Museum.

48 Xavier Domingo, 'Un "Chamorro", por favor', *Cambio 16*, 21 September 1981, 86–91 (p. 86).

49 Van Hensbergen, *Guernica*, p. 304.

50 Josep Palau y Fabra, 'Una obra de guerra, símbolo de paz', *El País*, 11 September 1981, 25.

51 'La guerra ha terminado', *El País*, 11 September 1981, 8.

52 'Editorial: UCD y el *Guernica*', *Deia*, 11 September 1981, 2.

53 Van Hensbergen, *Guernica*, pp. 310–11.

54 Tusell, *El 'Guernica' recobrado*, pp. 305.

55 Barcelona, Archive of the Museu Picasso, File 7282.

56 Antonio Saura, *Contra el 'Guernica'* (Madrid: Turner, 1982), p. 39. The official logo for the cultural activities designed to accompany the World Cup was Picasso's *El futbolista* (*The Football Player*), whilst Joan Miró prepared the design for the official poster for the football tournament, and each of the fourteen stadiums hosting matches were represented by a work from a contemporary artist from Spain. Giulia Quaggio, *La cultura en Transición: reconciliación y política cultural en España, 1976–1986* (Madrid: Alianza, 2014), pp. 231, 233.

57 Paul Julian Smith, *Contemporary Spanish Culture: TV, Fashion, Art and Film* (Cambridge: Polity Press, 2003), p. 80.

58 Contained in Box 62283 of the Ministry of Culture Archive.

59 For a more detailed discussion of the creation of the centre alongside ante-cedent projects, see Isaac Ait Moreno, 'Modernización y política artística: el Centro Nacional de Exposiciones entre 1983 y 1989', *Anales de historia del arte*, 17 (2007): 223–45; and 'Arte y estado en la España contemporánea: los orígenes del Museo Nacional Centro de Arte Reina Sofía (1979–1988)', *Anales de historia del arte*, special issue (2010): 9–22.

60 See Diego Jalón and Adolfo Suárez, 'El *Guernica* ingresa en el hospital', *ABC*, 26 July 1992, 46–7.

61 Fernando Samaniego, 'El *Guernica* pasa al Museo Reina Sofia a cambio de la ampliación del Prado', *El País*, https://elpais.com/diario/1992/05/20/cultura/706312802_850215.html (accessed 6 May 2020).

62 See Paul Julian Smith, 'Two televisual *Guernicas*. *Genius: Picasso* (National Geographic, 2018) and *El Ministerio del Tiempo* (RTVE, 2015–2017)', *Bulletin of Spanish Visual Studies*, 2.2 (2018): 167–79.

63 For a solid historical background to this museum, and its historical links with both Madrid and Toledo, see Selma Reuben Holo, *Beyond the Prado: Museums and Identity in Democratic Spain* (Washington: Smithsonian Institution Press, 1999), pp. 77–96.

64 Benito Gómez Oliveros, *General Moscardó: Sin novedad en el Alcázar* (Barcelona: AHR, 1956).

65 Van Hensbergen, *Guernica*, p. 177.

66 Amongst the archival records on the creation of this museum, there is some very angry correspondence from the Prado's director. Contained within Box 62286, Ministry of Culture Archive.

67 Trinidad Manchado, 'Cultural memory, commerce and the city: the Valencian Institute of Modern Art', in Barry Jordan and Rikki Morgan-Tamosunas (eds), *Contemporary Spanish Cultural Studies* (London: Arnold, 2000), pp. 92–100 (p. 95).

68 Pau Raussel Köster, *Políticas y sectores culturales en la Comunidad Valenciana* (Valencia: Universitat de Valéncia and Tirant lo Blanch, 1999), p. 214.

69 Paul Julian Smith, *The Moderns: Time, Space, and Subjectivity in Contemporary Spanish Culture* (Oxford: Oxford University Press, 2000), p. 54.

70 Correspondence contained in Box 75478 of the Ministry of Culture Archive.

71 This fourteen-minute programme titled 'Del hospital general de Madrid al Museo' (From Madrid's general hospital to the museum) is available for consultation in the reading rooms of the Reina Sofia library.

Chapter 11 The historical nationalities: Culture and community in the Basque Country, Catalonia and Galicia

1 Richard Gunther and José Ramón Montero, *The Politics of Spain* (Cambridge: Cambridge University Press, 2009), p. 73.

2 Marianne Heiberg, *The Making of the Basque Nation* (Cambridge: Cambridge University Press, 1989), p. 125.

3 Javier Moreno-Luzón and Xosé M. Núñez Seixas, 'The flag and the anthem: The disputed official symbols of Spain', in Javier Moreno-Luzón and Xosé M. Núñez Seixas (eds), *Metaphors of Spain: Representations of Spanish National Identity in the Twentieth Century* (New York: Berghahn, 2017), pp. 33–62 (p. 54).

4 Heiberg, *The Making of the Basque Nation*, p. 122.

5 Paul Preston, *The Triumph of Democracy in Spain* (London: Methuen, 1986), p. 135.

6 Diego Muro, *Ethnicity and Violence: The Case of Radical Basque Nationalism* (London: Routledge, 2008), p. 59.

7 Ludger Mees, *Nationalism, Violence and Democracy: The Basque Clash of Identities* (Basingstoke: Palgrave Macmillan, 2003), p. 13.

8 Stanley G. Payne, 'Nationalism, regionalism and micronationalism in Spain', *Journal of Contemporary History*, 26.3–4 (1991): 479–91 (p. 485).

9 Paloma Aguilar, 'The memory of the civil war in the transition to democracy: The peculiarity of the Basque case', *West European Politics*, 21.4 (1998): 5–25 (p. 20).

10 Muro, *Ethnicity and Violence*, p. 100.

11 *Ibid.*, p. 113.

12 John Sullivan, *ETA and Basque Nationalism: The Fight for Euskadi, 1890–1986* (London: Routledge, 2015), p. 70.

13 *Ibid.*, p. 92.

14 Luis Bilbao Larrondo, *El pueblo dirigido de Otxarkoaga. Del plan de urgencia social de Bizkaia al primer plan de desarrollo económico: la vivienda en Bilbao (1959–1964)* (Bilbao: Ayuntamiento de Bilbao, 2008), p. 100.

15 Gregorio Alonso, 'Children of a lesser God: The political and pastoral action of the Spanish Catholic Church', in Gregorio Alonso and Diego Muro (eds), *The Politics and Memory of Democratic Transition: The Spanish Model* (New York: Routledge, 2011), pp. 113–31 (p. 126).

16 Frances Lannon, *Privilege, Persecution and Prophecy: The Catholic Church in Spain, 1875–1975* (Oxford: Clarendon Press, 1987), p. 251.

17 Pamela Beth Radcliff, *Making Democratic Citizens in Spain: Civil Society and the Popular Origins of the Transition, 1960–78* (London: Palgrave Macmillan, 2011), p. 45.

Notes

18 María Antonia Calvo González, 'La figura del gobernador civil en el régimen franquista', unpublished Ph.D. thesis, Universidad Complutense de Madrid, 1977, unpaginated.

19 Audrey Brassloff, *Religion and Politics in Spain: The Spanish Church in Transition, 1962–96* (London: Macmillan, 1998), p. 28.

20 Joseba Gabilondo, *Introduction to a Postnational History of Contemporary Basque Literature (1978–2000)* (Woodbridge: Tamesis, 2019), p. 48.

21 Rob Stone and María Pilar Rodríguez, *Basque Cinema: A Cultural and Political History* (London: I.B. Tauris, 2015), p. 49.

22 Jon Kortazar, *Contemporary Basque Literature: Kirmen Uribe's Proposal* (Madrid: Iberoamericana/Vervuert, 2013), p. 29.

23 This unpublished report can be found alongside the minutes of the town hall meeting at the Municipal Archive of Bilbao. See Box C-023/79/001, pp. 12–13.

24 *Ibid.*, p. 13

25 CAT, *San Sebastián: Memoria 1977* (San Sebastián: CAT, 1978).

26 Mar Diestro-Dópido, 'San Sebastián: A film festival of contrasts', in Duncan Wheeler and Fernando Canet (eds), *(Re)viewing Creative, Critical and Commercial Practices in Contemporary Spanish Cinema* (Bristol: Intellect, 2014), pp. 405–18 (p. 407).

27 This letter, marked confidential, was contained in Box 89225 of the Ministry of Culture Archive. I made the mistake of asking for a photocopy. On seeing the letter, the archivists said that it had been misfiled and should not have been made available to me. It was removed from the file to an unknown (at least to me) location in the Ministry.

28 San Sebastián Muncipal Archive, File 6327-1.

29 Stone and Rodríguez, *Basque Cinema*, p. 76.

30 See Karlos Sánchez Ekiza, 'Radical rock: Identities and utopias in Basque popular music', in Sílvia Martínez and Héctor Fouce (eds), *Made in Spain: Studies in Popular Music* (New York: Routledge, 2013), pp. 42–52.

31 Miquel Siguan, 'La situación lingüística en España y los nacionalismos históricos', in Jean-Louis Guereña and Manuel Morales Muñoz (eds), *Los nacionalismos en la España contemporánea: ideologías, movimientos y símbolos* (Malaga: Servicio de Publicaciones, Centro de Ediciones de la Diputación de Málaga, 2006), pp. 239–58 (p. 248).

32 Gabilondo, *Introduction to a Postnational History*, p. 10.

33 *Ibid.*, p. ix.

34 *Ibid.*, p. 23

35 Bernardo Atxaga, *Obabakoak: A Novel* (London: Vintage, 1992), p. ix.

Notes

36 Tom Lewis, 'España "fuera de sí": Representing San Sebastián in Antonio Muñoz Molina's *El invierno en Lisboa* and *Ardor Guerrero*', in Brad Epps and Luis Fernández Cuenca (eds), *Spain beyond Spain: Modernity, Literary History, and National Identity* (Lewisburg: Bucknell University Press, 2005), pp. 331–59 (p. 355).

37 Robert Hughes, *Barcelona: The Great Enchantress* (London: Harvill, 1992), p. 11.

38 Interview with the author in London on 13 June 2015.

39 See, for example, AGA, Box 60323 for the instructions corresponding to the prize for 1962.

40 Kathryn Crameri, *Catalonia: National Identity and Cultural Policy, 1980–2003* (Cardiff: University of Wales Press, 2008), p. 27.

41 Andrew Dowling, *Catalonia since the Spanish Civil War: Reconstructing the Nation* (Brighton: Sussex University Press, 2013), p. 107.

42 Carme Molinero and Pere Ysàs, *La cuestión catalana* (Barcelona: Planeta, 2014), p. 26.

43 James Burns, *Barça: A People's Passion* (London: Bloomsbury, 1999), p. 220.

44 Josep Tarradellas, *Ja sóc aquí: record d'un retorn* (Barcelona: Planeta, 1989), p. 50.

45 Eduardo Mendoza, *Qué está pasando en Cataluña* (Barcelona: Seix Barral, 2017), p. 62.

46 Charles Powell, *Juan Carlos of Spain: Self-Made Monarch* (Houndmills: Macmillan, 1996), p. 95.

47 See Vicente Palacio Atard, *Carlos III, el Rey de los ilustrados* (Barcelona: Ariel, 2006), pp. 56–60.

48 John H. Elliott, *Scots and Catalans: Union and Disunion* (New Haven: Yale University Press, 2018), p. 233.

49 Caroline Gray, *Nationalist Politics and Regional Financing Systems in the Basque Country and Catalonia* (Bilbao: Foral Treasury Doctoral Thesis Collection, 2016), p. 204.

50 Molinero and Ysàs, *La cuestión catalana*, p. 271.

51 Tarradellas, *Ja sóc aquí*, p. 147.

52 Muro, *Ethnicity and Violence*, p. 128.

53 Alfons Quinta, 'Tarradellas: "Cataluña no puede ser tratatada como La Mancha"', *El País*, 22 January 1978, https://elpais.com/diario/1978/01/22/espana/254271617_850215.html (accessed 8 May 2020).

54 Serge Poisson-de-Haro, 'Gran Teatre del Liceu: Rising from the ashes', in Beatriz Muñoz-Seca and Josep Riverola (eds), *When Business Meets Culture: Ideas and Experiences for Mutual Profit* (New York: Palgrave Macmillan,

2011), pp. 83–101 (pp. 86–7). Madrid's Teatro Real was closed from 1925 to 1966; it was then a concert hall for twenty-two years before being closed and reopened as an opera house in 1997.

55 Lluís Homar, *Ahora empeiza todo* (Barcelona: Bow, 2017), p. 143.

56 Figures taken from Ministry of Culture Archive, Box 91974.

57 Moreno Luzón and Núñez Seixas, 'The flag and the anthem', p. 53.

58 Crameri, *Catalonia*, p. 112.

59 Kathryn A.Woolard amd Tae-Joong Gahng, 'Changing language policies and attitudes in autonomous Catalonia', *Language in Society*, 19.3 (1990): 311–30 (p. 316).

60 *Ibid.*, p. 327.

61 Kathryn A. Woolard, 'Linguistic consciousness among adolescents in Catalonia: A case study from the Barcelona urban area in longitudinal perspective', *Zeitschrift für Katalanistik*, 22 (2009): 125–49 (p. 147).

62 Benny Pollock, 'Spain: From corporate state to parliamentary democracy', *Parliamentary Affairs*, 31.1 (1978): 52–66 (p. 58).

63 Susan M. DiGiacomo, '*La caseta i l'hortet*: Rural imagery in Catalan urban politics', *Anthropological Quarterly*, 60.4 (1987): 160–6 (p. 164).

64 See Jesús Contreras Hernández, 'La cultura tradicional a la Catalunya d'avui', in Salvador Giner (ed.), *La societat catalana* (Barcelona: Institut d'Estadística de Catalunya, 1998), pp. 821–37.

65 Crameri, *Catalonia*, p. 169.

66 See Joan Soler i Amigó, *Cultura popular tradicional* (Barcelona: Pòrtic, 2001), pp. 95–7.

67 Ivan Serrano, 'Just a matter of identity? Support for independence in Catalonia', *Regional and Federal Studies*, 23.5 (2013): 523–45 (p. 531).

68 Miranda Joseph, *Against the Romance of Community* (Minneapolis: University of Minnesota Press, 2002), p. xviii.

69 Alejandro Quiroga, *Football and National Identities in Spain: The Strange Death of Don Quixote* (New York: Palgrave Macmillan, 2013), p. 176.

70 Najat El Hachmi, *Jo també sóc catalana* (Barcelona: Columna, 2004), p. 76.

71 *Ibid.*, p. 51.

72 Sarah Gore, 'The Catalan language and immigrants from outside the European Union', *International Journal of Iberian Studies*, 15.2 (2002): 91–102 (p. 101).

73 Thomas Jeffrey Miley, 'Democratic representation and the national dimension in Catalan and Basque politics', *International Journal of Politics, Culture and Society*, 27.3 (2014): 291–322 (p. 311).

74 Ramón del Valle-Inclán, *Luces de bohemia*, ed. Alonso Zamora Vicente (Madrid: Austral, 1987), p. 162.

75 Raphael Minder, *The Struggle for Catalonia: Rebel Politics in Spain* (London: Hurst, 2017), p. 79.

76 Kenneth McRoberts, *Catalonia: Nation Building without a State* (Oxford: Oxford University Press, 2001), p. 80.

77 *Ibid.*, p. 112.

78 *Ibid.*, p. 102.

79 Lourdes Orozco, *Teatro y política: Barcelona (1980–2000)* (Madrid: Publicaciones de la Asociación de Directores de Escena en España, 2007), pp. 48–9.

80 See Pilar de Yzaguirre, *Festival de Otoño en Madrid, 1984–1988* (Barcelona: Iberia, líneas aéreas de España, 1988).

81 Orozco, *Teatro y política*, p. 16.

82 See Xavier Fàbregas, *Aproximació a la historia del teatre català modern* (Barcelona: Curial, 1972).

83 Helena Buffery, *Shakespeare in Catalan: Translating Imperialism* (Cardiff: University of Wales Press, 2007), p. 47.

84 Duncan Wheeler, *Golden Age Drama in Contemporary Spain: The Comedia on Page, Stage and Screen* (Cardiff: University of Wales Press, 2012), p. 60.

85 Guillem-Jordi Graells (ed.), *Teatre Lliure, 1976–2006* (Barcelona: Fundació Teatre Lliure, 2007).

86 Keith Gregor, *Shakespeare in the Spanish Theatre: 1772 to the Present* (London: Continuum, 2010), p. 117.

87 Josep Maria Flotats, *Un projecte per al teatre nacional* (Barcelona: Ediciones de la Revista de Catalunya, 1989), p. 12.

88 Bruce McConachie, 'Towards a history of national theatres in Europe', in S. E. Wilmer (ed.), *National Theatres in a Changing Europe* (Houndmills: Palgrave Macmillan, 2008), pp. 49–60 (p. 51).

89 Marvin Carlson, 'National theatres: Then and now', in Wilmer, *National Theatres*, pp. 21–33 (p. 30).

90 André Lecours, *Basque Nationalism and the Spanish State* (Reno: University of Nevada Press, 2007), p. 101.

91 Xosé M. Núñez Seixas, 'What is Spanish nationalism today? From legitimacy crisis to unfulfilled renovation (1975–2000)', *Ethnic and Racial Studies*, 24.5 (2001): 719–52 (p. 719).

92 Montserrat Guibernau, *Catalan Nationalism: Francoism, Transition and Democracy* (London: Routledge, 2004), p. 6.

93 Bonnie N. Field, 'The evolution of substate nationalist parties as state-wide parliamentary actors: CiU and PNV in Spain', *Nationalism and Ethnic Politics*, 21.1 (2015): 121–41 (p. 122).

Notes

94   Cited in Stephen Burgen, ' "I'm no fascist": Film-maker hits back over opposition to Catalan independence", *Guardian*, 23 July 2017, www.theguardian. com/world/2017/jul/22/catalonia-independence-referendum-isabel-coixet (accessed 8 May 2020).

95   Andrew Dowling, 'Prohibition, tolerance, co-option: Cultural appropriation and Francoism in Catalonia, 1939–75', *Contemporary European History*, 27.3 (2018): 370–86 (p. 379).

96   Mary Nash, 'Mass tourism and new representations of gender in late Francoist Spain: The *sueca* and Don Juan in the 1960s', *Cultural History*, 4.2 (2015): 136–61 (p. 139).

97   Servicio Informativo Español, *Spain at a Glance* (Madrid: Ministerio de Información y Turismo, 1964), p. 13.

98   Begoña Barrera, *La Sección Femenina, 1934–1977: Historia de una tutela emocional* (Madrid: Alianza, 2019), p. 331.

99   Municipal Archive of Bilbao, Box C-0159091001.

100 José Ortega y Gasset, *España invertebrada* (Madrid: Revista de occidente, 1955), p. 52.

101 Dowling, 'Prohibition, tolerance, co-option', p. 382.

102 Kirsty Hooper, *Writing Galicia into the World: New Cartographies, New Poetics* (Liverpool: Liverpool University Press, 2011), pp. 41–2.

103 *Ibid.*, p. 1.

104 Lourenzo Fernández Prieto, 'Interpreting Galician history: The recent construction of an unknown past', in Kirsty Hooper and Manuel Puga Moruxa (eds), *Contemporary Galician Cultural Studies: Between the Local and the Global* (New York: MLA, 2011), pp. 24–39 (p. 27).

105 Clare Mar-Molinero, *The Politics of Language in the Spanish-Speaking World* (London: Routledge, 2000), p. 51.

106 Jaine E. Beswick, *Regional Nationalism in Spain: Language Use and Ethnic Identity in Galicia* (Clevedon: Multilingual Matters, 2007), p. 60.

107 Helena Miguélez-Carballeira, *Galicia, a Sentimental Nation: Gender, Culture and Politics* (Cardiff: University of Wales Press, 2013), p. 22.

108 Jonathan Dunne, *Anthology of Galician Literature/Antoloxia de literatura galega (1196–1981)* (Vigo: Edicións Xerais de Galicia, 2010), pp. 291.

109 See Javier Serrano Alonso, 'Galicia en una visión poliédrica de Don Ramón: Las manifestaciones de Valle-Inclán sobre asuntos gallegos', *Cuadrante: revista cultural de 'Asociación Amigos de Valle-Inclán'*, 16 (2007): 25–41.

110 Roberto Lima, *The Dramatic World of Valle-Inclán* (Woodbridge: Tamesis, 2003), p. 33.

111 *Ibid.*, p. 129.

Notes

112   Maria M. Delgado, 'Other' Spanish Theatres: Erasure and Inscription on the Twentieth-Century Spanish Stage (Manchester: Manchester University Press, 2003), p. 152.

113   Ibid., pp. 151–6.

114   Rosa Cal, 'Centro dramático gallego: duros y largos años de esfuerzo', Reseña (September–October 1985): 27–8.

115   See Elisa Serra Porteiro, Performing Irishness: Translations of Irish Drama for the Galician Stage (1921–2011), unpublished Ph.D. thesis, University College Cork, 2015.

116   Cited in Carmen Becerra, Guardo la voz, cedo la palabra: conversaciones con Gonzalo Torrente Ballester (Barcelona: Anthropos, 1990), p. 41.

117   Gonzalo Torrente Ballester, La saga/fuga de J. B. (Madrid: Alianza Editorial, 2019), p. 201.

118   Ibid., p. 454.

119   Ibid., p. 616.

120   Becerra, Guardo la voz, pp. 41–2.

121   See José Luis Calvo Carilla, 'La urgencia de dejar atrás un pasado incómodo: la Transición política y algunos ejemplos de silencios y recomendaciones', in Carmen Peña Ardid (ed.), Historia cultural de la Transición: pensamiento crítico y ficciones en literatura, cine y televisión (Madrid: Catarata, 2019), pp. 45–60 (pp. 52–9).

122   Carmelo Urza, Historia, mito y metáfora en 'La saga/fuga de J. B.' de Torrente Ballester (Ann Arbor: University Microfilms International, 1992), p. 433.

123   Cited in Becerra, Guardo la voz, p. 105.

124   Jaine E. Beswick, 'Borders within borders: Contexts of language use and local identity configuration in Southern Galicia', in Dominic Watt and Carmen Llamas (eds), Language, Borders and Identity (Edinburgh: Edinburgh University Press, 2014), pp. 105–17 (p. 105).

125   See José Saramago, 'Mi iberismo', in César Antonio Molina (ed.), Sobre el iberismo y otros escritos de literatura portuguesa (Madrid: Akal, 1990).

126   See John Patrick Thompson, 'Portuguese or Spanish orthography for the Galizan language? An analysis of the conflicto normativo', in Kirsty Hooper and Manuel Puga Moruxa (eds), Contemporary Galician Cultural Studies: Between the Local and the Global (New York: MLA, 2011), pp. 143–65.

127   Manuel Rivas, Galicia, el bonsái atlántico (Madrid: El País, 1989), pp. 17–18.

128   Manuel Fraga, En busca del tiempo servido (Barcelona: Planeta, 1987), p. 465.

129   Rivas, Galicia, el bonsái atlántico, p. 87.

Notes

130 Nacho Carretero, *Fariña: Historia e indiscreciones del narcotráfico en Galicia* (Madrid: Los libros del KO, 2015), p. 37.

131 *Ibid.*, p. 104.

132 *Ibid.*, p. 103.

133 Benito Leiro Conde, *Un lugar tranquilo: contrabando, droga e corrupcion nas rías baixas* (Vigo: Nigra, 1993), p. 84.

134 Cited in Antonio Papell, *Conversaciones con Miquel Roca Junyent* (Barcelona: Editorial Argos Vergara, 1984), pp. 74–5.

135 Carretero, *Fariña*, p. 87.

136 Jesús Ordovás, *Siniestro Total: apocalipsis con grelos* (Madrid: Guía de Música, 1993), p. 121.

137 See José Colmeiro, 'Peripheral *Movidas*: Cannibalising Galicia', in William J. Nichols and H. Rosi Song (eds), *Toward a Cultural Archive of 'La Movida': Back to the Future* (Madison: Fairleigh Dickinson University Press. 2014), pp. 107–33.

138 The information in this paragraph draws on the materials held in the unindexed press folders of Vigo's Municipal Archive.

139 See Paul Julian Smith, *Contemporary Spanish Culture: TV, Fashion, Art and Film* (Cambridge: Polity Press, 2003), pp. 34–60.

140 Ricardo Cantalapiedra, 'El encuentro de las "vanguardias" de Madrid y Vigo se dispersó en la algarabía de la fiesta', *El País*, 22 September 1986, https://elpais.com/diario/1986/09/22/cultura/527724005_850215.html (accessed 8 May 2020).

141 Leiro Conde, *Un lugar tranquilo*, p. 118.

142 Javier Becerra and Begoña R. Sotelino, '25 años de dos conciertos históricos en Galicia', *La voz de Galicia*, 21 April 2016, www.lavozdegalicia.es/noticia/sociedad/2015/07/28/25-anos-dos-conciertos-historicos-galicia/0003_201507G28P28991.htm (accessed 8 May 2020).

143 Manuel Rivas, *El periodismo es un cuento* (Madrid: Santillana, 1997), pp. 200–1.

144 Xosé Manoel Núñez Seixas, 'From National-Catholic nostalgia to constitutional patriotism: Conservative Spanish nationalism since the early 1990s', in Sebastian Balfour (ed.), *The Politics of Contemporary Spain* (London: Routledge, 2006), pp. 121–45 (p. 128).

145 María Reimóndez, 'Whose heritage is it, anyway? Cultural planning and practice in contemporary Galicia', in Hooper and Puga Moruxa (eds), *Contemporary Galician Cultural Studies*, pp. 190–201 (p. 194).

146 Salvador Rodríguez, *Entre Fisterras: conversas con Carlos Núñez* (Vigo: Xerais, 2003), pp. 20–1.

Notes

147   Javier Campos Calvo-Sotelo, 'We're on the celtic fringe! Celtic music and nationalism in Galicia', in Martínez and Fouce, *Made in Spain*, pp. 53–63 (p. 60). Campos Calvo-Sotelo cites as an example that 'the hammer and sickle (so widespread during the 1970s) fades in favour of a geometrical Celtic motif, just as the figures of Marx and Castelao are replaced by Ossian and Stivell' (p. 60).

148   Cited in Rodríguez, *Entre Fisterras*, p. 32.

149   Javier Campos Calvo-Sotelo, 'We're on the celtic fringe!', p. 57.

150   Helena Miguélez-Carballeira, 'Sentimentality as consensus: Imagining Galicia in the democratic period', in Luisa Elena Delgado, Pura Fernández and Jo Labanyi (eds), *Engaging the Emotions in Spanish Culture and History* (Nashville: Vanderbilt University Press, 2016), pp. 210–24 (p. 216).

151   Hooper, *Writing Galicia*, pp. 43–4.

152   Michael Keating, 'The minority nations of Spain and European integration: A new framework for autonomy?', *Journal of Spanish Cultural Studies*, 1.1 (2000): 29–42 (p. 38).

153   *Ibid.*

154   Manuel A. Castiñeiras, *Galicia e os camiños de Santiago* (Santiago: Xunta de Galicia, 2016), p. 226.

155   Walter Starkie, *The Road to Santiago: Pilgrims of St James* (London: John Murray, 1952), p. 25.

156   David Lodge, *Therapy* (London: Penguin, 1996), p. 289.

157   *Ibid.*, p. 300.

158   Juan Antonio García Barquero, *El camino de Santiago: primera ruta turística de España* (Jérez: Caja de Ahorros de Jérez, 1971), pp. 7–8.

159   René Freund, *The Road to Santiago: Walking the Way of St James* (London: Armchair Traveller, 2006), p. 89.

160   *Ibid.*, p. 22.

161   Lodge, *Therapy* p. 152.

162   *Ibid.*, p. 301.

163   Montserrat Guibernau, 'Nations within states in the EU: The Catalan case', in John McGarry and Michael Keating (eds), *European Integration and the Nationalities Question* (London: Routledge, 2006), pp. 216–24 (p. 216).

Notes

Chapter 12 What qualifies as Spanish culture? The State, autonomous communities and the culture wars

1 Germán Labrador Méndez, 'Lo que en España no ha habido: la lógica normalizadora de la cultura postfranquista en la actual crisis', *Revista hispánica moderna*, 69.2 (2016): 165–92 (p. 165).

2 Diana Holmes and David Looseley, 'Introduction. Imagining the popular: Lowbrow, highbrow, middlebrow', in Diana Holmes and David Looseley (eds), *Imagining the Popular in Contemporary French Culture* (Manchester: Manchester University Press, 2013), pp. 1–15 (p. 6).

3 Fundación FOESSA, *Informe sociológico sobre la situación social de España* (Madrid: Euramérica, 1966), p. 40.

4 Raymond Carr, *Modern Spain 1875–1980* (Oxford: Oxford University Press, 1980), p. 157.

5 Carmen Llorca, *Los teleclubs en España* (Madrid: Publicaciones Españolas, 1971), p. 4.

6 Joaquín Marco, 'Entre España y América', in Joaquín Marco and Jordi Gracia (eds), *La llegada de los bárbaros: la recepción de la literatura hispanoamericana en España, 1960–1981* (Barcelona: Edhasa, 2004), pp. 13–39 (p. 26).

7 *Ibid.*, p. 25.

8 Mercedes Cabrera, *Juan March (1880–1962)* (Madrid: Marcial Pons, 2011), p. 394.

9 José Manuel Sánchez Ron, *Cincuenta años de cultura e investigación en España: la Fundación Juan March (1955–2005)* (Barcelona: Edición Crítica, 2005), p. 82.

10 See Antonio Saura, 'Cuenca la vieja', in Antonio Saura, *Crónicas: artículos* (Barcelona: Círculos de lectores, 2000).

11 Elizabeth Thompson Goizueta, *Cuenca: City of Spanish Abstraction* (Boston, MA. McMullen Museum of Modern Art, 2019), p. 14.

12 Cited in *Discursos de Inauguración: 27 de marzo 1992* (Teguise: Fundación César Manrique Servicio de Publicaciones, 1992), p. 23.

13 Manuel Fraga, *Memoria breve de una vida pública* (Barcelona: Planeta, 1980), p. 229.

14 See Juan Marrero Portugués, *César Manrique y Pepín Ramírez: dos líderes canarios en su contexto histórico* (Taro de Tahíche: Fundación César Manrique, 2017), pp. 143–4.

15 *Ibid.*, p. 152.

16 César Carreño, 'Una comisión para exponer a la autoridad los deseos del pueblo', *La Provincia* (July 1968). Local press cutting with no date or page number, found amongst the papers of the Fundación César Manrique.

Notes

17 Cited in Patricia Juncosa Vecchierini, *Segous ells mateixos: Miró/Sert, correspondencia 1937–1980* (Palma de Mallorca: Fundació Pilar i Joan Miró, 2008), p. 431.

18 Alexandre Cirici, 'La Fundació Joan Miró obre les portes', *Serra d'or*, 15 June 1975, 79–85 (p. 82).

19 Tony Bennett, *Making Culture, Changing Society* (London: Routledge, 2013), p. 48.

20 *Memoria* (Oviedo: Ayuntamiento de Oviedo, 1977).

21 *Bienal Nacional de Arte Ciudad Oviedo* (Oviedo: Ayuntamiento de Oviedo, 1977), pp. 430–1.

22 Selma Reuben Holo, 'The art museum as a means of refiguring regional identity in democratic Spain', in Marsha Kinder (ed.), *Refiguring Spain: Cinema/Media/Representation* (Durham, NC: Duke University Press, 1997), pp. 301–26 (p. 302).

23 Tamar Groves, 'Everyday struggles against Franco's authoritarian legacy: Pedagogical social movements and democracy in Spain', *Journal of Social History*, 46.2 (2012): 305–34 (p. 323).

24 Andrés Amorós, 'Introducción: el momento cultural español', in Xesús Alonso Montero, Andres Amorós and José Luis Abellán, *El año cultural español* (Madrid: Castalia, 1979), pp. 7–26 (pp. 12–13).

25 See Alfonso E. Pérez Sánchez, *Presente, pasado y futuro del Museo del Prado* (Madrid: Fundación Juan March, 1977).

26 See Alberto Pancerbo La Blanca, 'Historia de la Fundación Amigos del Museo del Prado', unpublished Ph.D. thesis, Universidad Complutense de Madrid, 2016.

27 Leopoldo Calvo Sotelo, *Memoria viva de la Transición* (Barcelona: Plaza & Janes, 1990), p. 69.

28 Alfonso Guerra, *Dejando atrás los vientos: memorias, 1982–1991* (Madrid: Espasa Calpe, 2006), p. 26.

29 Eric Storm, 'A more Spanish Spain: The influence of tourism on the national image', in Javier Moreno-Luzón and Xosé M. Núñez Seixas (eds), *Metaphors of Spain: Representations of Spanish National Identity in the Twentieth Century* (New York: Berghahn, 2017), pp. 239–59 (pp. 253–4).

30 Javier Tusell, *Spain: From Dictatorship to Democracy*, trans. Rosemary Clark (Chichester: Wiley-Blackwell, 2011), p. 386.

31 Oliver Boyd-Barrett, 'University reform', in Oliver Boyd-Barrett and Pamela O'Malley (eds), *Education Reform in Democratic Spain* (London: Routledge, 1995), pp. 246–55 (p. 246).

Notes

32 Giulia Quaggio, *La cultura en Transición: reconciliación y política cultural en España, 1976–1986* (Madrid: Alianza, 2014), p. 288.

33 *Ibid.*, p. 290.

34 The report titled 'Estudios sobre el mecenzago de la empresa' is contained in the Ministry of Culture Archive, Box 67439; see p. 45.

35 In File 4 ("Correspondencia") of the Osorio archive held by the Fundación de la Transición.

36 Cabrera, *Juan March*, p. 425.

37 Antoni Tàpies, *Collected Essays*, Vol. II (Barcelona: Fundació Antoni Tàpies and Indiana University Press, 2011), p. 417.

38 See Ramón Guardiola Rovira, *Dalí y su museo: la obra que no quiso Bellas Artes* (Figueras: Editorial Empordanesa, 1984).

39 Cited in *ibid.*, p. 131.

40 Catherine Grenier, *Salvador Dalí: The Making of an Artist* (Paris: Flammarion, 2012), p. 140.

41 Ian Gibson, *The Shameful Life of Salvador Dalí* (London: Faber & Faber, 1997), p. 596.

42 José Luis Yuste, 'Poderes públicos y cultura', in *Cultura y sociedad: una promoción sociocultural* (Madrid: Ministerio de Cultura, 1984), pp. 80–112 (p. 103).

43 José Manuel Sánchez Ron, *Cincuenta años*, p. 93.

44 Óscar J. Martín García, '"Un deprimido trozo de España": la lucha por la democracia en una provincia subdesarrollada', in Manuel Ortiz Heras (ed.), *La Transición se hizo en los pueblos: el caso de la provincia de Albacete* (Madrid: Biblioteca Nueva, 2016), pp. 179–99 (p. 181).

45 José Bono, *Discursos del Presidente José Bono, 1983–1995* (Castilla La Mancha: Servicio de Publicaciones de la Junta de Comunidades de Castilla La Mancha, 1995), p. 80.

46 Richard Maddox, *The Best of All Possible Islands: Seville's Universal Exposition, the New Spain, and the New Europe* (Albany: State University of New York Press, 2004), p. 216.

47 César Oliva, 'Un festival en un lugar de la Mancha', in Luciano García Lorenzo and Andrés Peláez Martín (eds), *Festival Internacional de Teatro Clásico, 20 años (1978–1997)* (Toledo: Caja Castilla La Mancha and Festival de Almagro, 1997), pp. 37–46 (p. 41).

48 Eugenia Afinoguénova and Jaume Martí-Olivella, 'Introduction. A nation under tourists' eyes. Tourism and identity discourses in Spain', in Eugenia Afinoguénova and Jaume Martí-Olivella (eds), *Spain Is (Still) Different:*

Tourism and Discourse in Spanish Identity (Lanham: Lexington, 2008), pp. xi–xxxviii (p. xxii).

49 I have taken this information from Archive of the Diputación de Aragón, Files 004167 and 019949, available to the public for consultation via prior appointment in the Pignatelli Building.

50 See www.patrimonioculturaldearagon.es/ruta-de-goya (accessed 10 May 2020).

51 Ferran Alberich, Román Gubern and Vicente Sánchez-Biosca, 'Film clubs, festivals, archives, and magazines', in Jo Labanyi and Tatjana Pavlović (eds), *A Companion to Spanish Cinema* (Malden: Wiley-Blackwell, 2013), pp. 434–63 (p. 447).

52 Luisa Elena Delgado, *La nación singular: fantasías de la normalidad democrática española (1996–2011)* (Madrid: Siglo XXI, 2014), p. 102.

53 Paloma Pedrero, *Juego de noches/Nueve obras en un acto*, ed. Virtudes Serrano (Madrid: Cátedra, 2007), p. 115.

54 See Cristina Masanés, *Girona: 32 veus que fan ciutat* (Girona: Ajuntament de Girona, 2011), pp. 50–3.

55 *Encuesta de comportamiento cultural de los españoles: análisis de la Comunidad autónoma de Madrid* (Madrid: Ministerio de Cultura, 1986), p. 71.

56 *Ibid.*, p. 236.

57 *Girona i els seus barris* (Girona: Ajuntament de Girona, 1983), pp. 326–8.

58 Enrique Gil Calvo, *La era de las lectoras: el cambio cultural de las mujeres españolas* (Madrid: Instituto de la Mujer and Ministerio de Asuntos Sociales, 1993), p. 103.

59 Raquel Medina, 'Poesía y política cultural: las antologías de poesía en la España democrática', *Hispanic Review*, 80.3 (2012): 507–28.

60 David Looseley, *The Politics of Fun: Cultural Policy and Debate in Contemporary France* (Oxford: Berg, 1995), pp. 43–4.

61 Paloma Gay y Blasco, *Gypsies in Madrid: Sex, Gender and the Performance of Identity* (Oxford: Berg, 1999), p. 10.

62 Information taken from the correspondence sent to the City Council. Contained in Bilbao Municipal Archive, File C-028783/001.

63 Gay y Blasco, *Gypsies in Madrid*, p. 178.

64 María Luisa López Varas and Gonzalo Fresnillo Pato, *Margen y periferia: representaciones ideológicas de los conflictos urbanos entre payos y gitanos* (Madrid: Asociación Secretariado Gral Gitano, 1995).

65 Bennett, *Making Culture*, p. 14.

66 Susan Martin-Márquez, *Disorientations: Spanish Colonialism in Africa and the Performance of Identity* (New Haven: Yale University Press, 2008), p. 9.

Notes

67 Ian Gibson, *Aventuras ibéricas: recorridos, reflexiones e irreverencias* (Barcelona: Grupo Zeta, 2017), p. 333.

68 Maria M. Delgado, *Federico García Lorca* (Abingdon: Routledge, 2008), p. 193.

69 Richard A. Peterson, 'Understanding audience segmentation: From elite and mass to omnivore and univore', *Poetics*, 21 (1992): 243–58 (p. 252). See also Richard A. Peterson and Roger M. Kern, 'Changing highbrow taste: From snob to omnivore', *American Sociological Review*, 61.5 (1996): 900–7.

70 Peterson, 'Understanding audience segmentation', p. 252.

71 Robert M. Fishman and Omar Lizado, 'How macro-historical change shapes cultural taste: Legacies of democratization in Spain and Portugal', *American Sociological Review*, 78.2 (2013): 213–39 (p. 218).

72 William Washabaugh, *Flamenco Music and National Identity in Spain* (Farnham: Ashgate, 2012), p. 86.

73 Pedro Fernaud, 'La dimensión africana de Canarias', *Revista de occidente*, 69 (1987): 101–16 (p. 104).

74 Ignacio Tofiño-Quesada, 'Spanish orientalism: Uses of the past in Spain's colonization in Africa', *Comparative Studies of South Asia, Africa and the Middle East*, 23.1–2 (2003): 141–8 (p. 144).

75 Xavier Casals Meseguer, 'Franco "El Africano"', *Journal of Spanish Cultural Studies*, 7.3 (2000): 207–24.

76 Tofiño-Quesada, 'Spanish orientalism', p. 144.

77 Helen Graham, *The Spanish Civil War: A Very Short Introduction* (Oxford: Oxford University Press, 2005), p. 34.

78 See Gustau Nerín, *Guinea Ecuatorial: historia en blanco y negro* (Barcelona: Península, 1998).

79 Benita Sampedro Vizcaya, 'Theorizing Equatorial Guinea', *Afro-Hispanic Review*, 28.2 (2009): 15–19 (p, 16).

80 Michael Ugarte, *Africans in Europe: The Culture of Exile and Emigration from Equatorial Guinea to Spain* (Chicago: University of Illinois Press, 2010), p. 24.

81 Cécile Stephanie Stehrenberger, 'Folklore, nation, and gender in a colonial encounter: Coros y danzas of the Sección Femenina of the Falange in Equatorial Guinea', *Afro-Hispanic Review*, 28.2 (2009): 231–44 (p. 240–1).

82 Donato Ndongo, *Shadows of Your Black Memory* (Chicago: Swan Isle Press, 2007), pp. 15–16.

83 *Ibid.*, p. 19.

84 Martin-Márquez, *Disorientations*, p. 283.

85 Alicia Campos Serrano, 'Política exterior, cambio normativo internacional y surgimiento del estado post-colonial: la descolonizalación de Guinea Ecuatorial (1955–1968)', unpublished Ph.D. thesis, Universidad Autónoma de Madrid, 2000, pp. 290–1.

86 *Ibid.*, p. 294.

87 *Ibid.*, p. 353.

88 *Ibid.*, p. 378.

89 Information taken from document contained in Almeria, Archivo Histórico Provincial, Box 2566.

90 See Martin-Márquez, *Disorientations*, pp. 324–5.

91 See José Ramón Diego Aguirre, *Guerra en el Sáhara* (Madrid: Fundamentos, 2001).

92 Isaías Barreñeda and Raquel Ojeda García, 'Presentación', in Isaías Barreñeda and Raquel Ojeda García (eds), *Sáhara Occidental, 40 años después* (Madrid: Catarata, 2016), pp. 7–9 (p. 7).

93 José Ramón Diego Aguirre, *Historia del Sáhara español: la verdad de una traición* (Madrid: Kaydeda, 1988), p. 848.

94 Aguirre, *Guerra en el Sáhara*, p. 101.

95 Martin-Márquez, *Disorientations*, p. 337.

96 Carlos Robles Piquer, *Memoria de cuatro Españas: República, guerra, franquismo y democracia* (Barcelona: Planeta, 2011), p. 461.

97 See Antonio de Oyarzábal, *Recuerdos políticos* (Madrid: Cuadernos del laberinto, 2017), pp. 169–72.

98 Mark Kurlansky, *The Basque History of the World* (New York: Walker, 1999), pp. 174–5.

99 John H. Elliott, *Scots and Catalans: Union and Disunion* (New Haven: Yale University Press, 2018), p. 43.

100 Stehrenberger, 'Folklore, nation, and gender', p. 234.

101 José Abu-Tarbush, 'Canarias y la cuestión del Sáhara Occidental', in Barreñeda and Ojeda García, *Sáhara Occidental, 40 años después*, pp. 293–310 (p. 298).

102 See José Manuel Betancort, 'El carnaval de 1936 a 1976: de la guerra civil española a la democracia', in José Manuel Betancort, Ángel Marino Herrero, Juan María Luna and Juan Francisco Trujillo (eds), *Chicharrero de corazón, Santa Cruz en carnaval* (Santa Cruz: Ediciones Idea y Asociación Murga ni Pico ni Corto, 2011), pp. 83–102; Alberto Ramos Santana, *El carnaval secuestrado o historia del carnaval: el caso de Cádiz* (Cádiz: Quorum, 2002).

103 Gilberto Alemán, *El carnaval: la fiesta prohibida* (La Laguna: Centro de Cultura Popular Canaria, 1996), p. 65.

Notes

104 All quotations from *murgas* taken from the currently unindexed holdings of the Casa de Carnaval in Santa Cruz de Tenerife.

105 Amparo Santos Perdomo and José Solorzano Sánchez, *Historia del carnaval de Santa Cruz de Tenerife* (Santa Cruz: Ayuntamiento de Santa Cruz de Tenerife, 1983), p. 199.

106 Carmen Marina Barreto Vargas, 'El carnaval de Santa Cruz de Tenerife: un estudio antropológico', unpublished Ph.D. thesis, University of La Laguna, 1992–3, p. 361.

107 Antonio Muñoz Molina, *Todo lo que era sólido* (Barcelona: Seix Barral, 2013), pp. 62–3.

108 *Ibid.*, p. 63.

109 Terry Eagleton, *Culture* (New Haven: Yale University Press, 2016), p. 66.

110 Maddox, *The Best of All Possible Islands*, p. 25.

111 See Giulia Quaggio, '1992: la modernidad del pasado. El PSOE en busca de una idea regenerada de España', *Historia y política*, 35 (2016): 95–122 (pp. 101–6).

112 Ministry of Culture Archive, Box 67439.

113 José María Aznar, *El compromiso del poder: memorias II* (Barcelona: Planeta, 2013), p. 196.

114 Stephanie Dennison, 'National, transnational and post-national: Issues in contemporary film-making in the Hispanic world', in Stephanie Dennison (ed.), *Contemporary Hispanic Cinema: Interrogating the Transnational in Spanish and Latin American Film* (Woodbridge: Tamesis, 2013), pp. 1–24 (p. 5).

115 Soledad Becerril, *Años de soledad* (Barcelona: Galaxia Gutenberg, 2018), p. 114.

116 Alastair Reid, *An Alastair Reid Reader: Selected Prose and Poetry* (Hanover, NH: Middlebury College Press, 1994), pp. 56–7.

117 Maddox, *The Best of All Possible Islands*, p. 3.

118 Luz Sánchez Mellado, 'El motín de los nuevos descubridores', *El País*, 9 January 1992, https://elpais.com/diario/1992/01/09/ultima/694911601_850215.html (accessed 10 May 2020).

119 Maddox, *The Best of All Possible Islands*, p. 165.

120 *Ibid.*, p. 144.

121 *Ibid.*, p. 265.

122 Jesús Aguirre, *Crónica en la comisaria: memorias del cumplimiento* (Barcelona: Plaza & Janes, 1992), p. 120.

123 Soledad Becerril, 'Cuando el rio suena', *La ilustración regional* (November 1974): 17–19.

124 Information taken from Municipal Archive of Girona, File 109.092

125 See Quino Petit, 'Fuimos una máquina contra la droga', *El País*, 29 April 2012, https://elpais.com/cultura/2012/04/28/actualidad/1335638296_11687.html (accessed 10 May 2020).

Notes

126 'Los manifestantes anti-Expo emplazan a la policía a mostrar el material "bélico" que se les atibuyó', *El País*, 25 April 1992, https://elpais.com/diario/1992/04/25/espana/704152819_850215.html (accessed 10 May 2020).

127 Maddox, *The Best of All Possible Islands*, p. 63.

128 Marçal Sarrats, *Así en la tierra: Enrique de Castro y la iglesia de los que no se callan* (Barcelona: Lectio, 2013), p. 127.

129 Giles Auty, 'Marx on the wall', *Spectator*, 8 August 1992, 32–3 (p. 32). As the acerbic critic goes on to say: 'Of course it is only because I don't have to seek work on BBC or Channel 4 arts programmes, at the South Bank say, or on courses in supposed modern art history at the Courtauld or Leeds University that I dare ask such a question' (p. 32).

130 Gay y Blasco, *Gypsies in Madrid*, p. 33.

131 Victorino Ruiz de Azua and Jesús Duva, 'Los asesinos de una inmigrante en Aravaca dispararon munición de uso militar y policial', *El País*, 15 November 1992, https://elpais.com/diario/1992/11/15/espana/721782015_850215.html (accessed 10 May 2020).

132 See Vicente Rodríguez Ortega, 'Coda. From the Barcelona Olympics to Alcàsser: Two images of 1992 and their afterlives', *Journal of Spanish Cultural Studies*, 21.1 (2020): 97–117.

133 Joan M. Oleaque, *En éxtasis: el bakalao como contracultura en España* (Valencia: Barlin, 2017), p. 92.

134 Cited in Luis Costa, *¡Bacalao! Historia oral de la música de baile en Valencia, 1980–1995* (Barcelona: Contraediciones, 2016), p. 132.

135 See Duncan Wheeler, 'Barcelona, a musical olympus? Live concerts, club cultures, television and city branding', *Journal of Spanish Cultural Studies*, 21 (2020): 79–96.

136 Costa, *¡Bacalao!*, pp. 108, 194.

137 Tom Whittaker, 'Accelerated rhythms and sonic routes: Mapping the sound cultures of *bakalao*', *Journal of Spanish Cultural Studies*, 20.3 (2019): 287–99 (p. 290).

138 Ramón Freixas, '*Jamón, jamón*', *Dirigido por* (September 1992): 34–7 (p. 36).

139 Whittaker, 'Accelerated rhythms and sonic routes', p. 296.

140 See Nerea Barjola, *Microfísica sexista del poder* (Barcelona: Virus, 2018).

141 Aznar, *El compromiso del poder*, p. 154.

142 Josep Tarradellas, *Ja sóc aquí: record d'un return* (Barcelona: Planeta, 1989), p. 30.

143 Ferran Archilés and Manuel Martí, 'Ethnicity, region and nation: Valencian identity and the Spanish nation-state', *Ethnic and Racial Studies*, 24.5 (2001): 779–97 (p. 791).

Notes

144 See Josep Lluís Sirera, 'Noticia de un desencuentro', *Fiesta cultura* (October 2002): 10–11; Manuel V. Vilanova, 'Realidad y ficción del teatro romano de Sagunto', *Fiesta cultura* (October 2002): 6–9.

145 Fernando Sánchez Dragó and Santiago Abascal, *España vertebrada* (Barcelona: Planeta, 2019), p. 79.

146 Santiago Abascal and Gustavo Bueno, *En defensa de España: Razones para el patriotismo español* (Madrid: Asociación para la defensa de la nación española amd Ediciones Encuentro, 2008), p. 33.

147 Typical of the book's tone and content is the claim that 'The Spanish empire deserved historical justice and it will get it, but much more time is needed.' María Elvira Roca Barea, *Imperiofobia y leyenda negra: Roma, Rusia, Estados Unidos y el Imperio español* (Madrid: Siruela, 2017), p. 476.

148 Juan Pablo Fusi, 'La cultura de la Transición', *Revista de occidente*, 122–3 (1991): 37–64.

149 'Crece un 9,7 por ciento al presupuesto público destinado a la cultura'; *El cultural*, 14 January 2019, https://elcultural.com/Crece-un-97-por-ciento-el-presupuesto-publico-destinado-a-la-cultura (accessed 10 May 2020).

150 For details of UK government spending for 2019, see www.gov.uk/government/publications/spending-round-2019-document/spending-round-2019 (accessed 10 May 2020).

Conclusion

1 Chantal Mouffe, *The Democratic Paradox* (London: Verso, 2000), pp. 102–3.

2 Mikel Ayerbe and Mari Jose Olaziregi, 'Yup lala! Carrero Blanco como lugar de memoria en la canción y literatura vascas', in Patrick Eser and Stefan Peters (eds), *El atentado contra Carrero Blanco como lugar de (no-) memoria* (Madrid: Vervuert and Iberoamericana), pp. 215–30.

3 José Ignacio Torreblanca, *Asaltar los cielos: Podemos o la política después de la crisis* (Barcelona: Penguin Random House, 2015), p. 108.

4 *Ibid.*, p. 32.

5 Miguel Martínez Lucio, 'Trade unions and communism in Spain: The role of the CCOO in the political projects of the left', *Journal of Communist Studies*, 6.4 (1990): 80–99.

6 Robert M. Fishman, *Working-Class Organizations and the Return to Democracy in Spain* (Ithaca: Cornell University Press, 1990), p. 240.

7 Jordi Gracia, *Contra la izquierda: para seguir siendo de izquierdas en el siglo XXI* (Barcelona: Anagrama, 2018), p. 37.

Notes

8   Santos Juliá, *Transición: historia de una política española, 1937–2017* (Barcelona: Galaxia Gutenberg, 2017), p. 618.

9   See Duncan Wheeler, 'The long Transition', *Jacobin*, 12 June 2018, www. jacobinmag.com/2018/12/spain-transition-franco-gonzalez-constitution-podemos (accessed 10 May 2020).

10   Telephone interview with the author on 15 January 2020.

11   Amando de Miguel, *Los españoles: sociología de la vida cotidiana*, 2nd edn (Madrid: Temas de hoy, 1995), p. 125.

12   Cited in Miguel Fernández-Braso, *Conversaciones con Alfonso Guerra* (Barcelona: Planeta, 1983), pp. 201–2.

13   In 2019, Jordi Casanovas wrote a verbatim play, *Jauría*, about the initial trial. This was performed at the Teatro Kamikaze in Madrid in a production directed by Miguel del Arco. See Maria M. Delgado, 'Misogyny on trial: Miguel del Arco's verbatim production offers a new trial for "La Manada"', *Theatre Times*, 7 April 2019, https://thetheatretimes.com/misogyny-on-trial-miguel-del-arcos-verbatim-production-offers-a-new-trial-for-la-manada (accessed 10 May 2020).

14   Cited in Paula Ponga, *Carmen Maura* (Barcelona: Icaria, 1993), p. 56.

15   Interview with the author in Pamplona on 13 July 2018.

16   Bryan Cameron, 'Spain in crisis: 15-M and the culture of indignation', *Journal of Spanish Cultural Studies*, 15.1–2 (2014): 1–11 (p. 4).

17   Email sent on 26 November 2019. This academic and politician requested that I retain his anonymity.

18   Dominic Sandbrook, *Seasons in the Sun: The Battle for Britain, 1974–1979* (London: Allen Lane, 2012), p. xviii.

19   *Ibid.*, p. 479.

Select bibliography

Abella, Carlos (2006). *Adolfo Suárez: el hombre clave de la Transición* (Madrid: Espasa Calpe).

Aguilar, Paloma (2002). *Memory and Amnesia: The Role of the Spanish Civil War in the Transition to Democracy* (New York: Berghahn).

Alonso, Gregorio and Diego Muro (eds), *The Politics and Memory of Democratic Transition: The Spanish Model* (New York: Routledge).

Álvarez Junco, José (2011). *Spanish Identity in the Age of Nations* (Manchester: Manchester University Press).

Amorós, Andrés (1983). *Diario cultural* (Madrid: Espasa-Calpe).

Attlee, James (2017). *'Guernica': Painting the End of the World* (London: Head of Zeus).

Balfour, Sebastian and Alejandro Quiroga (2007). *The Reinvention of Spain: Nation and Identity since Democracy* (Oxford: Oxford University Press).

Balibrea, Mari Paz (2017). *The Global Cultural Capital: Addressing the Citizen and Producing the City in Barcelona* (London: Palgrave Macmillan).

Bernecker, Walther L. (1998). 'Monarchy and democracy: The political role of King Juan in the Spanish *Transición*', *Journal of Contemporary History*, 33.1: 65 84.

Beswick, Jaine E. (2007). *Regional Nationalism in Spain: Language Use and Ethnic Identity in Galicia* (Clevedon: Multilingual Matters).

Blakeley, Georgina (2004). *Building Local Democracy in Barcelona* (Lewiston: Edwin Mellon Press).

Brassloff, Audrey (1998). *Religion and Politics in Spain: The Spanish Church in Transition, 1962–96* (London: Macmillan).

Brennan, Jason (2016). *Against Democracy* (Princeton: Princeton University Press).

Select bibliography

Brooksbank Jones, Anny (1997). *Women in Contemporary Spain* (Manchester: Manchester University Press).

Buck, Tobias (2019). *After the Fall: Crisis, Recovery and the Making of a New Spain* (London: Weidenfeld and Nicolson).

Burns, James (1999). *Barça: A People's Passion* (London: Bloomsbury).

Cameron, Bryan (2014). 'Spain in crisis: 15-M and the culture of indignation', *Journal of Spanish Cultural Studies*, 15.1–2: 1–11.

Carr, Raymond (1980). *Modern Spain 1875–1980* (Oxford: Oxford University Press).

Carretero, Nacho (2015). *Fariña: historia e indiscreciones del narcotráfico en Galicia* (Madrid: Los libros del KO).

Carrillo, Santiago (2008). *Memorias* (Barcelona: Planeta).

Castells, Manuel (2008). 'Productores de ciudad: el movimiento ciudadano de Madrid', in Vicente Pérez Quintana and Pablo Sánchez León (eds), *Memoria ciudadana y movimiento vecinal: Madrid, 1968–2008* (Madrid: Catarata), pp. 21–32.

Cazorla Sánchez, Antonio (2010). *Fear and Progress: Ordinary Lives in Franco's Spain, 1939–1975* (Malden: Wiley-Blackwell).

Cercas, Javier (2009). *Anatomía de un instante* (Barcelona: Random House Mondadori).

Cervera, Rafa (2003). *Alaska y otras historias de la movida* (Barcelona: Random House Mandadori).

Chislett, William (2013). *Spain: What Everyone Needs to Know* (Oxford: Oxford University Press).

Closa, Carlos and Paul M. Heywood (2004). *Spain and the European Union* (Houndmills: Palgrave Macmillan).

Collins, Larry and Dominque Lapierre (1968). *Or I'll Dress You in Mourning: The Story of El Cordobés and the New Spain He Stands For* (London: Simon & Schuster).

Crameri, Kathryn (2008). *Catalonia: National Identity and Cultural Policy, 1980–2003* (Cardiff: University of Wales Press).

Crick, Bernard (2002). *Democracy: A Very Short Introduction* (Oxford: Oxford University Press).

Crumbaugh, Justin (2009). *Destination Dictatorship: The Spectacle of Spain's Tourist Boom and the Reinvention of Difference* (Albany: State University of New York Press).

Delgado, Maria M. (2003). *'Other' Spanish Theatres: Erasure and Inscription on the Twentieth-Century Spanish Stage* (Manchester: Manchester University Press).

Select bibliography

—— (2008). *Federico García Lorca* (Abingdon: Routledge).

—— (2015). 'Memory, silence and democracy in Spain: Federico García Lorca, the Spanish Civil War, and the law of historical memory', *Theatre Journal*, 67.2: 177–96.

Derrida, Jacques (1996). *Archive Fever: A Freudian Impression* (Chicago: Chicago University Press).

Desfor Edles, Laura (1998). *Symbol and Ritual in the New Spain: The Transition to Democracy after Franco* (Cambridge: Cambridge University Press).

Dowling, Andrew (2013). *Catalonia since the Spanish Civil War: Reconstructing the Nation* (Brighton: Sussex University Press).

—— (2018). 'Prohibition, tolerance, co-option: Cultural appropriation and Francoism in Catalonia, 1939–75', *Contemporary European History*, 27.3: 370–86.

Encarnación, Omar G. (2008). *Spanish Politics: Democracy after Dictatorship* (Cambridge: Polity Press).

Estruch, Joan (1995). *Saints and Schemers: Opus Dei and Its Paradoxes* (Oxford: Oxford University Press).

Faulkner, Sally (2006). *A Cinema of Contradiction: Spanish Film in the 1960s* (Edinburgh: Edinburgh University Press).

Fuentes, Juan Francisco (2011). *Adolfo Suárez: biografía política* (Barcelona: Planeta).

—— (2016). *Con el Rey y contra el Rey: los socialistas y la monarquía de la Restauración canovista a la abdicación de Juan Carlos I (1879–2014)* (Madrid: La esfera de los libros).

Fusi, Juan Pablo (1991). 'La cultura de la Transición', *Revista de occidente*, 122–3: 37–64.

Gabilondo, Joseba (2019), *Introduction to a Postnational History of Contemporary Basque Literature (1978–2000)* (Woodbridge: Tamesis).

Gallero, J. L. (1991). *Sólo se vive una vez: esplendor y ruina de la movida madrileña* (Madrid: Ardora).

Gillespie, Richard (2015). 'Between accommodation and contestation: The political evolution of Basque and Catalan nationalism', *Nationalism and Ethnic Politics*, 21.1: 3–23.

González, Felipe and Juan Luis Cebrián (2001). *El futuro no es lo que era: una conversación* (Barcelona: Alfaguara).

Graham, Helen (2005). *The Spanish Civil War: A Very Short Introduction* (Oxford: Oxford University Press).

—— (2016). 'Writing Spain's twentieth century in(to) Europe', in Helen Graham (ed.), *Interrogating Francoism: History and Dictatorship in Twentieth-Century Spain* (London: Bloomsbury), pp. 1–25.

Graham, Helen and Jo Labanyi (1995). 'Introduction', in Helen Graham and Jo Labanyi (eds), *Spanish Cultural Studies: An Introduction. The Struggle for Modernity* (Oxford: Oxford University Press), pp. 1–19.

Guerra, Alfonso (2006). *Dejando atrás los vientos: memorias, 1982–1991* (Madrid: Espasa Calpe).

Guibernau, Montserrat (2004). *Catalan Nationalism: Francoism, Transition and Democracy* (London: Routledge).

Harrison, Joseph (1995). *The Spanish Economy: From the Civil War to the European Community* (Cambridge: Cambridge University Press).

Hensbergen, Gijs van (2004). *'Guernica': The Biography of a Twentieth-Century Icon* (London: Bloomsbury).

Hooper, John (2006). *The New Spaniards*, 2nd edn (London: Penguin).

Hopewell, John (1986). *Out of the Past: Spanish Literature after Franco* (London: BFI).

Humlebaek, Carsten (2015). *Inventing the Nation* (London: Bloomsbury).

Huntington, Samuel P. (1991). 'Democracy's third wave', *Journal of Democracy*, 2.2: 12–34.

Iglesias, Pablo (2015). *Una nueva Transición: materiales del año del cambio* (Madrid: Akal).

Iglesias, Pablo and Enric Juliana (2018). *Nudo España* (Barcelona: Arpa & Alfil).

Juliá, Santos (2004). *Historia de las dos Españas* (Madrid: Taurus).

Kornetis, Kostis (2014). ' "Is there a future in this past?" Analyzing 15M's intricate relationship to the Transition', *Journal of Spanish Cultural Studies*, 15.1–2: 83–98.

Kornetis, Kostis, Eirini Kotsovili and Nikolaos Papadogiannis (2016). 'Introduction', in Kostis Kornetis, Eirini Kotsovili and Nikolaos Papadogiannis (eds), *Consumption and Gender in Southern Europe since the Long 1960s* (London: Bloomsbury), pp. 1–26.

Labanyi, Jo (2002). 'Introduction: Engaging with ghosts; or, theorizing culture in modern Spain', in Jo Labanyi (ed.), *Constructing Identity in Contemporary Spain* (Oxford: Oxford University Press), pp. 1–14.

—— (2009). 'The language of silence: Historical memory, generational transmission and witnessing in contemporary Spain', *Journal of Romance Studies*, 9.3: 23–35.

Labrador Méndez, Germán (2016). 'Lo que en España no ha habido: la lógica normalizadora de la cultura postfranquista en la actual crisis', *Revista hispánica moderna*, 69.2: 165–92.

—— (2017). *Culpables por la literatura: imaginación política y contracultura en la Transición española, 1968–1986* (Madrid: Akal).

Select bibliography

Lannon, Frances (1987). *Privilege, Persecution and Prophecy: The Catholic Church in Spain, 1875–1975* (Oxford: Clarendon Press).

Maddox, Richard (2004). *The Best of All Possible Islands: Seville's Universal Exposition, the New Spain, and the New Europe* (Albany: State University of New York Press).

Magone, José M. (2009). *Contemporary Spanish Politics*, 2nd edn (London: Routledge).

Mar-Molinero, Clare (2000). *The Politics of Language in the Spanish-Speaking World* (London: Routledge).

Martin-Márquez, Susan (2008). *Disorientations: Spanish Colonialism in Africa and the Performance of Identity* (New Haven: Yale University Press).

Maxwell, Richard (1995). *The Spectacle of Democracy: Spanish Television, Nationalism and Political Transition* (Minneapolis: University of Minnesota Press).

McRoberts, Kenneth (2001). *Catalonia: Nation Building without a State* (Oxford: Oxford University Press).

Medina, Alberto (2001). *Exorcismos de la memoria: política y poéticas de la melancolía en la España de la transición* (Madrid: Ediciones Libertarias).

Miguélez-Carballeira, Helena (2013). *Galicia, a Sentimental Nation: Gender, Cultural and Politics* (Cardiff: University of Wales Press).

—— (2017). '*Ocho apellidos vascos* and the poetics of post-ETA Spain', *International Journal of Iberian Studies*, 30.3: 165–82.

Minder, Raphael (2017). *The Struggle for Catalonia: Rebel Politics in Spain* (London: Hurst).

Molinero, Carme and Pere Ysás (2014). *La cuestión catalana* (Barcelona: Planeta).

—— (2018). *La Transición: historia y relatos* (Madrid: Siglo XXI).

Monedero, Juan Carlos (2013). *La Transición española contada a nuestros padres: nocturno de la democracia española* (Madrid: Catarata).

Mudde, Cass and Cristóbal Rovira Kaltwasser (2017). *Populism: A Very Short Introduction* (Oxford: Oxford University Press).

Muro, Diego (2008). *Ethnicity and Violence: The Case of Radical Basque Nationalism* (London: Routledge).

Núñez Seixas, Xosé M. (2001). 'What is Spanish nationalism today? From legitimacy crisis to unfulfilled renovation (1975–2000)', *Ethnic and Racial Studies*, 24.5: 719–52.

O'Brian, Patrick (2010). *Picasso: A Biography* (London: HarperCollins).

O'Connor, Patricia (1966). 'Government censorship in the contemporary Spanish theatre', *Education Theatre Journal*, 18.4: 443–9.

Orozco, Lourdes (2007). *Teatro y política: Barcelona (1980–2000)* (Madrid: Publicaciones de la Asociación de Directores de Escena en España).

Ortuño Anaya, Pilar (2002). *European Socialists and Spain: The Transition to Democracy, 1959–77* (New York: Palgrave).

Pack, Sasha D. (2007). 'Tourism and political change in Franco's Spain', in Nigel Townson (ed.), *Spain Transformed: The Late Franco Dictatorship, 1959–75* (Houndmills: Palgrave Macmillan), pp. 47–66.

Palacio, Manuel (2012). *La televisión durante la Transición española* (Madrid: Cátedra).

Pavlović, Tatjana (2011). *The Mobile Nation: España cambia de piel* (Bristol: Intellect).

Powell, Charles (1996). *Juan Carlos of Spain: Self-Made Monarch* (Houndmills: Macmillan).

—— (2011). *El amigo americano: España y Estados Unidos de la dictadura a la democracia* (Madrid: Galaxia Gutenberg).

Preston, Paul (1986). *The Triumph of Democracy in Spain* (London: Methuen).

—— (1995). *Franco* (London: Fontana Press).

—— (2004). *Juan Carlos: A People's King* (London: HarperCollins).

Pujol, Jordi (2007). *Memòries: història d'una convicció* (Barcelona: Proa).

—— (2012). *Memòries: temps de construir (1980–1993)* (Barcelona: Proa).

Quaggio, Giulia (2014). *La cultura en Transición: reconciliación y política cultural en España, 1976–1986* (Madrid: Alianza).

Radcliff, Pamela Beth (2011). *Making Democratic Citizens in Spain: Civil Society and the Popular Origins of the Transition, 1960–78* (London: Palgrave Macmillan).

—— (2017). *Modern Spain: 1808 to the Present* (Chichester: Wiley-Blackwell).

Ribas, Pepe (2007). *Los 70 a destajo: Ajoblanco y libertad* (Barcelona: Destino).

Schwartz, Kessell (1968). 'Posibilismo and imposibilismo: The Buero Vallejo–Sastre polemic', *Revista hispánica moderna*, 34.1–2: 436–45.

Semprún, Jorge (1977). *Autobiografía de Federico Sánchez* (Barcelona: Planeta).

—— (1996). *Federico Sánchez se despide de ustedes* (Barcelona: Fabula Tusquets).

Smith, Paul Julian (2000). *The Moderns: Time, Space and Subjectivity in Contemporary Spanish Culture* (Oxford: Oxford University Press).

—— (2003). *Contemporary Spanish Culture: TV, Fashion, Art and Film* (Cambridge: Polity Press).

—— (2006). *Spanish Visual Culture: Cinema, Television, Internet* (Manchester: Manchester University Press).

Solchaga, Carlos (2017). *Las cosas como son: diarios de un político socialista (1980–1994)* (Barcelona: Galaxia Gutenberg).

Select bibliography

Stapell, Hamilton M. (2010). *Remaking Madrid: Culture, Politics, and Identity after Franco* (New York: Palgrave Macmillan).

Thompson, Michael (2016). 'Conclusion: The power of theatre', in Catherine O'Leary, Diego Santos Sánchez and Michael Thompson (eds), *Global Insights on Theatre Censorship* (New York: Routledge), pp. 259–67.

Tofiño-Quesada, Ignacio (2003). 'Spanish orientalism: Uses of the past in Spain's colonization in Africa', *Comparative Studies of South Asia, Africa and the Middle East*, 23.1–2: 141–8.

Townson, Nigel (2007). 'Introduction', in Nigel Townson (ed.), *Spain Transformed: The Late Franco Dictatorship, 1959–1975* (Basingstoke: Palgrave Macmillan), pp. 1–29.

Treglown, Jeremy (2014). *Franco's Crypt: Spanish Culture and Memory since 1936* (London: Chatto & Windus).

Triana-Toribio, Nuria (2016). *Spanish Film Cultures: The Making and Unmaking of Spanish Cinema* (London: BFI Palgrave).

Tusell, Javier (1995). *Juan Carlos I: la restauración de la monarquía* (Madrid: Temas de hoy).

—— (2011). *Spain: From Dictatorship to Democracy*, trans. Rosemary Clark (Chichester: Wiley-Blackwell).

Usó, Juan Carlos (1996). *Drogas y cultura de masas: España (1855–1995)* (Madrid: Taurus).

Vincent, Mary (2007). *Spain, 1833–2002: People and State* (Oxford: Oxford University Press).

Woodworth, Paddy (2001). *Dirty War, Clean Hands: ETA, the GAL and Spanish Democracy* (Cork: Cork University Press).

Index

Index

Index

Index

Index

Index

Index

Index

Index

Index

Index

Index

Index

Index

Index

Index

Index